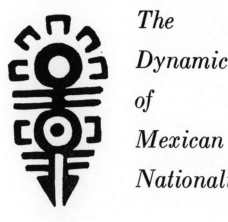

The
Dynamic
of
Mexican
Nationalism

The
Dynamic
of
Mexican
Nationalism

Frederick C. Turner

The University
of North Carolina Press
Chapel Hill   1968

To C. E. T. and N. C. T.

Preface

Little justification need be given for analyzing the causes of the rise of nationalism as a unifying social value in Mexico. With implications for analysis of Mexican economic growth and the link between political participation and national integration, the study of Mexican nationalism may point up specific elements that make the Mexican Revolution of 1910 appear to be an instrument of change. Such a study may develop a theory that can be applied and tested among other national groups in other periods of history. Analytical value comes not only from the study of new situations but also from investigations of situations previously studied without a particular set of theoretical problems in mind.[1] While histories of the Mexican Revolution fill numerous library shelves, the Revolution has never been approached as a progenitor of the kind of nationalism that has evolved in Mexico. With the emergence of nationalism in Asia and Africa, and the possibilities of social consensus and violent revolution in Latin America so frequently discussed today, study of the nature and causes of Mexican nationalism takes on added significance outside Mexico.

But too much should not be claimed for the study of Mexican nationalism. Such study analyzes the rise and causes of only one force in Mexican society: the sense of loyalty to the national community. The analysis has importance as more than an intellectual exercise, however, since the growth of Mexican nationalism has been one of

---

1. Talcott Parsons, *The Structure of Social Action* (Glencoe, Ill.: The Free Press of Glencoe, 1961), p. 8.

the most influential forces shaping Mexico's society, economy, and political system. Study of the growth of nationalism entails emphasis on the impact of the 1910 Revolution, because, as Gabriel Almond and Sidney Verba point out, the Revolution is the crucial event in the development of Mexican political culture. It "created a sense of national identity and a commitment to the political system that permeates almost all strata of the society."[2] Just as understanding of the Revolution's impact is impossible without careful consideration of the barriers and multiple impetuses to Mexican nationalism in the hundred years before 1910, so examination of the Revolution's impact through diverse changes in the social and literary milieu necessarily extend the study beyond the main period of revolutionary struggle that ended with the Querétaro Constitution of 1917.

In writing about the rising sense of community in a nation not his own, about the only advantage a foreigner can claim is his presumed objectivity. Although no foreigner can fully share a subjective appreciation of nationalism, researchers may develop a sincere liking for the country and its people which clouds their judgments. While frankly admitting this liking in my own case, I have been conscious of it in both research and writing and have endeavored to prevent its influencing observations or conclusions. Objective analysis of nationalism in Mexico or elsewhere should not attach value judgments to nationalism, although it may point to apparent effects of the rise of nationalism which may be regarded as either harmful or beneficial. Analysis should rather try to isolate the various elements leading to the rise of nationalism in an individual national context. In the case of Mexico, holding value judgments to a minimum facilitates investigation, not merely of the substance of Mexican nationalism, but also of the function that

2. Gabriel A. Almond and Sidney Verba, *The Civic Culture: Political Attitudes and Democracy in Five Nations* (Princeton, N.J.: Princeton University Press, 1963), p. 503.

nationalism plays in the political, economic, and social life of the Mexicans.

The research for this study is based upon consultation of primary and secondary sources and upon empirical observation and interviews carried on in Mexico during 1964. Much of the growing literature on nationalism and political development, as well as Mexican histories and polemics, elucidated causes for the rise of Mexican nationalism, while observation and interviews clarified some of the misconceptions and misplacements of emphasis that exclusive dependence on bibliographical research may develop. No questionnaire techniques were employed, although recent statistical surveys have yielded important information on Mexican behavior. It was found that information on present Mexican attitudes concerning the nature of the national community could be more strategically gathered through personal interviews with Mexican intellectuals and with a broad spectrum of Mexicans from diverse social and economic backgrounds. Conducted in Spanish in eleven Mexican states and the Federal District, the interviews reached a variety of Mexicans whose illiteracy or disinclination to answer would have prohibited the use of written questionnaires. The interviews also made it possible to tailor discussion to the particular contribution the subject could make: Villistas and other partisans discussed the conflict between factionalism and the ideal of national unity; educators discussed the contribution that nationalistic literature and education can make to Mexican nationalism. For purposes of comparison, standard questions calling for the evaluation of national heroes, opinions on the extent of Mexican social communication, and views on the causes of the growth of communication were asked in all interviews.

The debts incurred in the preparation of this study are many. William S. Barnes and Ruhl J. Bartlett of the Fletcher School of Law and Diplomacy, John N. Plank of the Brookings Institution, and K. H. Silvert of the Ford

Foundation have provided the advice and encouragement that made the study possible. Discussions with Howard F. Cline, Robert E. Scott, Luis González, Rafael Segovia, and Daniel Cosío Villegas pointed up early flaws in the analysis and suggested new paths of inquiry. The responsiveness and sympathetic co-operation of Mexicans with highly varied backgrounds and viewpoints added depth to the study not readily obtainable in other ways. Lewis Hanke, Joseph Sommers, Frank Dauster, Seymour Menton, and Boyd G. Carter read sections of the manuscript and offered helpful suggestions. Special thanks are due Hugh M. Hamill, Jr., Nathan L. Whetten, Robert G. Mead, Jr., Robert F. Smith, and Morris Singer, all colleagues at the University of Connecticut; insights derived from their own extensive research on Mexico in the fields of history, sociology, literature, and economics have aided greatly. The University of Connecticut provided a research grant to assist the study, and Judson DeCew, Jr., proved a most able graduate assistant. Caroline C. Turner provided the wifely support without which the study could not have been carried out. Finally, Dorothy Fox of the Edwin Ginn Library, Dolores Vasconcelos Vda. de García and Adelina Chávez de Crespo of the Biblioteca de México, and Baldomero Segura García of the Biblioteca Isidro Fabela provided special help in locating individual sources. They, like those who gave specific advice and insight, are in no way responsible for any errors of fact or interpretation that the following pages may contain.

FREDERICK C. TURNER

Storrs, Connecticut
March, 1968

Contents

Preface   vii

I. THE CONCEPT OF MEXICAN NATIONALISM   3
    The Dynamic of Mexican Social Cohesion   4
    The Elements of Mexican Nationalism   15

II. XENOPHOBIA, 1810-1910   22
    The Disparate Groups in New Spain in 1810   23
    Independence and the Influence of Spain   28
    The United States, Texas, and the War of 1847   35
    The Church   44
    France and Maximilian   48
    The Díaz Regime   53

III. SOCIAL CHANGE, 1810-1910   62
    Population   62
    Miscegenation and Class Differentiation   72
    Language   81
    Education   88
    Transportation   95

IV. THE REVOLUTION AS A CATALYST OF SOCIAL CHANGE   101
    The New National Heroes   102
    Migration   120
    Status, Class Structure, and Family Solidarity   129
    Clerical Aspirations   136
    Destruction as an Impetus to Unity and the
        Theory of Economic Equality   144

V. SOCIAL GROUPS AND THE REVOLUTION   156
   A Note on Military Technology   157
   The Inclusiveness of Revolutionary Appeals   163
   Indianism   170
   Workers   179
   Women   183

VI. XENOPHOBIA AND THE REVOLUTION   202
   The Intensity of Xenophobia and Its
      Manifestations   203
   North American Provocations   216
   A Multiplicity of Elements   231
   Verbal Attacks   242
   The Limitations on Xenophobia and Its Over-all
      Effect   248

VII. LITERATURE, THE ARTS, AND NATIONALISM   254
   Antecedents and the Mexican Novel   256
   Histories and School Textbooks   266
   Poetry, Plays, and Oratory   274
   Music   279
   Art   287
   Films and the New Media   295

VIII. AN OVERVIEW   307

   Bibliography   317

   Index   323

The
Dynamic
of
Mexican
Nationalism

I
The Concept
of Mexican Nationalism

The Mexican people have achieved a remarkable degree
of political consensus within a political and social framework that allows for dissent and encourages economic
growth in per capita terms. Since the mid-1930's, political
stability, steady economic advances, a lack of military
intervention in the political process, and consistent foreign
policies upholding national self-determination in the face
of North American interests have differentiated Mexico
sharply from nearly all of the other Latin American republics. What is it that causes Mexico to be the exception
in Latin America? Is it the heavy domestic investment
that fosters per capita economic growth despite a yearly
population growth of over 3 per cent? Is it the integral
acceptance of racial diversity that has set Mexico off so
sharply from Ecuador or Peru? Is it the social consensus
that distinguishes Mexico from Argentina's fractionalized
polity? Is it the Mexican party structure in which, despite
presidential predominance, the official interest groups have
some room to maneuver within the single dominant party?

   In answering that "the Revolution" causes Mexico's
distinctiveness, Mexicans are in a sense only restating the
question. Their conception of the Mexican Revolution as
a continuous process of social change proceeding from its

violent phase between 1910 and 1917 becomes a way of summarizing and expressing pride in the development of distinctiveness. The causes of Mexican uniqueness are multiple, of course, and no single concept elucidates the Mexican panorama. One element pervading each area of distinctiveness, however, is the development of a brand of nationalism that has given the Mexican national community a particular cohesiveness and flexibility.

THE DYNAMIC OF MEXICAN SOCIAL COHESION

Nationalism is a concept that may be defined in many ways, and its relevance in any discussion depends on the particular definition. One of the most useful concepts of nationalism views it as "social value,"[1] a set of attitudes widely held within a "national community" which facilitate social intercourse among the inhabitants of contemporary nation-states. The "national community" is that segment of the inhabitants of a national territory whose actions are in part shaped by their subjective, internalized acceptance of nationalist attitudes. This view of nationalism as a social value affecting human attitudes and actions is useful because it suggests the social function of nationalism. It raises questions of who holds the attitudes, what attitudes are held, and how the possession of these attitudes affects the relationships among individuals and social groups within a national polity.

Nationalism varies "quantitatively" as changes occur in the number of individuals comprising the national community and as the relationship between the size of the national community and the size of the national population varies. The national community does not usually include persons who lack the status of legal nationality as defined by the laws of the country in question, although long-time foreign residents or persons forced to change their legal

1. K. H. Silvert, ed., *Expectant Peoples: Nationalism and Development* (New York: Random House, 1963), pp. 18-19.

nationality may hold attitudes and values of a nation-state not legally their own. The national community never includes all inhabitants of a given territory, since mental incompetents, small children, and culturally isolated individuals do not pertain to it. In the sense of achieving active loyalty and participation in national affairs from a maximum number of inhabitants, the Mexican "nation," like all "nations," remains a goal to be approached rather than an accomplished fact.[2]

As individuals accept nationalist attitudes, the size of the national community increases numerically and proportionally. If, in the process of socialization, most children acquire national loyalties that replace the exclusively parochial attitudes of their parents, the size of the national community becomes larger in relation to the national population as the older inhabitants gradually pass away. Around the world today, "nationalism," as defined in these quantitative terms, varies greatly, since the countries of the world contain national communities of widely varying size in relation to the national populations.

Nationalism varies "qualitatively" in the sense that the degree of consensus in nationalist attitudes among the members of the same national community may be large or small. Consensus may apply only to the vague concept of national unity for which citizens are willing to give up a bare minimum of personal prerogatives. By contrast, it may include general agreement on the kinds of public and private programs required to further the prosperity of the national population.

Consensus does not necessarily exist among individuals who voice identical nationalistic phrases. Invocations of patriotism may be used to hide appeals to special group interests. Here nationalism does not mark common attitudes but rather creates the appearance of common attitudes. Since individuals frequently respond to appear-

2. Juan Roura Parella, "Formación de la conciencia nacional," *Revista Mexicana de Sociología*, Año 16, Vol. 16, Núm. 1 (enero-abril, 1954), 53-54.

ances and fail to question the underlying viewpoints of patriotic orators, the appearance as well as the reality of nationalism affects the social relationships within a nation-state. The differences between Mexican and Spanish nationalism illustrate the operation of nationalism at different levels of consensus. Mexican nationalism, as it has existed since the 1910 Revolution, contrasts sharply with the appeals to nationalism that attempt to maintain existing social stratification and political nonparticipation. Mexican nationalism is categorically opposed to the Spanish nationalism that during the twentieth century has served primarily as a device through which the Spanish Army and the monied classes have deferred social and political change.[3]

Paradoxically, invocations of nationalism that cloak the demands of special interests embody divisive forces in society, while nationalism, as a means of resolving the conflict of special interests, is a unifying, cohesive social force. The myth of nationalism and national unity is— in polities like Mexico, which have achieved a high degree of consensus on national goals—one means of resolving intergroup conflict. Even in highly developed societies, groups with conflicting interests, such as labor-management bargainers arguing over wage increases, do not concede their positions when, as nationalists, they are told that conceding is in the "national interest." Shared beliefs and loyalty to an inclusively defined national community, however, make their opposing interests appear ultimately more compatible. Nationalism does not dissolve group conflict, but it can help to channel conflict into the peaceful give and take that results in compromise and mutual acceptance.

The rise of nationalism in nation-states with a high degree of consensus has, in part, replaced religious and familial loyalties with a system of national allegiance. "Right" actions are still those actions which allow organ-

3. Stanley G. Payne, "Spanish Nationalism in the Twentieth Century," *Review of Politics*, Vol. 26, No. 3 (July, 1964), 418-22.

ized society to continue functioning, such as altruism, industry, and the avoidance of antisocial actions (incest, murder, and theft). The rationale for such injunctions is no longer merely that they injure an individual's family or anger his God but that they conflict with the welfare of his "nation." Injunctions that are internalized in the value structures of individuals sometimes influence behavior more than external threats, so that increases in national loyalty within a population significantly affect the degree of cohesiveness with which the individuals and groups within it work together. In addition to the rise of internalized national loyalties, nation-states have also imposed codes of national law that attempt to prevent antisocial behavior. In conjunction with national statutes, the rise of both national loyalty and a sense of personal responsibility toward the nation provides a meaningful device of social control.

Nationalism varies, not only in the size of the segment of the population holding nationalist values and the degree of consensus on them, but also in the specific content of the values held. The attitudes and values held within one national community differ from those held in another. "Variants" of nationalism develop depending on the stress placed on various elements of the nationalist ideology. Patriotism, referring to a citizen's devotion to his country and to such symbols as its flag, is a common element in all variants of nationalism, as is a desire for national autonomy and independence from foreign domination. National ideologies and systems of loyalty differ radically, however, in the value they place on their own attempts at foreign conquest.

The content of Mexican nationalism varies sharply from the kind of aggressive German nationalism that characterized Hitler's Third Reich. Mexican nationalism lacks what Hans Morgenthau calls "nationalistic universalism," what Boyd C. Shafer describes as "the doctrine that the nation (the nationalist's own) is or should be dominant if not supreme among other nations and should take aggressive action to this end."[4] Although a few Mexican nationalists have wanted to extend the bases of Mexican power in order to increase her international influence, particularly in relation to the United States and Central America, it is not rewarding to view Mexico in terms of aggressive nationalism. Mexican nationalism has been, in Arthur P. Whitaker's terms, "introvert" rather than "extrovert,"[5] in that it has promoted internal unity among Mexicans rather than the aggrandizement of Mexico in relation to neighboring countries. As Mexican leaders point out, Mexican nationalism has no need to be aggressive or expansionistic.[6]

This differentiation between aspects of nationalism resolves the question of ethical approaches to Mexican nationalism. Nationalism as a phenomenon has been regularly defended or condemned depending on the definition given to it. When seen as an aspiration for national identity, integrity, and self-determination, nationalism appears to be "good," whereas persons viewing it as an impetus to the domination of other states see it as "bad."[7] The present approach to Mexican nationalism views it as "good," because—far from serving as a justification for domination or aggression—Mexican nationalism has been a search for national integrity and a social consensus.

Mexican nationalism involves a mode of perception and an emotional reaction rather than a process of intellectual reasoning. If you say, for example, that a Mexican tree is

4. Boyd C. Shafer, *Nationalism: Myth and Reality* (New York: Harcourt, Brace and Company, 1955), p. 6.

5. Arthur P. Whitaker, "Nationalism and Social Change in Latin America," in Joseph Maier and Richard W. Weatherhead, eds., *Politics of Change in Latin America* (New York: Frederick A. Praeger, 1964), p. 87. See also Arthur P. Whitaker, "Varieties of Nationalism in Latin America," *Orbis*, Vol. 10, No. 4 (Winter, 1967).

6. Antonio Carrillo Flores, *El nacionalismo de los países latinoamericanos en la postguerra* (México: El Colegio de México, 1945), p. 27.

7. Kenneth W. Terhune, "Nationalism among Foreign and American Students: An Exploratory Study," *Journal of Conflict Resolution*, Vol. 8, No. 3 (September, 1964), 256.

beautiful, it seems to nationalists to possess beauty because it is Mexican rather than simply because it is a tree.[8] Nationalism relates directly to the perception of an increased opportunity for social mobility, of a chance to rise in both social and economic status on one's merits and to gain greater access to the levers of political influence. Nationalism, with its corollary insistence that the barriers to advancement be personal rather than ascriptive, promotes a more equalitarian society. As Bert F. Hoselitz suggests, nationalism establishes strong common ties without hierarchical subordination and maintains "the principle of equality as a significant political value."[9]

The political value of equality can coincide with popular neglect of social inequalities. When all citizens are proclaimed to be equal and given equal chances for advancement as through expanded educational opportunities, the inequalities of status in a society appear to be less permanent. Slogans such as "We are all Mexicans" and "The Revolution was fought for the Mexican people" draw attention away from the existing inequalities of wealth, social position, and power among the Mexican people. Workers are more likely to accept a pattern of highly skewed income distribution when they are fed on assurances of the equality of all citizens. Industrialists receiving large incomes, who as nationalists may perceive their own goals partly in terms of the welfare of the national community, are at least aware that domestic social cohesion lessens the chances for violent revolution. Seeing no need to send their profits abroad and in some cases feeling an urge toward nationally beneficial domestic investment, they invest at home and help to finance economic growth. Growth and increasing productivity in turn allow elites to keep the lion's share of material profits and political power, and at the same time the masses of

8. Jacques Séverin, "Démocratie mexicaine," *Esprit*, 20e Année, No. 190 (Mai, 1952), 800.

9. Bert F. Hoselitz, "Nationalism, Economic Development, and Democracy," *The Annals of the American Academy of Political and Social Science*, Vol. 305 (May, 1956), 6.

urban and rural workers acquire a somewhat greater share of both.

Mexicans exhibit strong national pride in their political system. On the basis of extensive survey material, Gabriel Almond and Sidney Verba find that the frequency with which Mexicans express pride in their political system is considerably higher than that of the Germans or the Italians. The Mexican Revolution of 1910 is a primary object of this pride. A sense of political participation and pride in the Revolution exists despite the fact that Mexico ranks behind the United States, Britain, Germany, and Italy in the impact attributed to the government and the equal treatment that is expected from it.[10]

The rise of nationalism as a unifying social value helps to foster individual participation in the political system, but in itself it does not produce such participation. Robert E. Scott estimates that in 1910 nearly 90 per cent of the Mexican people as traditional subsistence agriculturalists lacked a meaningful concept of the nation and its government, another 9 per cent as "subjects" saw what government might do to or for them in terms of output, and only 1 per cent participated in the input functions of government policy making. As Mexico's population has risen from about 15 million in 1910 to more than 45 million in 1968, the proportion of political activists has also increased. Today, about 25 per cent of the Mexican people remain traditionalists, 65 per cent have become subjects, and 10 per cent are participants,[11] in terms of the traditionalists' subjective unawareness of the national government, the subjects' view of themselves as essentially passive consumers of its actions, and the participants' appreciation of their role as producers of governmental decisions.

10. Gabriel A. Almond and Sidney Verba, *The Civic Culture: Political Attitudes and Democracy in Five Nations* (Princeton, N.J.: Princeton University Press, 1963), pp. 102-4, 108-9, 414-15.

11. Robert E. Scott, ''Nation-Building in Latin America,'' in Karl W. Deutsch and William J. Foltz, eds., *Nation-Building* (New York: Atherton Press, 1963), p. 81.

Scott's categories of political participation reflect the rise of nationalism as a cohesive social value, since the increase in the combined "subject" and "participant" categories corresponds to the growth in the proportion of Mexican citizens who feel themselves to be part of the Mexican national community. The 25 per cent of the Mexican population which today remains substantively unaware of governmental functions in either output or input terms is in fact the same quarter of the population that, despite extensive and consequential government programs to incorporate it into national life, still remains effectively outside the national community.

Nationalism as a cohesive value now affects the 75 per cent of the population included in the national community rather than the mere 10 per cent that participates actively in policy formation. Nationalism is one of the most important social links between the 10 per cent and the 65 per cent, as it eases the acceptance of participants' decisions by the mass of the population that still sees the government in terms of output functions. The strong positive value that Mexican leaders place on the social value of nationalism underlies the determined efforts in education and economic development which are yearly reducing the proportion of individuals outside the national community. The rise of nationalism as a cohesive social value has thus shaped and continues to shape Mexico's political structure.

While particularly applicable in the Mexican case, the approach to nationalism as an instrument of social cohesion does not contradict other approaches to nationalism. To say that nationalism may be an integrating social force is not to imply that it cannot be anything else. The cohesive tendency of nationalism coincides with Karl W. Deutsch's assumption that nationalism "essentially consists in wide complementarity of social communication. It consists in the ability to communicate more effectively, and over a wider range of subjects, with members of one large group than with outsiders.''[12] Heightened social cohesion results from effective communication. Similarly, Hans Kohn's concept of a living and active corporate will and Rupert Emerson's emphasis on consciousness of national identity elucidate the basically subjective acceptance of nationalism that leads to greater social cohesion.[13]

The concept of cohesive nationalism differs, however, from the common but imprecise connotations of the term "nation" and the more sophisticated but equally irrelevant concept of an exclusivistic nationalism that attempts to preclude all individual loyalties other than those to the nation. In common usage the term "nation" appears as a synonym for "state" or "country." The concept of nationalism as an element of social cohesion, on the other hand, considers the effect that shared values and loyalties may have on the social relationships of the inhabitants of the country.

Other loyalties are not terminated with the rise of nationalist attitudes, even though in any action-oriented decision a nationalist may be expected to place national loyalty above loyalty to his class or his religion but seldom to his family. No group, including the national community, fully absorbs an individual, and the individual formulates and expresses only a fraction of his attitudes in relation to any group to which he belongs.[14] Mexico is and always has been very far from being a totalitarian state. The extensive competition between individuals and groups in Mexico shows that most Mexicans work for themselves, for their families, or for their religion as well as for the benefit of their countrymen. It is perfectly possible to consider

12. Karl W. Deutsch, *Nationalism and Social Communication* (New York: John Wiley & Sons, 1953), p. 71.

13. Hans Kohn, *The Idea of Nationalism: A Study in Its Origins and Background* (New York: The Macmillan Company, 1961), Ch. 1; and Rupert Emerson, *From Empire to Nation: The Rise to Self-Assertion of Asian and African Peoples* (Boston: Beacon Press, 1962), Chs. 5-9.

14. David B. Truman, *The Governmental Process: Political Interests and Public Opinion* (New York: Alfred A. Knopf, 1960), p. 157.

nationalism without making it an all-exclusive end in itself, as some actions and some parts of many actions are motivated by the national consciousness that in Deutsch's terms facilitates communication among the inhabitants of Mexico.

While not inferring nationalist exclusivism, analysis of Mexican nationalism as an element of social cohesion prevents confusion between the Mexican love for public show and the achievement of nationalism. The love of fiestas and national holidays, which for Mexicans serve the special function of allowing escape from inner solitude and the ordinary set of social relationships,[15] shows no personal commitment on the part of the spectators to the nationalistic phrases so often expressed on such occasions. As K. H. Silvert suggests, "Glorification of the race, military pomp and ceremony on the occasion of national holidays, martial anthems, and homage to the symbolic baggage of the nation are celebrated on many occasions in Latin America. These evocations of a national spirit were the custom of small upper groups imitating European practice long before Latin-American governments could, in fact, even dream of claiming to represent nationally conscious peoples."[16] Patriotic displays in Mexico, like the prolonged and enthusiastic welcome given to Santa Anna when he returned a year after disgracing Mexico at San Jacinto, have probably resulted more from a need among Mexicans for periodic exuberance than from any subjective commitment to nationalism. Here again the Mexican case illustrates a general problem. The need in any country to distinguish between patriotic display and the nationalist consensus that the display may or may not manifest makes the concept of cohesive nationalism relevant outside the Mexican sphere.

Suggesting the potential applicability of the concept of

15. Octavio Paz, *The Labyrinth of Solitude: Life and Thought in Mexico,* Lysander Kemp, trans. (New York: Grove Press, 1961), pp. 47-53.

16. K. H. Silvert, "Nationalism in Latin America," *The Annals of the American Academy of Political and Social Science,* Vol. 334 (March, 1961), 3.

nationalism outside Mexico as an element of social cohesion does not deny the unique level that cohesive nationalism has achieved in Mexico. Whereas conflicts between ideologically antagonistic groups now fractionalize Argentina, preventing its social cohesion and economic progress,[17] the degree of national solidarity achieved by Fidel Castro in Cuba has been won at the cost of political liberty and a sharp economic decline. Brazilians exhibit little agreement on how to achieve the common goals of economic development and an independent foreign policy. Although Chileans have now swung strongly behind President Eduardo Frei, for the past quarter-century Chile has shown neither the economic growth nor the self-assured cohesion of the Mexicans. The long aftermath of Colombia's 1948 revolution shattered the illusion of cohesion that Colombia had long presented, and the lack of effective Venezuelan nationalism reflects in the failure of national leaders before Rómulo Betancourt to use the huge oil revenues to increase substantially an equality of opportunity among Venezuelan citizens. Most of the smaller countries of Central America and the Caribbean display the trappings of patriotism rather than a thoroughgoing national consensus. Uruguay and Costa Rica have achieved high levels of social consensus, but their limited populations, racial homogeneity, and geographic compactness have made the problems of nation-building comparatively simple. While encouraging diversity and political freedom within the national community, Mexico alone in Latin America has achieved a consensus on national goals and the methods for achieving them, and she is now systematically trying to incorporate into the national community that quarter of the population still remaining effectively outside. The uniqueness of Mexican nationalism, particularly in its Latin American context, adds significance to the study of its origins.

17. K. H. Silvert, ''The Costs of Anti-Nationalism: Argentina,'' in Silvert, ed., *Expectant Peoples*, especially pp. 364-72.

THE ELEMENTS OF MEXICAN NATIONALISM

A number of factors combine to produce the common attitudes and loyalties of cohesive nationalism. Societal elements traditionally regarded as attributes of nationalism, such as xenophobia, language, and racial homogeneity, give rise to nationalism as they develop through time. The presence of a common race, a common language, and a common fear of outsiders in Mexico demonstrates the same underlying causes for the rise of nationalism which are found in other parts of the world. Similarly, protestations of equality and greater opportunity advance the possibilities of common attitudes among nationalists everywhere. The kind of social change imposed by a violent revolution depends largely on the size and nature of the revolution. Changes in technology, demography, and literature affect the rise of nationalism. Since the forces operating on nationalism are so diverse, it seems advisable to trace a hypothetical framework for the rise of nationalism suggested by social theorists and the experience of groups outside Mexico.

One of the forces that facilitates cohesion within a group is xenophobia, the common fear or hatred of foreigners outside the group. Xenophobia is too often looked upon as an exclusively destructive social force, but it can be one of the major forces leading to greater unity within a national polity. Xenophobia sometimes leads to foreign wars that destroy life and property, and it may incite forms of "economic nationalism" that erect barriers to mutually beneficial international trade, but it also stimulates greater national cohesion by focusing common antipathy toward foreigners. It increases internal cohesion within nation-states while it fractionalizes loyalties in the international community.

Xenophobia influences future as well as present inhabitants of the national territory. As citizens share common emotional responses toward outsiders, they develop mutual attitudes. Furthermore, although groups within a state initially respond differently to foreign influences, their descendants may in retrospect develop a common antipathy toward outsiders which was not originally present. The national myths growing up after historical events require a minimum of historical fact, and popular history is interpreted according to the desires of the popularizers. The mythology of the American West, for example, romanticizes desperate and unenviable men and so gives Americans today a national history with which they can readily identify, but some historical precedent was needed on which to build the myth. The history of Mexico before 1917, like that of the American West, was significant for later manifestations of nationalism because it shaped the interpretations that could be given to it.

The effects on nationalism, both immediate and subsequent, of struggles with outsiders are evident in a variety of historical events. The expulsion of the Dutch from Brazil in 1654 showed groups within the colony that they could work together, and this proved to be an event that later generations of Brazilians look back upon with pride. Common pride in Andrew Jackson's victory over the British at New Orleans in 1815 helped to solidify a sense of nationalism in the deeply divided American people. The role that the foreign invaders had played for the early Brazilians and Americans was repeated in Mexico by Spain, by France, and by the United States.

Xenophobia is in no way limited to the Western Hemisphere or to colonial and newly independent states. It has proved particularly important as a factor contributing to the rise of nationalism in Asia, where a close correlation has existed between the emergence of national feeling and the intensity of foreign danger.[18] The Bolsheviks, despite their international ideology, first won control of the Soviet Union with the help of xenophobic nationalism. The Allied

18. Delmer M. Brown, *Nationalism in Japan: An Introductory Historical Analysis* (Berkeley, Calif.: University of California Press, 1955), p. 3.

intervention from 1917 to 1920 unified Russians behind the Communists, and the Bolsheviks might never have triumphed had their Russian opponents not been compromised by collaboration with the foreigners.[19]

Through the impact of xenophobia, Irish nationalism strikingly resembles Mexican nationalism. Both are cohesive social forces partially induced by strong antiforeign feeling. With an effect similar to that in Mexico, the force of nationalism unites Irishmen despite the sharp class and religious divisions within Irish society. As the function of Anglophobia in Ireland resembles that of "gringophobia" in Mexico, so the deep respect that Irish Catholics and members of all Irish social classes give to Protestant or aristocratic national heroes—Theobald Wolfe Tone, Thomas Davis, Charles Stewart Parnell, or Roger Casement— has stimulated a cohesiveness among the antagonistic groups within the Irish polity similar to the cohesiveness found in Mexico.[20] While opposition to foreigners operates as a unifying device in such isolated contexts as seventeenth-century Brazil or Bolshevik Russia, it also stimulates cohesive nationalism in the case of Ireland or Mexico where the foreign pressure is heavy and continuous over an extended period of time.

Cohesion among members of a state is also increased by forces, whether domestic or foreign, that break down sharp economic and social differences, giving individual members of the state new attitudes and vested interests. In 1916 Manuel Gamio wrote:

If, as has always been the case in Mexico, certain families live in plenty and others, the majority, suffer the torment of hunger, nakedness, and intellectual neglect, it is clear that a harmonious whole cannot result, that nationality cannot sprout from their

19. George F. Kennan, *Russia and the West under Lenin and Stalin* (Boston: Little, Brown and Company, 1960), p. 117.

20. For different approaches to Irish nationalism, see Alice Stopford Green, *Irish Nationality* (London: Williams and Norgate, 1911); E. Strauss, *Irish Nationalism and British Democracy* (London: Methuen & Co., Ltd., 1951); and Brian Inglis, *The Story of Ireland* (London: Faber and Faber, Ltd., 1956).

artificial union, because as in all times and in all countries, instead of any idea of motherland and nationality there has been that of self-interest.[21]

Wide differences in income, status, and opportunity prevent common attitudes and a sense of community. By selecting either the path of exploitation or that of constructive investment, wealthy citizens and foreign managers affect the economic growth upon which a more egalitarian community can be built.

The recent research of Wendell Bell substantiates this relationship between egalitarianism and nationalism. In an extensive study of the rise of Jamaican nationalism carried out between 1956 and 1962, Bell concludes that egalitarian attitudes were a prime cause of Jamaican nationalism and conversely that antiegalitarianism stimulated antinationalist sentiments. Bell finds that the desire for political independence from Britain was expressed as "equality" for Jamaicans in relation to other peoples of the world and that Jamaican nationalist attitudes were produced by a "desire for civil, political, economic, social and cultural equality," which through internal reform would create parity of opportunity among the Jamaican social classes.[22]

Violent revolution can under certain conditions speed the development of nationalist and egalitarian attitudes. The ordinary Latin American barracks revolt does not produce changes in attitude or social structure. Only the personnel in top leadership positions changes unless the small group of successful revolutionaries has a plan for

21. Manuel Gamio, *Forjando patria* (México: Editorial Porrúa, S.A., 1960), p. 11. The term "patria" is here and afterwards translated as "motherland," because Mexicans envisage the representative of their nation-state in feminine form. The figure most often used to represent the nation in Mexican plays and popular art—a figure comparable to Uncle Sam or John Bull—is a beautiful, young, and defiant girl with Indian characteristics. Mexicans often portray and visualize her as in danger of being molested by Uncle Sam.

22. Wendell Bell, *Jamaican Leaders: Political Attitudes in a New Nation* (Berkeley, Calif.: University of California Press, 1964), pp. 142-46.

social reform or can give effective leadership of the revolutionary movement to a group that does. Here the real revolution is not the initial acquisition of power but the more substantial battles waged when the reforms are first carried out. Mass revolutions such as those that began in France in 1789 or Mexico in 1910 do affect the egalitarian element of nationalist attitudes, however, as their early stages are marked by proclamations of individual equality.[23] Although the extreme emphasis on equality diminishes after revolutionary fervor begins to quiet, it does not disappear. One of the major social changes initiated by both the French and the Mexican revolutions has been the underlying sense of equality in a national community which forms an important element of the nationalism that is so strikingly evident in France and Mexico.

Violent periods of massive and prolonged revolution also affect nationalist attitudes in other ways. Civil wars such as Mexico experienced in 1910 contrast in their effect with both separatist revolts where intense loyalties are already channeled (the United States Civil War, 1861-65) and with revolts that become a stage for confrontation with a third power (the Spanish Civil War, 1936-39). In civil wars of the 1910 Mexican variety where competing factions range widely over the national territory, leaders are likely to make broadly based appeals for support to diverse groups and individuals. The destruction of such revolutions causes an immediate impetus to group unity in the process of reconstruction. The heroes of victorious factions appear to be cultural heroes whose stature legitimizes the common goals for which popular historians declare the revolution was fought.

In addition to xenophobia, equality, or the inclusive appeals of revolutionary heroes, a wide range of other social forces advances an individual's commitment to his

23. Pitirim A. Sorokin, *The Sociology of Revolution* (Philadelphia, Pa.: J. B. Lippincott Company, 1925), p. 354.

national community. Many developments within a state both influence nationalism at the time and provide a foundation for its later growth. Innovations in transportation, for example, reduce geographic barriers to communication and have a cumulative impact on nationalism in the future. The state of transportation, communications media, and literacy establishes an important limit to the spread of national values at any given time.

The cultural patterns of groups within the national population affect nationalism, as they reflect degrees of national identification and as they later serve either as precedents for nationalism or as foils against which nationalism reacts. Literary themes and attitudes mark the development of nationalism and successively stimulate its rise. Changing language patterns and the extent of education immediately affect nationalism and establish the basis for its future development. Through the biological fusion of originally antagonistic racial groups, miscegenation creates pride in common racial nationality.

Foreigners and foreign states often affect these essentially domestic influences upon nationalism. When one group of people copies the cultural patterns of a foreign group, they fail to develop a unique national culture. Immigration of foreigners introduces a variety of languages, races, and customs, and the acquisition of preponderant wealth and privilege by the foreigners creates an impetus to the xenophobia and demands for equality that can give a nationalist cast to the violence of mass revolutions. The foreign influences, like the social changes that are essentially domestic, have an effect on the growth of a sense of national community extending well beyond the period of their instigation. A basic reason for analyzing the Mexican case is to study the effect of time on these various "protonationalist" forces, the social forces that lead to the rise of cohesive nationalism. By detailed consideration in one national context of the changes in social structure and social attitudes leading to the development of nationalism as a unifying social value, it is hoped that one might raise questions and develop tools of analysis that can be tested in relation to other groups in other periods and national contexts.

II Xenophobia, 1810-1910

Consideration of nineteenth-century Mexican nationalism
has strict limitations, because a marked absence of cohesive
nationalism characterized this period. In the young Mexican state the factionalism that manifested domestic dis-
unity was a prime cause of early foreign conflicts, although
those conflicts in turn produced greater Mexican unity.
When examining the rise of a sense of community among
a people, it is helpful to separate foreign and domestic
influences, to examine successively in "partial equilibrium
analysis" first the effects of outsiders upon the group and
then of changes within the group itself. By temporarily
excluding such influences upon nationalism as common
language and common religion, one can isolate issues such
as the extent to which religion may be alien to nationalism,
the effects of loss of territory, and the rise of national
heroes in foreign wars. The categories of domestic and
foreign influences upon nationalism correspond with what
Mexican writers refer to as Mexico's "internal battle"
and her "external battle."[1] Although nationalism is most
conspicuous by its absence in nineteenth-century Mexico,
it is significant to view both the forces working for and

1. Leopoldo Zea, *El occidente y la conciencia de México* (México: Porrúa
y Obregón, S.A., 1953), p. 41.

against it during that period in order to understand the background for the effective Mexican nationalism of the twentieth century.

The major forces that had shaped the colony of New Spain up to 1810, forces that the first century of Mexican history was to modify but not to change, were, in John J. Johnson's phrase, "basically antinationalistic."[2] Racial distinctions were precise, as the confrontation and initial miscegenation of Indians, Spaniards, and Negroes had created not a feeling of common brotherhood but a sense of separateness attested by the multitude of Spanish terms denoting the gradation of intermixture. Geographical differences among the rugged mountain areas, the coastal lowlands, and the arid regions of the north and west created separate environments so that "diversity is also produced by the physical land itself."[3] The mountain and arid regions combined to make transportation and communications particularly difficult, and the sparsely populated areas of Texas, New Mexico, and California had little contact with the Spanish culture of the southeast. Economic competition, the desire for political influence, and opposing interests regarding free trade set the regions of New Spain in conflict with one another.[4] No powerful neighboring states

2. John J. Johnson, *Political Change in Latin America: The Emergence of the Middle Sectors* (Stanford, Calif.: Stanford University Press, 1958), p. 22.

3. Preston E. James, *Latin America* (3d ed.; New York: The Odyssey Press, 1959), p. 585.

4. On the conflict between regionalism and nationalism in Mexico, see the chapter entitled "Mexico: The Nation and the States," in Harry Bernstein, *Modern and Contemporary Latin America* (New York: J. B. Lippincott Company, 1952), pp. 56-77; Bernstein's 1944 article on "Regionalism in the National History of Mexico," which is reprinted in Howard F. Cline, ed., *Latin American History: Essays on Its Study and Teaching, 1898-1965* (2 vols.; Austin, Texas: University of Texas Press, 1967), Vol. 1, pp. 389-394; and Charles C. Griffin, "An Essay on Regionalism and Nationalism in Latin American Historiography," *Journal of World History*, Vol. 8, No. 2 (1964).

bordered the colony to unite its people in fear and common action. The extensive methods of cultivation in the predominantly agricultural economy, like the sweat shops of the early textile industry or the comparatively well-paying mining industry, depended on cheap labor and so emphasized differences between rich and poor.

The Spanish crown had administered New Spain as part of the greater Spanish empire, so for three centuries the nominal political allegiance of its people was to a group outside the colony. Despite such figures as Hernando Cortés or Sor Juana Inés de la Cruz, New Spain lacked its own military heroes and separate cultural tradition. The leaders of the colony had inherited the Spanish tendency toward strong local loyalties; their immediate loyalty outside the family was often to the isolated *patria chica*. Throughout the colonial period the church and its educational institutions had preached Catholic brotherhood, but this concept of brotherhood was designed to link the diverse groups within New Spain, not with each other, but with both human and divine forces outside the colony. The various factors of race, geography, income levels, a lack of powerful neighbors, an absence of unique military and cultural traditions, and universalistic religion and education united to prevent a feeling of community among the inhabitants of New Spain.

A review of the mutually exclusive groups into which the variety of antinationalistic forces had split the colony of New Spain indicates the difficulties preventing greater cohesion. Indian groups remained separate both from each other and from the Spaniards. Before the Spanish conquest, the powerful Aztecs had been united by their common acceptance of a world in which elemental forces of superhuman, if little understood, strength held sway,[5] although this sense of common subjugation to the force of

5. Jacques Soustelle, *La vida cotidiana de los aztecas en vísperas de la conquista*, Carlos Villegas, trans. (México: Fondo de Cultura Económica, 1956), pp. 101-11.

nature gave the Aztecs no sense of unity with the other Indian tribes. During the colonial period, the attitudes, values, and patterns of life of the Indian groups continued to differ radically among themselves, for the Indian population of New Spain varied from the ancient Maya and advanced Aztec civilizations of the south to the savage Comanches of Texas and Apaches of Arizona. Attempts at religious instruction of the Indians often produced nominal converts, but the severe limitations of higher education in the colony meant that most Indians could not realize more than the most superficial aspects of Spanish culture and religion. To Spaniards, as to many Anglo-Saxons, the Indians appeared to be inferior, lazy, and childlike groups, fit only to be used for pleasure or profit. Even the colonial friars and missionaries who became the Indians' defenders attempted to press them into the mold of Spanish religion and culture rather than accepting the inherent value of the native cultures.

As long as the Indian was regarded as inferior, the members of the mestizo class that had grown up from the beginning of the conquest could not feel themselves to be full participants in the national community. While one may speculate on the extent to which the *indigenismo* of the twentieth century reflects a desire of mestizos to legitimize a part of their ancestry, it is clear that the full-blooded Spaniards of 1810 did not accept the mestizo as an equal. The time had not yet come when writers like José Vasconcelos would take pride in miscegenation and find that "the mestizo represents an entirely new element in history."[6]

Economic as well as racial differences sharply divided the inhabitants of New Spain. Feudal divisions existed in the countryside, where great haciendas grew up subject to the personal decisions of their owners, the privileged *hacendados*. In Mexico City a small upper-class aristocracy

6. José Vasconcelos and Manuel Gamio, *Aspects of Mexican Civilization* (Chicago: University of Chicago Press, 1926), p. 83.

contrasted sharply with the mass of Indians, Negroes, mulattoes, and mestizos whose lack of wealth, status, and regular employment pressed them into positions of lassitude, beggary, and thievery. Vast differences in economic status retarded the growth of nationalism by providing the members of the Mexican state with widely different backgrounds and values and by creating a society with which the majority of its members were unable to identify. Economic division also fed on itself, as the possession of extreme wealth created in a privileged few both pride and fear that an easing of social barriers would ultimately destroy their pre-eminence. The dichotomy between the rich and the poor perpetuated the antagonisms that retarded a sense of national community, as aristocrats, who might have been the most effective champions of national values, isolated themselves in narrow attitudes of self-interest.

Finally, the upper classes within New Spain were divided among themselves. The separate status of military and clerical groups received legal recognition in their *fueros,* the conditions of privilege under which they received separate trials and punishment. The competition among clerical, military, and lay groups for the wealth that each group denied the mass of Indians proved to be a source of friction among the upper classes until they came to share it under Porfirio Díaz. One of the strongest divisions among the upper classes was that between the *criollos* and the *gachupines,* between persons of Spanish blood born in the colony and those born in Spain. The deep hatred between these groups split the religious orders, with *criollos* and *gachupines* withdrawing into separate convents. Although some *criollos* amassed great fortunes, they remained unable to win political influence.[7]   The split continued

7. Catalina Sierra, *El nacimiento de México* (México: Universidad Nacional Autónoma de México, 1960), p. 72. For an excellent general discussion of the incipient *criollo* nationalism, see Hugh M. Hamill, Jr., *The Hidalgo Re-*

throughout the colonial period and is often given as a reason for the wars of independence, as the *criollos* came increasingly to resent the *gachupines'* air of social superiority and the fact that they received the highest positions in both the colonial government and the church.

The divisions among the various Mexican groups, which became particularly evident after independence removed the unity of Spanish rule, have retarded the enlargement of the Mexican national community from the date of independence to the present. They caused Frank Tannenbaum, in 1933, to say, "Mexico is not a nation. It is becoming one, but the process is painful and harsh. Mexico can never have peace unless it achieves internal unity and harmony. It cannot do that unless it destroys the enormous disequilibrium that lies at its roots."[8] Despite conscious attempts to increase national loyalty and cohesion after the 1910 Revolution, as in the murals of Diego Rivera and José Clemente Orozco or in the extensive efforts of the Mexican government to spread the Spanish language, a quarter of the Mexican population remains effectively outside the national community in terms of its subjective loyalties and attitudes. Concentrating on the number of citizens in the national community rather than on the degree of social cohesion that the community has achieved, K. H. Silvert ranks Mexico distinctly behind Argentina, Uruguay, Costa Rica, and Chile in the achievement of national identity.[9] The study of Mexican nationalism, therefore, is the study of a process that is still going on.

---

volt: Prelude to Mexican Independence (Gainesville, Fla.: University of Florida Press, 1966), pp. 38-41. See also Gloria Grajales [Ramos], *Nacionalismo incipiente en los historiadores coloniales* (México: Universidad Nacional Autónoma de México, 1961); and Xavier Tavera Alfaro, *El nacionalismo en la prensa mexicana del siglo XVIII* (México: Club de Periodistas de México, 1963).

8. Frank Tannenbaum, *Peace by Revolution: An Interpretation of Mexico* (New York: Columbia University Press, 1933), p. 111.

9. K. H. Silvert, "Nationalism in Latin America," *The Annals of the American Academy of Political and Social Science*, Vol. 334 (March, 1961), 5.

INDEPENDENCE AND THE INFLUENCE OF SPAIN

Writing of the states in Africa and Asia which have recently gained independence, Henry Kissinger notes that "contrary to the nations of Western Europe, from which they drew their ideal of nationhood, many of the newly independent states are based neither on a common language nor on a common culture. Their only common experience is the former colonial rule. Their leaders require anti-colonialism to achieve not only a sense of personal but also of national identity."[10] Mexico in the early nineteenth century resembled the modern states that Kissinger describes. She drew both her ideas of nationhood and the occasion to effect them from outside states. Attempts to remove colonial rule pointed up the disparate groups in the colony which lacked a common language and a common culture. The fact that many leaders gained their sense of personal identity by identifying with the Hispanic past rather than with anti-Hispanicism served only to show in Mexico, as it may show in Asia and Africa, the difficulty of achieving national culture. Moreover, the actions of Spain from 1821 to 1836, and to a lesser extent thereafter, created a kind of anticolonialism in Mexico which provided a greater sense of national identity.

Foreign influences were decisive in the early formation of Mexican nationalism. The three centuries of Spanish "meddling" that preceded Mexican independence implanted the initial seed for an excitable Mexican nationalism that later events were to nourish.[11] The development of constitutional government and religious toleration in England gradually inspired liberal ideas in New Spain which the censors could not totally suppress. The North American colonies east of New Spain came to espouse democracy

10. Henry A. Kissinger, *Nuclear Weapons and Foreign Policy* (Garden City, N.Y.: Doubleday & Company, Inc., 1958), p. 216.

11. Daniel Cosío Villegas, "Nacionalismo y desarrollo," *Foro Internacional*, Vol. 3, Núm. 3 (enero-marzo, 1963), 323-24.

and equality before the law, made possible in part by their comparatively even distribution of wealth; their successful revolt provided New Spain, after the victory of Yorktown in 1781, with an enduring example of the possibility of independence. Spain's inability to prevent the new United States from acquiring Louisiana in 1803 or Florida in 1819 showed New Spain that her connection with Spain served as no bulwark against neighboring states. The French Revolution raised doubts as to the permanence of monarchical or church domination with its introduction of secularism and overthrow of an entrenched aristocracy. The French Revolution served as a precursor of nationalism in Mexico, as well as in a number of other countries, by its assertion of the liberty, equality, and fraternity of a national community in which all citizens might participate.

Besides establishing much of the ideological framework for the independence movement, events abroad contributed substantially to the accomplishment and maintenance of Mexican independence. Napoleon's conquest of Spain provided the occasion for the early revolts in New Spain, and, to the extent that Napoleon's invasion weakened Spain internally and diverted Spanish troops to other revolts in South America, it also contributed directly to the achievement of Mexican independence in 1821. Both the United States and Britain favored Mexican independence, recognizing Mexico in 1826. In George Canning's proposal of a mutual guarantee of Spanish American independence and in the Monroe Doctrine, both Britain and the United States denounced any attempt at reconquest by the Holy Alliance. Finally, events in Spanish America also affected Mexican independence. The collaboration between the regions of South America to oust Spanish rule and the Panama Congress of 1826 to which Mexico sent representatives showed that, if the danger of Spanish reconquest should actually become imminent, Mexico might expect some help from the other Spanish American republics.

Although foreign ideas of liberty and events abroad undoubtedly shaped the expression of Mexican independence, the early uprisings of Miguel Hidalgo y Costilla and José María Morelos have allowed Mexicans to look back on their own movements as the forerunners of Mexican nationalism. In the war that Hidalgo declared against the *gachupines* in 1810, he called various racial groups together in what became a social revolution. While the violence of the revolt was a precedent for the bloodshed of the Three Years' War and the 1910 Revolution, Hidalgo's concern for the Indians presaged Juárez' attempts at social reform and the *indigenismo* of the twentieth century. Although masses of Indians fought beside the creole officers who followed Ignacio Allende and the regiments of Celaya and Valladolid, their action did little to improve the Indians' poverty over the next hundred years. Like their original possession of the land or the simple fact of their physical presence in Mexico, however, it serves as a further argument for their incorporation into the Mexican nation.

Detractors of Hidalgo find him something other than an ideal national hero. He led a bloody revolt that Lucas Alamán, then a witness at eighteen, condemned with horror in his *Historia de México*. Vanity allowed Hidalgo to lead his forces despite his lack of military knowledge rather than giving Allende command or following Allende's advice to advance on Mexico City without delay after Colonel Trujillo's defeat, and Hidalgo seems to have renounced his own deeds in what appears to be an authentic *mea culpa*. Nevertheless, Hidalgo was a figure who easily became a national hero. He now appears in textbooks and popular literature as Mexico's champion, a symbol of resistance to foreign rule and domestic oppression. His Grito de Dolores provides Mexicans with their largest national holiday. On the night of September 15, huge crowds still gather in the Zocalo at Mexico City to see the president of Mexico ring Hidalgo's bell as they join clamorously in shouting long life to all the heroes of the independence movement. The president's words are broadcast to each city and hamlet in Mexico, where the celebration is duplicated in miniature.

In José María Morelos, Mexicans gained an advocate of most of the programs that later reforms were to incorporate. In the plans he made at Chilpancingo in 1813, Morelos proposed not only separation from Spain for his republic of Anáhuac but also racial equality, the abolition of clerical and military *fueros,* and the distribution of land from the haciendas to the peasants. Mexicans today remember proudly that Morelos' program of reform envisioned independence with sovereignty residing in the people, an end to slavery and economic exploitation of the poor, and complete equality before the law for all citizens.[12] Morelos' program anticipated much that developed after the 1910 Revolution, and Morelos himself was a man whom the revolutionaries could look back upon with genuine pride. He proved to be a brilliant military strategist, and he never repented of his program although he was shot for it. His selfless devotion to national goals is reminiscent of George Washington's refusal to become a despot.

The wars for independence from Spain provided Mexico with a variety of national heroes in addition to Hidalgo and Morelos. Vicente Guerrero,[13] a man who was dedicated to Morelos' ideas and whose ancestry happened to combine the Indian, Spanish, and Negro races, continued his resistance after Morelos' death and finally helped Agustín de Iturbide win independence. He was joined in the final victory by such heroic men as the self-styled Guadalupe Victoria, who survived alone for two years in the hinterland

12. For an example of the contemporary process of hero-creation, see Ubaldo Vargas Martínez, *Morelos, siervo de la nación* (México: Secretaría de Educación Pública, 1963), especially pp. 155-56, 189-90, 220.

13. For an early piece of literary hero-creation that typifies coeval tracts written about the other heroes of independence, see *Al ciudadano . . . al general . . . al venemérito de la patria en grado heroíco ¡Vicente Guerrero . . .! con los amigos, con los enemigos en la paz y en la guerra, fue magnánimo* (San Luis Potosí, S.L.P.: Imprenta del Estado, 1833).

to avoid capture, and Nicolás Bravo, who had the humanity to release three hundred prisoners after the Spaniards had shot his father. Bravo also distinguished himself later by putting Iturbide on a boat for Europe after he had declared himself emperor. The folkloric creation of national heroes is strikingly apparent in the case of Hidalgo, whose attack on the Alhóndiga in September, 1810, is recorded in pamphlets and school textbooks, not as the massacre that Lucas Alamán describes, but as the occasion for the heroism of El Pípila. Protecting himself by tying a huge flagstone on his back, Juan José Martínez, famous under his nickname of El Pípila, crawled to the door of the fortress and set it afire to let the revolutionaries enter. El Pípila is one of the individuals most frequently mentioned when one asks Mexican schoolchildren about the heroes of their nation.

Although the clergy, army, and landowners originally opposed the plans of Hidalgo and Morelos for social reform, they came to join later Mexican heroes in opposing the *gachupines* and continued Spanish rule. After all, they stood to gain most from the nomination of clerical and military leaders in Mexico and an end to subsidies to the Spanish crown. Liberal and reactionary groups were brought together by Iturbide, who used their support to seize power for himself. In confining his revolt to political separation from Spain, Iturbide accomplished more than Hidalgo and Morelos by attempting less, but in furthering Mexican nationalism by achieving independence, he also retarded it by trying to retain the stratification of colonial society. Iturbide's revolt served in later years as but a small stimulus to nationalism, because he tried to establish a monarchy based on all the old divisions of race and income in Mexican society. Nevertheless, Iturbide and the groups that he represented did gain for Mexico the political independence from Spain so necessary for the establishment of a separate Mexican nationalism.

After independence the influence of the Spanish state

continued to further Mexican nationalism. It is quite true that in one sense the inheritance of Spanish culture, like the aping of French culture later in the century, retarded the development of a separate Mexican culture, although it did provide Mexico with a feeling of distinct separateness from the United States. The influence of Spanish culture is distinct from the influence of the Spanish state, however, and may be better discussed in connection with the rise of Mexican literature and art forms. The influence of Spain itself after independence was evident enough in the Spanish troops remaining in the island fortress of San Juan de Ulúa and in a Spanish attempt at reconquest. When, in 1829, Ferdinand VII sent an expeditionary force to Mexico under General Isidro Barradas, Santa Anna defeated Barradas' men, who were sick and lacked sufficient food, in a short but violent action. Even though Mexicans could gain little national consciousness from the small affair, it did create further hostility to Spain. Anti-Spanish feeling manifested itself in a series of expulsions of the Spaniards left in Mexico, but these expulsions hurt the Mexican economy by depriving Mexico of much of her small middle class and the considerable capital the Spaniards took with them. Spain generated further Mexican hostility by adamantly refusing to recognize Mexican independence. It was not until December, 1836, that a treaty of peace and friendship was signed between Spain and Mexico, and Mexico received Spanish ratification of the treaty in February, 1838.[14]

Even after recognizing Mexican independence, Spain gave Mexican nationalists some cause for fear. In the 1840's Mexicans were concerned with Spanish influence among the separatists of Yucatán, particularly the activity of the Spanish commercial agent in Campeche.[15] Spain

14. Carlos Bosch García, *Problemas diplomáticos del México independiente* (México: El Colegio de México, 1947), pp. 188, 191.
15. Jaime Delgado, *España y México en el siglo XIX* (3 vols.; Madrid: Consejo Superior de Investigaciones Científicas, Instituto Gonzalo Fernández de Oviedo, 1950-53), Vol. 2, p. 281.

continued to control Cuba and Puerto Rico until 1898; the repeated revolts there and the resulting number of Spanish soldiers sent to quell them remained a source of potential friction long after Mexicans had given up plans to liberate the islands as a means of safeguarding their own independence. Spanish troops again came to Mexico when General Prim landed at Veracruz in December, 1861, and the British and French detachments who were to act in conjunction with Spain in settling problems of claims did not join the Spanish army until January, 1862. When Prim left Mexico, partly because he discovered Napoleon's desire to intervene in Mexico and partly in order to watch political events in Madrid, Spanish activity elsewhere in the Americas showed that Spain was not free of colonial designs. Spain annexed the neighboring Dominican Republic from 1861 to 1865, and seized the Chincha Islands from Peru in 1864. Like the actions of the Spanish state, the private investments and economic power of Spanish citizens in Mexico, which increased further under the Díaz regime, allowed Mexicans to continue their hostility to Spain long after independence had been won.

Spain, therefore, influenced Mexican nationalism in several ways during the nineteenth century. It was against Spanish and *gachupín* power that Iturbide finally established the Mexican independence that was a basis of nationalism, as both liberals and conservatives within Mexico joined against opposing movements within Spain. The social and economic reforms of Hidalgo and Morelos could have produced the greater individual equality that Manuel Gamio later found necessary for the establishment of a viable national community, so they can be looked back upon as progenitors by later promoters of Mexican nationalism. The process of cultural hero-creation that began soon after independence gave Mexicans a set of historical figures in whom to take common national pride. If the Spanish resistance to Mexican independence helped to create national heroes, it also helped throughout the nineteenth century to remind Mexico of her former status. The garrison at San Juan de Ulúa, the attempt at reconquest, the intrigues with separatists and monarchists, the long delayed recognition, the troops of General Prim, and the continuing economic power of Spanish citizens made Mexicans repeatedly aware of their nationality, as did their inheritance of Spanish cultural patterns which set them off from the expanding Anglo-Saxon culture of the north.

THE UNITED STATES, TEXAS, AND THE WAR OF 1847

Extrapolating from the national history of the United States, it would be easy for North Americans to discount the potential influence of foreign states in shaping national attitudes.[16] The strength, independence, and long isolation of the United States make it difficult for most Americans to conceive of the sentiments of fear, anxiety, and belligerence that an overpowering and apparently hostile state may provoke in a neighboring populace. Between 1810 and 1910, the power of the United States, as measured by such standards as territorial size, population, and economic potential, increased decisively, and in so doing it provided Mexico with that strong neighboring state that the colony of New Spain had lacked. Successive friction between the United States

16. For the United States, nationalistic feelings were certainly heightened by the wars with Britain which began in 1775 and 1812, although significant groups within the United States preferred to move to Canada after independence, to trade with Britain during Jefferson's Embargo, or to oppose the War of 1812 at the Hartford Convention. Despite incipient conflicts with Britain, settled by the Webster-Ashburton and Clayton-Bulwer treaties, and even the potential intervention of European powers in the Civil War, the geographic isolation of the United States formed a severe barrier to foreign invasion until the radical improvements in world-wide transportation in the twentieth century. The Mexican and Spanish-American Wars hardly threatened United States territory. The effect of our own western frontier was far more significant in shaping American attitudes and values than fear of strong foreign states. The very fact that the growing strength of the United States as compared to that of Canada and Mexico relieved American citizens of potential anxiety in the nineteenth century was in itself a source of anxiety for those neighboring states.

and Mexico in the nineteenth century gave all Mexicans an opportunity to work in a common cause, and, whatever the motives of the United States government or its citizens, it also gave advocates of Mexican nationalism a set of historical precedents on which to base claims for the need for national unity.

Friction underlay the initial cordiality between the United States and Mexico. The achievement of independence from European control and the mutual desire to maintain that independence gave Mexico and the United States nominal claim to a common experience and a common interest in 1821. Iturbide declared his admiration for Henry Clay and his appreciation of Clay's championship of Mexico in Congress. What benefit the United States had derived from common experience, friendly declarations, and early American recognition of Mexican independence was undone in large part, however, during the first fifteen years of Mexican-American relations. By the time of Joel R. Poinsett's arrival in Mexico in 1825, a number of conflicts were evident. The United States resented growing British influence in Mexico, and both Mexico and the United States feared that the other was planning to seize Cuba. The differences between North American democracy and Protestantism and the aristocratic dominance and Catholicism of Mexico became sharper as the danger of Spanish reconquest receded. Poinsett failed to dispel this discord but rather increased the hostility by his intervention in Mexican politics. The friction caused by Poinsett's promotion of democracy and American business interests, his countering of British activity, and his siding with the York Rite Freemasons of Mexico against those of the Scottish Rite was increased still further by the second United States minister, Anthony Butler. Butler was, as North American historian Justin H. Smith readily admits, "a national disgrace . . . personally a bully and swashbuckler, ignorant of the Spanish language and even the forms of diplomacy

... wholly unprincipled as to methods, and, by the testimony of two American consuls, openly scandalous in his conduct."[17] Poinsett's attempt to purchase Texas and Butler's open advocacy of annexation by the United States increased Mexican fears of Yankee expansion.

The historical causes of the Texas secession in 1835, the annexation of Texas to the United States in 1845, and the War of 1846 to 1848 in which Mexico lost the California territory do not have as much bearing on Mexican nationalism as do the causes that the Mexicans themselves have attributed to them. J. Fred Rippy may be essentially correct in saying that the early settlers in Texas "were entirely innocent of conspiracy or of ulterior motives of any sort."[18] Justin H. Smith attempts objectivity in his exhaustive study of *The War with Mexico* when he lays blame for the Texas secession primarily on Mexican politicians and the Mexican military.[19] The overwhelming opinion among most Mexicans, however, has been that the United States encouraged secession, annexation, and war in order to expand its territory. The majority of them would accept the blunt statement by José Vasconcelos, in his popular *Breve historia de México*, that "the Texas colonists were the advance guard of yankee imperialism."[20] Even writers who do not speak of imperialism, such as Carlos Bosch

17. Justin H. Smith, *The War with Mexico* (2 vols.; New York: The Macmillan Company, 1919), Vol. 1, p. 62.

18. J. Fred Rippy, *The United States and Mexico* (New York: Alfred A. Knopf, 1926), p. 8.

19. While fully cognizant of Smith's painstaking scholarship, Mexicans find his work to be "a late expression of Manifest Destiny." See Silvio Zavala, "La historiografía americana sobre la guerra de 47," *Cuadernos Americanos*, Año 7, Vol. 38, Núm. 2 (marzo-abril, 1948), especially 202-5.

20. José Vasconcelos, *Breve historia de México* (3d ed.; México: Editorial Continental, 1959), p. 327. A more specialized tirade which, in bitterly emphasizing the frictions in Mexican-American relations from the early nineteenth century to 1959, concludes that the United States has risen to greatness largely at the expense of Mexico is Mario Gill, *Nuestros buenos vecinos* (4th ed.; México: Editorial Azteca, S.A., 1959). Gill's treatment of the Texas secession and the War of 1847 on pages 17 to 89 exemplifies those accounts that consciously try to arouse fierce Mexican pride and xenophobia. The Cuban regime of Fidel Castro has republished a special edition of *Nuestros buenos vecinos*.

García in his objective and unemotional *Historia de las relaciones entre México y los Estados Unidos, 1819-1848,* can find good reason to fear American acquisitiveness in the pro-Texas and pro-expansion American press.[21]

The loss of Texas, New Mexico, and California has furthered Mexican nationalism in at least four ways. First, it provided an outside focus in the Republic of Texas and the United States against which Mexicans of the time could join in opposition. All classes and groups can set aside their struggles with one another to oppose a foreign foe, and as they continue to oppose forces from outside the national unit over a period of time, their makeshift co-operation proves the feasibility of internal unity. The need to resist foreigners leads to ideological emphasis on the need for unity to make that resistance effective.

At first glance, it seems that Mexicans had little to rally them to a national cause, considering the perfidy and incompetence of Santa Anna and the series of defeats like that at San Jacinto, where Texans, with 3 men killed and 18 wounded, managed to kill nearly 400 Mexicans, wound 200, and take 730 prisoners. What is under consideration is the feeling of common purpose that grows up among the inhabitants of a state, and this feeling is furthered by mutual fear of renewed foreign oppression or a shared sense of wounded pride as well as by a shared joy in common victory that in itself removes the original cause of joint action. It is quite natural that promoters of nationalism should re-examine their history with the idea of pointing out the positive achievements of the national group. It would be a far different matter, however, to say that all feelings of national community that arose among men in the earlier period could be motivated only by victory. The loss of Texas, New Mexico, and California may have increased Mexican nationalism at the time, even though the

21. Carlos Bosch García, *Historia de las relaciones entre México y los Estados Unidos, 1819-1848* (México: Escuela Nacional de Ciencias Políticas y Sociales, Universidad Nacional Autónoma de México, 1961), pp. 173-78.

final proof of Texas' self-assertion and the apparent inefficiency of the central government stimulated *cacique* autonomy and the assertion of *patria chica* loyalties in the aftermath of the War of 1847. It is possible, of course, that the war had no positive immediate effect on Mexican nationalism but rather destroyed loyalties to the national state by demonstrating the state's ineffectiveness. Although the war may or may not have initially stimulated any great degree of national loyalty, the fact that factionalism was not immediately reduced indicates the extent of the divisions within Mexican society and the limited effectiveness of xenophobia in counteracting them.

Second, the loss of Texas, New Mexico, and California provided Mexico with a permanent focus for xenophobia, a focus made particularly effective where low educational levels made most of the population lacking in reasoned analysis and historical objectivity. The "myth of the treasure of Texas and California"[22] remains a potent emotive force in Mexican society. Mexicans can still be rallied by a sense of their lost territory, and when something goes wrong in Mexico, it is possible to say, "Yes, but that would not matter if we had Los Angeles or San Francisco or Houston." The incompetence of Santa Anna can be left unnoted when prominent writers like José Vasconcelos continue to stir Mexican nationalism with references to "Yankee imperialism."

Third, the loss of half of her territory deprived Mexico of the need to incorporate it into an effective national unit. After 1848 the Indians of the north became the gringos' problem. Only massive border fortifications could have prevented the westward movement of individual Anglo-Saxons, particularly after the discovery of California gold, and if Mexico had retained title to her northern territories, she would only have been faced with the problem of in-

22. Jorge Carrión, ''Efectos psicológicos de la guerra de 47 en el hombre de México,'' *Cuadernos Americanos*, Año 7, Vol. 37, Núm. 1 (enero-febrero, 1948), 127, 131.

corporating yet another disparate group into her national community.

Finally, it may be argued that the territorial losses proved to be one of the most conclusive of a series of recognized needs for national unity. The Texas secession was the result of an internal conflict that directly alienated a large part of Mexico's territory and, to the extent that the war with the United States was brought on by Mexican intransigence over the Texas issue, indirectly alienated California as well. Furthermore, internal conflicts prevented Mexico from putting up an effective military or diplomatic resistance to United States expansion. Mexicans were increasingly to reflect Justo Sierra's fear that the United States would absorb Mexico and extinguish her nationality if she were found weak. Like a variety of other events in the nineteenth century, and like the violence and destructiveness of the Revolution of 1910, the early losses of territory to the United States indicated the need for an effective unification of the Mexican citizenry.

In retrospect, the war with the United States injected the Mexican people with a deep national consciousness. Although Santa Anna tried to save face after the 1847 defeats by associating his personal honor with the national honor of Mexico,[23] his symbolic importance to the Mexican national community is that of a scapegoat and an ''antihero'' against whom Mexicans join in disgust. Mexicans look back with little pride on their generals and on the outcome of major battles, but they take pride in the tenacity of their common soldiers. Recent Mexican accounts consciously appeal to nationalist sentiments by charging American soldiers with pillage, by accusing General Winfield Scott of stealing Mexican archives, and by denouncing ''the lack of patriotism'' that some Mexicans displayed in col-

23. *Al pueblo mexicano: Relación de las causas que influyeron en los desgraciados sucesos del día de agosto de 1847* (México: Imprenta de Vicente García Torres, 1847), p. 8.

laborating with the United States "enemy."[24] The American attack on the Military College at Chapultepec Castle on September 13, 1847, gave Mexico a new set of national heroes in the Niños Héroes, the young cadets who died fighting the American invaders. In order to prevent the Yankees from defiling his country's flag, Cadet Juan Escutia wrapped himself in the Mexican colors that flew above the castle and leaped to his death from the battlements. Mexico today celebrates the Niños Héroes in popular textbooks, in colorful pictures with which children decorate their homes, and even in cinema newsreels that show the president of Mexico awarding swords on September 13 to the contemporary cadets of the Colegio Militar.

Anyone wishing to promote a sense of Mexican nationalism by stimulating fear of the United States can find ample precedents following the War of 1846 to 1848. After the acquisition of Texas and California, a vocal minority within the United States supported annexation of all Mexico. The Gadsden Treaty of 1853, although drawn up primarily to settle boundary disputes and to facilitate a southern railroad route for the United States, did add more Mexican territory to the United States. The desire for right of transit and protection on the Isthmus of Tehuantepec aroused some fear of American expansion, for Nicholas P. Trist was authorized to pay extra for the right and certain rights were later incorporated into the Gadsden Treaty. Since these rights were not canceled until 1937, Mexicans had a number of years in which to ponder the potential limitations on their sovereignty.

Mexican conservatives even see Secretary of State William H. Seward's efforts to aid Benito Juárez and remove the French from Mexico as undue American influence. Mexican writers such as Rafael de Castro orig-

24. Alberto María Carreño, *México y los Estados Unidos de América: Apuntaciones para la historia del acrecentamiento territorial de los Estados Unidos a costa de México desde la época colonial hasta nuestros días* (México: Editorial Jus, S.A., 1962), pp. 154-56.

inally justified French intervention and the monarchy of Maximilian as necessary for the realization of Mexican nationalism by claiming that they would prevent United States invasion and cure Mexico's "social disorganization."[25] Although standard Mexican histories now approve and give importance to Secretary Seward's diplomatic pressure on Napoleon III,[26] a more conservative line of Mexican thinking represented by José Vasconcelos still violently resents the United States "interference." Vasconcelos, as quoted by Erico Verissimo, expresses this viewpoint when he says, "the year 1865 saw the Empire consolidated. But unfortunately the Civil War in the United States ended that same year with the victory of the Unionists, and the first thing they did was to invoke the Monroe Doctrine, threatening us with the invasion of Mexico by Grant's troops."[27]

The final assertion of United States government influence before the conciliatory policies of the Díaz regime eased official Mexican-American relations occurred in 1877, when talk of war arose from President Rutherford B. Hayes's need to divert attention from his doubtful electoral victory. In response to bellicose North American statements, Díaz sent General Treviño to the border to establish order and to counter a possible United States offensive. It is a mark of the increased national unity that Mexico had achieved from its previous friction with the United States and from other sources that this order rallied Mexicans from all factions solidly behind Díaz.

A number of other irritants in Mexican-American rela-

25. J. Rafael de Castro, *La cuestión mexicana, ó esposición de las causas que hacian indispensables la intervención europea y el restablecimiento de la monarquía en México como unicos medios de salvar la nacionalidad y la independencia del país* (México: Imprenta de J. M. Andrade y F. Escalante, 1864), pp. 70, 87.

26. See Alfonso Toro, *Compendio de historia de México: La revolución de independencia y México independiente* (11th ed.; México: Editorial Patria, S.A., 1959), p. 534.

27. Quoted in Erico Verissimo, *Mexico*, Linton Barrett, trans. (New York: The Orion Press, 1960), p. 197.

tions promoted nationalistic sentiment among particular groups of Mexicans. Raids of American filibusters such as those of William Walker into Sonora in 1853, Callahan and Henry in 1855, or the Crabb expedition of 1857 in which over sixty filibusters were shot after surrendering stirred a national consciousness in the inhabitants of the northern states and rekindled general fears of annexation. The fact that Yucatán remained neutral and maintained its own agent in Washington during the War of 1847 exemplified the divided nature of the Mexican polity. Not only did the inhabitants of Yucatán feel an intense local loyalty that separated them from the inhabitants of Mexico living outside the peninsula, but the Yucatecos themselves were also typically split by the division between the Spanish and Maya populations and the sharp rivalry between the city of Campeche and the rest of the peninsula.[28] When an Indian uprising in 1848 made the inhabitants of Yucatán seek annexation to the United States, Mexicans in touch with the Yucatán situation were made additionally aware of the need to forge a truly national state.

The mounting number of claims by and against American citizens for damage to property, seizure of cargoes, personal injury, or imprisonment forced many Mexicans to turn for settlement to their national government, thus developing a personal stake in the effectiveness of that government. Claims involving officials of the American government sometimes aroused considerable public bitterness, as did those involving Consuls John A. Robinson and Francis W. Rice. It was from a variety of lesser incidents that directly involved only a small number of Mexicans —the filibuster raids and the international claims—and from events of more general relevance—the loss of Texas, New Mexico, and California; Seward's Mexican policy;

28. Ricardo Molina Hübbe, ''Yucatán en el siglo XIX,'' *Ciencias Políticas y Sociales,* Año 2, Núm. 3 (enero-marzo, 1956), 104-5, 121-27. See also Nelson Reed, *The Caste War of Yucatan* (Stanford, Calif.: Stanford University Press, 1964).

and Díaz' dispatch of General Treviño—that Mexicans became increasingly aware of their powerful neighbor.

The influence of the Catholic church worked against secular
nationalism in nineteenth-century Mexico. As a body of
doctrine claiming universal applicability and supreme importance, its precepts vied with national allegiance for
the loyalty of the Mexican people. As a world-wide movement directed from Rome, its official position repeatedly
resembled that of other foreign powers who tried to impose
their will on the Mexican people. Finally, as a vested
economic interest within Mexico, the church tried to maintain its privileged position and so inevitably aligned itself
with those secular conservatives who were trying to maintain a system that effectively excluded the majority of the
Mexican people from a sense of national participation.

In its role as a body of universalistic doctrine, the
church faced the same barriers of geography and tradition
that faced the growth of a sense of national community
in the nineteenth century. Frank Tannenbaum cogently
argues that "the Mexican Indian is parochial. His universe
is exceedingly limited; the mountains that circumscribe his
horizon define his intellectual and spiritual world. The
gods he worships are local gods. . . . The notion of an
organized church, of a universal Catholic Church, is beyond the experience of the isolated primitive communities."[29] While devotion to universalistic doctrine worked
against an exclusively national orientation for the comparatively few Mexicans who had received a higher education, it is doubtful that it was a major factor in delaying
a sense of nationalism among the masses.

The economic position of the Mexican church prompted
considerable political concern. The church owned half the

29. Tannenbaum, *Peace by Revolution*, p. 61.

real estate in Mexico and collected vast income from its investments, tithes, and payments for religious services. In addition to its fundamental doctrines of charity and salvation that were universal rather than nationally exclusive, the Mexican church emphasized such virtues as obedience and humility that favored the wealthier classes and its own vested interests.

During the struggles for independence and immediately thereafter, the papacy remained hostile to the establishment of a separate Mexican state, while the Mexican clergy attempted to use the new state for its own purposes. Although Hidalgo and Morelos were priests, the church could not be associated with the independence movement when these two were denounced, excommunicated, and turned over to secular authorities to be shot as traitors to Spain. After political independence from Spain was achieved, the church insisted that the clergy should retain its privileged status but that the rights of patronage formerly vested in Spain should revert to the Holy See. While on the surface this would appear to be a separation of church and state, it would in fact have greatly increased the power of the church. In 1824 Pope Leo XII urged Mexican prelates to support Ferdinand VII. When the archbishop of Mexico and the bishop of Michoacán left Mexico for Spain, the pope refused to fill the vacancies. The papal policy went so far that, within three years, seven of the ten bishoprics and seventy-nine of the cathedral benefices lacked incumbents.

After independence the church fought to maintain its power in Mexico. Under the leadership of Valentín Gómez Farías in 1833 a Liberal Congress passed legislation to curb the power of both the papacy and the Mexican clergy. The Congress declared that the *patronato* belonged to the state and limited state support for the church by making tithes voluntary and abolishing civil enforcement of monastic vows. In retaliation, the church joined forces with the army, under the opportunistic leadership of Santa

Anna, to oust the Liberals. The Ley Juárez of 1855 elimi-
nating the jurisdiction of ecclesiastical courts over civil
cases but not criminal cases met clerical rebellion in Puebla.
The Ley Lerdo a year later provided for the sale of church
property. In retaliation for the resulting clerical attacks,
cemeteries were placed under civil control, and the Ley
Iglesias removed the civil rights of the clergy. When the
Constitution of 1857 incorporated previous measures to
limit clerical power, Pope Pius IX simply declared that the
document had no validity. The constitution received similar condemnation within Mexico, as Archbishop of Mexico
Lázaro de la Garza y Ballesteros declared that the sacraments would be denied to any official who swore allegiance
to it.

But not all of the clergy opposed the establishment of
a more independent Mexican state; some continued to give
the sacraments to all who asked, and a few died for their
liberal views, as did Father Rodrigo Victoria who was shot
by General Mejía. Some clerics shared the views of Father
Ignacio Hernández, who wrote that the "Constitution is
the expression of a free country which no one has the right
to oppose" and that the "clergy has been wrong in resisting
openly and with forbidden weapons—through the pulpit
and pastoral and in other ways—profaning the church of
Jesus Christ, defeating the purposes of His supreme authority, causing incalculable harm to the country, and while
proclaiming defense of the church, in reality injuring
and ruining it."[30] Despite the occasional voicing of such
clerical views, however, the church as a whole was so opposed to reform that, in conjunction with secular conservatives, it fought a long and bloody war between 1858
and 1861 for the retention of its authority.

The legislation of the Mexican Reforma did not attack
the religious convictions of the Mexican people but rather

30. Quoted in Ernest Gruening, *Mexico and Its Heritage* (New York:
The Century Company, 1928), p. 205. See also Robert J. Knowlton, "Clerical
Response to the Mexican Reform, 1855-1875," *The Catholic Historical Review*,
Vol. 50, No. 4 (January, 1965).

curbed the economic privileges and the secular power of the church. As the law of December 4, 1860, stated, the church could be constituted only by the spontaneous consent of its members and could exercise over them no more than "simply spiritual" authority.[31] By reducing the economic and political power of the church, the Liberals divested a group within Mexico of the unique privileges and status that set it apart from other groups.

When the Liberal victory in the Three Years' War confirmed the limitations imposed on the secular power of the church, the church turned for restoration of its privileges to foreign intervention and Maximilian of Austria. The pope blessed the imposition of Maximilian as emperor of Mexico, and the Mexican clergy at first also supported Maximilian, declaring that all who opposed the French armies that he led would be excommunicated and that they would not minister to wounded Liberal soldiers. When Maximilian refused to completely restore church power, however, suggesting support for the church but toleration of other religions and questioning the practicality of returning church lands, the clergy turned against him. The breach between the emperor and the clerical party within Mexico was so complete that, when French troops withdrew, Maximilian was left without any effective support within the state that he nominally ruled.

31. Jesús Reyes Heroles, *La integración de las ideas* (Vol. 3, *El liberalismo mexicano*; 3 vols.; México: Universidad Nacional Autónoma de México, 1957-61), p. 226. On the power of the Mexican church, see also Wilfred H. Callcott, *Church and State in Mexico, 1822-1857* (Durham, N.C.: Duke University Press, 1926); Ernest Galarza, *The Roman Catholic Church As a Factor in the Political and Social History of Mexcio* (Sacramento, Calif.: Capital Press, 1928); José María Luis Mora, *El clero, el estado y la economía nacional* (México: Empresas Editoriales, 1950); William Marion Clawson, "The Influence of the Catholic Church on the Development of the Mexican Government and Its Relationship to Protestant Missions" (unpublished D.Th. dissertation, New Orleans Baptist Theological Seminary, 1960); and Martín Quirarte, *El problema religioso en México* (México: Instituto Nacional de Anthropología e Historia, 1967). On the legislation through which the Mexican government curbed the power of the church, see Walter V. Scholes, *Mexican Politics During the Juárez Regime, 1855-1872* (Columbia, Mo.: The University of Missouri Studies, 1957), pp. 47-55.

The battles to strip the church of privileges during the first fifty years of the Mexican Republic contributed substantially toward the achievement of Mexican nationalism. The reforms clearly illuminated the extranational motivations of nineteenth-century papal authority, as the pope invalidated the Constitution of 1857 and supported the candidacy of Ferdinand VII and Maximilian. While the church regained prestige and some secular influence under the Díaz regime, it never won back its economic dominance. The revolutionaries of 1910 held up the Juárez reforms as a glowing precedent for the final limitations on church power which the Revolution had imposed. In trying to limit the church to the separate sphere of purely religious authority, the reforms indicated the extent to which the church itself could later be incorporated as one of the groups promoting Mexican nationalism. When the church was shorn of its worldly privileges, beliefs like those of Father Hernández could become more general. The church could then join, as it has done to some extent as a result of the increased tolerance of the revolutionary party since the late 1930's, other groups on an equal footing and acknowledge the coexistence of national and spiritual loyalties.

FRANCE AND MAXIMILIAN

During the colonial period, France often appeared in the role of New Spain's enemy. French pirates captured the first ship that Cortés sent back to Spain laden with Aztec treasure, and in 1562 Menéndez de Avilés liquidated a colony of French Protestants who had settled in Florida. French acquisitions in Louisiana and the Caribbean came to rival Spanish dominance in New Spain. French trade with the colony, which rose sharply in the eighteenth century, posed an increasing threat to the legitimate authorities. At the end of the colonial period, France did not recognize Mexican independence until well after the American and British treaties of July and December, 1826. She signed only a provisional declaration with Mexico in 1827 and did not conclude a treaty of friendship, commerce, and navigation until 1831.

After independence the claims of French citizens against Mexico increased commensurately with the amount of French foreign investment, and seventeen years later her first foreign war, the Franco-Mexican War of 1838 and 1839, resulted. The limited nature of the war and the fact that Mexicans have given it the jocose name of the "Pastry War" after a French restaurant owner who was one of the claimants indicate that it had little effect on Mexican nationalism. Only passing note was taken of the French seizure, under Admiral Baudin, of the previously invulnerable fortress of San Juan de Ulúa or of the fall of Veracruz after what Frank E. Lally calls "a wretched resistance."[32] The loss of Santa Anna's leg and his statement that he might now die happy if his fellow citizens conceded him to have been a "Good Mexican" gave Mexico an object of ridicule rather than a true national hero, as it was obvious that Santa Anna had no thought of dying. Mexicans have taken some national pride in the war, however, as histories, such as Guillermo Prieto's written for Mexican military cadets, single out the heroism of individual Mexican defenders like Blas Godines and Antonio Gaona.[33]

It was never essential that the Mexicans unite against a large-scale French invasion, because British influence and yellow fever actually won the war. Britain, whose primary concerns in nineteenth-century Mexico were unimpeded trade and further British investment, repeatedly sought to bring Mexico and France together and mediated the final accord. In the spring of 1838, scurvy and yellow fever

32. Frank Edward Lally, *French Opposition to the Mexican Policy of the Second Empire* (Baltimore, Md.: The Johns Hopkins University Press, 1931), p. 23.

33. Guillermo Prieto, *Lecciones de historia patria, escritas para los alumnos del Colegio Militar* (3d ed.; México: Oficina Tip. de la Secretaría de Fomento, 1891), p. 355.

reduced the original French blockade force by one-half, so
the French were more than ready to accept conciliation
when the pestilence returned in 1839. Although the Pastry
War did little to arouse Mexican nationalism, it did confirm
the pattern of earlier French hostility and emphasize the
menace that foreign states presented.

In 1862 the further accumulation of French claims
served as the excuse for a second military intervention
that was to have a much more formidable effect on the rise
of Mexican nationalism. Claims, the United States preoccupation in the Civil War, the desire of Napoleon III to
solidify his rule by a foreign triumph, the dissatisfaction
of the Mexican clerical party after its defeat in the
Three Years' War, and the tales of easy conquest spun by
a group of Mexican *émigrés* at the French court combined
to bring the French armies to Mexico again in 1862. The
Spanish and the British forces originally accompanying
the French soon found that claims were not the only issue,
and by April, 1862, they decided to leave. Napoleon sent a
new French army under General Lorencez, which was able
until 1867 to enforce loyalty to Maximilian, the Hapsburg
prince whom Mexican conservatives called upon to accept a
Mexican throne. The Mexicans who fought against French
troops from 1862 to 1867 developed a strong sense of Mexican patriotism, and resentment developed between the
French troops and their Mexican allies, as the French
contemptuously found the Mexicans difficult to train and
openly accused the Mexican officers and soldiers of widespread dishonesty, deceit, and a tendency to embezzlement.[34]

Maximilian tried and failed to identify himself with
Mexican nationalism. By dressing in the Mexican style,
by referring to himself as a Mexican, and by replacing
many European counselors with Mexicans, he seems from

34. Jack Autrey Dabbs, *The French Army in Mexico, 1861-1867: A Study
in Military Government* (The Hague: Mouton & Co., 1963), p. 263. For an
annotated bibliography of Mexican studies of the French intervention, see
Ernesto de la Torre Villar and Arturo Gómez Camacho, ''La Intervención
Francesa,'' *Historia Mexicana*, Vol. 25, Núm. 4 (abril-junio, 1966).

the beginning to have only estranged the Mexican people. His attempts to win favor among Mexican Liberals and his refusal to restore church lands and privileges alienated him from those conservative groups that at first had supported him. On October 3, 1865, Maximilian tried to end all resistance quickly by decreeing the death penalty for all who opposed his forces, but in carrying out the decree he only increased Mexican resentment. Paradoxically, in trying to associate himself with the Mexican nation, Maximilian strengthened Mexican nationalism by turning more and more Mexicans against himself.

Maximilian and the French army served, as had the United States in the War of 1847, as a focus for Mexican nationalism. Mexico gained a new national holiday in the victory over Laurencez at Puebla, when on May 5, 1862, the French army was forced back to the coast with the loss of a thousand men. The period of defeat for Benito Juárez, when in the spring of 1865 he controlled only a small portion of the far north, in retrospect makes his final triumph seem all the grander. Mexican nationalism finds a solid foundation in the fact that Mexicans did defeat the foreign invader. The Juárez forces received indirect aid both from groups within France which opposed Napoleon's costly and imperialistic enterprise and, after Robert E. Lee's surrender in April, 1865, from Secretary Seward's heavy diplomatic pressure on Napoleon to withdraw French troops. But the forces working within France and the diplomatic pressure of a foreign government were by no means as obvious to the Mexican people as were the victorious soldiers of Juárez.

Long-range anti-French feeling similar to that engendered earlier against the Spanish and the North Americans did not develop in the struggles of the 1860's. Maximilian is not a villain but a misguided hero, and today many Mexicans look back upon him with pride and make him one of "their own" important leaders of the past. French cultural dominance in Mexico during the period following the French intervention indicates the lack of anti-French feeling. Widespread study of the French language among the upper classes, acceptance of the positivist philosophy of Auguste Comte, and the predominance of French architecture attest to Mexican acceptance of French influence in the late nineteenth century. Although French intervention caused no long-range xenophobia, it did give Mexicans a set of common emotional responses and a sense of common pride in their victory over foreigners.

The struggle against the French and the clerical party also contributed to Mexican nationalism by producing a valid national hero in the person of Benito Juárez. A mythology has certainly grown up around him, but in fact, as well as in story, Juárez was an heroic figure. A Zapotec Indian whose parents and grandparents died while he was very young, Juárez gained an education through perseverance and remained scrupulously honest during his rise from lawyer, legislator, and governor of Oaxaca to the presidency of Mexico. His modesty, his strong sense of public responsibility, and the taste for simplicity manifest in his conservative dress and plain black coaches now displayed in Chapultepec Castle contrast sharply with the pomp and pretension that characterized Santa Anna. Like Morelos, Juárez endeavored to inspire not personalistic but nationalistic loyalty, loyalty not to himself but to all inhabitants of Mexico. Finally, he struggled relentlessly against two forces that threatened the consolidation of the Mexican nation: the church and the troops of Napoleon III.

Juárez helped to shape nationalism during the 1910 Revolution because he provided the image of a Mexican patriot fighting for many of the same principles that the revolutionaries of 1910 said they wanted to effect. By the time of the Revolution, Mexican writers had already turned Juárez into a national hero and associated him with the formation of the Mexican national community. Andrés

Molina Enríquez in his *Juárez y la Reforma,* originally
published in 1906, wrote, "Juárez represented not only the
inner formation of nationality but also the incommensur-
able pledge to impose this nationality on the outside. . . .
As a whole, the work of Juárez was to establish, with two
terrible wars, Mexican nationality in the mestizo element
of the population."[35] Justo Sierra, who educated many of
the revolutionaries and whom they made ambassador to
Spain, found that French intervention had made Mexico a
nation. He declared:

The Republic was then the Nation; with unknown exceptions, all
partook of the triumph, all understood that it was a definitely
consummated event, that conquests which would be eternal in
history had been realized, that the Reform, the Republic and the
Motherland formed, from that moment, the same thing and that it
was nothing else than the national flag, the Constitution of 1857;
under it all turned to be citizens, to be Mexicans, to be free. Victors and vanquished had, by the incontestable force of an idea
which contained all the future of Mexico, to unite in a common
longing: to realize law, to realize right, to enthrone justice.[36]

Juárez, like the concepts of internal reform and unity
against foreign invasion for which he stood, was to have
a lasting effect on Mexican nationalism, not only through
his own efforts, but through the efforts that his example
inspired in others.

THE DÍAZ REGIME

Under the regime of Porfirio Díaz from 1876 to 1911, Mexican nationalism was furthered not so much by conflicts
with foreign governments as by the growth of private for-

35. Andrés Molina Enríquez, *Juárez y la Reforma* (México: Libro-Mex,
1956), pp. 155-56. For examples of the more blatant kind of hero-creation,
see *En honor de Juárez* (México: Tipografía de José Vicente Villada, 1887);
and Rafael Martínez and Heriberto Frías, *Juárez inmortal: Edición popular
para ser distribuída gratis entre niños, soldados, obreros y campesinos de la República Mexicana* (México: Talleres Gráficos "Soria," 1925).

36. Justo Sierra, *Evolución política del pueblo mexicano* (México: La
Casa de España en México, 1940), p. 410.

eign investment and influence within Mexico. The early friction between Díaz and the Hayes administration, in which Hayes sent General Ord to the border and Díaz gained widespread public support by sending General Treviño north, served to unite Mexicans behind the policy of their government. In his reaction to the crisis of 1877 to 1879, however, Díaz began to make concessions to American private enterprise even though he made no direct concessions to the American government. Díaz' disposition to grant concessions, which originally showed the Hayes administration that its hostility to Mexico would hurt American investors, developed into a hallmark of the Díaz regime. In doing so, it received favor from foreign governments but rallied nationalistic sentiment within Mexico against foreigners, setting the stage for the Revolution of 1910.

The concessions of Díaz to foreign enterprise grew to staggering proportions, as foreign speculators bought up huge tracts of Mexican land. American holdings in railways, which in 1902 were valued at just over $335 million, rose in value by the end of 1911 to over $644 million. A report by Consul Marion Letcher in 1912 found that North American investment in Mexico, having just passed the $1 billion mark, exceeded the total amount of capital invested by Mexicans themselves.[37] Although the United

37. William H. Seamon, a mining engineer, prepared the table that Letcher submitted. Although Seamon's estimates of British and French investments in Mexico fall far below those of other contemporary reports, his estimate of a total North American investment of just over one billion dollars agrees with that of Sir Edmund Walker, the president of the Canadian Bank of Commerce. The disinterested Letcher estimate is more reliable than that of the Fall Committee which, in emphasizing United States claims against Mexico, set the total United States investment in Mexico at the beginning of the Revolution at closer to $1.5 billion. See Andrew D. Barlow, ''United States Enterprises in Mexico,'' *Commercial Relations of the United States with Foreign Countries during the Year 1902* (Washington: Government Printing Office, 1903), pp. 433-503; Marion Letcher, ''Wealth of Mexico'' in U.S., Department of Commerce and Labor, Bureau of Manufacturers, *Daily Consular and Trade Reports*, 15th Year, Vol. 3, No. 168 (July 18, 1912), 316; and U.S., Congress, Senate, Committee on Foreign Relations, *Investigation of Mexican Affairs*, 66th Cong., 2d sess., Sen. Doc. 285 (2 vols.; Washington, 1920), Vol. 2, p. 3322.

States was the largest single source of foreign investment funds, European countries also invested heavily in Mexican development. Whereas United States money went predominantly into railroads and mining, Britain's three largest investments included public utilities as well as railroads and mines. Numerous Spaniards and Chinese worked as local merchants, although most of their funds were originally earned in Mexico rather than invested from abroad. With French investment heaviest in financing the Mexican public debt, Frenchmen (like North Americans, Britons, and other foreigners) also invested in mines, railroads, agriculture, banking, commerce, oil, and industry.[38]

Despite such reliance on foreign capital, the Díaz regime did not fail to pay lip service to Mexican nationalism. The men around Díaz wanted to unify Mexico, as had their predecessors, around their own ideas, in their case the Positivist ideas of order and progress through science. Conservatives had always been as willing to unify Mexico around the maintenance of their wealth as the church had been to unify Mexico around ecclesiastical authority and the *fueros*. Each group claimed that the satisfaction of its interests promoted the welfare of the Mexican "nation."

But the *científicos*, the Positivist ideologues of the Díaz regime, lacked a sense of cohesive nationalism. They refused to share political power or national wealth more equally with the Indian masses. To the men around Díaz, nationalism became a convenient excuse for dictatorship and the maintenance of privilege. This was the concept of Mexican nationalism that the Revolution of 1910 was to overcome. As Federico González Garza wrote in 1917, a

38. One of the most balanced summaries of foreign investment under the Díaz regime is Luis Nicolau D'Olwer, "Las inversiones extranjeras," in Francisco R. Calderón and others, *El porfiriato, la vida económica*, Vol. 2 of *Historia moderna de México*, Daniel Cosío Villegas, ed. (México: Editorial Hermes, 1965), pp. 973-1185. For carefully estimated comparisons of the investments by country and by type of investment, see Tables LXV and LXVI on pp. 1154, 1155.

cardinal error in Mexico's *científico* leadership during the *porfiriato* was the belief that the "white population constitutes, forms and exclusively incarnates the Mexican people, the Mexican nation, and the Mexican motherland," that the interests of the people, nation, and motherland are solely the interests of the white population.[39] At the conclusion of the violent years of the Revolution, Luis Cabrera, in a moving appeal for a concept of Mexican nationalism that would include all the citizens of Mexico, similarly emphasized the traditional differences in Mexico's "two patriotisms": the exclusivistic patriotism of the upper classes of Iturbide, Santa Anna, and the *científicos* which resembled a form of class loyalty; and a second true patriotism and reverence of national heroes which Cabrera ascribed to the Mexican masses.[40]

With their own brand of nationalism, the *científicos* argued that social reform and defense of national sovereignty could be based only on the Díaz dictatorship's enforcement of internal peace and encouragement of economic development. What this argument failed to consider was that a dictatorship might become satisfied with its own wealth and power, so that social reform would finally result from its overthrow rather than its maintenance. The influence of foreigners in this situation was first to provide the capital for material progress under the dictatorship and then to bear the brunt of xenophobia under its reform.

While some Mexicans stood to gain from the kind of nationalism that Díaz espoused, the majority of Mexicans was alienated from it. Only about 4 per cent of the Mexican electorate was ever allowed to vote under Díaz, and the controlling aristocracy amounted to no more than 1 per cent of the population. Those few Mexicans who had ac-

39. F. González Garza, *¿Cumplen las escuelas oficiales, especialmente las llamadas preparatorias, su misión educativa en México?* (Habana: Imprenta "El Siglo XX," 1918), p. 20.

40. Blas Urrea [Luis Cabrera], *Obras políticas del lic. Blas Urrea . . .* (México: Imprenta Nacional, S.A., 1921), pp. 331-36.

cumulated savings to be invested with the foreign capital clearly stood to profit. Díaz' highly efficient rural constabulary, the *rurales,* took pleasure in their summary powers, and those Mexicans who found employment as managers or foremen on haciendas or in expanding industries such as railroad-building enjoyed comparative prosperity. Díaz was careful not to alienate the church, so nunneries and monasteries again appeared. A heavy immigration of Spanish, French, and Italian priests pleased the church hierarchy but aroused resentment in the lower ranks of the native-born Mexican clergy.

As the native clergy came to resent the influx of foreign priests, so other groups came to resent the foreigners with whom they were thrown into competition. The lack of sufficient domestic capital and skilled labor within Mexico and the wealth of the Mexican upper groups prevented complete hostility to foreigners, but some jealousy was inevitable in the Mexican financiers or skilled workers who were denied a particular concession or job only to have it given to a foreigner. Most significant was the fact that the masses remained in a state of abject poverty and even lost some of the privileges enjoyed before the influx of foreign capital and personnel. Using a statute originally designed to break up church lands and to make the Indians small independent landowners, Díaz deprived them of their land, and resentment was only natural when foreigners received these properties. The resentment that built up among the Indians supplied ready troops after 1910 to Emiliano Zapata and any other revolutionary leader who promised change and won an initial victory, and for this reason the Revolution became a mass movement rather than a barracks revolt.

Anticipating the Revolution, the bloody copper company strike at Cananea in June, 1906, combined xenophobia and nationalism, for the major cause of the strike was discrimination against Mexican workers in favor of Americans

and armed American forces crossed the border to suppress
the strike. The outcries of Manuel M. Diéguez and Esteban
B. Calderón for equal pay for Mexicans at Cananea re-
sulted in demands among the followers of Ricardo Flores
Magón and later among the revolutionaries of 1910 that
Mexicans and foreigners receive equal pay for equal work.
The potential strength of xenophobia and nationalism
throughout Mexico in 1906 is reflected in the unanimity
with which the Mexican press denounced Governor Rafael
Izábal of Sonora for allowing armed Arizona rangers under
Captain Thomas Rynning, a veteran of the Spanish-Amer-
ican War and frontier campaigns, to assist in putting down
the Cananea strike.[41]

Although most writers during the Díaz regime praised
its stability, writers both inside and outside Mexico came
to denounce it as a betrayal of Mexican national interest.
In 1909 Andrés Molina Enríquez wrote in *Los grandes
problemas nacionales,* which in effect discusses various
barriers to the extension of Mexican nationalism, that a
culminating factor was the presence of a new racial group,
the North American, that confronted the diverse groups
already in Mexico.[42] One of the most outspoken opponents
of Díaz was John Kenneth Turner, whose book, *Barbarous
Mexico,* was written after two trips through Mexico in 1908
and 1909 and first appeared as a series of articles in the
American Magazine from October, 1909, to January, 1910.
In no uncertain terms, Turner finds that "the partnership
of Díaz and American capital has wrecked Mexico as a
national entity" and that the "United States has virtually
reduced Díaz to a political dependency, and by so doing
has virtually *transformed Mexico into a slave colony of*

41. See the major compilation of Manuel González Ramírez, *La huelga de
Cananea* (Vol. 3, "Fuentes para la Historia de la Revolución Mexicana";
México: Fondo de Cultura Económica, 1956), especially pp. xxi-xxii, xxviii,
xxxv, 57, 59, 88-89.

42. Andrés Molina Enríquez, *Los grandes problemas nacionales* (México:
Imprenta de A. Carranza e Hijos, 1909), p. 76.

the United States." Furthermore, "all over the tropical section of Mexico, on the plantations of rubber, sugar-cane, tropical fruits—everywhere—you will find Americans buying, beating, imprisoning, killing slaves."[43] Whether Turner's statements are historically accurate or not, they form the basis for effective appeals to xenophobia. The first contribution of the Díaz regime to Mexican nationalism, therefore, was the maintenance of a situation that produced antagonism in the Mexican people to a group of domestic and foreign managers, both during and after the regime.

The foreign concessions of the Díaz regime also promoted Mexican nationalism by the material progress these brought to Mexico. Bringing with them the capital and technical skills that Latin American states still desire, foreigners sharply advanced the Mexican economy, and economic progress was gradually to undermine the old social relationships and attitudes. Industrialization ultimately freed many rural laborers by offering them employment in oil fields or cities, allowing workers to give loyalty to the nation that had formerly been reserved for the *hacendado* and *patrón.* Improvements in transportation, such as the railroads that were financed by foreign capital, reduced the isolation of the *patria chica.* Supervision of foreign concessions helped to create a government bureaucracy, which grew by 900 per cent between 1876 and 1910 and developed a personal interest in the achievement

43. John Kenneth Turner, *Barbarous Mexico* (Chicago: Charles H. Kerr & Company, 1911), pp. 254, 260. The italics are Turner's. Although Turner's North American citizenship removes any taint of "Mexican ethnocentrism" from his appraisal, his dedication to radical socialism and his activity among the followers of Flores Magón colored his interpretation fully as much as a sense of outraged patriotism might have done. Turner's accusations encouraged xenophobia, and despite his exaggerations he is still revered in some Mexican historiography. For Mexican appreciation of Turner's work, see Moisés González Navarro, *El porfiriato, la vida social,* in *Historia moderna de México,* Daniel Cosío Villegas, ed. (México: Editorial Hermes, 1957), pp. 260-65; and Manuel González Ramírez, *La revolución social de México. I. Las ideas—la violencia* (México: Fondo de Cultura Económica, 1960), pp. 107-11.

of national goals. A middle class that was to actively champion Mexican nationalism rose in response to the need for technical skills in the new economy. Although the foreigners who invested in Mexico under the Díaz concessions were naturally motivated by their own desire for profits, one result of their investment was to further the long-run changes in the economy and society of which nationalism was to be a part.

Finally, the economic progress that foreign capital brought to Mexico had an immediate effect on Mexican society. In a static society, men accept their poverty because they feel that it cannot be changed. As the "revolution of rising expectations" in the underdeveloped countries today suggests, once men see the benefits of a richer society, they come to expect more and more of their own. The foreigners who came to Mexico under the Díaz regime demonstrated the benefits of a comparatively high standard of living to the Mexicans around them and encouraged various economic developments that brought increased prosperity, at least to some upper and middle groups in Mexican society. With material wealth more evident among the privileged upper groups, peasant wages fell in real terms in the years preceding the Revolution. Toribio Esquivel Obregón points out that with 250 days' work a laborer could buy 42.50 hectoliters of corn or 9.71 measures of flour in 1891 but only 23.51 hectoliters of corn or 5.25 measures of flour in 1908.[44] Peons could nevertheless see evidences of the new prosperity that was reflected in the balanced budget, the paid-off foreign debt, and the 400 per cent rise in the value of foreign trade between the 1870's and the end of the century. Higher wages for some urban workers and middle groups served only to whet their ap-

44. T. Esquivel Obregón, *Influencia de España y los Estados Unidos sobre México* (*ensayos de sociología hispano-americano*) (Madrid: Casa Editorial Calleja, 1918), p. 343. Compare the statistics in Eyler N. Simpson, *The Ejido: Mexico's Way Out* (Chapel Hill, N.C.: The University of North Carolina Press, 1937), pp. 37-38.

petites. As a result, one reason that the early intellectual and business leaders of the Mexican Revolution found the Indians, peasants, and workers so ready for rebellion may well have been that they were prepared for revolution by the example of economic progress, created in part by those foreign interests that they were to denigrate and destroy.

III
Social Change, 1810-1910

Developments in the demographic, racial, linguistic, educational, and transportational structure of Mexico paralleled the influx of foreigners during the hundred years before the Revolution of 1910. Changes in population patterns and immigration, in the size and attitudes of classes and racial groups, and in the knowledge of language as well as changes in the language itself shaped nationalism in varying degrees. The rise of education that stressed national values helped to create a sense of unity among Mexican citizens which transportation improvements significantly increased. While the changes in nineteenth-century Mexican society are not viewed with the same intensity of patriotic sentiment as are Mexican battles against foreigners, the changes, nevertheless, provided an indispensable basis for Mexican social cohesion in the twentieth century.

POPULATION

Changes in the size, distribution, and foreign components of the Mexican population between 1810 and 1910 contributed to the process of nation-forming. Although a great variety of population statistics prove helpful in estimating

degrees of nationalism and in indicating reasons for changing loyalty patterns within the national group, some statistics lie outside the immediate area of population considerations.[1] A comparison of the estimated size of the
nationally conscious minority and the total population
provides the "quantitative" measure of the degree of
nationalism within a state. Problems of changing racial and
occupational compositions within the population and the
complications of educating a rapidly increasing population
should be examined separately, because they are part of
larger class and educational considerations.

Increases in the total population, shifts in its density,
and the size and type of immigration also affect the national consciousness of the individual inhabitants of a state.
A small population tends to give its members less physical
contact with other nationals and does not require the degree of economic or ideological integration required by a
larger population. Shifts of population through internal
migration not only reduce parochialism but also increase
interpersonal communication in areas of low population.
Immigration can temporarily retard the growth of nationalism if large foreign groups move into a society whose
members are in the process of forming their own national
values, but it also stimulates nationalism by providing a
group of foreigners against which the national group can
measure its distinctiveness. In nineteenth-century Mexico,
as in any other context, consideration of the effects of
different population trends requires careful examination
of the trends themselves.

During the nineteenth century, the population of Mexico
rose from an estimated 6.5 million in 1808 to just over 15
million in 1910,[2] and this growth in total population facili-

1. For a more complete analysis of the relationship between nationalism
and population, see Frederick C. Turner, ''The Implications of Demographic
Change for Nationalism and Internationalism,'' *Journal of Politics*, Vol. 27,
No. 1 (February, 1965).

2. For a good summary of the increase, see Gilberto Loyo, *La población de
México, estado actual y tendencias, 1950-1980* (México: Investigación Económica, 1960), pp. 3-4.

tated the integration of the Mexican national community. By cutting the land/labor ratio in half, the doubling of population during the nineteenth century brought Mexicans closer together in a physical sense. As the over-all density of population in the republic doubled, Mexicans became more aware of their compatriots as human beings if not as fellow Mexicans. Pointing up one aspect of an individual's propensity to associate himself with his national state, Katherine and A. F. K. Organski note the importance of "mental associations of fertility with strength and of declining numbers with impotence, old age, and death. There is a displacement of feelings about our individual selves onto groups or nations, with a consequent pleasure in large numbers as a source of self-esteem."[3] Certainly the Mexicans have derived pride and national self-esteem from their expanding population. When, for example, during the 1910 Revolution, a journalist praised Argentina as the outstanding cultural and economic center of Latin America, the Mexicans with whom he was talking retorted simply, "But Argentina has only seven million people" while "there are fifteen million Mexicans."[4]

The nineteenth-century population increase also provided a substantially enlarged internal market on which economies of scale and the more industrialized, nationalistic society of the future could be built. Population growth of necessity creates pressure to provide more food by modernizing agriculture, and this tends to break down the feudal hacienda that excludes national allegiance. Population growth also promotes a more specialized division of labor that ultimately makes the entire national community more economically interdependent, creating the markets and internal transportation that in turn increase personal contact among members of the national group. The ex-

3. Katherine Organski and A. F. K. Organski, *Population and World Power* (New York: Alfred A. Knopf, 1961), p. 196.

4. V. Blasco Ibáñez, *Mexico in Revolution*, Arthur Livingston and José Padín, trans. (New York: E. P. Dutton & Company, 1920), pp. 220-21.

tension of national economic interdependence encourages a superstructure of nationalistic values that discourage the disruption of the pattern of interdependence. The disguised rural unemployment, which after the Revolution was to lure Mexicans to the cities where they could more easily absorb nationalistic values, resulted from the nineteenth-century increase in population as well as from improved agricultural techniques. Finally, proletarian populations may resort to revolutions such as that of 1910 if the productivity of their society does not increase by enough to provide for the new wants created by population increases and by rising expectations.

The rural isolation of the Mexican population before the Revolution helps to explain the lack of widespread nationalism up to that time. In 1900 the population of Mexico was 83 per cent rural—at a time when localities of under 2,500 inhabitants were considered rural—and by 1910 the rural proportion of the population had decreased but slightly, to 80 per cent.[5] In 1862 only four Mexican cities had more than 50,000 inhabitants, and the population of Mexico City was about 210,000.[6] In 1900 only six cities, Mexico City, Guadalajara, León, Puebla, San Luis Potosí, and Monterrey, had over 50,000 inhabitants, and all of these cities except Monterrey were in the center of the republic. The number of Mexicans living in cities of over 50,000 totaled scarcely 700,000, or just over 5 per cent of the total population.[7] In 1910 Mexico had only sixty-eight cities with over 10,000 population and only two, Mexico City and Guadalajara, with over 100,000. Urban congregations remained sharply limited before 1910, and the only

5. Daniel Moreno, *Los factores demográficos en la planeación económica* (México: Ediciones de la Cámara Nacional de la Industria de la Transformación, 1958), pp. 39-40, 63.

6. José María Pérez Hernández, *Estadística de la República Mejicana* (Guadalajara, Jal.: Tip. del Gobierno, a Cargo de Antonio de P. González, 1862), p. 63.

7. Moreno, *Los factores demográficos en la planeación económica*, pp. 70-71.

numerical increase of these Mexican cities occurred on market days when villagers from the surrounding region converged to sell their produce and exchange information.[8]

This lack of urbanization in nineteenth-century Mexico partially explains the absence of cohesive nationalism, because urbanization is one of the social forces that provides a prime stimulus to nationalist attitudes. In Africa, as in Mexico during the twentieth century, it has significantly affected the rise of nationalism by loosening kinship ties and accelerating social communication between "detribalized" ethnic groups.[9] The city dweller can be more easily incorporated into the national community, because he is closer to communications media and has readier access to the educational facilities that provide literacy and allow an understanding of nationalistic literature. Urban residents have contact in physical terms with the variety of people who comprise the nation, whereas individuals living in rural isolation at best develop only a parochial and limited impression of the nation.

The small population of the more nationally oriented urban areas in pre-revolutionary Mexico coincided with a sparse population in the outlying territories. In 1900 the population of the northern states was far less dense than the central regions, as Baja California had only 7,585 inhabitants and the large states of Sonora and Chihuahua only 221,780 and 327,685, as compared to Jalisco and Guanajuato with over 1,000,000 and Michoacán and Mexico with over 900,000.[10] In 1904 the Federal District reported over 735 persons per square kilometer, while this figure

8. Sumner W. Cushing, "The Distribution of Population in Mexico," *Geographical Review*, Vol. 11, No. 2 (April, 1921), 233.

9. James S. Coleman, "Nationalism in Tropical Africa," *American Political Science Review*, Vol. 48, No. 2 (June, 1954), 411. For an excellent summary of Mexican urbanization in the twentieth century, see *Distribución geográfica de la población en la República Mexicana* (México: Instituto de Geografía, Universidad Nacional Autónoma de México, 1962), pp. 46-52, 57-89.

10. Moreno, *Los factores demográficos en la planeación económica*, p. 31.

for the states and territories ranged from 42 for Tlaxcala to 0.3 for Baja California.[11]

Despite the comparatively sparse population in the north, a sizable influx of population had come to the region by 1910 which may have stirred a national awareness that Pancho Villa and Álvaro Obregón were later to mold. Coinciding directly with the expansion of railroads, the annual rate of population increase in the north rose from 1.1 per cent (1857-80) to 3 per cent (1880-1900), compared with the smaller rates of 1.6 per cent in the central states and 2.4 per cent in the south. Between 1900 and 1910, the shift to the periphery continued although with less intensity. Official programs in colonization, irrigation, industrialization, and transportation favored the population shift, as the proportion of Mexicans living in the central region steadily declined from 57 per cent in 1869 to 49 per cent in 1910.[12] The migrants representing these figures brought their own attitudes and values to their new environments, reducing the isolation of the older inhabitants. Their increased appreciation of the national state developed during the migration, the extra-regional values that they brought to indigenous residents, and the fact that the migrants were still recently uprooted newcomers at the time of the Revolution may help to explain the widespread support for revolution in the countryside after 1910.

Throughout the nineteenth century, Mexican governments endeavored to stimulate immigration, but in quantitative terms their efforts were wholly unsuccessful. The immigration law of 1823 encouraged colonization, and it was not until 1830 that a law was passed requiring that North Americans have a passport to cross the Texas border. Santa Anna authorized agents in Europe to procure colonists, and the Mexican government tried to promote the

11. Mexico, Department of Finance, *The Mexican Year Book 1909-10* (London: McCorquodale & Company, Limited, 1910), p. 11.

12. Julio Durán Ochoa, *Población* (México: Fondo de Cultura Económica, 1955), pp. 221-23.

immigration of civilized Indians and freed Negroes from the United States in an effort to counteract the violent Indians of the northern frontier. Immigrants failed to come to Mexico, however, because of her early political instability and the arid colonization areas. Immigration opportunities seemed more favorable in countries like Argentina, Brazil, and the United States. In the early years after independence, between 600 and 900 immigrants came yearly to Mexico and between 150 and 300 emigrated. Although there is little reliable data for nineteenth-century immigration, twentieth-century data tends to confirm extremely limited immigration and emigration.[13]

Although the aims of governmental immigration policies did not counteract the consolidation of the Mexican national community, greater national consolidation may have been achieved because the policies were largely unsuccessful. Immigration policy during the nineteenth century attempted to rectify the over-all deficiency and uneven distribution of the population, to exploit natural resources, and to attract white immigrants of alleged superiority. Francisco Pimentel showed that the aim of this policy was often to achieve rather than retard the integration of the nation, when in 1866 he wrote that "foreign colonization not only augments but also betters our population because it adds physically or mentally . . . it not being either just or possible to destroy the Indians, it is necessary to confess that his only remedy, and with him that of the entire nation, consists in *transformation* by means of European immigration."[14]

Despite Pimentel's argument, a flood of foreign immigrants might well have merely added another discordant element to the Mexican polity, disturbing the growing sense of community among older residents of Mexico and re-

13. Durán Ochoa, *Población,* pp. 150-53, 166-67.
14. Francisco Pimentel, *La economía política aplicada á la propiedad territorial en México* (México: Imprenta de Ignacio Cumplido, 1866), pp. 179, 183. The italics are Pimentel's.

quiring time for the acculturation of the immigrants themselves. Widespread Spanish immigration would certainly have helped the dominant aristocracy to postpone acceptance of Indian and mestizo elements. Countries in which nationalism grew despite immigration usually lacked an Indian population or decimated it, as was the case with Argentina and the United States, or they had special characteristics like the Brazilians' facility to accept diversity or Canada's stark need for more inhabitants. Nationalism has grown in the United States in spite of Harlem and the little Italies rather than because of them. Mexico's experience in Texas remains a classic example of the dangers of immigration, even if it ultimately increased a sense of community in the remainder of Mexico.

The immigrants who did come to Mexico made little effort to incorporate themselves into the national community. One-fifth of the immigrants were illiterate, and a large part of them neither knew Spanish nor tried to learn it.[15] The attempt to bring in Italian agricultural workers brought in pickpockets and beggars instead. Naturalization statistics dramatically illustrate the nonassimilation of foreign groups. Although by 1900 there were already 57,634 resident foreigners in Mexico, the number of immigrants who manifested their loyalty to the Mexican national community by becoming naturalized citizens numbered only 30,560 for the entire period from 1828 to 1952—an average of 244 persons each year.[16]

While foreign immigration was not large enough to overwhelm or greatly retard the growth of Mexican nationalism, it was large enough to serve as a foil against which Mexicans could define their own nationality. The 57,634 foreigners living in Mexico in 1900 had increased from 26,975 in 1862 and increased rapidly again by 1910.[17]

15. Daniel Moreno, ''Problemas de México, 1877-1910,'' *Historia Mexicana,* Vol. 7, Núm. 3 (enero-marzo, 1958), 426.

16. Durán Ochoa, *Población*, pp. 151, 164, 243.

17. Mexico, Department of Finance, *The Mexican Year Book 1909-10*, p. 12.

An influx of both North American and German merchants joined the British merchants who had resided in Mexico for generations. The United States by the 1880's and Germany by 1906 had surpassed Great Britain in their share of the Mexican import market.[18] Although the 5,820 Guatemalans registered in Mexico in 1900 may have felt as little national allegiance to Guatemala as their Mexican neighbors in Chiapas felt toward the Mexican nation, the 16,280 Spaniards, 15,820 North Americans, and 3,970 Frenchmen living in Mexico had come from countries in which the growth of their sense of nationalism served to set them apart.

The Mormon colonies in northern Mexico clearly illustrate the process by which limited foreign immigration stimulated Mexican nationalism. A Mormon battalion volunteered for service with the United States Army in the War of 1847, and in the 1870's Anthony W. Ivins, Moses Thatcher, and other missionaries first went south into Mexico. As part of the program to encourage immigration, Díaz welcomed the Mormon apostles and said that his government would welcome Mormon colonists who might help develop the country. By the time of the Revolution, the resulting Mormon colonies in Sonora and Chihuahua had grown to include 4,000 persons, mostly American citizens, who comprised between 700 and 800 families and owned property valued at between $7 million and $8 million.

The Mormons kept even more aloof than the other immigrants, maintaining a policy of no social mixing and "strict neutrality" in the Revolution itself.[19] Thomas Cottam Romney, the Mormon historian of the colonies that his father had helped to lead, writes that "socially, the colonists were exclusive and seclusive, having few if any contacts with their neighbors." While Romney is careful to point

18. Alfred P. Tischendorf, ''The Loss of British Commercial Preeminence in Mexico, 1876-1911,'' *Inter-American Economic Affairs*, Vol. 11, No. 1 (Summer, 1957), 87.

19. Thomas Cottam Romney, *The Mormon Colonies in Mexico* (Salt Lake City, Utah: The Deseret Book Company, 1938), pp. 37-38, 59, 182, 195.

out that the Mormons' exclusiveness "was not born of a
'race superiority' complex,"[20] this aloofness, added to the
Mormons' evident prosperity and American citizenship,
made the Mexicans aware of their foreignness. By providing the contrast of a foreign group and stimulating
jealousy among the Mexicans with whom they came in
contact, the Mormon immigrants increased the Mexicans'
sense of national identity.

Looking from the Mormon point of view at the process
by which the Mexicans gained a sense of their separate
identity, Romney writes:

> It is historically true that the immediate cause for the wholesale
> migration of the Mormons from Mexican soil was the demand
> made by the rebel forces for their firearms. But the ultimate,
> therefore more fundamental causes, were to be found in the con-
> trasting natures, traditions, habits and ideals of the colonists and
> their neighbors; in the envy and covetousness of the natives de-
> veloped over a long period of years and resulting from the ma-
> terial and social progress of the colonists as expressed in thriving
> settlements, well-cultivated orchards and farms, and convenient
> and comfortable homes.[21]

Romney finds that it was not merely rebel forces from other
parts of Mexico that caused the Mormons to leave but that
"a large measure of blame must be attached to the natives
living adjacent to the Mormon colonies," some of whom
were "early selecting the Mormon homes they expected to
occupy following the departure of their owners from the
country."[22] Mexicans, as Mexicans, wanted to take over the
fine Mormon homes.[23] Confirming the jealous antagonism
towards the Mormons, Consul Thomas D. Edwards in
Ciudad Juárez reported that the hostility of the lower-class
Mexicans towards the Americans in his district, the ma-

20. *Ibid.*, p. 147.
21. *Ibid.*, p. 148.
22. *Ibid.*
23. U.S., Congress, Senate, Committee on Foreign Relations, *Investigation
of Mexican Affairs*, 66th Cong., 2d sess., Sen. Doc. 285 (2 vols.; Washington,
1920), Vol. 2, p. 2729.

jority of whom were Mormon colonists, was "a social or pecuniary dislike or hatred born of jealousy."[24] Although the Mormons' degree of exclusiveness makes their case a striking example, other immigrants also stimulated jealousy and a sense of separateness in the Mexicans with whom they came in contact. Like the over-all growth of the Mexican population, the internal migration toward the periphery, and the lack of overwhelming immigration, the immigrants who did come to Mexico in the nineteenth century helped to create a sense of national identity in the Mexicans who were already there.

MISCEGENATION AND CLASS DIFFERENTIATION

The composition and attitudes toward nationalism of Mexican classes and social groups shifted significantly in the hundred years before 1910. Changes in the racial composition of the population through miscegenation brought changes in mestizo influence and attitudes, but of equal importance for the process of social integration were the comparatively stable attitudes of *criollo* and Indian groups. In addition to attitudes in part traceable to a sense of race, the national allegiance of such diverse groups as illegitimate offspring and members of the industrial sector of the economy also affected social integration.

The process of miscegenation by which the Indian and white races intermarried to form the mestizo group greatly changed the racial composition of Mexico during the nineteenth century. In 1824 Humboldt estimated that 1,860,000 mestizos made up 27.3 per cent of the Mexican population,[25] while Ramón Beteta estimates that on the eve of the Revolution 8,000,000 mestizos comprised 53 per cent of the popu-

24. Thomas D. Edwards to Huntington Wilson, March 21, 1911, State Department Files of the National Archives, 812.00/1063. Unless otherwise indicated all correspondence from the Department of State will be from the 812.00 files and will be identified only by the slash number.
25. Durán Ochoa, *Población*, p. 229.

lation.[26] According to Humboldt's and Beteta's figures, the number of white Mexican citizens fell from 1,230,000 in 1824 to 1,150,000 in 1910, and the proportion of white citizens decreased from 18 per cent of the total population to only 7.5 per cent. Although the number of Indians rose from approximately 3.7 million to 6 million, the Indian portion of the population fell from 54.4 per cent to 39 per cent. Even if we accept Ramón Beteta's opinion that a larger number of Mexicans were mestizos in the early nineteenth century, the proportion of mestizos still rose from 38 per cent to 53 per cent in the hundred years before 1910. The biological miscegenation of the Mexican population was a gradual and irreversible process, because both the union of whites and Indians and that of mestizos with either of the other groups produce mestizo offspring. This process had reached such a point by 1908 that Frederick Starr, a contemporary anthropologist from the University of Chicago, stated that "in some parts of Mexico, it almost seems as if what white-blood once existed is now breeded out."[27]

In the early nineteenth century when mestizos were still numerically inferior, they lacked both power and prestige. They enjoyed neither the security of the *criollo* in being the legitimate heirs of their fathers nor the paternal protection that the white Spaniard was obliged to offer the Indian. In trying to improve their own positions, mestizos came to champion the idea of a national community. Increasingly in the nineteenth century, the mestizos took command of Mexico and used appeals to common Mexican nationality to legitimize their place in society. Mestizos wanted to change the basis of economic and social advancement from ascription to achievement, to eliminate race

26. Ramón Beteta, ''Social Forces in Mexican Life,'' in Hubert C. Herring and Katharine Terrill, eds., *The Genius of Mexico: Lectures Delivered before the Fifth Seminar in Mexico, 1930* (New York: The Committee on Cultural Relations with Latin America, 1931), p. 34.

27. Frederick Starr, *In Indian Mexico: A Narrative of Travel and Labor* (Chicago: Forbes and Company, 1908), p. 396.

and inherited social position as criteria for the acquisition of status. The steady increase in the number of mestizos as well as their drive to gain status through achievement increased their power within Mexican society.

Mexicans came to associate the process of racial mixture with the formation of their national community, as Andrés Molina Enríquez and other writers before 1910 emphasized the mestizo's role in national affairs. The new pride in the mestizo race comes out strongly in José Vasconcelos' 1925 study, *La raza cósmica*. Carlos Chávez has even defined Mexican music as mestizo music, writing that the "new music of Mexico, that is, *mestizo* music, the fruit of the two races and the two cultures put into contact by the Conquest, is very rich and varied."[28] Associating the mixing of races with a growing equality of opportunity for citizens of all racial backgrounds, Mexicans proclaim that all citizens should be "incorporated into the nationality economically as well as spiritually" in order to aid the process of breaking down the "artificial and antipatriotic barriers to national unity."[29]

In taking national pride in the fusion of races, Mexicans in one sense differ widely from other nations where allegations of racial unity are a unifying force. Mexicans were patently not of common origin, and the rise of nationalism among them demonstrates just how unnecessary a common racial base is. Just as the Swiss prove that a common language is not necessary, so the Mexicans have proved that a viable national group may be created from antagonistic races. In demonstrating the lack of need for racial unity, the Mexicans also prove that nationalism is effectively promoted by the fusion of races and the pride taken in the new race that is thus formed.

Miscegenation also removed the underlying mutual de-

28. Carlos Chávez, "Mexican Music," in Hubert Herring and Herbert Weinstock, eds., *Renascent Mexico* (New York: Covici, Friede, 1935), p. 212.

29. Emilio Uribe Romo, "México y las implicaciones demográficas de la postguerra," *Revista Mexicana de Sociología*, Año 9, Vol. 9, Núm. 3 (septiembre-diciembre, 1947), 340.

pendence of Mexico's races which, together with their superficial antagonism, retarded the advance of nationalism. Despite the conquest and subsequent racial friction, an element of truth lies in the notion that the Spaniard needs an Indian to be Spanish just as the Indian needs a Spaniard to be Indian. The Spaniard could acquire a proper sense of *dignidad* when he had someone like the Indian to do the ordinary, manual work that he rejected, leaving him free for less mundane feats such as conquest or intellectual stimulation. Before the conquest, most Mexican Indians lived in highly stratified societies, and Spanish subjugation reinforced their inherited cultural patterns. The proportion of the Mexican population that either as Spaniards or Indians could derive their sense of identity from being "above" or "below" steadily declined, however, with the process of assimilation of the races.

The gradual effects of miscegenation should not obscure the fact that a massive Indian population remained largely unassimilated before the Revolution of 1910. Frequent claims that the Indian was endowed with "sloth and languor" and the meager desire to obtain only physical necessities reflected his cultural acceptance of traditionally low consumption standards, his unbegrudging subsistence in a world of hostile forces, and his physical and mental endurance. Indians continued to be set apart economically as well as culturally, as they received the lowest wages in the city and countryside. They also failed as a group to participate in any of the formal political processes. As an observer of the Mexican Congress commented in 1885, nine-tenths of the Mexican congressmen were pure white and the remaining tenth had "no more color than fashion demands of a stylish brunette."[30]

Such diverse writers as Francisco Pimentel, Lucas Alamán, Andrés Molina Enríquez, and Francisco Bulnes recognized that Mexico was split into two opposing nations,

30. T. S. Van Dyke, "Mexican Politics," *Harper's*, Vol. 71, No. 425 (October, 1885), 762.

one western and one Indian. Pimentel said that the difference between whites and Indians meant that "Mexico can not aspire to the rank of a *nation* properly defined." Whereas the white man speaks Spanish or French, is Catholic or indifferent, and has wealth and fine clothes, the Indians speak a hundred languages, are idolaters, possess little wealth, and go almost bare.[31] Alamán found that even Indians and mestizos kept apart, as they differed in dress, language, occupation, foods, and their ways of life.[32]

Many individuals in the nineteenth century became concerned with giving the Indians equality and actively incorporating them into the nation. In the Plan de Iguala of February 24, 1821, Iturbide announced that all citizens of his monarchy, including Indians, should have the right to any employment according to their merit. Orders passed in 1822 declared that sick Indians must be admitted to hospitals along with other citizens and that no public or private document could classify citizens by origin. In practice, however, Indian distinctiveness remained evident in the separate registration of "Mexicans" and "Indians."[33] Typifying later Indianist attitudes in *La redención de una raza: Estudio sociológico* published in 1887, Rafael de Zayas Enríquez declared that the Indian required the help of other Mexicans to gain assimilation since he could not redeem himself and learn true patriotism on his own.

Although the success of the individuals who wanted to incorporate the Indians was limited in the nineteenth century, changes at that time—the decline of clericalism, the

31. Francisco Pimentel, *Memoria sobre las causas que han originado la situación actual de la raza indígena de México, y medios de remediarla* (México: Imprenta de Andrade y Escalante, 1864), p. 217. The italics are Pimentel's.

32. Lucas Alamán, *Historia de Méjico desde los primeros movimientos que prepararon su independencia en el año de 1808 hasta la época presente* (5 vols.; Méjico: Imprenta de J. M. Lara, 1849-1852), Vol. 5, p. 879.

33. Alfonso Caso and others, *Métodos y resultados de la política indigenista en México* (México: Ediciones del Instituto Nacional Indigenista, 1954), pp. 115-18, 143.

personal achievements of individual Indians, their army service, and repeated Indian rebellions—foreshadowed later acceptance. The growth of secularism contributed to the eventual incorporation of Indian groups in the national community by reducing the church power that had protected the Indians. It was not until after the removal of church jurisdiction and Díaz' consequent sale of Indian lands that the Indian was obliged to enter the same battle with all other Mexicans. As the decrease in church power forced Indian groups into articulation of their demands within the national framework, the early nationalistic fight against ecclesiastical power advanced nationalism in a manner that the anticlericals had not wholly expected.

The fact that Indians like Benito Juárez, Tomás Mejía, and Ignacio Manuel Altamirano could become president of the republic, conservative general, and leading literary critic in the nineteenth century proves that the bars of Indian poverty and cultural separation were not insurmountable. The examples of these men also substantiated the claims of twentieth-century Indianists concerning the importance of the Indian population. Service in the regular or revolutionary armies also changed some Indian attitudes. Although Mexicans themselves find the army to have been lacking in morality, honor, and discipline,[34] it at least provided some rudimentary training in Spanish and a new sense of punctuality. The seeds of Indian incorporation also became manifest in expressions of their separation, in the Indian revolts that occurred almost every year between 1821 and 1910. From Juan Banderas' rebellion, 1825, to those of Cajeme and Tatabiate, ending in 1887 and 1901, an almost uninterrupted series of revolts took place, including the serious insurrections in Yucatán in 1847, Juchitán from 1847 to 1851, and Chiapas in 1868. Although the Indians often fought to be left alone rather than to be accepted in the national society, their rebellions

34. Agustín Cue Cánovas, *Historia mexicana* (México: Editorial F. Trillas, S.A., 1959), p. 171.

at least registered a discontent with the status quo which was again evident after 1910.

At the top of Mexican society there remained a class that was the antithesis of the Indian masses in wealth and prestige but strikingly similar to the Indians in its failure to accept Mexican national values. By tradition the rich *criollo* did not work and remained indifferent to the life of the country. Traditional Spanish courtesy rather than a sense of mutual unity in the national community explains such contemporary comments as John G. Bourke's that the "proudest gentleman in the land will take off his hat to return the salutation of the beggar who begs a light for his cigarrito."[35]

The rich *criollo* class rejected Mexican culture and aped foreign manners largely because they were foreign. The *criollo* built his house in the style of the Second Empire and claimed that the house was beautiful because there was *"nothing Mexican in it!"*[36] Although the attitudes of this comparatively small but influential *criollo* group retarded the spread of nationalism in the nineteenth century, the desire for a purely Mexican culture later arose partly in reaction to this total rejection of things Mexican.

The high rate of technical illegitimacy before the Revolution also affected nationalism. From 1922 to 1930 an estimated 48.6 per cent of the births in Mexico were illegitimate, and this statistic dropped to 28.2 in 1950. Julio Durán Ochoa concludes, on the basis of the trend in illegitimacy statistics in the twentieth century, that at the beginning of the century illegitimate birth must have been more than 60 per cent of general birth.[37] This failure to seek

35. John G. Bourke, "Notes on the Language and Folk-Usage of the Rio Grande Valley," *Journal of American Folk-lore*, Vol. 9, No. 33 (April-June, 1896), 104. For a more extensive discussion of nineteenth-century Mexican customs, see Howard T. Fisher and Marion Hall Fisher, eds., *Life in Mexico: The Letters of Fanny Calderón de la Barca* (Garden City, N.Y.: Doubleday and Company, Inc., 1966).

36. Lesley Byrd Simpson, *Many Mexicos* (Berkeley, Calif.: University of California Press, 1952), p. 260. The italics are Simpson's.

37. Durán Ochoa, *Población*, p. 73.

either civil or ecclesiastical marriage was the result of a variety of causes: the Indian cultural patterns that rejected imposed ceremonies, a lack of funds to pay for the ceremony and the accompanying fiesta, and the rural isolation of much of the Mexican population which made reaching the officials who could legitimize a marriage extremely difficult. Formal marriage often proved to be an exorbitant luxury, as it cost a minimum of 8 pesos and often considerably more.[38] The fact that the high cost of marriage ceremonies considerably reduced the number of formal unions appears in the 1942 decision of over 50,000 Mexican couples to be legally married under a government-sponsored campaign providing free marriage ceremonies throughout the republic.[39]

Since many of the technically illegitimate births resulted from common-law marriages, it would be wholly unjustified to conclude that Durán Ochoa's estimate of 60 per cent illegitimacy meant that 60 per cent of Mexican children lacked the discipline and sense of security that comes from family associations. The high rate of illegitimacy does emphasize the lack of national identification, however, as 60 per cent of the births were to parents who lacked enough allegiance to the nation to solemnize their union according to its laws. The rate also supports the hypothesis that a significant portion of the Mexican population was ready to gain a sense of identity from a revolutionary movement, that they were not tied down to legalized relationships and so could join the armies of Zapata and Villa in search of something else to which they could become loyal. An illegitimate child who lacks a sense of loyalty to a family may give loyalty to the national group when transportation changes or historical events make him aware of

38. Manuel Gamio, *La población del valle de Teotihuacán* (3 vols.; México: Dirección de Talleres Gráficos, Dependiente de la Secretaría de Educación Pública, 1922), Tomo 2, p. 247; and Charles Jenkinson, ''Vera Cruz: What American Occupation Has Meant to a Mexican Community,'' *Survey*, Vol. 33, No. 6 (November 7, 1914), 137.

39. Nathan L. Whetten, *Rural Mexico* (Chicago: University of Chicago Press, 1948), p. 378.

that group. Like the mestizo, he gains a sense of identity from membership in the national community which he otherwise might have derived from family or social relationships.

The attitudes that had arisen by 1910 in the industrial segment of the population also favored the rise of nationalism. Although agriculture still claimed 68 per cent of the working force, industry employed over 19 per cent in 1910. Commerce employed almost 5 per cent of the working force, and public administration, the professions, and communications each employed over 1 per cent.[40] The acquisitive values of an industrialized society had not yet spread beyond the industrial sector, as the attitudes of rural Mexicans contrasted sharply with the hard-driving spirit of Yankee entrepreneurship.

Nevertheless, Mexico's industrial revolution had begun to create the groups of industrial workers and employers whose attitudes more easily encompassed nationalism. With the publication of many working-class periodicals after the inauguration of *El Socialista* in 1871 and the founding of the Gran Círculo de Obreros Mexicanos in 1872, Mexican industrial workers were not content with the defense of their own interests and became the mouthpiece for mine workers and peons on the haciendas who did not defend themselves. Some 250 strikes occurred under the Díaz regime, mainly in textiles, railroads, and the cigar industry.[41] Employers developed both managerial attitudes and contentions with such labor leaders as Ricardo Flores Magón, and the aims of both labor and management became divorced from the attitudes prevalent in the older agricultural and mining sectors. The Revolution of 1910 developed in one sense out of the contradiction between the maturing feudal system and the growth of industrialism.[42] Although

40. Moreno, *Los factores demográficos en la planeación económica*, p. 240.
41. On the strikes, see Moisés González Navarro, "Las huelgas textiles en el porfiriato," *Historia Mexicana*, Vol. 6, Núm. 2 (octubre-diciembre, 1956).
42. Luis Chávez Orozco, *Historia económica y social de México: Ensayo de interpretación* (México: Ediciones Botas, 1938), p. 171.

the more stable attitudes of Indians and *criollos* delayed the rise of nationalism, the new attitudes of industrial workers and employers, like those of the increasing mestizo group and illegitimate offspring, favored the process of change that would bring both nationalism and the Revolution.

LANGUAGE

Changes in language patterns affected nationalism in nineteenth-century Mexico by the spread of Spanish which facilitated communication, by the formidable language barriers that still made communication difficult in 1910, and by the rise of idiosyncrasies in the Spanish dialect spoken in Mexico. Although a number of Mexicans came to see the implications of language in the development of their national community, its effects on nationalism arose more from unconscious social interaction than from conscious human manipulation.

A passage in *The Mexican Year Book 1909-10,* a publication of the Díaz Department of Finance issued in English, indicates both the problem that divergent languages posed for the consolidation of the Mexican nation and the attitude of the Díaz regime toward this problem. Copying the passage from a previous edition, the *Year Book* says:

Spanish is the official language of the Republic, and is spoken and understood almost everywhere, but there are about 2,000,000 individuals whose mother-tongue is some Indian language. These languages belong to at least 13 families, which are mutually unintelligible. In certain remote districts Spanish seems even now to be almost unknown. This is especially true in Yucatán, where 83.7 per cent claimed Maya as their native language. With the exception of the last-named, however, the Indian languages possess no influence over the destinies of the nation. The entire social, educational and political life of the Republic is carried on in Spanish.[43]

43. Mexico, Department of Finance, *The Mexican Year Book 1909-10,* p. 9.

The *Year Book* here evidences the disparate character given Mexican society by its variety of languages, divided not only between Spanish and Indian but also into a variety of mutually exclusive Indian languages.

Such a divergence of languages clearly retards inter-personal communication and social cohesion. Linguistic unity is not a prerequisite for nationalism, for it is obvious that shared value systems and similar socio-economic backgrounds produce rapport among the Swiss people despite their various languages. In the Mexican case, however, where language differences have coincided with social and economic division between the Indian and Spanish-speaking groups, language formed a final barrier to communication. The divergent backgrounds and experiences of the inhabitants of Mexico were reflected in the fact that they quite literally did not speak the same language. The Díaz regime took pride in the Spanish language, for it excluded from national participation those who could not speak it or those who could only speak it in a halting, newly learned manner. By carrying on the "entire social, educational and political life of the Republic" in Spanish, the *científicos* kept the Indians apart from the national society. It was not merely the "Indian languages" as the *Year Book* states but the Indians themselves who possessed "no influence over the destinies of the nation."

The diversity of languages impeded the rise of Mexican nationalism throughout the nineteenth century. Most books translated into the Indian languages promoted ecclesiastical rather than national values, as the early civic texts translated into Zapotec in 1887 and Náhuatl in 1888 were few indeed compared to the various clerical texts published in Huicol, Kekchí, Maya, Mixtec, Tarahuman, and Tzotzil.[44] Ignacio Ramírez observed that language barriers protected the separate nationality of individual Indian tribes, because the only Spanish learned by most Indians was the "sterile

44. Caso and others, *Métodos y resultados de la política indigenista en México*, p. 138.

formulas'' of business transactions or the ''odious expressions'' exchanged between a master and his servant.[45] Even if an Indian did speak some Spanish, he usually did not speak it well enough to see himself as part of the national community that it represented.

Mexican writers were well aware that diversity of language prevented Mexican unity. In the introduction to *Las lenguas indígenas de México*, Francisco Pimentel quotes Babbi as saying that ''language is the characteristic sign which distinguishes one nation from another'' and Pedro Felipe Monlau as saying that *''the language is the nation.''*[46] In 1902 Justo Sierra wrote that, while the existing presence of many languages was an obstacle to ''the complete formation of the consciousness of the Motherland,'' uniformity of language would be the ''invaluable vehicle of social unification.''[47] He hoped that the use of Spanish in schools would cause local languages to atrophy and be destroyed.

Despite the problem of Indian languages, the spread of Spanish in the nineteenth century worked to facilitate the social unification for which Justo Sierra hoped. Different languages have roughly equivalent value for the purpose of social integration, although one may be better than another if it is easier for other groups to learn or if it is initially spoken by the largest language group. Mexico could have received an impetus to nationalism if all her inhabitants had learned Náhuatl, and the distinctiveness of such a language would even have set Mexico off from other national groups as the propagation of Hindi does in India today. Since the dominant group in New Spain

45. From Ramírez' speech of July 7, 1856, collected in Emilio del Castillo Negrete, ed., *Galería de oradores de México en el siglo XIX* (3 vols.; México: Tipografía de Santiago Sierra, 1877-80), Vol. 2, p. 264.

46. Francisco Pimentel, *Cuadro descriptivo y comparativo de las lenguas indígenas de México* (2 vols.; México: Imprenta de Andrade y Escalante, 1862 y 1865), Vol. 1, pp. xvi-xviii. The italics are Pimentel's.

47. Justo Sierra, *Discursos* (Vol. 5, *Obras completas del maestro Justo Sierra;* 14 vols.; México: Universidad Nacional Autónoma de México, 1948), p. 297.

spoke Spanish, however, it came to be the spread of Spanish that facilitated communication within the Mexican community.

Spanish spread along with the growth of markets and internal transportation; Mexicans needed it as a medium for economic transactions. The basic educational policy for the Indians was instruction in Spanish because, since few teachers could lecture in the Indian languages, Indians could not learn other subjects until they had learned Spanish. Even the factional wars of the nineteenth century increased the knowledge of Spanish, as Spanish provided the common language for the diverse groups banding together to travel and to fight. The increase in spoken Spanish became particularly evident when Díaz imposed civil tranquility. In 1877 Antonio García Cubas estimated that 38 per cent of the Mexican population spoke Indian languages, although he probably exaggerated or included some bilingual persons. By 1895 the proportion of Mexicans speaking Indian languages fell to 16.6 per cent, and it fell successively to 15.3 per cent in 1900 and 12.9 per cent in the census of 1910.[48] This growing knowledge of Spanish undergirded national unity and made the appeals of the revolutionary leaders of 1910 more widely intelligible than those of nineteenth-century Mexican leaders.

As one group remains geographically or culturally isolated from another, language changes imperceptibly. Differences arise in the pronunciation and meaning of words, in syntactic forms, and in locutions and idioms.[49] As the type of Spanish spoken in Mexico changed in the nineteenth century, taking on distinctively Mexican phrases and intonations, it produced a language variant that set Mexicans off from the inhabitants of Spain and the rest of Spanish America. A language has to change only slightly for the speakers of two states to be aware of their dis-

48. Moreno, *Los factores demográficos en la planeación económica*, p. 16.
49. José Ortega y Gasset, *Man and People*, Willard R. Trask, trans. (New York: W. W. Norton & Company, Inc., 1957), pp. 228-29.

tinctiveness. Idioms and accents creep in which, although they do not prevent the communication of ideas, give the speakers a sense of separateness. Mexicans increasingly gained a sense of their distinctiveness from their national dialect, just as North Americans did from the British spoken accents and written idioms that became "foreign." The efforts toward linguistic purity of the Academia Mexicana de la Lengua were certainly less effective than the inclusion of the Indian words that enriched the Spanish spoken in Mexico.

The brand of Spanish spoken in Mexico became distinctive through the incorporation of Indian words and the development of Mexican slang. Words like *maguey, pulque, chiquihuite, ahuacate, metate, metlapil, tortilla, molcajete,* and *tejolote* came into the language to describe the plants, drinks, and utensils of the country. *Escuintle,* the term for the hairless Aztec dog, came into Mexican slang to refer to little boys. Mexican slang has continued to develop, including such words as *lana* for "money," *tiliche* for bits of wearing apparel, and *chivas* for "things." Mexicans use variants of *pos* for *pues, trais* for *traes, mano* for *hermano,* and *changa* for *charla.*[50] The Revolution brought new words such as the verb *carranciar,* "to steal like a Carrancista."[51] Increasing verbal communication between Spanish-speaking countries and the international impact of media such as radio, television, and the cinema now retard the growth of a distinctive "Mexican language." But, as both Francisco J. Santamaría's massive *Diccionario de mejicanismos* and Miguel Velasco Valdés' smaller *Vocabulario popular mexicano* attest,[52] the brand of Spanish spoken in Mexico still contains a number of words whose

50. Oscar Álvarez Andrews, "Aspectos sociológicos del lenguaje popular," *Revista Mexicana de Sociología,* Año 11, Vol. 11, Núm. 2 (mayo-agosto, 1949), 181.

51. Edith O'Shaughnessy, *Diplomatic Days* (New York: Harper & Brothers, 1917), p. 166.

52. Francisco J. Santamaría, *Diccionario de mejicanismos* . . . (Méjico: Editorial Porrúa, S.A., 1959); and Miguel Velasco Valdés, *Vocabulario popular mexicano* (México: Editorial "Olimpo," 1957).

form and meaning set them apart from the forms of Spanish spoken elsewhere.

While Mexicans generally agree that the brand of Spanish spoken in Mexico sets them apart from foreigners, they do not feel that regional linguistic differences set Mexicans apart from one another. Whereas a Mexican in Spain is immediately recognized by his language as a Mexican, differences in language within Mexico do not make a man feel "I am a Veracruzano" or "I am from the border." Any Mexican feels linguistically at home in any part of Mexico, partly as a result of the unity that communications media have encouraged in the twentieth century. Regional accents and idioms have manifested distinctions between *patrias chicas,* but the preponderance of interpersonal contact within Mexico has tended to make regional dialects less pronounced and more generally acknowledged as a mere local variant.

Linguistic parochialism was more pronounced in the nineteenth century. The extensive dictionary published by Feliz Ramos i Duarte in 1895 testifies to both the pride that some Mexicans were taking in their language and the extent of its regional diversity at that time. With the avowed purpose of unifying and purifying the brand of Spanish spoken in Mexico, Ramos i Duarte remarks in his preface that "the intimate life of a people is revealed in its language, which is its mode of being: its heart, its intelligence, its thought, its dignity, its essential element of existence, its motherland, its all."[53] In turn, however, Ramos i Duarte's study chronicles for over five hundred pages the provincialism of Mexican Spanish by pointing out the distinctive meanings that a multitude of words had come to have in different states and regions of Mexico.

53. Feliz Ramos i Duarte, *Diccionario de mejicanismos* . . . (Méjico: Imprenta de Eduardo Dublán, 1895), p. 5. On the parochialisms of Mexican Spanish, see also Joaquín García Icazbalceta, *Vocabulario de mexicanismos, comprobado con ejemplos y comprobado con los de otros países hispano-americanos* . . . (México: Tip. y Lit. "La Europea," de J. Aguilar Vera y Ca., 1899).

While various regional linguistic differences persist, the incorporation of English words along the border has had the most effect on Mexican nationalism. Veracruzanos still speak the dialect that set them apart linguistically in 1810, but Yankee terms like *jaibol, beisbol, plogas, fuente de sodas,* and Yankee phrases such as *usar la cabeza, esperar por,* and *una chanza de chino* have extended past their use on the border into more general use in Mexico.[54] The substitution of words like *truke* for *camión* arouses resentment, and Mexicans have cried out against North American "linguistic imperialism," the alleged attempt of the United States to rob the Mexican language of its beauty, replacing words like *martillo* with *jamo* and *lápiz* with *pencilo* and conjugating English verbs like "love" in the ugly manner of *loveo, loveas, lovea.*[55]

Some of the strongest outbursts against linguistic imperialism occurred during the 1910 Revolution. In the circular distributed by Mexican students during the riots over the 1910 burning of Antonio Rodríguez in Rock Springs, Texas, the description of the burning includes verbal attacks made on Rodríguez "in a rabid and barbarous English."[56] Articles in the Mexican press stated that, rather than allowing Indians along the border to learn English, Mexican schoolmasters should concentrate on teaching them Spanish because this language would help form the Indians' "nationality."[57] The revolutionary government of Francisco I. Madero required all railroad workers to pass an examination in Spanish which, since not more than 5 per cent of the American employees could speak Spanish well enough to pass the examination, implemented the government's determination to eliminate Americans from the service.[58] Later, as part of the campaign

54. Joseph H. Matluck, "The Comic Strip: A Source of Anglicisms in Mexican Spanish," *Hispania,* Vol. 43, No. 2 (May, 1960), 228-29, 231.
55. Juan T. Burns, *El pulpo* (Madrid: Editorial Reus, S.A., 1921), p. 312.
56. *The Mexican Herald,* November 10, 1910, clipping enclosed in Henry Lane Wilson to Philander C. Knox, November 10, 1910, /385.
57. *El Sufragio Libre,* November 9, 1910, p. 1:1-2.
58. Wilson to Knox, February 20, 1912, /2889.

against the Constitutionalists, Carranza's ministers were calumniated as Yankeephiles who ate, worked, and even slept in the English language.[59]

The impact of opposition to linguistic imperialism should not be overemphasized, since it is not the major linguistic force stimulating Mexican nationalism. The greatest single linguistic effect on nationalism has clearly been the growth of the Spanish language in Mexico with the gradual fading of Indian languages. Like the spread of Spanish, the rise of a Mexican variant of Spanish has worked to facilitate the national communication that Mexico's variety of languages still makes difficult. Throughout the nineteenth and into the twentieth century, divisions of language have remained a barrier, but a diminishing barrier, to cohesion within the Mexican national community.

EDUCATION

Despite limitations in the size of the school population, formal education furthered Mexican nationalism significantly in the century before 1910. Since education can promote loyalty to any group, the type of education disseminated, as well as the spread of education, affected the rise of nationalism. Mexican Liberals early championed the lay education that would allow representatives of the state rather than the church to instruct Mexican youth, and later educators worked consciously and with increasing effect to unify the nation through education. Even where the school population is small, nationalistic education may be highly significant when school graduates become the most active and articulate part of the population. Mexican educators affected the national community, therefore, not only through the ideas that they gave their students but also in the ways in which their students themselves later initiated or channeled the violence of the Revolution.

59. T. F. Serrano and C. del Vando, *Ratas y ratones: O Carranza y los carrancistas* (El Paso, Texas: n.p., 1914), p. 92.

Formal education effectively propagates group loyalties, including loyalty to the national group. Children may be educated to give loyalty to many groups besides the nation, to feel themselves a part and so to further the interests of a particular religious sect or military order. They can be made aware of the total human collectivity with which world federalists hope all individuals will increasingly identify themselves. Compulsory state-wide courses on Texas history help to explain Texans' unique loyalty to their state, and new multinational schools have attempted to break down barriers of nationalism within the European economic community. Education also serves as a prime promoter of nationalism, because it can indoctrinate students in loyalty to the national community and also provide them with a fundamental knowledge of geography, language, and history, giving them a common basis of communication. Language training provides the possibility of communication for groups who do not speak the national language, provides them with the opportunity to read and discuss nationalistic literature, while the study of geography creates awareness of the physical limits of the fatherland and of the foreign states against which the fatherland must contend.

Study of the history, art, and music of the national community tends to make many students associate themselves with it, lessening the antagonisms of social classes by giving them a basis for common responses. Even if students go on to acquire a specialized facility of communication as part of narrower groups such as lawyers or physicians, they retain the facility of communication within the national group gained in elementary education. As Octavio Véjar Vázquez writes from the Mexican point of view, "in order to form a true nation and preserve it a common and lasting basic spiritual formation is indispensable," and education is the means to "fuse all Mexicans in that spiritual communion which engenders true nationality.''[60] The potential power of education in furthering national unity gives particular relevance to the size of the school population, to the group that teachers represent, and to the awareness and effectiveness of educators in promoting national values.

Historical and economic forces counteracted the spread of national values through education in nineteenth-century Mexico. A 1916 North American study of Mexican education points up the widespread lack of education among the less wealthy Indian and mestizo groups, tracing the prolonged failure of popular government in Mexico to what it calls the failure to educate the ''real people.''[61] In 1906 only 5.42 per cent of the total Mexican population attended school, as compared to rates of 14 per cent in France, 15 per cent in Germany, 16 per cent in England, and 18 per cent in the United States. In Mexico City only 11.3 per cent of the total population attended school.

Many Mexican children could not attend school because their work helped to sustain their families. The introduction and development of machinery during the nineteenth century made sustenance less dependent on daily increments of human labor, potentially freeing Mexican citizens for educational opportunities that could indoctrinate them with nationalistic values. In 1910, however, many Mexican children remained tied to patterns of subsistence farming or wage earning for family support. Parents prod their children but little if they themselves never went to school and if they see that education, although allegedly bringing economic advantages, separates their children from them and from family traditions. Furthermore, since the church controlled a large part of the education in nineteenth-century Mexico, the children who could attend school often received training primarily in universalistic and eccle-

60. Octavio Véjar Vázquez, *Hacia una escuela de unidad nacional* (México: Ediciones de la Secretaría de Educación Pública, 1944), pp. 53, 59.

61. Charles William Dabney and others, *A Study of Educational Conditions in Mexico and an Appeal for an Independent College* (Cincinnati, Ohio: The Committee for the Study of Educational Conditions in Mexico, 1916), p. 27.

siastical loyalty. For many years after independence, as well as before, clerical and military education produced individuals who were enemies of all secular change, men with ecclesiastical or military loyalties rather than loyalty to the Mexican nation.

Despite the historical and economic drawbacks, education and particularly nationalistic education rose sharply before 1910. At the end of the colonial period only 60,000 out of 1.5 million children of school age attended school, but by the end of the Díaz regime 3 out of every 10 children of school age attended. Literacy figures dramatically illustrate the effect of new schools because, while the population of Mexico rose from over 6 million to over 15 million persons, the rate of illiteracy fell from 99.5 per cent at the time of independence to 78.4 per cent in 1910. To counteract the specific problem of Indian education, many states established schools especially for Indians: Chiapas in 1882 and 1900, Guerrero in 1867, Chihuahua and San Luis Potosí in 1889.

Changes in the type of education were at least as important as the rise of education itself, for secular representatives of the state replaced clerics as the formal instructors of Mexican youth. Although the church enjoyed a nearly complete monopoly on education at the time of independence, secular education and secular attitudes increased decisively by the time of the Revolution. In 1910 Mexico City had 436 public schools as compared to 235 private schools of all denominations. By 1910 the public schools maintained neutrality in the religious field, abandoning the old anticlericalism in order to affirm all-inclusive national unity. Church schools had similarly lessened their insistence on the rigid exclusiveness of secular loyalties and allowed more civic education, thus placating government officials, some elements of public opinion, and the more nationalistic segment of the Mexican clergy.

The Liberals who fought for lay education up to the victory over Maximilian wanted to make education a basis for Mexican patriotism.[62] Then, in the comparatively peaceful years of the Díaz regime, education increasingly promoted national cohesion despite the *científico* concept of nationalism. Evidencing the Díaz clique's definition of nationalism as its own self-interest, Mexican Positivists like Gabino Barreda and Manuel Ramos saw the strengthening of the nation through education as the strengthening of the "small group that feels itself to be representative of the nation."[63] The National Preparatory School that Barreda founded under Benito Juárez actively disseminated Positivism, and the Positivists' emphasis on achieving realizable material goals, rather than following the "utopian" ideals of the liberalism inherited by Díaz, allowed Mexico to achieve the material progress that in itself brought a society more receptive to nationalism.

Influential educators under Díaz developed a theory of education that counteracted Barreda's and Ramos' emphasis on material progress and explicitly acknowledged the relationship of education to nationalism. Joaquín Baranda, the minister of justice and public education just before Justo Sierra, wrote that "social organisms, from family to nationality, must pay attention to the bases of their existence" and "the fundamental base of society is the instruction of youth." Applying his concept to Mexico, Baranda found that the school, "in a democratic country, must extend to the borders of the motherland, since only in this way is it possible to create true *national unity*."[64] Enrique C. Rébsamen, who came to lead the model school that Enrique Laubscher founded at Orizaba in 1883, as-

62. See, for instance, *La educación pública en México a través de los mensajes presidenciales desde la consumación de la independencia hasta nuestros días* (México: Publicaciones de la Secretaría de Educación, 1926), pp. 3-164; and Irma Wilson, *Mexico: A Century of Educational Thought* (New York: Hispanic Institute in the United States, 1941).

63. Leopoldo Zea, *Del liberalismo a la Revolución en la educación mexicana* (México: Biblioteca del Instituto Nacional de Estudios Históricos de la Revolución Mexicana, 1956), pp. 103-4.

64. Quoted in Leopoldo Zea, "Hacia un nuevo liberalismo en la educación," *Historia Mexicana*, Vol. 5, Núm. 4 (abril-junio, 1956), 542, 545-46.

serted the necessity of bringing education to all the people in order to secure liberties and give unity to what would be the Mexican nation. Justo Sierra proved to be one of the most influential as well as one of the most eloquent of Mexican educators. He wanted to "realize the religion of the motherland in the soul of the child," to create what he called "the civic religion, the religion which unites and unifies, destined, not to replace the others . . . but to create 'one' social soul."[65]

The educators worked steadily within the Mexican community to implement their ideas and their hopes. A major congress on education, to which such important educators as Rébsamen, Sierra, Porfirio Parra, and Francisco Bulnes came as delegates in December, 1889, formulated a program promoting nationalism. The program required primary education, civic instruction, and national language training, and the work of the congress stimulated state support for normal schools and increased the number of primary schools.[66] The congress found that rural education required special attention and that education would help to incorporate the Indian, whose alleged intellectual inferiority was a great falsehood. The repeated linking of education and national unity at the congress suggests that its members, like other Americans both then and now, saw public education as a panacea for economic and social problems in that it furthered the nationalism they so desired. Many educators made distinctive personal contributions. Baranda, for example, unified the educational system and founded the Normal School for Teachers in 1887 and the Normal School for Women Teachers in 1890. In 1910 Justo Sierra founded the National University, which was as he predicted "to nationalize learning, to Mexicanize knowledge."[67] The specific accomplishments as well as the

65. Quoted in Zea, *Del liberalismo a la Revolución en la educación mexicana*, p. 181.
66. Wilson, *Mexico*, pp. 312-13.
67. Quoted in Zea, *Del liberalismo a la Revolución en la educación mexicana*, p. 186.

educational philosophy of Baranda and Justo Sierra became the basis for Mexican education after the Revolution.

Educators like Sierra, Baranda, and Carlos A. Carillo also greatly affected Mexican nationalism in their capacity as shapers of the revolutionary generation. As Leopoldo Zea writes, "the *porfiriato* did not bring the school to the mass of the people, but it exposed ideas which would bring it." The generation that revolted against Díaz was not "spontaneous" but rather reacted to the antidictatorial ideas in its environment.[68] Revolutionaries after 1910 fought to implement the principles of liberty and democracy they had learned in Baranda's Normal School for Teachers. In stories of Montezuma and his warriors exploiting other Indian groups, Carlos Carillo drew an analogy that his students readily applied to Díaz' contemporary exploitation of the same groups. Carillo was in a sense preparing his students for both the violence and the objectives of the Revolution when he said that *"injustice,* in nations as in individuals, always carries in itself the source of punishment. Only *justice* elevates and aggrandizes nations."[69]

Although the school population was small in 1910, liberal educators trained both initiators of the Revolution and the middle-class intellectuals who shaped its later course. The sharp rise in the number of primary students from over 738,000 in 1906 to over 889,000 in 1910 helped to facilitate national communication on the eve of Díaz' overthrow, and the cumulative effect of increases in education that stressed justice and national unity combined with other trends in Mexican society to form the Revolution. Like the rise of education, the new supremacy of lay education and the increasing awareness of the educator's role in forming the national community, the effects of education on the revolutionaries themselves had a lasting impact on the self-consciousness of the Mexican community.

68. Zea, "Hacia un nuevo liberalismo en la educación," pp. 528, 530.
69. Quoted in *ibid.,* p. 539. The italics are Zea's.

Unprecedented changes in transportation and communications facilities in the century before 1910 provided the physical means for more effective contact and communication among the inhabitants of Mexico. The increase in the miles of railroads was the most significant single innovation in its implications for nationalism, but a variety of other innovations occurred, including the initiation of the telegraph and the improvement of port facilities. Although Mexican writers have criticized these innovations for not going far enough in facilitating communication within the Mexican community, the changes did help to overcome the isolation that geography had imposed upon many small groups. The innovations in transportation not only allowed increasing contact among Mexicans during the nineteenth century but also provided a network of facilities that gave revolutionary forces the physical mobility necessary to achieve a national consciousness after 1910.

Limited means of transportation discouraged communication at the time of independence. The difficulty of travel prevented both internal migration and commercial intercourse, as pack mules were the only means for transporting merchandise and the only paths of communication were the rough roads leading out from Mexico City to towns like Acapulco, Veracruz, and Santa Fe. The roads and paths that wound through the mountains or crossed the arid plains became difficult in times of storms, and few roads ran into Baja California or Yucatán. Transportation was still limited to mules, horses, and human beings.

The enlargement of the railway system in the nineteenth century greatly increased the ease of travel and communications. The first Mexican railway was built in 1850, and Mexicans completed a line from Mexico City to Veracruz, laying 1,073 kilometers of track, between 1850 and 1880. The early railroad between the metropolis of Mexico City and the suburban religious center of Guadalupe, completed about a year after it was begun in 1855, increased its annual passenger load from 153,588 passengers in 1869 to 677,671 passengers by 1877.[70] Religious pilgrims making this excursion paid homage to the distinctively Mexican Virgin of Guadalupe, and the train trip itself provided contact with a creation of the industrial society. After 1880 the Mexican government gave strong official support to railroad construction, and by 1884 numerous railroads in different parts of the country provided 5,731 kilometers of track. Running up to Nuevo Laredo and what are now Ciudad Juárez and Piedras Negras to connect with United States lines, Mexican railways had a total track of 13,615 kilometers in 1900 and 19,280 kilometers in 1910.[71] By the end of the Díaz regime, railroads connected all states of the republic except Tabasco and the territories of Quintana Roo and Baja California, and regional networks were operating in Yucatán and all the way from the Arizona border to below Mazatlán. Once the railroads were built, they not only allowed but stimulated increased travel and merchandise transport, as raw materials and food could move more easily to the cities while manufactured products flowed back to the countryside.

Numerous other innovations in communications, such as the telegraph, postal service, telephone, and improved port facilities, also supplemented the network of roads that existed in New Spain. In 1852 the first telegraph line went up from Mexico City to Veracruz, and by 1862 Mexico had

70. Ernesto de la Torre Villar, ''La capital y sus primeros medios de transporte: Prehistoria de los tranvías,'' *Historia Mexicana*, Vol. 9, Núm. 2 (octubre-diciembre, 1959), 230-31, 241.

71. While estimates of Mexican railway mileage constructed in each year before 1910 differ among themselves, one of the best summaries of Mexican railway development, with maps showing the lines built by 1880, 1884, 1898, and 1910, is Francisco R. Calderón, ''Los ferrocarriles'' in Calderón and others, *El porfiriato, la vida económica* in *Historia moderna de México*, Daniel Cosío Villegas, ed., (México: Editorial Hermes, 1965), Vol. 1, pp. 483-634.

912 miles of telegraph lines. Railroads put up separate telegraph lines for their own use and the use of passengers en route, and some state governments developed and owned their own lines. By 1910 the extensive federal telegraph system under the Department of Communications and Public Works operated aerial and wireless installations and even used submarine cables such as the one running 735 kilometers from Veracruz to Frontera. Mexico established the office of postmaster in 1850, and by 1862 the postal service in Mexico City employed 25 administrators and 196 subordinates. Telephones came to Mexico in 1882. Although few citizens could afford telephones and the high rate restricted use of the postal service, both telephones and letters provided comparatively inexpensive means of communication. Like the telegraph, they gave quick access to geographically isolated areas. The number of Mexican sea ports increased during the nineteenth century to ten Gulf ports and fourteen Pacific ports in 1900, and the $22 million Puerto Mexico project in 1906 and the $42 million Salina Cruz project in 1910 were among the numerous port improvements made by the Díaz government. Besides facilitating the inflow of foreigners against which Mexicans could define their nationality, these ports permitted increasing coastal trade and the circulation of Mexican goods and citizens which a lack of overland communications in areas like Baja California and Yucatán made difficult.

Mexican writers have criticized the fact that Mexico did not create more extensive communications facilities with which to unify the nation. On the eve of the 1910 Revolution, Mexicans such as Félix F. Palavicini were pleading for the extension of roads, highways, and railroads precisely because these means of communication would change the thinking of geographically isolated Mexicans and make it possible to bring them into the Mexican national community.[72] Daniel Moreno, who is well aware that com-

72. Félix F. Palavicini, *Pro-patria: Apuntes de sociología mexicana* (México: Tip. "La Ilustración," 1905), pp. 25-26.

munications did further "the integration of the motherland," finds that the railroads "were not constructed to
serve the national interests." They linked the United States
to Mexico City, allowing foreign exploitation of natural
resources rather than promoting the union of the population.[73] Built largely with foreign capital that sought private
profit, the railroads left the vast regions of Yucatán and
Baja California unconnected with the rest of the country.
Carlos M. Ibarra similarly finds that the railroads "bene-
fited one class and not all," that landowners received a
disproportionate share of the railroads' benefits.[74] Certainly the highly unequal income distribution in the Díaz
period did give landowners a major portion of the agricultural and industrial profits that transportation improvements helped to increase, and the *hacendado* naturally
traveled more by train than the peon who was tied to one
area by servitude and could seldom afford the price of a
ticket. Many of the areas connected by the railroads were
in fact regions that had been connected by roads in the
colonial period. Reducing his argument to personal terms,
Ibarra writes that the "citizen of Yucatán knows Havana
or New Orleans better than his own country, as the Sonoran
or Californian prefers Los Angeles or San Francisco to
Mexico because he remains closer to them. Many citizens
of Chiapas know Guatemala better than their motherland."[75]

While Moreno and Ibarra are right in showing that the
railroads were no panacea for problems of Mexican transportation, the railroads did significantly help to unify the
Mexican nation. Indian crews were forced to learn some

73. Moreno, *Los factores demográficos en la planeación económica*, pp.
283-85.
74. Carlos M. Ibarra, *Economía política mexicana* (Puebla, Pueb.: Lino-
tipografía Económica, 1940), p. 498.
75. *Ibid.*, p. 499. For North American corroboration, see Frank Tannenbaum, "Technology and Race in Mexico," *Political Science Quarterly*, Vol.
61, No. 3 (September, 1946), 375.

Spanish while they were building the railroads, and contact among travelers on the railroad network tended to break down local dialects, unifying the Spanish dialect spoken in Mexico. Railroads facilitated the distribution of nationalistic novels and histories, and they gave students easier access to the centers of education. Railroads also aided the process of mixing the races by bringing the white and widely dispersed Indian groups into physical proximity, and they increased occupational mobility both for the workers needed to establish and maintain railroad equipment and for the other workers who could now move with greater ease between regions. Trains also proved to be a startling manifestation of the industrial society to the isolated rural worker who saw them rumble through his countryside, often stimulating the desire to know more about society outside the *patria chica* if not the desire to see it.

The railroads also served as a focus for xenophobia and aided national communication more than ever after new railroad construction virtually stopped in 1911. Bringing both foreign capital and foreign citizens into Mexico, the railroads carried the North Americans who financed both the railroads and the industries that the railroads were exploiting. In 1908 the Mexican government took control of many railways that had grown up under foreign concessions. Jaime Gurza summed up the fear of the United States which underlay popular support for the government action when he wrote in 1911 that, since Mexico had such a rich and energetic neighbor, "every effort which, like the nationalization of our railroads, gives us more independence and more influence in our internal matters and relations, must be eminently patriotic."[76] After 1910 boxcars of revolutionaries replaced the regularly scheduled trains. One crucial difference between the Revolution of 1910 and those of 1810 and 1857 was the new railroad network, as

76. Jaime Gurza, *La política ferrocarrilera del gobierno* (México: Tipografía de la Oficina Impresora de Estampillas, 1911), p. 116.

the armies that contended after 1910 had a mobility unknown to the followers of Hidalgo and Juárez. After 1910 masses of common soldiers and their women gained access to the transportation that economic circumstances previously had reserved for the Mexican elite.

IV
The Revolution as a Catalyst of Social Change

Between 1910 and 1917, the evolution of Mexico's civil war revised the process of social change in Mexico. This period of violence underlay the later development of more systematic social change, of course, but shifts in the parameters significant for the growth of Mexican nationalism also occurred in the period of violence itself. The Revolution speeded up the pre-existing processes of internal migration, miscegenation, and even linguistic assimilation, while it reversed such trends as the growth of clerical prerogatives which opposed the rise of nationalism. With the breakdown of authority and the new-found physical and economic mobility of revolutionaries came discussions and programs for wide-ranging societal changes. The idealized leaders of revolutionary factions, who encouraged aspirations and articulation among their followers, appeared to subsequent generations of Mexicans as a new galaxy of national heroes invoked to sanction the process of social change.

Individual concern for the unprecedented material and human destruction of the Mexican Revolution created an immediate and fairly durable impetus to national unity and the peaceful harmonizing of opposing interests. The ideal of greater social and economic equality within the national community, as a concomitant of more effective social communication among Mexican citizens, received support from revolutionary leveling and redistributions and from the increasing possibility of acquiring social status through achievement rather than ascription. Although destruction also imposed restrictions on the momentum of change and although the serious impediments of unaltered class structure, restricted educational opportunities, and isolation—geographic, racial, and linguistic—remained after 1917, the years of revolutionary upheaval altered the course of Mexican social change and provoked a continuing commitment to change among the leaders and the people of Mexico.

THE NEW NATIONAL HEROES

Shortly before the epic Revolution began, Mexicans celebrated the centennial of their 1810 movement for national independence. The celebrations and the extensive preparations for them throughout the republic subjected citizens of varying social status to the brainwashing oratory, military parades, and demonstrations that stirred at least superficial concern for the meaning of Mexican nationality. A flood of highly nationalistic books and pamphlets appeared in 1910 to honor the heroes and events of Mexican independence.[1] Newspapers and periodicals carried patriotic articles and stories throughout the year.[2] A year of

1. For examples of the regional studies that, subsuming regional loyalties into the broader Mexican national loyalty, tried to make Mexicans from different sections of the republic feel loyalty to the nation, see Eduardo Gómez Haro, *La ciudad de Puebla y la guerra de independencia. Historia de la participación que Puebla tomó en el movimiento bélico que emancipó a México de España. Obra escrita para celebrar el centenario de nuestra independencia* (Puebla, Pueb.: Imprenta "El Arte Tipográfico," 1910); *El monumento a la independencia en Zacatecas* (Zacatecas, Zac.: n.p., 1910); and Luis Villa y Gordoa, ed., *El movimiento revolucionario de independencia en Aguascalientes* (Aguascalientes, Ags.: Tip. "El Clarín," 1910). A typically stirring, illustrated account of Hidalgo's heroism as father of Mexican independence, written for the centennial celebration, is José M. de la Fuente, *Hidalgo íntimo* . . . (México: Tipografía Económica, 1910), especially pp. 239-385.

2. For exemplary articles that stress the fraternal solidarity of Mexican citizens and describe such events as the celebrations, the receipt of relics as "national treasures," the erection of the spire to independence in Mexico

anticipation culminated in what pretended to be an extravaganza of national fraternalism in September, 1910, just two months before the official beginning of the Maderista revolution in November.

In one sense the centennial celebrations offer an interesting test case in the influence of nationalistic paraphernalia on the emerging of nationalism as a cohesive social force. The speeches, writings, and glittering parades clearly contained a theatrical irrelevance to problems of conflict within the national society. Moreover, as lower-class Mexicans were partially excluded because they might be offensive to the foreign visitors present, the celebrations pointed up the narrowness of the *científicos'* concept of the Mexican national community. The convivial parties that welcomed foreigners rather than fellow Mexicans, the official praise of a material progress that was limited to the small upper strata of Mexican society, and the attempt to portray Mexico to the world and to itself as a country of homogeneous and progressive Spanish-speaking people mirrored the exclusivistic *científico* attitudes against which the Revolution was to turn.

Despite the window dressing and the evidencing of *científico* attitudes, the centennial celebrations gave Mexicans a dose of nationalistic sentiment that carried over to shape the nature of the succeeding Revolution. The bands playing national airs, the parading columns of plumed Mexican cavalry, and the orations on how "Mexicans" had fought "foreigners" to be free stirred fleeting feelings of national pride in countless Mexicans whose actions during the following years were in part influenced by that pride. The celebrations also awakened nationalist resentment and a vague desire for wider membership in the national com-

City, and the special issue of commemorative stamps, see "En la celebración del centenario, se impone la fraternidad," *El Sufragio Libre*, August 24, 1910, p. 1:1-2; "De manos de la hidalguía español recibe México jubiloso, un histórico presente," *El Imparcial*, September 18, 1910, p. 1:2-6; and "Solemne inauguración de la columna de la independencia," *El Imparcial*, September 17, 1910, pp. 1:4-7, 9:1-3.

munity among those excluded from full participation in
the festivities and among those who saw distinctions of
class, wealth, and political nonparticipation as separating
Mexicans from one another. The atmosphere of incipient
nationalism fostered by the centennial celebrations thus
helped to give the continuing revolutionary struggle its
strongly nationalistic overtones in the years following 1910.
In doing so, it created an atmosphere in which Madero and
the other leaders who rose to prominence could more readily
resemble the national heroes of the past.

The leaders of major factions competing for power
between 1910 and 1917 differed in backgrounds, careers,
and objectives. During the revolutionary turmoil and subsequent years of reconstruction, however, their subordinates' loyalty to them and their deeds and violent deaths
made them uniformly lionized as reformers, heroes, and
prototypes. Francisco Madero, Venustiano Carranza, and
Álvaro Obregón have become the most widely respected
heroes of the 1910 Revolution. Francisco Villa enjoys a
romantic popularity that makes him the frequent hero of
films and comic books, and Emiliano Zapata has a staunch
band of devotees among farmers and residents of the states
of Morelos and Mexico. In order to analyze the impact that
the process of hero-creation may have in sanctioning social
change, the actual careers of the individual leaders must be
separated from their lionization.

When one asks Mexicans who was the greatest man of
the Revolution, a majority usually answers that it was
Francisco I. Madero. As the wealthy heir to a cotton
plantation in Coahuila and a man who had developed a
sense of egalitarianism through study in France and the
United States, Madero sparked political interest by the
1908 publication of a book on the presidential succession
of 1910. In accepting the re-election of Porfirio Díaz but
calling for wider political participation and free selection of
a vice-president, the book, like much of Madero's subsequent
career, showed him to be not so much an economic, agrarian,

or social reformer as a *laissez-faire* liberal in the nineteenth-century or European sense who wanted to give Mexicans a system of democratic elections under which they could select responsible representatives to devise the laws that Mexico needed.[3] Basing his plans for the Mexican national community chiefly upon revisions in the political super-structure, Madero sincerely hoped to create a government that would represent and unite all Mexicans. The nature of Madero's nationalistic thrust appears in the dedication to *La sucesión presidencial en 1910.* He aptly dedicated the volume to Mexico's national heroes, to "the heroes who with their blood have won the independence of the mother-land" and shown Mexicans how "to work, all united, pursuing the great principle of fraternity, to obtain, through the means of liberty, realization of the magnificent democratic ideal of equality before the law."[4]

Madero began to acquire hero status with his addresses to Mexican crowds in what became a popular campaign against Díaz' re-election and by calling for revolution after the campaign failed to overthrow the dictatorship. In his three campaign swings of 1909 and 1910, he promised partial agrarian and labor reforms, advocated a large state-financed system of education, denounced wars against the Yaqui and other Indian groups, and played upon anti-Yankee sentiment by chiding Díaz' cordiality toward the United States. These nationalist stands gained support for Madero and underlie his depiction as a reformer. The ig-

3. One of the most objective and best documented accounts of Madero's viewpoint is Stanley R. Ross, *Francisco I. Madero: Apostle of Mexican Democracy* (New York: Columbia University Press, 1955), p. 219. See also Charles Curtis Cumberland, *Mexican Revolution: Genesis Under Madero* (Austin, Texas: University of Texas Press, 1952).

4. Secondary dedications also praised Mexican journalists who suffered espousing liberty and "all Mexicans in whom the idea of the motherland has not died." Francisco I. Madero, *La sucesión presidencial en 1910* (3d ed.; México: Librería de la Viuda de Ch. Bouret, 1911), pp. 3-6. Madero's original call and the overt stirrings of other opposition groups resulted partly from Díaz' own protestations that he would allow an opposition party and not run for the presidency again. This was contained in the widely publicized interview with James C. Creelman in the March, 1908, edition of *Pearson's Magazine.*

norance of the rural Mexican proletariat made its members unable to understand the political motives of Madero and his group of intellectuals, but in his revolution, as in most revolutions, men with different interests and causes of discontent came together in a single armed protest.[5]

Madero's stature increased with his revolutionary triumph over Díaz. The Maderista insurgents took nationalist garb even though they lacked regular uniforms; they wore ribbons with the red, white, and green Mexican tricolor and some even displayed in addition impressive badges with pictures of Madero, Juárez, and Hidalgo.[6] After the triumph of Madero's forces at Ciudad Juárez, it did indeed seem as though a more inclusive national community might soon be realized. With a visionary's optimism, Madero proclaimed to his "fellow citizens" on May 27, 1911, that now "liberty will extend its ample wings over all Mexicans, and fraternally united we will work for the aggrandizement of our country."[7] Continuing civil strife mocked Madero's statement for the next decade, although his vision of fraternal union and progress became surprisingly pertinent to the following fifty years of Mexican history. As Madero's struggle for influence reached a climax in the weeks before his death, he gained in heroic stature through glowing accounts of himself as a leader who, with flag in hand, brought courage to his troops.[8] Eighty thousand copies of a pamphlet by Rogelio Fernández Güell described Madero's battlefield heroism and dedication to the Mexican people in typ-

5. Lucio Mendieta y Núñez, *Teoría de la revolución* (México: Biblioteca de Ensayos Sociológicos, Instituto de Investigaciones Sociales, Universidad Nacional, 1959), pp. 113-14.

6. *New York Herald*, March 7, 1911, in U.S., Library of Congress MSS collection, *Newspaper Clippings pertaining to Mexico, 1911-1913*, 3 vols., III-48-C,1, Ac. 6194, Vol. 1; *The New York Times*, May 21, 1911, p. 1:7; and Edith O'Shaughnessy, *Diplomatic Days* (New York: Harper & Brothers, 1917), p. 37.

7. From a manifesto reproduced in Antonio P. González and J. Figueroa Domenech, *La Revolución y sus héroes* . . . (México: Librería de Ortega y Compañía, 1911), pp. 281-85.

8. See *Nueva Era*, February 10, 1913, p. 4:2-3.

ical fashion while refuting in detail the arguments of Madero's detractors.[9]

Despite such defenses, Madero's popularity diminished sharply after he acquired power. Although Madero and José María Pino Suárez won the presidency and vice-presidency in one of the freest elections in Mexican history, critics bitterly attacked the election, denouncing Madero's strong support of Pino Suárez as an "imposition" similar to that of candidates under the old Díaz regime. Satisfying the clamorous demands of the opposing groups within the Mexican polity proved impossible, and Madero became caught between the old federal army and the Zapatistas, who now turned against him for not fulfilling their demands for agrarian reform. He suffered vilification from a massive opposition press that, in attempting to realize the conditions of true democracy, he had allowed to exist. Madero experienced a general unpopularity that Mexicans today rarely remember, although sympathetic contemporaries found him to be the most unpopular president Mexico had ever had.[10] Even Madero's staunchest defenders acknowledged his rapid loss of popularity.[11]

Madero's stature as the most widely respected revolutionary derives partly from his assassination by agents of Victoriano Huerta, the general to whom he entrusted the defense of Mexico City during the insurrection of Bernardo Reyes and Félix Díaz. Madero's assassination solidified revolutionaries in opposition to Huerta as the president's earlier invocations for unity had never done. When the victorious Constitutionalists finally overthrew Huerta, they staged a large celebration for the "martyred" Madero and Pino Suárez in whose names they had been fighting, initiat-

9. Rogelio Fernández Güell, *El moderno Juárez: Estudio sobre la personalidad de D. Francisco I. Madero* (México: Tip. "Artística," 1911).

10. Manuel Calero, *Un decenio de política mexicana* (New York: Printed by L. Middleditch Co., 1920), p. 100.

11. M. Márquez Sterling, *Los últimos días del presidente Madero (mi gestión diplomática en México)* (Habana: Imprenta "El Siglo XX," 1917), pp. 343-44.

ing with a parade and eulogies a series of official government tributes to the early heroes which has continued ever since.[12] As in the case of such valid North American heroes as Abraham Lincoln and John Fitzgerald Kennedy, Madero's assassination reduced the asperity of contemporary and subsequent criticism. In doing so, it allowed Mexicans to remember and respect Madero primarily for his deep devotion to political democracy and Mexican unity.

Venustiano Carranza and Álvaro Obregón took up Madero's mantle. As a former senator under Díaz whose early support for Madero had made him governor of Coahuila after the Maderista triumph, Carranza declared against Huerta in March, 1913, and became over-all leader of the Constitutionalist coalition that ultimately forced Huerta into exile. As a gradualist with a basically political orientation, Carranza was not the strenuous social reformer he is often pictured to have been. The distinctiveness of his nationalist attitudes was not advocacy of social and economic reforms that would work to equalize opportunities for members of the Mexican national community but rather a fierce upholding of Mexican national honor against the Veracruz occupation and the Pershing expedition of President Woodrow Wilson. Carranza aroused the antipathy of the Zapatistas, and they reviled the "First Chief" of the Constitutionalists as "intolerant and exclusivistic, treacherous and deceitful, full of duplicity and hypocrisy, false in everything, faithless to everyone, autocratic and exclusivistic, stubborn, plotting, perverse, a traitor to the Revolution and a usurper who to complete his work wanted, like Huerta, to bring the country to the edge of international conflict."[13] The image of Carranza that predominates in

12. Narrative and pictorial coverage of the celebration with long excerpts from encomiums by Álvaro Obregón, Luis Manuel Rojas, Félix F. Palavicini, and José I. Novelo appear in "Grandioso homenaje de los vengadores al mártir de la democracia," *El País,* August 18, 1914, pp. 1:2-6, 8:1-7; and *Revista de Revistas,* Año 5, Núm. 228 (23 agosto 1914), 2-3.

13. Alfonso Taracena, *La tragedia zapatista* (México: Editorial "Bolívar," 1931), p. 85.

Mexican folklore, however, was created by Isidro Fabela, who wrote in August, 1913: "Do you know who Venustiano Carranza is? He is the Law; he is the symbol of Justice; he is, in these solemn moments of our history, the incarnation of the Motherland."[14] When, after becoming president, Carranza found opposition from Obregón too powerful, he fled in May, 1920, with a small band of friends and money from the Mexican treasury. Waylaid while trying to escape by train to Veracruz, Carranza rode northward and was later treacherously murdered while asleep in a peasant hut.

Álvaro Obregón, as a former schoolteacher and factory worker, developed a more personal commitment to social change than had either Madero or Carranza. With his early support of Madero and recognized service in the Constitutionalist cause against Huerta, Obregón won fame as a military tactician whose knowledgeable use of barbed wire and trench warfare stopped the previously invincible attacks of Villa's *dorado* cavalry. Obregón received labor support and acquired an additional political debt when members of the Casa del Obrero Mundial sent six "Red Battalions" to aid his military victory. Obregón helped frame the 1917 Constitution before solidly entrenching himself in the presidency from 1920 to 1924, yielding control for four years to Plutarco Elías Calles, and being elected president for a second term on July 1, 1928. Obregón, too, died violently; two and a half weeks after the 1928 election victory, he was shot by a religious fanatic.

Although the image of Emiliano Zapata has come to be revered as a national symbol, the loyalty of Zapata and his men was actually confined to their *patria chica* of Morelos rather than extended to the wider Mexican Republic. Zapatistas wanted agrarian reform in their own area. They fought with Madero against Díaz but turned against Madero when he failed to meet agrarian demands. They fought as

14. From an article reprinted in Isidro Fabela, *Arengas revolucionarias, discursos y artículos políticos* (Madrid: Tipografía Artística, 1916), p. 88.

Constitutionalists against Huerta but joined Francisco Villa in opposition to Carranza and Obregón. The parochialism of their ultimate loyalty is demonstrated by the fact that after the victory at Puebla on December 16, 1914, the Zapatistas melted back into the sanctuary of their small homeland rather than pursuing with Villa what seemed to be the clear and final destruction of Carranza and Obregón.[15] On April 10, 1919, Zapata was tricked to his death in a meeting with Jesús Guajardo, who had pretended to go over to Zapata's side and even had murdered a detachment of Carranza's troops to prove it. The tragic death of this revolutionary hero provided opportunity for endless romanticization, and Zapata came to symbolize the Mexican peasants' struggle for land, a struggle that became officially dedicated to greater equality within the national community.

The striking career of Francisco Villa won for him a popularity not shared by the more intellectual but less well remembered Mexican revolutionaries. Before the Revolution, Villa lived as a bandit, according to popular history, after being outlawed for killing an *hacendado* who had raped his sister. He duly fought under Madero and against Huerta, amassing over 100,000 followers who, with Huerta's defeat, looked like the strongest force in Mexico. He won striking victories, like the 1913 capture of Ciudad Juárez, that are now celebrated in popular literature. In addition to showing Villa's military heroism, the literature usually describes amorous exploits that make him approach the Mexican ideal of "manliness."[16] After Obregón's victories limited Villa's power to his own region of Chihuahua, Villa gained fame throughout Mexico by the daring raid on Columbus, New Mexico, which provoked the North Amer-

---

15. Robert E. Quirk, *The Mexican Revolution, 1914-1915: The Convention of Aguascalientes* (Bloomington, Ind.: Indiana University Press, 1960), p. 141.

16. "Amanecer en el otro mundo," *Cabalgando con Villa*, Núm. 9 (30 noviembre 1964). See also, "Memorias de un periodista yanqui," *Leyendas de Pancho Villa*, Año 1, Núm. 34 (9 mayo 1964); "Villa sabe perdonar," *Leyendas de Pancho Villa*, Año 1, Núm. 44 (n.d.); "La piadosa," *Leyendas de Pancho Villa*, Año 1, Núm. 23 (20 febrero 1964); and 'Nubarrones sobre Columbus," *Cabalgando con Villa*, Núm. 4 (30 abril 1964).

ican retaliation of General Pershing's punitive column. Villa's death was immediately proclaimed as the assassination of a hero when, on July 20, 1923, he was shot from ambush while driving from his hacienda to Parral with his secretary and three *dorados*.[17]

Besides the major figures in the hagiology of the Mexican Revolution, a variety of somewhat less widely known men receive regular tribute as revolutionary heroes. Former revolutionaries still remember the lieutenants of the major chiefs—men like Felipe Ángeles and Genovevo de la O, who are now lauded in textbooks and biographies. Andrés Molina Enríquez is remembered for his contribution in drafting the important agrarian reform article of the 1917 Constitution. Although Ricardo Flores Magón is less widely known in Mexico today than the major leaders, he is respected as a true liberal rather than an anarchist. Mexican intellectuals attribute important revolutionary impetus to his call for economic and political reform, his violent *Regeneración* paper, and the widely circulated 1905 platform of the Mexican Liberal party. Statues and monuments commemorate heroes such as Aquiles Serdán, who died with his family in the first Maderista uprising of November, 1910, and Belisario Domínguez, a senator murdered for opposing Huerta. The intellectuals around the revolutionary leaders, Luis Cabrera, José Vasconcelos, Manuel Gamio, and Isidro Fabela, have through their own actions, writings, and subsequent careers as educators, Indianists, and statesmen carved out impressive personal reputations. Appeals for national pride can be made to all Mexican citizens in the names of these leaders, and each leader may be invoked in particular instances to sanction the continuing "revolutionary" process of social change.

17. *Vida, hazañas y muerte del Gral. Francisco Villa: Su juventud audaz, su esplendor guerrero, su vuelta a la vida pacífica del campo y su trágica muerte* (San Antonio, Texas: Librería de Quiroga, n.d.), pp. 139-43. On the mythology which has grown up around Villa, see Enrique Beltrán, "Fantasía y realidad de Pancho Villa," *Historia Mexicana*, Vol. 26, Núm. 1 (julio-septiembre, 1966).

Victoriano Huerta is an "anti-hero" to the Mexican national community, a man who unifies Mexicans by the revulsion of his memory. In his contribution to the growth of nationalism, Huerta resembles Santa Anna, the archetype Mexican anti-hero, and the foreign bogeymen of the Revolution castigated by Mexican patriots, American Ambassador Henry Lane Wilson and President Woodrow Wilson. There are but few sympathetic accounts of Huerta's life and death. Rómulo Velasco Ceballos' account praises Huerta as a nationalist above all, showing him valiantly confronting Yankee authorities at Fort Bliss, Texas, and claiming that he died a "victim of vengeance, because he wanted to be Mexican, but a Mexican proud of his dignity rather than the vile slave of businessmen."[18] The circumstances did contain elements of pathos and heroism. Before his quiet death on the evening of January 13, 1916, his health had deteriorated during his confinement in a run-down American jail with drunks and petty criminals. His lack of money and the financial plight of his family cast doubts on reports of his large-scale raiding of the Mexican treasury.[19]

The propaganda needs of a society, however, help to determine what segments of a national figure's life will be emphasized and remembered. Huerta is remembered in Mexico as a symbol of retrogression and the murderer of Madero and Pino Suárez. A hero to no one, his name is still invariably linked with the term "usurper" as it was during the campaign to unseat him. Although Huerta voiced his appeals for support in terms of Mexican nationalism, he stimulates Mexican nationalism today only through denunciations as a self-seeker and a social re-

18. R. Velasco Ceballos, *El General Huerta. La prisión de Fort Bliss, sucia e incómoda, y los inhumanos tratamientos que recibió en la misma, determinaron la muerte del General VICTORIANO HUERTA.—Sensacionales revelaciones.—Ante la humanidad elevamos nuestra protesta* (El Paso, Texas: Imprenta Juárez, n.d.), p. 25.

19. George J. Rausch, Jr., "The Exile and Death of Victoriano Huerta," *Hispanic American Historical Review*, Vol. 42, No. 2 (May, 1962), 143-51.

actionary who would have erased the impetus of Madero's revolution by reverting to a Porfirian dictatorship. Huerta's lasting effect on Mexican nationalism, therefore, remains basically that of other Mexican anti-heroes of the Revolution such as Jesús Guajardo, the betrayer and murderer of Emiliano Zapata.

As an individual Porfirio Díaz never fully lost the heroic aura built up around him before 1910, so that he has gradually come to assume a unique position beside the leaders of the revolt against him. Although vituperative denunciations of Díaz appeared during the violence of his overthrow,[20] the departure of the deposed dictator for Europe illustrates the degree of sympathy still felt for him. When Díaz sailed on the *Ypiranga* on May 31, 1911, Veracruzanos joined to pay him a surprisingly unanimous tribute. He and his party left the house in which he had been quartered without announcement and took carriages along a circuitous route, but soldiers, two military bands, and a large crowd of both working people and socialites jammed the way to the Sanitary Pier where the *Ypiranga* lay. Commenting that on May 31 Veracruz gave Díaz only cheers whereas before his name had evoked only hisses, the foreign press described the departure scene in which a dozen pretty girls threw great bunches of roses, the guns of Fort Santiago fired a final salute, and every hat came off as the ship's band played the Mexican national anthem. Díaz "received an ovation on the walk to the ship rarely accorded to any one in Vera Cruz and never before to Gen. Díaz," as the "crowd was cheering itself hoarse, with never a cry for Madero."[21] Convincing proof that this send-off for Díaz was exceptional and not simply an excuse for exuberance is shown by the lack of enthusiasm five days later for Bernardo Reyes' return from Europe to Vera-

20. See Federico de la Colina, *Porfirio Díaz. Su vida militar. Sus perfidias políticas. Sus odios. Sus traiciones. Su decadencia. Su cobardía* (México: Talleres del "Diario Republicano," 1911), especially pp. 11, 37.

21. *The New York Times*, June 1, 1911, p. 1:7.

cruz. Soldiers attended but the people stayed at home, and only a fringe of peons stood behind the soldiers.[22] Strengthening his image as an exiled patriot, Díaz proclaimed shortly after he reached Spain—and repeated over and over again until his death on July 2, 1915—that he would not return to Mexico unless foreign intervention demanded it: "Only some international difficulty necessitating a supreme effort on the part of all Mexicans in a close union could make me alter my decision, but if such an eventuality arose nothing could stop me from going to the end of my life—as in the first years of my manhood—rifle in hand."[23]

Since the Revolution, Díaz has failed to acquire the anti-hero status of Santa Anna and Huerta. The social elite that amassed wealth and great prestige under his regime long continued to look upon Díaz as the representative of their own "real" Mexico. While Díaz has always been revered by the wealthy families opposing the 1910 Revolution, his general acceptance as a hero represents in part the amalgamation in a new elite of the old aristocracy and the revolutionary leaders. Today a resurrected Díaz is esteemed; his early heroism against the French is praised as is the material growth that his maintenance of political stability engendered. As a national champion in his early days, he is remembered as "a fierce anticlericalist and a Jacobin Liberal who was both xenophobic and anti-imperialist."[24] Films and literature that show him as a zealous young officer and as a white-haired patriarch sometimes even take pride in the regal adornments that the upper fringe of Mexican society enjoyed under him. Mexicans retrospectively differentiate sharply between Díaz and his governmental system, simultaneously respecting Díaz and criticizing the *continuismo* and arbitrary quality of the *porfiriato*. In acquiring respect as an individual national

22. *Ibid.*, June 5, 1911, p. 2:1.
23. Quoted in *ibid.*, June 19, 1911, p. 4:2.
24. Daniel Cosío Villegas, *The United States versus Porfirio Díaz*, Nettie Lee Benson, trans. (Lincoln, Neb.: University of Nebraska Press, 1963), p. xi.

hero, Díaz differs from both the lesser-known revolutionary heroes and reformers and the anti-heroes who affect Mexican unity only by generating unanimous opposition.

The process of hero-creation vitally affects the subsequent sanctioning of social change. Revolutions lead to the creation of heroes when, as P. A. Sorokin writes with primary reference to the Soviet Revolution, "crime and brutality are dubbed heroic deeds; pygmies grow into giants; babblers into heroes; persons of lax morality are canonized; parasites looked upon as saviours."[25] Mass revolutions, in contrast to the ordinary Latin American *cuartelazos* and *golpes d'estado,* serve the dual purpose of drawing members of the populace into the movement and of creating heroes for the community after the violence is over. In Lucio Mendieta y Núñez' terms, the victorious generals and great battles first influence the creation and maintenance of a revolutionary spirit, give prestige to the revolutionary movement, and "attract military contingents from the passive part of the population, convert many spectators into actors."[26] Desire for profit and, where subsistence becomes difficult, hunger further impel men to join the revolution. With the revolution's triumph, legends arise which elevate the participants to the category of heroes, so creating a basis in national folklore for the new social order.

The violence of the Mexican Revolution incorporated this process of revolutionary hero-creation. Many of the peasant participants who had no effective sense of identification with the "nation" could identify themselves with a personalistic leader. As the persistence of "personalism" in Latin American politics testifies, it is easier to identify first with a person than with the nation. In the maturing situation of the Mexican Revolution, individuals gradually developed a new sense of nationalism as their personalist

25. Pitirim A. Sorokin, *The Sociology of Revolution* (Philadelphia, Pa.: J. B. Lippincott Company, 1925), p. 360.
26. Mendieta y Núñez, *Teoría de la revolución,* p. 85.

leaders came to be invoked as national heroes. Mexicans today view the revolutionaries of 1910 as representing the highest point of national devotion, sometimes questioning whether Mexicans who currently profess national loyalty might deny that loyalty when it conflicts with personal, family, or religious interests, while the actions of the 1910 revolutionaries show that they put the interests of the national community first.[27] The objective validity of this view varies considerably among different leaders like Madero, Obregón, and Villa, but what is important for Mexican nationalism is the viewpoint itself.

The availability of heroes whose invocation unifies the national community and shapes its values sets Mexico apart from other Latin American states, as the latter lack a purposeful sense of social cohesion and, incidentally, find national heroes much harder to come by. Sharp contrasts in the quality of national heroes and the pervasiveness of cohesive nationalism differentiate Mexico and Peru. With a paucity of national heroes who might be invoked to stimulate national identification and participation, attempts at hero-creation in Peru have had to look to such men as José Gálvez, a Peruvian minister of war killed by a chance shot in 1866 while observing a naval engagement between Spain and Peru.[28] Jorge Chávez, a young Peruvian aviator who died in September, 1910, after becoming the first man to fly the Alps, inspired a large monument built in Lima to his memory in 1937, but Chávez makes a shallow national hero. Born in Paris of Peruvian parents, he lacked a personal sense of loyalty to Peru and chose to live in Europe.

The nationalist view of Mexican heroes gains support from legendary re-creations of the Revolution. Factional histories and memoires have so often portrayed leaders in terms of factional interests that for every literary attempt

27. Interview with Roberto Zaínos in San Jerónimo Lídice, D.F., October 11, 1964.
28. John Nathan Plank, ''Peru: A Study in the Problems of Nation-Forming'' (unpublished Ph.D. dissertation, Harvard University, 1958), p. 193.

at hero-creation there is a damning chronicle portraying the same leader as weak, immoral, or traitorous. The over-all effect of the myriad revolutionary accounts has been one of hero-creation, however, because readers—whether Maderista champions of political democracy, agrarian reformers invoking Zapata, or industrial workers looking back to Obregón's Red Battalions—tend to associate their personal interests with their own "heroic" revolutionary leaders. Furthermore, the passage of time has mellowed indictments of one faction by another, and accounts in general histories and school textbooks emphasize the accomplishments of every major leader.

The case of Emiliano Zapata aptly demonstrates the manner in which revolutionary hero-creation has sanctioned the process of social change. Even before his death, writers acclaimed Zapata as "the idol of the humble people" of Morelos and Mexico.[29] The manifesto signed by Zapata's lieutenants and supporters five days after his death significantly linked his deification to the concept of a Mexican national community. Renewing their oaths "in the presence of the Mexican Nation," the Zapatistas proclaimed that "the national soul was awakened to new life by the ardent and overwhelming call of Emiliano Zapata, the apostle and prophet" and dedicated themselves to "complete the work of the reformer, avenge the blood of the martyr, follow the example of the hero."[30] Sincere propagandists evoke a sense of continuity in the line of national heroes by comparing Zapata to José María Morelos, as Zapata becomes a symbol of all Mexicans who "defend the lands of their fathers" and "a man sprung from and immersed in the life of his people who is a prototype in the history of Mexico."[31]

29. Antonio D. Melgarejo, *Los crímenes del zapatismo (apuntes de un guerrillero)* (México: F. P. Rojas y Cía., 1613 [*i.e.* 1913]), pp. 165-66.

30. Quoted in Porfirio Palacios, *Emiliano Zapata: Datos biográfico-históricos* (México: Libro Mex Editores, 1960), pp. 289-91. On pp. 305-23 Palacios presents an interesting tabulation of verbal tributes and monuments erected to Zapata in Mexico.

31. Jesús Sotelo Inclán, *Raíz y razón de Zapata* (México: Editorial Etnos, 1943), pp. 190, 199.

Zapata has become a special hero among the people of his home state of Morelos, where the state shield bears the Zapatista slogans of "Land and Liberty" and "The Land Belongs to Those Who Work It with Their Hands."

Most importantly, however, Zapata is the hero of agrarian reformers, who have employed his image to promote the extensive redistributions of land to peasant farmers, thus counteracting peasant alienation from the national community. The token redistributions after Zapata's death, the massive redistributions under Lázaro Cárdenas in the 1930's, and the continuing redistributions (along with extensive irrigation, agricultural education, and the mechanization of efficient larger tracts since 1940) invoke the memory of Zapata. Portraits and busts of Zapata now adorn offices of the Confederación Nacional de Campesinos throughout Mexico, and the CNC, as the voice of Mexico's farmers within the official party and national government, perpetuates the battle for land and opportunity for Mexico's rural workers.

Because Zapata has achieved the status of a national hero, Mexican writers today express their own points of view in his name. Leftists invoke Zapata, for instance, to support not only the continuation of agrarian reform but also the efficacy of the Russian Revolution, the current Soviet regime, and the solidarity of the Cuban and Mexican peoples.[32] Moreover, responsible leaders of Mexican political and economic development shape the emphasis of particular ideas attributed to Zapata and other revolutionary heroes, just as Soviet and Chinese theoreticians select different sections of Lenin's writings to support their opposing strategic plans for the Communist victory. The invocation of national heroes proves an effective sanction of social change even in pragmatic, nonideological states like Mexico. With the continuing Mexican emphasis on education, Zapata is typically portrayed as having had a "pro-

32. Alberto Domingo, "Vamos a 'echarnos' a Zapata otra vez!" *Siempre!* Núm. 576 (8 julio 1964), 44.

found preoccupation'' with education, with literacy campaigns, and even with the autonomy of the University of Mexico.[33]

The process of hero-creation in the case of other major factional leaders similarly allows them to appear in retrospect as apostles of social change. With Madero's martyrdom as a precedent, the assassinations of Carranza, Zapata, and Villa in factional conflict and even Obregón's murder by a religious fanatic take on a romanticized aura of heroism. Venustiano Carranza is portrayed in a majority of Mexican and North American accounts as a reformer whose Veracruz decrees—actually concessions for support when his fortunes ebbed—proved his dedication to change and foreshadowed the later Querétaro Constitution that he helped to engineer. Obregón appears, not as a reconciler and enforced spokesman for the reform-minded intellectuals and groups that supported him, but as the special champion of social reform who led the fight for constitutional Article 123, the ''Magna Charta of Mexican Labor.''

Francisco Villa is held up as a Mexican ideal, a prototype of that sense of separate nationality that serves as a spur to unity, social cohesiveness, and the peaceful harmonization of opposing interests. All Mexicans join Villistas in taking umbrage at foreign vilification of their hero. H. H. Dunn, who traveled in Mexico during the Revolution yet wrote his description from Hollywood, California, in 1932, described Villa as a ''negroid bandit'' who, ''with the distorted mind of a sadistic child,'' was ''the closest approach to the long-sought ape-man the New World has seen.''[34] Mexicans, however, remember him as the heroic figure who escaped Pershing after the ''daring'' raid on Columbus. Midway in the account of Pershing's expedition, Miguel Alessio Robles, in his popular *Historia política de la Revolución,* chronicles all of Villa's past

33. Palacios, *Emiliano Zapata,* p. 246.
34. H. H. Dunn, *The Crimson Jester: Zapata of Mexico* (New York: National Travel Club, 1934), p. 166.

victories, going on to sympathetically describe Villa's pursued troop as being "in rags, wounded, without food, dead with thirst, frozen with cold, pursued everywhere, . . . now trampled upon by the cursed foot of the invading soldier."[35] Mexicans of stature like Andrés Molina Enríquez praise Villa as "the greatest man of the Revolution," as "a beautiful model of the composition and potentiality of the men who are forming the Mexican nationality."[36]

The revolutionary heroes have significantly influenced political participation and concern for national progress. Individual participation in the political process through voting and party allegiance, the articulation of individual and group interests through representation within the now dominant Partido Revolucionario Institucional, and increasing personal concern for the national problems of poverty and educational deficiencies are crucial determinants in the advancement of nationalism as a social value. By stimulating articulation in others through military and political action, each revolutionary leader affected these determinants even before his image was invoked as a national hero.

MIGRATION

Social change results from numerous alterations in the economic, demographic, and cultural environment as well as from the social values that national heroes instill or are later said to have instilled. In the area of demographic change, population growth leveled off in Mexico from 1910 to 1917; a major influenza epidemic, military and civilian deaths in battle and reprisals, and severe food shortages sharply increased the death rate. As the Revolution impeded population growth, it slowed down the component of na-

35. Miguel Alessio Robles, *Historia política de la Revolución* (3d ed.; México: Ediciones Botas, 1946), pp. 210-11.

36. Andrés Molina Enríquez, *La revolución agraria de México* (5 vols.; México: Talleres Gráficos del Museo Nacional de Arqueología, Historia y Etnografía, 1933-37), Vol. 5, p. 145.

tional consciousness that arises from the increased pressure of population. The Revolution also advanced the rise of nationalism, however, by occasioning a substantial increase in migration. Extensive travel between regions in Mexico, temporary urbanization, and travel by Mexican citizens to the United States contributed to the stimulation of nationalism. The 1910 Revolution lessened regional loyalties by forcing Mexicans to fight, travel, and work outside their *patrias chicas*. In the analogy of Samuel Ramos, who goes so far as to claim that regional loyalties no longer affect Mexican national unity, the Mexico of 1910 to 1917 resembled a cocktail shaker in which men of all regions were blended into a new national mixture.[37]

The enforced travel of government troops and revolutionary armies during the decade of violence after 1910 took men outside their village environments, giving them a wider view of the various regions and peoples encompassed in the Mexican nation. Although revolutionary bands fought primarily in their home regions and traveled to other areas only in major campaigns such as the convergence of Constitutionalist armies on Mexico City for the ousting of Huerta, the over-all effect of revolutionary troop movements was to increase travel and internal migration, in terms of both the number of Mexican migrants and the diversity of regions visited.

The extensive new railroad system established under the Díaz regime received expanded use, as peasants previously unable to afford travel were shuttled in revolutionary armies around the republic. Military leaders commandeered passenger trains and sent their men in boxcars when coaches were unavailable. The revolutionary troop trains provided a unique experience for their riders which is now memorialized in stories, pictures, and *corridos,* as the trains carried not only soldiers but their horses, live-

37. Samuel Ramos, ''En torno a las ideas sobre el mexicano,'' *Cuadernos Americanos,* Año 10, Vol. 57, Núm. 3 (mayo-junio, 1951), 105-6.

stock, and the women who served as their companions and commissariats.

Conscription of federal troops under Victoriano Huerta forcibly pulled men out of their local environments to serve in other parts of the country. Since Huerta's strategy was to hold key fortified cities on the railroad lines from the American border to Mexico City, the Constitutionalist strategy came to be one of capturing city after city along the lines. The gradual approach to the national capital in 1913 and 1914 led Constitutionalist forces and the retreating federal troops to travel and live in a large portion of the national territory. Here, as in the later captures of the capital by Villa, Zapata, and Obregón, men from the hinterland came to Mexico City to fight, while men from the core area of the capital dispersed under orders to outlying districts. Migration increased when federal troops were assigned to posts throughout Mexico, when northerners and southerners followed Madero and Zapata to the capital, when the adherents of Obregón and Villa fought pitched battles from Veracruz up into Chihuahua, and when roving bands traveled in regional campaigns such as that for Yucatán. Mexicans also derived new appreciation of the dimensions of their national territory by sailing around it in the transports that carried soldiers and female commissariats from port to port as military exigencies demanded.[38]

This travel in revolutionary armies was particularly important in giving Mexicans a wider conception of their Motherland, because even after the Revolution permanent migration in Mexico remained sharply limited. Indicating a low rate of internal migration for permanent residence, Nathan Whetten, on the basis of 1940 statistics, notes that in twelve states primarily in southern Mexico 95 per cent or more of the total state population was born in their state

38. See William W. Canada to William Jennings Bryan, December 2, 1913, /10015; William E. Alger to Bryan, December 9, 1913, /10114; and Alphonse J. Lespinasse to Bryan, December 10, 1913, /10329.

of residence. Furthermore, with the four exceptions of the Federal District, Tamaulipas, Baja California Norte, and the territory of Quintana Roo, over 75 per cent of the inhabitants resided in 1940 in the state in which they were born.[39] Since the revolutionary period, Mexicans have recognized that internal migration fosters nationalism and have voiced interest in promoting it. Stating directly that internal migration or "national tourism" is "one of the primary means of attaining another basic principle of the Revolution: national unification, which is the strengthening of our Mexicanness and the securing of our sovereignty,"[40] Alfonso García González promoted this means of strengthening Mexican nationalism while serving as chief of the Department of Tourism under President Adolfo López Mateos.

Government migration programs during the Revolution took the form of enforced colonization in the remote and unhealthy territory of Quintana Roo at the end of the Yucatán peninsula. In July, 1913, alone over 800 prisoners from the interior of Mexico were sent to Quintana Roo,[41] where Díaz also had kept a prison colony. In January, 1914, John Lind reported that consignments of women, young girls, and men passed daily through Veracruz for Quintana Roo and the plantations of Campeche, where they were sold into peonage or prostitution.[42] The prisoners sent into Yucatán, many of whom soon died in the deadly Quintana Roo territory or remained on the henequin plantations, usually resented their enforced migration. After some 280 prisoners brought from northern Mexico to Progreso, Yucatán, were given arms and incorporated into the sixteenth federal battalion on August 18, 1913, they demon-

39. Nathan L. Whetten, *Rural Mexico* (Chicago: University of Chicago Press, 1948), p. 58.
40. Alfonso García González, ''La Revolución Mexicana y el turismo,'' in Norman Thomas and others, *Homenaje a la Revolución Mexicana, Combate,* edición especial, Vol. 2, Núm. 13 (noviembre, 1960), 97-98.
41. Canada to Bryan, July 20, 1913, /8094.
42. John Lind to Bryan, January 17, 1914, /10773.

strated their lack of loyalty by rioting, trying to escape, and attacking their barracks guard.[43] Although this mutiny against Huertista officials proved unsuccessful, it demonstrated a remaining spirit of resistance in the Constitutionalist deportees. In this resistance, as in the later reforms under General Salvador Alvarado and the powerful Socialist Party of the Southeast, the migrants came to work for the social and economic progress of Yucatán within the Mexican union and so counteracted the old force of Yucatecan separatism.

The process of temporary urbanization encouraged nationalism in many parts of the republic, as the uncertainties and atrocities of the long years of revolutionary violence impelled refugees to migrate for varying periods of time from villages to cities and towns. Thousands of Mexican families, especially those threatened by factional recriminations and those having young daughters, poured into Mexico City, where the population allegedly swelled to 750,000.[44] In each area where fighting occurred and the breakdown of authority produced extensive bandit activity, this pattern of temporary urbanization recurred. Many of the temporary urban residents returned to their homes after immediate threats had passed, but their experience of traveling even temporarily into a more urbanized setting broke into the isolation of their village routine. Through contact with the larger urban congregations and the men of varied regional and ethnic backgrounds who passed through in federal and revolutionary armies, Mexicans developed a broader conception of the actual bases of their national community.

Mass migrations to the United States for sojourns of varying length provided an intermittent stream of Mexican refugees who, through the contrast of living in the United States, gained perspective on their national distinctiveness.

43. John W. Germon to Bryan, August 20, 1913, /8511; and Germon to Bryan, August 20, 1913, /8757.
44. Dunn, *The Crimson Jester*, p. 159.

Mexicans crossed the border to escape violence, to seek work and a livelihood, to serve out exile after defeat, and as combatants to be interned by American authorities. Several large-scale migrations occurred. In June, 1913, between 5,000 and 7,000 Mexicans crossed over from the state of Tamaulipas, and remained in Texas through the summer and fall, often living in tents and rude huts on the banks of the Rio Grande.[45] From Coahuila, 8,000 Mexican refugees passed over the international bridge between Piedras Negras and Eagle Pass in a single day when Huertista federals took Piedras Negras in October, 1913.[46] Migration became so extensive that in November and December, 1913, the Huertista press along the Texas border tried to prevent emigration with allegations of a Negro revolution in the United States, involving eleven North American states and considerable destruction.[47] *El Heraldo Nacional* even claimed that two battalions of Negroes rose in Denver, Colorado, to cry out for President Wilson's death, sack banks, and set fire to private homes in an attempt to win the Negroes' long denied "claims for citizenship" in the North American nation.[48]

Many Mexicans from the interior as well as the border regions crossed over into the United States to find employment, as revolutionary activity severely curtailed job opportunities in their districts of Mexico.[49] The large irrigation projects and agricultural interests in southern Texas provided work for many refugees, and some repudiated their Mexican nationality by choosing to stay in the United States. Other Mexicans who traveled to the United States

45. George J. Head to A. Caminetti, October 28, 1913, /9482.
46. F. W. Berkshire to Caminetti, October 21, 1913, /9482.
47. *El Correo de Saltillo*, November 29, 1913, p. 1. See also John R. Silliman to Bryan, December 1, 1913, /10001.
48. *The Mexican Herald*, December 5, 1913, clipping enclosed in Canada to Bryan, December 6, 1913, /10271.
49. U.S., Congress, Senate, Committee on Foreign Relations, *Investigation of Mexican Affairs*, 66th Cong., 2d sess., Sen. Doc. 285 (2 vols.; Washington, 1920), Vol. 2, pp. 2145-48.

lived leisurely at the expense of their relatives and spent their time in billiard parlors, "moving picture" houses, cantinas, or in the street. These indigent individuals became antagonistic to Americans and American authorities when the thefts to which they resorted[50] resulted in their punishment and imprisonment. The frequent failure of Mexican immigrants in the United States to receive full justice in American courts, equal schooling for their children, and general acceptance on a basis of social equality created antipathy and a sense of separateness.[51] As reports of the Mexicans' ill-treatment in the United States filtered back to the immigrants' families, friends, and compatriots, the reports similarly increased a sense of national distinctiveness among the Mexicans who had stayed behind.

Despite some friction and griping, the Mexican soldiers interned in the United States generally enjoyed more favored treatment. Some of the internees traveled in the United States after their confinement, as was the case with 230 Mexican federal prisoners held at Fort Bliss, Texas, who were sent in August, 1913, to Fort Rosencrans at San Diego, California, before attorneys could obtain writs of *habeas corpus* for them.[52] A telegram from Major Adolfo Duhagon of the Mexican Army to President Woodrow Wilson dated October 29, 1913, complained of bad treatment given Mexicans at Fort Rosencrans, protesting that prices were very high at the camp store and that Mexicans refusing to work were put in the guardhouse on bread and water.[53] It has been established that the Mexican internees at Fort Rosencrans ate the same food as the American troops, although several Mexicans were confined for brief

50. "Condición económica de la colonia mexicana en los E. U. de América," *El Cosmopolita*, Kansas City, Mo., October 22, 1914, p. 2:2-4.

51. Samuel Guy Inman, *Intervention in Mexico* (New York: George H. Doran Company, 1919), p. 140.

52. *El Paso Herald*, August 5, 1913, clipping enclosed in W. R. Smith to Bryan, August 9, 1913, /8295.

53. Adolfo Duhagon to Woodrow Wilson, October 29, 1913, /9479.

periods on a bread and water diet for refusing to work and for fighting among themselves. Mexicans were allowed passes to leave Fort Rosencrans when authorized by Colonel Kosterlitzky, the ranking Mexican officer at the fort. In an investigation of Major Duhagon's charges, most Mexican internees reported that they were entirely satisfied with their treatment.[54] Like civilian refugees, the soldiers gratefully accepted what courtesy and assistance were given them by American Army representatives and private citizens.[55]

Migration to the United States variously affected the nationalist attitudes of the migrants. Some actively rejected their Mexican nationality in favor of loyalty to the United States, as had the Mexicans of Spanish descent who considered themselves "Texans" and fought for Texas independence in 1835. On the night of April 22, 1914, during the American occupation of Veracruz, about 600 Mexicans who had become citizens of the United States demonstrated just such loyalty when they met at the courthouse in El Paso, Texas, and adopted resolutions tendering their services to the United States government "to do anything whatsoever we may be called upon to do to preserve [the] peace and dignity of the city and country and to serve the United States in whatever capacity."[56] Many Mexicans remained in the United States until the 1920's and 1930's. A large body of Mexican nationals returned to Mexico between 1929 and 1932 when economic depression made jobs scarce in the United States. Between 1927 and 1944 a total of 646,460 Mexican nationals returned to Mexico.[57] The retention of national loyalty and pride in cultural heroes by the Mexican residents of the southwestern United States still reflects in names like Hidalgo and Zapata given to counties in southern Texas where a large

54. Report of Major William C. Davis, November 17, 1913, /9984.
55. Philip C. Hanna to Bryan, January 17, 1914, /10578.
56. *The Christian Science Monitor*, April 23, 1914, p. 4:2.
57. Whetten, *Rural Mexico*, p. 62.

segment of the population is American by birth but Mexican by race and tradition. During the Revolution, some of these Mexican expatriates in the United States evidenced a strong sense of loyalty to Mexico. When North American filibusters were invading Baja California in February, 1911, approximately 140 Mexicans residing in San Diego and other parts of American California offered to return to Mexico in order to enlist in the army and to fight the Yankees.[58]

Although the "alienness" of the North American environment that these migrants entered should not be overemphasized, it was sufficiently foreign to help them define their own Mexican nationality. The refugees who moved back into Mexico after short stays usually lived and associated with other refugees while in the United States, as did to a lesser extent the military internees and Mexicans who stayed for a period of years to work north of the border. American border cities and Mexican colonies in the cities in the Southwest present less "cultural shock" than do other North American regions. Spanish is widely spoken; Yankee values such as punctuality are not so rigorously enforced; and much of the surrounding populace is racially Mexican. But like the large groups of *braceros* who came to harvest North American crops from World War II to 1964, the earlier migrants of the Revolution found a degree of "alienness" in the United States. Even when North American associates proved kind and courteous, they overtly differed in speech, appearance, and attitude. The Mexicans who crossed the American border received a prolonged although seldom comprehensive view of another country, and from their view of racial, linguistic, and cultural differences in their temporary North American surroundings, the returning migrants gained a heightened sense of their own Mexican nationality.

58. R. Velasco Ceballos, *¿Se apoderará Estados Unidos de América de Baja California? (La invasión filibustera de 1911)* (México: Imprenta Nacional, S.A., 1920), pp. 60-61.

STATUS, CLASS STRUCTURE, AND FAMILY SOLIDARITY

The revolutionary upheaval between 1910 and 1917 shifted the immediate determinants of individual status from ascription to achievement, making an individual's influence and power in the revolutionary context depend not so much on his inherited position as on his own ability and initiative. Untutored men without wealth, education, or family standing such as Villa, Zapata, and thousands of subordinates rose from social obscurity to temporary positions of tremendous influence over the lives and fortunes of their fellow citizens. Mass revolutions through the years have proved to be great social levelers. Men of previously acquired status may stand out because of prior training or the devotion of financial resources to the revolution. Financial subsidization by Francisco Madero's family allowed his revolution to continue; Obregón's education added to his articulateness and circumspection; and Carranza's position as a senator under Díaz gave significance to his support of Madero. In such a revolution, however, men with leadership ability soon achieve advantages initially held by the previously advantaged, as talent in taking command gives them influence over followers, the ability to win battles, and the opportunity to appropriate the spoils.

No revolutionary situation is permanent, and with the gradual decline of violence in Mexican politics after 1917, the inheritance of wealth, family connections, and a consequently increased opportunity for education took on renewed importance in determining the status that individual Mexican citizens could acquire. Through effort, luck, and talent, "self-made" men could rise after the Revolution as Juárez and Altamirano had risen before it. But the chances that military victory might catapult a man into wealth and prominence gradually gave way to the pre-revolutionary criteria of political manipulation, economic entrepreneurship, and inherited position. Besides creating an influx of revolutionaries into the higher echelons of prestige and influence, however, the period of revolutionary violence set important precedents for the future acquisition of status.

Revolutionary pronouncements in favor of increased social and economic mobility abounded. After the Maderista victory over Díaz, Governor Abraham González of Chihuahua demonstrated the Maderista orientation of achievement rather than ascription in naming a shoemaker to the powerful office of *jefe político* in Chihuahua City. He optimistically declared that the aristocracy of northern Mexico would no longer be recognized and that government officials would henceforth be selected on the basis of their "ability and moral standing."[59] Repulsion of the symbols of ascriptive status reflects in Carranza's making a military hospital out of the old and prestigious Jockey Club,[60] an institution that still symbolizes wealth in Mexico and from which a new club has now been formed. Drawing upon the multiple plans and pronouncements of revolutionary leaders which promised greater equality of opportunity, contemporary commentators found that Mexicans were developing a new dedication to equality of rights and opportunity among themselves. In 1916 Professor C. Trejo Lerdo de Tejada wrote that the Revolution had "transformed the national conscience" and created "a demand, a reality, a new and indisputable tendency of justice and equality" for Mexico's serfs, proletariat, and "subjugated majority."[61]

Revolutionaries combined praise of social mobility with constitutional provisions to implement mobility. Some Mexican democrats linked the idea of political democracy with that of a greater degree of social equality. *El Sufragio Libre* proclaimed before the electoral contest between Díaz and Madero that democracy in Mexico had not existed, did

59. As quoted in *The New York Times*, June 15, 1911, p. 2:5.
60. *El Pueblo*, October 8, 1914, p. 8:4; and *El Pueblo*, October 15, 1914, p. 1:3-5.
61. C. Trejo Lerdo de Tejada, *La Revolución y el nacionalismo: Todo para todos* (Habana: Maza y Ca., 1916), p. 214.

not exist, and would not exist "short of the condition of social equality between all the individuals of the populace."[62] Provisions of the 1917 Constitution incorporated revolutionary promises to facilitate upward mobility through educational opportunities, agrarian reform, legal rights for women and illegitimate children, work rules, and legalized trade unionism. The ideal of increased social and economic mobility set forth in the 1917 Constitution and its partial realization in Mexico have themselves generated national loyalty among the upwardly mobile individuals, as was the case in Russia after the Bolshevik Revolution.[63]

Although the 1910 Revolution introduced greater fluidity into the structure of Mexican social classes, that structure remained the antithesis of increased Mexican nationalism. Class loyalty opposed the wider Mexican national loyalty that would include members of all classes. As Consul Wilbert L. Bonney at San Luis Potosí reported to Secretary of State Knox in April, 1912, "The class feeling is so much stronger than national feeling that no system will be successful which does not recognize their social differences."[64] The Revolution did not completely destroy the Mexican upper class of the *porfiriato*. Many of them took refuge in Europe or the United States, retained a large part of their capital, and later frequently mixed in a new upper class with members of the old middle class to whom the Revolution gave new social mobility.[65] A nucleus of the old aristocracy remains intact today, and a sense of social distinction still exists between the descendants of the pre-1910 aristocracy and the families that have risen to prominence since the Revolution.[66]

62. *El Sufragio Libre*, March 10, 1909, p. 2:1.
63. Frederick C. Barghoorn, *Soviet Russian Nationalism* (New York: Oxford University Press, 1956), p. 180.
64. Wilbert L. Bonney to Knox, April 30, 1912, /3814.
65. Lucio Mendieta y Núñez, "La clase media en México," *Revista Mexicana de Sociología*, Año 17, Vol. 17, Núms. 2, 3 (mayo-diciembre, 1955), 525.
66. This view is based upon interviews with a number of Mexicans and on an extended discussion with Frances Ann Ursúa de Chávez in Pachuca, Hgo. on October 25, 1964.

Changes in the determinants of class structure accompanying the Revolution clearly facilitated the spread of nationalism. In the Mexican case, as in periods of mass revolution in other countries, both the generality and the velocity of "circulation" among social groups increased.[67] The heightened prominence and influence that the Revolution gave to the intellectual spokesmen of the Mexican middle class, both during and after the violence, proved important, because the middle class even then was intensely nationalistic. Members of the middle class—schoolteachers and notaries—were the strongest backers of the idea of ousting foreign workers and winning "Mexico for the Mexicans" from the early days of the Madero revolt.[68]

Although limitations of land and capital have prevented radical shifts in the proportions of Mexican social classes, Mexico has achieved a more open class structure. Agrarian reform, an enlarged governmental bureaucracy, social legislation, labor union organization, minimum wage scales, expanded educational facilities, and growth in transportation systems have worked to open paths of social mobility. Besides creating increased opportunity to rise in the social scale, they have quickened the hope of workers and peasants to achieve middle-class status.[69] As Andrew Whiteford's extended studies of class structure in the city of Querétaro have shown, despite the survival of a vestige of the earlier aristocracy, the actual locus of power shifted first to the generals and politicians of the Revolution and then to the economic entrepreneurs of the mid-twentieth century.[70] This shift in power simultaneously bears out revolutionary promises of greater social mobility and invites a more inte-

67. Sorokin, *The Sociology of Revolution*, p. 236.
68. Senate, *Investigation of Mexican Affairs*, Vol. 1, p. 1431.
69. Nathan L. Whetten, ''El surgimiento de una clase media en México,'' in Miguel Othón de Mendizábal and others, *Las clases sociales en México* (México: Colección Tlapali, Sociedad Mexicana de Difusión Cultural, n.d.), pp. 54-61.
70. Andrew H. Whiteford, *Two Cities of Latin America: A Comparative Description of Social Classes* (Garden City, N.Y.: Doubleday & Company, Inc., 1964), p. 248.

grated national community, because by participation in nationally beneficial economic development, members achieve status in a more fluid if still self-conscious class structure.

Although family solidarity in Mexico is by no means as strong as the social value that Mexicans attach to it, the disruptions of the Revolution further broke down ties among family members and so prompted national loyalty to compare favorably with competing family loyalties. Mexicans revere the idea of family solidarity. The church holds up the ideal of large and cohesive families, forbidding divorce and remarriage. Cohesive families aid their members in both emotional and economic terms, as they provide an added sense of security through nepotism and the degree of care extended to family members.

Family solidarity is, however, as Oscar Lewis points out, an ideal that is only rarely achieved among a large part of Mexico's urban poor.[71] Paternal desertion, sexual promiscuity, and the masculine practice of keeping more than one household and family have prevailed in the urban proletariat. Family structures differ substantially in size, organization, and patterns of authority and solidarity among the remaining indigenous groups of Mexican Indians, but many Indian groups accept divorce.[72] Where extra-marital liaisons occur in the Mexican middle and upper classes, they seldom cause the divorce and public conflict that make marital tensions more apparent in the United States. Despite the sincere devotion of many fathers to the idea of family unity, the attitude of sexual license long condoned by Mexican males still works to undermine the

71. Oscar Lewis, *The Children of Sánchez* (London: Penguin Books, 1964), p. xxvii. The data gathered through Lewis' extensive system of interviews in Mexico repeatedly bear out his observation.

72. Roberto Mac-Lean y Estenós, *Status socio cultural de los indios de México* (México: Instituto de Investigaciones Sociales, Universidad Nacional Autónoma de México, 1960), p. 97. For comparisons of the family structures of the Indian groups, see pp. 95-125 of the Mac-Lean y Estenós study and *Etnografía de México: Síntesis monográficas* (México: Instituto de Investigaciones Sociales, Universidad Nacional Autónoma de México, 1957).

relationships of trust upon which lasting familial unity is built.

The 1910 Revolution made some family members more interdependent. Family loyalties increased in cases of families joining together to oppose violations of their rights and possessions. A sense of common family partisanship, which developed when family members fought for the same faction, has ultimately coincided with nationalistic pride in common revolutionary participation. When family members who fought on the same side now look back on being Villistas or Zapatistas, an element of family solidarity and pride in common revolutionary participation joins with their feelings of national pride, a pride now aroused and manipulated by the official inclusion of all factions in the revolutionary hagiology.

Supplementing the basic defects in the Mexican ideal of family unity, the revolutionary situation repeatedly disrupted family loyalties and made individuals dependent on the wider community. The rate of paternal desertion increased, as peon fathers left to join revolutionary armies or were conscripted by federal press gangs. Even though many wives, sweethearts, and babies went along on the treks, many also remained behind. As Consul Wilbur T. Gracey reported on Huerta's conscriptions in Yucatán, "the fact that married men are being taken, leaving their families without support, is arousing scenes of great sorrow, and the trains of men coming into Progreso under military guard, followed by their weeping women and children, is heartbreaking to witness."[73] Mrs. Nelson O'Shaughnessy, wife of the American *chargé d'affaires* who remained in Mexico after Ambassador Wilson left, repeatedly recounts similar actions of federal press gangs in the letters she wrote to her mother. Describing a situation that she found to typify "thousands of cases," Mrs. O'Shaughnessy tells of a pregnant mother and her four children under seven years of age whom she found sitting

73. Wilbur T. Gracey to Bryan, November 22, 1913, /10019.

homeless on the curb after a press gang had conscripted the father.[74]

Other family disruptions were inherent in the revolutionary situation. Besides the separations occasioned when a father was removed by enlistment, conscription, or death, families were split when the mother was forced to take separate employment or when children from necessity found second homes or roamed the streets and countryside looking for work or food. In increasing internal migration and breaking down established means of law enforcement, the violence and peregrinations of revolutionary armies increased miscegenation and illegitimate births. In contrast to the situation in which family members fought for the same faction, when the civil war placed members of the same extended family on opposing sides, it cut the ties of family altruism. Higher rates of separation, new sexual liaisons, and feuds among members of the same family aligned with different revolutionary factions created tension and discord within families. The individuals thus displaced gained a more personal appreciation of the national community when, temporarily uprooted from family dependencies, they sought and gained sustenance from other members of the national community. With this basis of familial disruption in the Revolution, the lack of family solidarity has been continued in twentieth-century Mexico by increasing urbanization, the exigencies of poverty combined with greater geographical mobility, feminine emancipation, and the ineffectiveness of religious prescriptions in some areas.[75] The dilution of familial loyalties in the cases of revolutionary family disruption permitted increasing national loyalty, as men, women and children who ordinarily would have derived their paramount sense of "belonging" from family relationships now derived a heightened sense

74. Edith O'Shaughnessy, *A Diplomat's Wife in Mexico* (New York: Harper & Brothers, 1916), pp. 54, 84, 89.

75. José E. Iturriaga, *La estructura social y cultural de México* (México: Fondo de Cultura Económica, 1951), pp. 13-17.

of belonging from their participation in revolutionary enterprises.

CLERICAL ASPIRATIONS

In the area of church-state relations, the 1910 Revolution reversed the trend toward political power and secular ambitions within the Mexican church, encouraged the church to express its goals in terms compatible with the goals of the national community, and so ultimately helped to make religious loyalty and national loyalty in Mexico more compatible and mutually reinforcing. By 1910 the limitations of the nineteenth-century reform movement on clerical prerogatives outside the religious sphere were only partially realized. During the *porfiriato,* many Mexican Catholics had learned to live with the secularization of laws which the 1857 Constitution and the Liberal victory under Juárez had imposed. Catholics acquiesced in matters of religious toleration and bans against church ownership of property, while the Catholic position on the oath to the constitution typically changed from complete condemnation to unreserved permission. The church hierarchy revoked early prohibitions against sending children to non-Catholic public schools, and it came to tolerate performance of the civil marriage after the religious ceremony.[76]

Under the regime of Porfirio Díaz, the church in Mexico also regained considerable prestige and increasing political influence, although it won back comparatively little economic power.[77] Confiscation of church property ended by the mid-1880's, and clerical garb and bell-ringing processions reappeared in the countryside. Díaz, partially under the influence of his devoutly Catholic wife and the preeminent social position that he had acquired since his days

76. Karl M. Schmitt, ''Catholic Adjustment to the Secular State: The Case of Mexico, 1867-1911,'' *The Catholic Historical Review,* Vol. 48, No. 2 (July, 1962), 203-4.

77. Karl M. Schmitt, ''The Díaz Conciliation Policy on State and Local Levels, 1876-1911,'' *Hispanic American Historical Review,* Vol. 40, No. 4 (November, 1960), 532.

as a fighter against the French, winked at nonenforcement
of anticlerical statutes. Observers in 1910 found that,
whereas Mexican men were often freethinkers or agnostics
who would nevertheless defend the church when it was
impugned or attacked, Mexican women were almost all
attached to their church "to the point of fanaticism."[78]
With this basis of support, the church seemed likely to
win a dangerous degree of political influence when a Catholic political party largely run by laymen reappeared at the
end of the *porfiriato*. After Madero's victory and the
signing of an armistice with federal forces, the Catholic
party under Gabriel Somellera, prelates, and landed aristocrats increased its organizational activity throughout Mexico.[79] The support of clerical elements for the reactionary
regime of Victoriano Huerta brought against them the
decisive opposition of the victorious Constitutionalists.

Constitutionalists loudly denounced clerical intromis-
sion in secular affairs. Dr. Atl claimed that the Roman
Catholic church opposed the Mexican Revolution because,
since "our revolution is a great force for the realization of
high and ineluctable human aspirations," it enjoyed world-
wide appeal and had become a danger to "bourgeois civilization."[80] General Alvarado in Yucatán frankly denounced
the church as an exploiter of human sentimentality, particularly the sentimentality of women. To Alvarado the
church was an enemy terrible to combat, an enemy who
must be deprived of the secular power it should not have, a
subtle enemy who surrounds the people with enchanting
music, penetrates them with incense, and impresses them
with the ornate scenery of cathedrals which simultaneously
"charms and oppresses."[81] In such attacks, Constitutional-

78. *The New York Times*, November 27, 1910, Part 5, p. 4:3.

79. *Ibid.*, May 23, 1911, p. 1:7.

80. Dr. Atl [Gerardo Murillo], *Palabras de un hombre al pueblo americano*
(Orizaba, Ver.: n.p., 1915), pp. 43-44.

81. Reprint entitled *Speech of General Alvarado, Governor of the State
of Yucatán, At the Closing Session of the Second Pedagogic Congress, Held
at Mérida* (n.p.: n.p., 1916), p. 13.

ists protested that they were not persecuting the Catholic religion but only trying to reduce church influence and involvement in politics. These protestations were supported by the fact that the Constitutionalists did not disturb Protestant clergymen and much of the lower Roman Catholic clergy who continued to minister and attend to spiritual duties without mixing in political questions.[82]

In addition to pronouncements, the Constitutionalists took active measures to reduce clerical influence. When the forces of Álvaro Obregón gathered at Tepic on May 19, 1914, they sentenced Bishop Andrés Segura to eight years in prison and expelled other Huertista churchmen for attacks made on them by clerics and the clerical periodicals, *El Hogar Católico* and *El Obrero de Tepic*.[83] While in control of Mexico City during February, 1915, Obregón demanded that the church pay 500,000 pesos to relieve the suffering of the poor. He deported foreign clerics and imprisoned archdiocesan Vicar-general Antonio de Jesús Paredes, and 167 other priests. Obregón declared in an interview with a correspondent of *The Mexican Herald* that no good could come from the "accursed" clerical organization that had been in league with Porfirio Díaz and Huerta and that had defiled Hidalgo, Morelos, and Juárez.[84]

The 1917 Constitution sharply delimited the bases of church political power. Article 3 reiterated freedom of belief and proscribed clerical intervention in primary and secondary education; Article 27 made the property of all religious associations legally the property of the nation; Article 130 prohibited Congress from passing laws that established or prohibited any religion. It also made marriage a civil contract, required ministers practicing within the national territory to be Mexicans by birth, and allowed

82. A. Paganel [Carlo de Fornaro], *What the Catholic Church Has Done to Mexico* (New York: Latin-American News Association, 1916), p. 5.
83. Álvaro Obregón, *Ocho mil kilómetros en campaña* (Vol. 5, "Fuentes para la Historia de la Revolución Mexicana," Manuel González Ramírez, ed.; México: Fondo de Cultura Económica, 1959), p. 123.
84. Quirk, *The Mexican Revolution, 1914-1915*, pp. 188, 191.

state legislatures to establish a maximum number of such
ministers within their jurisdictions. It directly prohibited
clerics from political participation and criticism of government laws and authorities, forbade clerical periodicals to
comment on political matters, and denied clerics the right
to pass on property by inheritance.

Subsequent conflict upheld the proscriptions on clerical
prerogatives which had been proclaimed during the violent
stage of the Revolution and incorporated in the Querétaro
Constitution. For eight years the anticlerical provisions
were not rigorously enforced, although some zealous state
governments did begin to exercise their delegated power
by restricting the number of priests in their jurisdictions.
Then in 1926 the strong regime of Plutarco Elías Calles
began stricter enforcement by actually prohibiting alien
priests, closing religious schools, and ordering priests to
register with civil authorities so that their political activities could be checked. In retaliation, priests went on a
three-year strike and refused to perform Catholic ceremonies of baptism, marriage, and burial. Lay Cristeros
resorted to armed rebellion against the government, and
they burned government schools, stoned teachers, and blew
up trains. The conflict after 1926 became a basic confrontation, a showdown between church and state. Its cause was
not that the church wanted to mix in the formalities of
Mexican politics but that both church and state wanted exclusive control of the Mexican people.[85] Although the clerics
took up the ministry again in 1929, hostilities flared in the
early 1930's, and accord between the church and state was
not established until the presidency of Lázaro Cárdenas
in the last half of the decade.

In restricting church power, the opposition of Mexican
revolutionaries to the continuance of secular influence and
aspirations of the church worked ultimately to harmonize

85. Robert E. Quirk, ''The Mexican Revolution and the Catholic Church,
1910-1929: An Ideological Study'' (unpublished Ph.D. dissertation, Harvard
University, 1950), p. 250.

the religious and national loyalties of Mexican citizens. In 1935, Earle K. James predicted that "if the government, as it professes, is not motivated by a desire to extirpate the Church, and the Church, as it argues, is not seeking return of the exclusive privileges it enjoyed under the old order, it would seem reasonable to suppose that many of the restrictions which at present incapacitate the Church in the exercise of its religious duties could be modified or alleviated."[86] The passage of time has upheld James's prediction and made plausible the hypothesis of mutual sincerity on which it was based. The increasing mutual toleration of church and state since 1936 does not represent a covert sellout to church interests by Mexican politicians or a mere swinging of the pendulum away from anticlericalism. Rather it indicates the evolution of church utterances into a position of compatibility with Mexican nationalism.

Religious and national loyalties could not be compatible while members of the church hierarchy within Mexico actively sought secular influence. Revolutionary curtailment of this search for influence had been realized by 1935, when Archbishop Pascual Díaz emphatically declared to a non-Catholic North American interviewer that the church in Mexico claimed no temporal power at all and asked only "the right to perform her spiritual mission of teaching and to exercise her charitable and welfare activities."[87] It was believed that church participation in education could supplement and complement governmental educational programs as long as what the clerics taught was strongly nationalistic and did not attempt to establish secular prerogatives for the church. One of the most significant results of the Revolution has been increasing acceptance by younger Mexican clerics of the absolute separation of church and state and a consequent emphasis on ministering to the

86. Earle K. James, "Church and State in Mexico," *Foreign Policy Reports*, Vol. 11, No. 9 (July 3, 1935), 116.

87. Charles S. MacFarland, *Chaos in Mexico: The Conflict of Church and State* (New York: Harper & Brothers, 1935), p. 162.

spiritual needs of the Mexican people. With the acceptance of essentially separate spheres of influence, competition for influence between clerical and national officials is reduced.

A continuing rapprochement of church and state reflects in the present leniency in clerical dress and the operation of church schools. Although Mexican law still forbids the wearing of clerical garb in public, the wearing of such apparel has now spread beyond the rural, isolated areas to which it was confined twenty-five years ago. Now nuns and priests may be seen wearing special attire and even formal habits in the streets and on the buses of Mexico City, and nuns seek charity from table to table in the downtown restaurants of the capital. Religious schools today significantly supplement public schools in the major population centers, and recently federal aid has gone to privately supported teacher-training schools in which the church plays a major role.

A Mexican can win acceptance as a full member of the national community—from the other members of that community, the majority of whom profess Catholic beliefs—whether or not he shares this religious faith. Catholicism may open some doors to him in the social, intellectual, or business communities just as Masonic affiliation aids a man in political circles, but religious association is significantly not the prime criterion for acceptance within the national community. With the smoothing over of church-state friction, religious affiliation has become an important additional bond. Catholics can generally feel the unifying xenophobic antagonism toward the United States which is traditionally fostered by conservatives on the proclaimed grounds of religious difference. The different shadings of Catholic belief in Mexico do not greatly reduce the effect of apparent religious homogeneity in furthering national allegiance. The intellectually devout, the patrons of Catholic bookstores, and the paganish Indians who worship Christian forms join solidly together in their reverence for the Virgin of Guadalupe.

With time, the Virgin of Guadalupe has gained effectiveness as a symbol of both Mexican religion and nationalism. Since her apparition in 1531, she has always appealed strongly to the Indian population, in part because of the darkness of her skin and also because she appeared to an Indian, Juan Diego. Although in colonial times the creole population often preferred to revere the light-skinned Virgen de los Remedios, the Virgin of Guadalupe has gained prominence as miscegenation turned Mexico into a mestizo nation. Hidalgo made her the symbol of his revolt in 1810,[88] and in the Revolution of 1910, Maderista and Zapatista troops carried her picture into battle on banners and on medallions attached to their hats. Now, with the new compatibility between church and state which has gradually emerged from the Revolution, deep devotion to the Virgin of Guadalupe throughout Mexico evidences the conjunction of loyalties.

Common professions of a single religious faith thus serve as a cohesive force within the nationalist framework. President Álvaro Obregón hinted that this might be the outcome when he wrote that, with the Catholic desire to "guide the souls of believers" and the necessity for post-revolutionary Mexican governments to materially and nationalistically "nourish the stomach, the brain and the soul of each and every Mexican," in these complementary programs "there is not only nothing mutually exclusive, but there should be on the contrary indisputable harmony."[89] Church leaders came increasingly to back the

88. On the political significance of the Virgin of Guadalupe, see Hugh M. Hamill, Jr., "The Virgin of Guadalupe and the Origins of Mexican Nationalism," paper read before the Ohio Academy of History, April, 1961; Edward Henry Worthen, "The Reconquest of Mexico: A Panoramic View of Mexican Literary Nationalism" (2 vols.; unpublished Ph.D. dissertation, University of Michigan, 1965), Vol. 1, pp. 66-69; and Francisco de la Maza, *El guadalupanismo mexicano* (México: Porrúa y Obregón, 1953).

89. Quoted in Arturo M. Elias, *The Mexican People and the Church* (New York: n.p., n.d.), p. 48.

programs of national leaders after Archbishop Luis Martínez, appointed in February, 1937, urged all Mexicans to stand behind their government in the oil crisis with the United States. The present concern of the Mexican clergy and papal hierarchy for improved social conditions in Mexico and their recognition that the problems—agriculture, the reduction of latifundia, and improved living standards for Mexican workers—are national problems confronting the "Motherland"[90] make church goals coincide with national goals. The conflict of loyalties is reduced when priests like Father José Cantú Corro announce that the Mexican race is powerful because it is made up of the equally illustrious Indian and Spanish strains, because "there throbs in our heart the spirit of El Cid and of Cuauhtémoc." Father Cantú Corro continues, "Mexico must not be for foreigners; no, a thousand times no. . . . Mexico, idolized Motherland, nest of affections, mansion of happiness, noble Republic; Mexico, my Motherland, let the Saxons never assault your soil, nor implant their false religion, nor tarnish your flag."[91]

In the reconciliation of church and state since the 1930's, the church has come to terms with the kind of Mexican nationalism preached by the revolutionary leaders. It continues to "modify" patriotism in Mexico by encouraging a sentiment of universal fraternalism, without working for its own prerogatives and power as a separate political force. Assumptions of religious uniformity in the Catholic faith strengthen social cohesion, while Catholic pronouncements on the need for social progress reinforce national goals. Movements within the Roman Catholic church in the 1960's for decentralization and greater autonomy for prelates within their national spheres show that the church is now coming to terms with the power of nationalism as a

90. For a typical statement of this modern viewpoint, see Joaquín Márquez Montiel, *La doctrina social de la iglesia y la legislación obrera mexicana* (2d ed.; México: Editorial Jus, 1958), pp. 203, 206.

91. José Cantú Corro, *Patria y raza* (México: Escuela Tipográfica Salesiana, 1924), pp. 33-35, 53-54.

world-wide phenomenon. Although some Roman Catholic writers still seek the disappearance of nationalism and the rise of a Christian or Catholic universalism,[92] the recent moves for a greater degree of national autonomy within the Roman Catholic church suggest the possibility of continuing and increasing compatibility between national and religious loyalties in Mexico as well as elsewhere.

DESTRUCTION AS AN IMPETUS TO UNITY
AND THE THEORY OF ECONOMIC EQUALITY

By wreaking great destruction in physical and human terms, the long years of revolutionary violence provided Mexicans with startling examples of the need for national unity. Between 1910 and 1917, the Revolution destroyed property, brought financial chaos, and killed and maimed unprecedented numbers of Mexican citizens. It loosed bandit activity and imposed hardships on most of the civilian population as well as on revolutionaries. As groups of Mexicans were split apart in destructive conflict, a more harmonious national community in which conflicts of interest could be settled peacefully became more and more appealing. The destruction wrought during the period of violence created stark needs for co-operation and reconstruction in what Mexicans call ''the constructive phase of the Revolution.'' The destructiveness of the Revolution thus exemplified the need for harmonizing conflicting interests which has formed the basis of Mexican nationalism as a cohesive social value.

Revolutionary violence undermined the daily workings of the Mexican economy in various ways. Revolutionary armies in the course of battles, maneuvers, and retreats devastated fields, houses, and businesses. Living as scavengers upon the land, revolutionaries destroyed property and appropriated other property to their own uses. Some

92. Raimundo Paniker, *Patriotismo y cristiandad: Una investigación teológica-histórica sobre el patriotismo cristiano* (Madrid: Ediciones Rialp, S.A., 1961), pp. 119-21.

outright destruction was not accidental but preventive; railroad lines, buildings, and commodities were willfully destroyed so that they would not fall into the hands of the enemy. Mexico suffered another economic loss when revolution forced citizens to emigrate, as was the case in Spain in 1938, Bolivia in 1952, and Cuba in 1959. Through emigration Mexico lost talented and prosperous citizens along with what possessions they could carry or send abroad, and foreign managers in mining, industry, and agriculture who best knew the operation of their individual enterprises were forced out by violence and the mounting tide of nationalist sentiment.

The loss by emigration coincided with losses of trained manpower by executions and the decimation of revolutionary armies. Further economic disruption resulted from the incidental destruction of titles, deeds, mortgages, and other documents and their purposeful destruction when Emiliano Zapata and his lieutenants dynamited the halls of record in areas they captured. Revolutionaries also destroyed economically useful information, as when Orozquistas destroyed Pablo Hoffman's manuscript on "Tropical and Sub-Tropical Agriculture," a three-volume study representing fourteen years of research of which only an initial section had been published in Berlin.[93]

These elements of destruction accompanied severe economic disruption in areas of revolutionary activity. As early as March 2, 1911, the *New York Herald* reported that business in Chihuahua was grinding to a halt as railroads were demolished, banks refused to make loans, and professional men such as physicians slipped out of the state.[94] In a report typical of later descriptions of havoc in revolutionary areas, Consul Theodore C. Hamm at Durango in August, 1913, informed Secretary of State Bryan that the agricultural, mining, industrial, and commercial pursuits

93. *The New York Times,* February 9, 1913, Part 4, p. 6.
94. *New York Herald,* March 2, 1911, in Library of Congress MSS collection, *Newspaper Clippings pertaining to Mexico, 1911-1913,* Vol. 1.

in his district remained "completely paralyzed."[95] Newspaper advertisements mirrored the economic upheaval. A reader of advertisements in Mexican newspapers of the time is struck by the fact that—beside the ever-present, illustrated coffin advertisements—there appeared innumerable ads for country estates and city homes of the rich being sold "very cheap."[96]

A particular impediment to financial stability was the multiplicity of currencies that were placed in circulation as the Revolution progressed. After 1910 state banks and revolutionary chieftains issued a great variety of paper money. Although some was quite well printed, other paper certificates that passed for money were easily forged.[97] Constitutionalist pesos bearing the inscription "Death to Huerta" competed with Huerta's official scrip. With pesos selling at a premium of 15 per cent and banks holding all specie in order to guarantee their outstanding bills, the Chamber of Commerce in Mérida, Yucatán, issued in November, 1913, its own special *vales* or notes which, although not accepted for the payment of government bills, went into general circulation among the local residents.[98] A British observer recalls that, in addition to the dozens of presses and printing plates turning out currency throughout Mexico, someone had passed off a great number of new American cigar store coupons as American currency to the peons and Indians for goods received.[99]

Revolutionary factions naturally refused to honor the currencies issued by opposing groups, but in doing so they sharply increased the difficulties of the Mexican merchants.

95. Theodore C. Hamm to Bryan, August 19, 1913, /8726.

96. See the advertisements consistently run in government and opposition newspapers collected in the Hemeroteca Nacional in Mexico City or *Juvenal*, September 12, 1912, p. 2, enclosed in Lespinasse to Knox, September 18, 1912, /5114.

97. For a discussion and numerous illustrations of revolutionary currency, see Gustavo Casasola, *Historia gráfica de la Revolución Mexicana, 1900-1960* (4 vols.; México: Editorial F. Trillas, S.A., 1960), Vol. 1, pp. 724-27.

98. Gracey to Bryan, November 22, 1913, /10019.

99. I. Thord-Gray, *Gringo Rebel: Mexico 1913-1914* (Coral Gables, Fla.: University of Miami Press, 1960), pp. 112, 114.

When, for example, in February, 1915, Venustiano Carranza declared invalid the enormous quantities of currency with which Pancho Villa had flooded Mexico City during his occupation, the merchants of the capital suffered.[100] Enemy scrip was liable to confiscation; the persons holding it were subject to military trials and punishment. As currency crises hurt merchants and forced them to close their shops and refuse to exchange goods for currency, the structure of Mexican finance began to break down. Just as inflation does not pose as severe a problem for underdeveloped countries in which the bulk of trading is on a barter basis, so the currency crisis did not affect subsistence agriculturalists in the Mexican hinterland as much as it did the monetary sector of the Mexican economy. It did, however, impose severe hardship on Mexicans caught with the wrong types of currency, restrict business and commercial activity, and threaten economic anarchy in the monetary sphere.

Privations imposed by economic deterioration bore in forcefully on the personal lives of Mexican families. Many Mexicans lived at close to subsistence level, and the bad harvest of 1909 had initially caused starvation among peasants in some areas. In the March, 1911, siege of Chihuahua City by Madero's forces, *The New York Times* reported that food became "so scarce that the poorer people were starving and the merchants had raised their prices so high that it was almost impossible for men in moderate circumstances to procure enough food to feed their families."[101] Destruction of crops and their appropriation by armed forces deprived Mexican civilians of food, and with transportation facilities disrupted and monopolized for military uses, starvation became possible in areas only a short distance from food supplies. In the year preceding Madero's overthrow, the price of food in Mexico City more than doubled, and prices of all other commodities rose

100. *El Pueblo*, February 7, 1915, p. 1:1-2.
101. *The New York Times*, March 18, 1911, p. 2:1.

considerably.[102]   The suffering caused in the subsequent
ouster of Huerta and strife among the victorious Constitutionalists was particularly evident during Obregón's occupation of Mexico City between January and March, 1915.
The forced circulation of Constitutionalist currency closed
many businesses; Obregón sent out trainloads of machinery,
factory equipment, and even teachers to the Carrancista
headquarters of Veracruz; and Zapata's blockade cut off
food supplies to the city. The Convention of Aguascalientes
consented to the destruction of the Xochimilco pumping
station, cutting off the city's supply of clean water and
causing serious sanitation problems when there was no
longer sufficient water pressure to force drainage from the
household pipes or the city sewer system.[103]

Human losses increased the suffering of revolutionary
privation. No accurate compilations exist on the exact
numbers of people killed as a result of the Revolution, but
estimates run as high as one million. What had been a steadily climbing over-all population actually declined during the
years of violence, and in April, 1914, before the major campaigns against Villa and Zapata, Mrs. O'Shaughnessy estimated that several hundred thousand men, women, and
children had already been killed in Mexico since Madero
started for Mexico City.[104] Masses of Mexican troops died
in the series of contests between Villa and Obregón and in
such engagements as the defense of Mexico City against
Félix Díaz in February, 1913, where both sides used heavy
artillery at close range. The deaths of Mexican citizens
summed up in the battle statistics brought both grief and
resentment. The psychological pressure that the atmosphere of violence placed on passive bystanders is reflected
in the intense relief the noncombatants expressed after
hearing church bells announce an end to the Madero-Félix
Díaz hostilities. Crowds poured into the streets, and there

102. Henry Lane Wilson to Knox, February 4, 1913, /6068.
103. Quirk, *The Mexican Revolution, 1914-1915*, pp. 181-85.
104. O'Shaughnessy, *A Diplomat's Wife in Mexico*, p. 286.

arose "the hysterical cries of men and women, who welcomed eagerly the relief from the strain under which they had lived."[105]

Atrocities and outrages were a glaring evidence of the ineptitude of violence as a continuing method of resolving conflict. The Revolution freed abject criminals as well as political prisoners from jail, and they joined brigand bands to rob, loot, and pillage. In 1912 Consul John B. Glenn estimated that 3,000 bandits were operating in his state of Guanajuato alone.[106] In addition to the brigands, revolutionary bands upon occasion resorted to extreme forms of brutality. While factional interests undoubtedly embellished or fabricated some reports of atrocities, disinterested reports of extreme brutality also exist. When one looks behind the roseate façade that now enshrines revolutionary accounts, it becomes apparent that some of the worst atrocities were immediately concealed.

Credible reports show wounded rebels burned alive, mass rapes, and the venting of lust and sadism. North American witnesses reported scores of instances of extreme cruelty by Huertista forces, such as that of a federal officer who overtook four carts in which between forty and fifty wounded men were being escorted by sixteen rebels under a white flag. The officer ordered the sixteen shot and then had crude petroleum poured over the wounded and set afire.[107] In another instance, a local chieftain and his men swooped down to loot a camp and then outraged all the women; no minors, old women, prostitutes, or married women escaped and "at night it was pitiful to hear the wails of the young women in the houses and the ravines."[108] Documented reports also attest to sadistic attacks in which pregnant women were repeatedly raped and finally cut open while their husbands watched, men were crucified on

105. *The New York Times*, February 20, 1913, p. 2:5.
106. John B. Glenn to Arnold Shanklin, August 19, 1912, /4713.
107. Lind to Bryan, December 13, 1913, /10170.
108. Rosendo G. Duarte to C. S. Westbrook, n.d., /3846.

trees, federal soldiers were killed by tying hot wires about their necks, and men and women were tortured by cutting off parts of their bodies.[109]

The economic disruption, the privation, the personal losses, and the atrocities demonstrated to all Mexicans on a personal level the pitfalls of violence in settling national conflicts of interest. A spirit of national solidarity arose in Mexico just as it had arisen in France after the Jacobin intemperances of the French Revolution; nationalism offered a handy rubric to bind together and protect the war-weary populace that remained. The spirit of nationalism offered a common rallying ground for the surviving activists who wanted to consolidate the gains of their faction, and it offered a bond to the more passive segment of the population which wanted an end to violence and economic destruction. The economic destruction of the Revolution created a situation in which co-operative effort among Mexican citizens was needed to provide the modicum of food, shelter, and clothing required by the members of various groups, thus emphasizing the need for an ideology of co-operation to unite the groups in joint effort. One element of the resulting nationalist credo became a theory of greater economic equality.

One vital aid in the rebuilding process and the subsequent establishment of solid economic growth has been the theory of economic equality, a theory proposing that Mexicans can be and should be more nearly equal in terms of economic opportunity and wealth. The *Revista de Revistas* indicated the logical basis for this viewpoint in 1913 when it declared that the violence of the Revolution resulted from the extreme inequalities of wealth among Mexicans, that a more equitable distribution of wealth in Mexico was inevitable sooner or later, and that disinterested patriotism on all sides was a necessary part of the solution.[110]

109. John L. Mathews to Knox, October 9, 1912, /5261.
110. ''Los grandes problemas nacionales: Distribución de la riqueza,'' *Revista de Revistas*, Año 4, Núm. 174 (22 junio 1913), 1.

Appeals for greater equality became central pronouncements in the expression of revolutionary goals. With a
basis in the program of Ricardo Flores Magón, the debates
over the Querétaro Constitution show a deep concern among
the delegates to the Constitutional Convention for setting
up the legal equality among Mexican citizens which had
preoccupied nineteenth-century Mexican Liberals.[111] A key
tenet of Mexico's admittedly nonideological Revolution became a dedication to the economic and social betterment of
the many as opposed to the few, an awareness that Mexicans could participate and should participate in raising the
living standards of all their countrymen.[112]

By 1917 the Industrial Revolution had brought about the
existence of technological know-how that, for the first time
in Mexican history, made it economically feasible to raise
the bare level of subsistence of the mass of the Mexican people. As one of the major forces producing the egalitarian
revolution that has risen side by side with nationalism since
the time of the French Revolution, the application of science
and technology to industry and agriculture indicated possibilities for a society of comparative abundance in which
Mexicans would no longer be so unalterably stratified in
social or economic terms. Increasing prosperity is compatible with a somewhat wider distribution of economic
benefits, as the effectively larger internal market created
by expanding incomes raises demand for agricultural and
manufactured goods. The technological innovations of the
Industrial Revolution allow a greater degree of ''economic
democracy,'' and this, in the long run, influences social
stratification, political participation, and equality in the
national community.

Protestations of economic egalitarianism also fit the
sequence of Mexican revolutionary events. The immediate,

111. L. Melgarejo Randolph and J. Fernández Rojas, *El congreso constituyente de 1916 y 1917* . . . (México: Departamento de Talleres Gráficos
de la Secretaría de Fomento, Colonización e Industria, 1917), pp. 454, 463.

112. For a particularly moving statement of this theme, see Daniel Cosío
Villegas, *Extremos de América* (México: Tezontle, 1949), p. 14.

as opposed to the long-range, impact of the Mexican Revolution was, as Sorokin says of the Bolshevik Revolution in
Russia, to produce ''economic equalization, not by enriching
the poor, but by making the rich poor and by contributing
to a general impoverishment.''[113] Some Mexicans retained
much of their wealth and some revolutionaries gained new
fortunes, but these cases did not counterbalance the general
poverty. In the long run, Mexicans have striven toward
increased economic equality through per capita economic
growth and land distribution stimulated in large part by
the Revolution, but the short-run impact of the Revolution
was to produce greater economic equality through destruction—the burning of haciendas, theft, and the required
contributions to revolutionary armies. Members of poorer
classes appropriated the property and possessions of the
rich. An immediate impetus to greater economic equality
came, therefore, from destruction of the property of the
rich, from acquisition of property and possessions from the
rich by the poor, and from a general lowering of economic
resources through mass destruction.

Internal reforms and attitudes toward foreign investment continued to support protestations of egalitarianism.
The Revolution spurred plans for regeneration such as that
directed by General Salvador Alvarado in Yucatán which
attempted to restore railroad service, to fight social evils
such as alcoholism, and to create greater social and economic equality among the people of Yucatán by raising the
standard of living.[114] Despite fluctuations in the force with
which successive national leaders supported the ideal of
greater equality, continuing distributions of land made
peasants feel that they were indeed gaining a larger material share of the national wealth. Internationally, Mexicans found the result of their 1910 Revolution to be the
elimination of foreign economic domination. Nationaliza-

113. Sorokin, *The Sociology of Revolution*, p. 225.
114. Salvador Alvarado, *Mi actuación revolucionaria en Yucatán* (México:
Librería de la Vda. de Ch. Bouret, 1918), pp. 52, 77, 128.

tion of foreign oil holdings under Lázaro Cárdenas in 1938 came at a time when Mexicans were capable of taking over petroleum production. Requirements of 51 per cent Mexican capital in joint ventures now allay nationalist fears of foreign domination and draw Mexican capital into domestic development. Rather than a sterile economic nationalism that rejects foreign capital, however, the economic nationalism enunciated in the 1917 Constitution and afterwards has tamed foreign capital and harnessed it to work for the economic benefit of the Mexican people.[115]

Protestations of egalitarianism have, paradoxically, also allowed the highly skewed income distribution and domestic reinvestment that have quickened Mexican economic growth. It is a question to both Mexicans and foreigners as to whether all but an elite group of Mexican workers and peasants are now better off in terms of buying power than before the Revolution. While wealth, as measured in terms of dress, housing, and living conditions, has increased somewhat for the majority of Mexicans outside chronically depressed areas, it is also clear that the share of the national wealth going to entrepreneurs and financiers has remained demonstrably large. From a balanced comparison of all the available data, Morris Singer concludes that in the 1950's 5 per cent of the Mexican population received about one-third of total personal income, the top 10 per cent of the population received 45 per cent of total personal income, and some one-eighth of the families in Mexico accounted for one-half of the income.[116] This unequal distribution has

115. For a Mexican defense of this position, see Moisés Sáenz, *Las inversiones extranjeras y el nacionalismo mexicano: Conferencia sustentada en la Universidad de Chicago, Ill., E. U. A., el mes de julio de 1926* (México: Talleres Gráficos de la Nación, 1927), pp. 15-16. Compare Miguel S. Wionczek, *El nacionalismo mexicano y la inversión extranjera* (México: Siglo Veintiuno Editores, S.A., 1967), pp. 19-25.

116. The best over-all summary of income distribution and its relation to theories of equality in Mexico is Chapter 5, "Income Distribution and Development," in Morris Singer, "Growth, Equality, and Mexico's Experience" (unpublished manuscript, 1966). On Mexican economic development, see also Robert Jones Shafer, *Mexico: Mutual Adjustment Planning* (Syracuse, N.Y.: Syracuse University Press, 1966); William P. Glade, Jr., and Charles W.

produced economic growth in national per capita terms despite Mexico's annual population increase of over 3 per cent, because Mexicans have reinvested the skimmed off profits in domestic ventures. While some North American aid has come to Mexico since World War II from direct investment as well as from tourists and *bracero* savings, nearly 90 per cent of the capital invested in Mexico since the early 1940's has been Mexican. With the Mexican government providing close to 40 per cent of direct investment since 1939,[117] the private sector has also contributed heavily to savings and growth.

The theory of egalitarianism has helped to make this possible, first by encouraging the lower classes to accept highly skewed income distribution. Men on the lower end of the scale hear and come to feel that the ''Revolution was fought for the economic benefit of all Mexicans.'' As long as they can see some improvement in personal status which seems to bear out the theory, it is easier to accept the acquisition of greater wealth by other Mexicans. They develop a delayed time perspective similar to that which permits Marxists to continue accepting the ultimate goal of fraternal harmony under communism. As Mexican workers see manifestations of wealth among entrepreneurs, their resentment is reduced by their acceptance of the notion that in the long run the Revolution works for the economic benefit of all. This notion permits the over-all growth in per capita terms which may someday justify its premise, because it defers the increased spending on immediate consumer goods and gives entrepreneurs capital for reinvestment.

Anderson, *The Political Economy of Mexico* (Madison, Wis.: University of Wisconsin Press, 1963); Robert L. Bennett, *The Financial Sector and Economic Development: The Mexican Case* (Baltimore, Md.: The Johns Hopkins University Press, 1965); Dwight S. Brothers and Leopoldo Solís M., *Mexican Financial Development* (Austin, Texas: University of Texas Press, 1966); and Mary Goldring, ''South of the Border,'' *The Economist*, May 13, 1967, pp. 683-9.

117. James G. Maddox, ''Economic Growth and Revolution in Mexico,'' *Land Economics*, Vol. 36, No. 3 (August, 1960), 275.

Acceptance of the theory among workers also promotes growth by establishing the peaceful domestic environment in which reinvestment is feasible. Nationalism and social consciousness have motivated the responsible entrepreneurship of the private sector of Mexico's mixed economy.[118] Neither patriotism, social concern, nor the profit motive, however, would guarantee domestic reinvestment of profits without the environment of harmony and pacific settlement of conflicting interests that reiterations of equalitarian nationalism have fostered. Flight capital poses a severe problem in Latin America; in the first years of the Alliance for Progress, the flight of Latin American capital abroad roughly equalled the yearly flow of North American public funds under the Alliance program. Mexico has enjoyed levels of both political stability and domestic reinvestment which make it stand out in Latin America, and the impetus to stability from protestations of nationalism is one basis of economic growth. The growth itself in turn wins over the Mexican participants whom it is aiding and draws formerly isolated individuals into economic participation in the nationalist framework. It advances commitment that has been and is being shaped by other elements of the revolutionary catalysis, from invocations of the new national heroes and the heightened national awareness of revolutionary migrations to increasing acquisition of status by personal achievement and the evolving harmony of national and religious loyalties.

118. See Frank Brandenburg, ''A Contribution to the Theory of Entrepreneurship and Economic Development: The Case of Mexico,'' *Inter-American Economic Affairs*, Vol. 16, No. 3 (Winter, 1962), 15.

V
Social Groups
and the Revolution

The Revolution of 1910 to 1917 established a precedent for actively incorporating the individual members of Mexican social groups within the national community. In 1910 the stage of military technology emphasized the importance of large ground forces rather than giving final military power to a small coterie of Homeric champions, feudal knights, or decision-makers in thermonuclear war. The military decisiveness of large ground forces meant that revolutionary leaders had to win and hold the loyalty of large numbers of Mexican citizens, and it naturally followed that leadership appeals came to be expressed in inclusive and nationalistic terms. In the context of a civil war that was not fought on the basis of geographical section or of international ideology, appeals were made in terms of patriotism, national unity, and the specific interests of domestic groups. From active participation in revolutionary struggles, Mexicans of previously marginal membership in the national community gained new status; the appeals and promises of revolutionary leaders gave recognition to unenfranchised groups within the national polity.

Those who gained increased national status make up a variety of categories. Mexican intellectuals as a group developed a more cohesively nationalistic outlook that soon gained expression and impact through literature and art. A large element of Mexican youth participated actively in the revolutionary fighting, and since the Revolution, Mexican youth has been drawn into the socioeconomic system and tried to reform it by pressure from within rather than by outside violence. The nationalist orientation of Mexican teachers has proved crucial for the subsequent rise of nationalism.

While it is important to keep in mind the impact of the Revolution on the intellectuals, youth, and teachers, the Revolution did not in these cases raise group status as much as it did in the cases of Indians, workers, and women. The members of these latter three groups fought actively in the revolutionary conflicts and won increased national recognition because of it. After violence abated, the status that each group had won continued to give its members claim to a place in the national community. With the Mexicans' tendency to associate themselves with the Indian heritage, the increased size and articulation of urban and rural working forces since 1917, and entreaties for the national participation of Mexican women, the tendency for members of these extended groups to perceive themselves in national terms becomes particularly important. The Revolution here affected nationalism not only as an immediate stimulant of group participation but also as a continuing precedent for the attitudes of inclusiveness that characterize the national community.

A NOTE ON MILITARY TECHNOLOGY

The stage of military technology available in the 1910 decade deserves consideration, because it shaped the mode of warfare of the Mexican Revolution and the immediate social relationships that this warfare produced. Military technology affects the kinds of appeals made in any context where conflicts of interest are settled through armed engagements. In the context of medieval Europe where small groups of highly skilled knights with costly equipment became militarily predominant, sharp social stratification and appropriation of political power by the knights mirrored their military control. These knights had to make no broadly based appeals for support outside of their personal retainers and subordinates, as even the military control of a kingdom depended on winning the allegiance of only a handful of earls, barons, and their vassals.

In a modern industrial state of the kind developed or developing in Nazi Germany, the United States, Russia, or Communist China, the capture and manipulation of broad popular loyalties is contrastingly important. Co-ordinated national loyalties and the degree of willingness with which the policies of national leaders are accepted and implemented vitally affect the ground forces still required in conventional wars. Such loyalty is necessary to fight nerve-testing guerrilla wars such as that in South Vietnam in which the patience and support of the domestic populaces of the major powers may prove decisive, just as this motivation must be present to provide the economic, technological, and industrial bases that underlie the development of thermonuclear devices and delivery vehicles. The military technology of the Mexican Revolution in no way matched the demands for loyalty of industrialized superpowers, but in requiring a high degree of broadly based support, there is resemblance.

The Mexican revolutionaries in 1910 used and devised new weapons. Machine guns, heavy artillery, and barbed wire came into use. Dynamite bombs made from tin cans appeared, and charges of nitroglycerin were used to blow up barracks. Revolutionaries utilized the soft, expanding dumdum bullets expressly forbidden by the 1899 declaration of the Hague Conference which Mexico had signed, and they attached Maxim silencers to rifles that they fired into trains. The Díaz government built the first of several specially armored railway cars and painted them in black and white checkered squares to conceal the portholes from which riflemen fired. Victoriano Huerta, Venustiano Carranza, and Pancho Villa all had Cadillacs with "nobby tread" tires in service in their armies, and foreign military planners watched with interest to discover what functions automobiles could perform in military campaigns. In what Mexicans proudly describe as the first use of an airplane for exclusively military ends, the biplane *Sonora,* piloted by Captain Gustavo Salinas with naval engineer Teodoro Madariaga as copilot, dropped bombs on Huerta's ships near Topolobampo in April and May, 1914.

Despite the use of several automobiles and airplanes in a rudimentary form of mechanized warfare, the real battles of the contesting armies were fought between individual foot soldiers and horsemen. The major weapons of the Revolution were rifles, both German Mausers with which Díaz had supplied federal troops and Winchester 30-30's smuggled in from the United States. The battles were largely those of attrition, in which opposing forces hammered away at each other with rifles plus some machine guns and artillery pieces. Victory came to those with the better tactical position and the heavier firepower; it regularly depended on the number of followers assembled, the quantities of rifles and ammunition, and the determination to fight. Villa's famous cavalry attacks in effect brought mounted riflemen into a position of tactical advantage. Obregón's use of trenches and barbed wire was a means of stopping the Villista cavalry charges while bringing heavy firepower against them from protected positions.

The 1910 style of warfare made peons militarily effective as it required a minimum of learning and military sophistication. It placed a higher premium on loyalty than on discipline and drill in the manual of arms. As Obregón's culminating trench warfare victory of Celaya showed, previously untutored recruits could in the course of campaigns gradually acquire the degree of discipline required even in the most advanced military tactics. Operation of rapid-fire machine guns did entail such skill that their operators were

at times in short supply,[1] but in comparison to the numbers
of rifles, pistols, and machetes in action, the number of
machine guns was very limited indeed. Handling a rifle
required only rudimentary knowledge, and marksmanship
improved with practice even for men who possessed no
prior skill. Riding came naturally to horsemen like Villa's
northern *vaqueros,* who made an easy transition from
cattle-tending to irregular cavalry.

Revolutionary warfare also left wide room for impro-
visation. In contrast to the scientists and experts now
required to manage atomic and bacteriological warfare,
peons could easily employ charges of dynamite. Noting that
dynamite "played a terrible role in the fighting" at Cholula
on May 29, 1911, *The New York Times* commented that "the
facility with which a cap can be fitted to the end of a fuse
and then thrust into a stick of dynamite, lighted, and tossed
anywhere with ease, with little danger to the thrower, makes
it a favorite weapon. Owing to their experience in the
mines nearly all peons are familiar with the use of this terrible explosive."[2] Dynamite squads fashioned bombs out of
tin cans and pieces of iron pipe fitted with nails and rocks,
attached and lighted a fuse, and projected them with a
crude slingshot. Particularly effective at night, the bombs
facilitated the taking of trenches and adobe forts.[3] Pascual
Orozco's rebels improvised spectacularly in the demolition
of armored railway cars. At Corralitos they sent an engine
loaded with dynamite hurtling at full speed into a train of
armored cars from which Maderistas were fighting, and
about sixty Maderistas were killed in the shock and ex-
plosion.[4]

The stage of military weaponry of the early twentieth
century thus made Mexicans of varied backgrounds essen-

1. John Lind to William Jennings Bryan, February 21, 1914, /10949.
2. *The New York Times,* May 31, 1911, p. 1:1.
3. See the description and photograph enclosed in Frederick Simpich to
Bryan, April 18, 1913, /7227.
4. Marion Letcher to Philander C. Knox, March 31, 1912, /3525.

tially equal on the field of battle. Familial, regional, occupational, linguistic, racial, aspirational, and even sexual differences counted for comparatively little in the revolutionary situation, as the background of the combatants paled in importance beside their ability to fight. Mass revolutions are social levelers not only by their decimation or exiling of once privileged classes but also because they temporarily change the rules of the game for the acquisition of privilege. Capability on the battlefield depended— after arms were bought and reasonably good tactics devised —on attracting wider and deeper support from Mexican citizens than one's opponents attracted. Rifles and pistols required individual wielders, and from the military standpoint, it mattered not whether the wielder was from Durango or Oaxaca, an Indian or a mestizo, a man or a woman. Unlike other weapons that require long training or masculine strength, a Mauser at short range is effective even in inexperienced hands. One reason that Mexican women participated in the 1910 to 1917 struggles as actual fighters was that the stage of military technology allowed them to do so. Since with the weapons of the early twentieth century one man or one woman was essentially the equal of another, the style of warfare itself helped to foster increasing sentiments of equalitarianism.

The exigencies of the military campaigns compelled revolutionary leaders to seek support among a variety of previously unenfranchised groups. Men were needed to achieve the ambition of each revolutionary leader, whether that ambition was for personal wealth and power or for a higher national goal such as Madero's desire for political democracy or Zapata's hope for land distribution. Wealth could be stolen and guns could be bought, but men had to be cajoled or rewarded into loyal service. *Esprit* and motivation proved crucial elements in victory. Villa's taking of Torreón between March 26 and April 2, 1914, evidenced the effectiveness of spirited recruits against better trained and entrenched army units that lacked the will to fight.[5] The defeating of the Díaz and Huerta regimes showed that, under a style of warfare that did not give central authorities overwhelming military superiority such as the force that crushed the Hungarian freedom fighters in 1956, the revolutionaries' will to fight could provide the margin of victory.

The revolutionaries' will to fight and their support by noncombatants resulted in part from the kinds of appeals made to them. Indians and members of labor unions were promised a share in the revolutionary enterprise because of the actual contributions that they could make to the goals of individual leaders. As each enterprise was nominally, if not actually, carried out for the benefit of "the nation," the sense of participation in each of the groups took on national implications. The Mexican Revolution was not fought on the basis of geographical sectionalism as the United States Civil War had been or on the basis of conflicting international ideologies like the Spanish Civil War of 1937 and 1938. It lacked the ready-made definitions of who should be on what side, which sectional or ideological loyalties have given in other contexts. There was a need to win the loyalty and support of Mexicans away from competing domestic chiefs. In the type of guerrilla warfare that interspersed major campaigns of the Revolution, support from local residents as well as fighters could be decisive. The armies and guerrilla bands of revolutionaries needed wide civilian support to supply food, shelter, and sanctuary. Support was more effective when induced voluntarily rather than enforced, and as a result the military leaders found it convenient to keep civilians as well as soldiers loyal by promises and concessions given in the name of the nation. Leaders won support from specific domestic groups by promising reforms specially aimed at group interests. In seeking a general common ground, leaders of opposing

5. Robert E. Quirk, *The Mexican Revolution, 1914-1915: The Convention of Aguascalientes* (Bloomington, Ind.: Indiana University Press, 1960), p. 24.

temperaments and tendencies clothed their appeals in the garb of "patriotism" and "national unity." In order to measure the types of appeals that Mexican revolutionary warfare helped to fashion, it is first necessary to analyze the content of the appeals themselves as a prelude to the consideration of their effects.

THE INCLUSIVENESS OF REVOLUTIONARY APPEALS

The revolutionary contests between 1910 and 1917 presented the anomalous situation in which men, now regarded in Mexico as the grandest heroes and the greatest villains of the era, were making their appeals for Mexican support on the same basis and frequently in the same phrases. The presentation of the Huerta and Félix Díaz programs made them appear not to differ radically from the promises of Madero, Carranza, and Obregón. Insurgent leaders made appeals for broad support based upon an inclusive concept of the national community, while the leaders of movements now branded as reactionary appealed to all citizens of Mexico on this same basis. As both heroes and villains reiterated concepts of national unity, nationalism, and patriotic duty, greater awareness of the concepts of Mexican nationalism and national community was awakened in individual Mexican citizens. The uniformity of nationalistic verbiage, while belying differences in factional programs and objectives, turned one aspect of the revolutionary contests into a struggle for wider national participation and allegiance.

One value uniformly stressed in revolutionary programs was the need for "national unity." The fact that each group actually meant "national unity in support of our candidate" did not detract from the breadth with which appeals were made but rather underlined the leaders' need for wider backing. The appeals for national unity and for support of Madero, Carranza, and Obregón are well known, but what is less well remembered is that their opposition expressed similar desires in similar terms. José Yves Limantour claimed that the "salvation of Mexico" depended on everyone's subordinating his personal conduct to the "highest interests of the nation,"[6] while Bernardo Reyes proffered the slogan of "ALL FOR THE MOTHERLAND," warning that Europe and America saw Mexico divided in dangerous factionalism.[7] The anti-Madero campaign of 1912 also pleaded for unity, professed complete loyalty to "the poor, wounded and bloody motherland," but found Madero incapable of leading that Motherland.[8] The manifesto that Félix Díaz issued during the abortive Veracruz uprising of October, 1912, called for "all Mexicans" and "all true patriots" to unite in restoring the national welfare.[9] Victoriano Huerta unrelentingly pleaded after his coup for the fraternal unity of all Mexicans in peace and prosperity,[10] while Huertista literature went so far as to claim that in Madero's overthrow "there was no conspiracy, no barracks revolt" but "a supreme and united force of national salvation."[11]

Reminiscences of the Revolution and its heroes contain only expressions of unity and fraternity in a common cause. In describing the assembling of Maderistas, Carrancistas,

6. Quoted in *The New York Times*, March 21, 1911, p. 2:1.

7. *Manifiesto del señor Gral. Bernardo Reyes y comité reyista á la nación* (México: Tip. Vda. F. Díaz de León, Sucs., 1911), p. 5. The capitalization is that of the manifesto.

8. See "México para los Mexicanos," *Ojo Parado*, Año 1, Núm. 7 (16 febrero 1912), 1.

9. Quoted in José Fernández Rojas, *La Revolución Mexicana de Porfirio Díaz a Victoriano Huerta, 1910-1913* . . . (México: F. P. Rojas & Cía., 1913), pp. 234-39.

10. For striking examples of Huerta's stress on the unity theme, see *La Tribuna*, February 22, 1913, p. 1:6-7; *Mensaje oficial y patrióticas alocuciones extraoficiales del Sr. Gral. D. Victoriano Huerta, Presidente de la República Mexicana, en la solemne apertura del Congreso de la Unión, el 1° de abril de 1913* (Mérida, Yuc.: Imprenta de la "Empresa Editora Yucateca, S.A.," 1913), p. 11; and Carlos Toro, *La caída de Madero por la revolución felicista* (México: n.p., 1913), pp. 54-64.

11. Salvador Hernández Chávez and Alfonso López Ituarte, *La angustia nacional en 16 meses del gobierno de don Francisco I. Madero* . . . (México: Imprenta de Alfonso López, 1913), pp. 72-73.

Obregonistas, Villistas, and Zapatistas at the death of Luis Cabrera, for example, General Francisco L. Urquizo writes that "grief again united us one to another, as formerly in our youth we united to fight tyranny with pen, with words or with arms."[12] The nationalist outcries of Huerta lie discredited and forgotten, as the memory of common opposition to him erases the sting of factionalism among those who struggled against one another after his defeat.

One reason for the expanding sense of unity in the Revolution was the fact that the Madero revolt and the insistence on greater social justice that grew out of it received support and sympathy from the great body of the Mexican people.[13] Catering to the heterogeneous elements of revolutionary armies, successive leaders each called for varying degrees of increased social welfare. Porfirio Díaz conceded political reforms and announced plans for nationalization of the public domain, heavy government spending on irrigation, and the opening of between 4 and 5 million acres of land to be divided into small farms. John Lind, as President Woodrow Wilson's personal representative, concluded from Constitutionalist propaganda that the great majority of the forces rising against Huerta did so in an attempt to gain popular economic and social reforms for Mexico rather than in the desire to fulfill personal ambitions.[14] Pancho Villa justified his later break with Carranza by proclaiming that Carranza was not fulfilling the Constitutionalist commitment to establish "not only a democratic government, but also the socioeconomic reforms

12. Francisco L. Urquizo, "Obregón, militar," in *Álvaro Obregón, Ocho mil kilómetros en campaña* (Vol. 5, "Fuentes para la Historia de la Revolución Mexicana," Manuel González Ramírez, ed.; México: Fondo de Cultura Económica, 1959), pp. xvii, xxx.

13. Contemporary analysts declared that the Revolution was receiving such sympathy and support and claimed that it did so because it was "a genuinely national phenomenon." See C. Trejo Lerdo de Tejada, *La Revolución y el nacionalismo: Todo para todos* (Habana: Maza y Ca., 1916), p. 204.

14. Constitutionalists welcomed such an appraisal and republished it. See John Lind, *La gente de México,* traducido por la Secretaría de Instrucción Pública y Bellas Artes (Veracruz, Ver.: Tip. de la Sría. de I. P. y B. A., 1915), pp. 12-13.

which are indispensable in order to assure the betterment of the disinherited classes."[15]

Proposals for reform broadened as the Revolution progressed. The plan advocated at the Convention of Aguascalientes in April, 1916, suggested extensive reforms to distribute land, legalize divorce, protect illegitimate children, raise teachers' salaries, create progressive inheritance taxes, remedy voting frauds, and guarantee limited working hours, industrial hygiene, and the right to strike.[16] Incorporation of these demands in the Constitution of 1917 took them out of the factional context, formalized them, conferred upon them a sense of national legitimacy, and made them lastingly invocable. Here appeals for unity and greater social justice coincided with frankly patriotic and nationalistic appeals.

The revolutionary campaigns encouraged patriotic adjurations, a sense of national participation in revolutionary armies, and an active seeking after national identity that made contemporary observers stress the strength of Mexican nationalism. Each group of combatants sought support by appeals to patriotism. Before 1910 Mexico had enjoyed a long and celebrated tradition of political "plans" with nationalistic invocations, but from 1910 to 1917 the number of plans issued increased sharply. In Madero's 1910 Plan of San Luis Potosí, Zapata's 1911 Plan of Ayala, and the Constitutionalists' 1913 Plan of Guadalupe, each group appealed directly to Mexicans as Mexicans. Like the program of Ricardo Flores Magón's Liberal party, they asked "Mexicans" to think of "the significance for the Motherland" of the proposals made.[17]

15. *Manifiesto del C. Gral. Francisco Villa a la nación, y documentos que justifican el desconocimiento del C. Venustiano Carranza como primer jefe de la Revolución* (Chihuahua, Chih.: Tipografía del Gobierno, 1914), p. 6.

16. Gustavo Pérez Jiménez, *Vigencia del pensamiento político, económico y social de la Revolución Mexicana en la vida institucional de la nación* (México: Editorial B. Costa-Amic, 1961), pp. 108-13.

17. Manuel González Ramírez, ed., *Planes políticos y otros documentos* (Vol. 1, "Fuentes para la Historia de la Revolución Mexicana"; México: Fondo de Cultura Económica, 1954), pp. 24ff.

Both defenders of constituted authority and their challengers clothed declarations in patriotic vestments. When Pascual Orozco rose in revolt against the Madero government, for example, he asked the men who had followed him in support of Madero to join him in opposition because the *"high duties of patriotism"* required it.[18] Circulars disguised themselves in patriotism when announcing a change in factional control in a region. When General Esteban Ramos delivered Matamoros to the Félix Díaz faction on February 17, 1913, the circulars claimed that the sole cause of such a change was the welfare of the Motherland.[19] As part of Huerta's campaign of patriotism, posters for the election of October 26, 1913, asked Mexicans to support the Huerta-Blanquet ticket because their work was "patriotic and eminently Mexican."[20] Even cigarette packages told Mexicans that theirs was a national struggle; a special-brand wrapper made by E. Pugibet showed a portrait of Huerta in uniform on one side and proclaimed in large letters on the other that Victoriano Huerta was "Defender of the National Integrity."[21]

The flags and emblems carried by the various insurgents also revealed a uniformity of patriotism. Revolutionary factions as well as defenders of authority all fought under the Mexican national flag. In addition to the national colors, Maderistas carried emblems on which the Virgin of Guadalupe was pictured along with the slogan "Effective Suffrage, No Re-election."[22] This slogan still appears on Mexican government stationery. Zapatistas sometimes substituted center emblems for the snake and eagle, but they

18. Ramón Puente, *Pascual Orozco y la revuelta de Chihuahua* (México: Eusebio Gómez de la Puente, 1912), pp. 110-11. The italics are Puente's.

19. Circular enclosed in Jesse H. Johnson to Knox, February 18, 1913, /6337.

20. Poster enclosed in William W. Canada to Bryan, October 31, 1913, /9630.

21. See illustration in Obregón, *Ocho mil kilómetros en campaña*, Fig. 39, facing p. 256.

22. See reproduction in Gonzalo G. Rivero, *Hacia la verdad: Episodios de la Revolución* (México: Compañía Editora Nacional, S.A., 1911), p. 154.

too generally used a slight variation on the national flag. The inconsistency of opposing sides fighting under the same emblems, although incongruous, accurately reflected a situation in which each side claimed to be fighting for what it defined as the national welfare.

A surprising sense of national camaraderie characterized Madero's early victory over Porfirio Díaz and lasted in modified form throughout the Revolution. Mexicans from differing factions joined in deriving common pride from the valor of their countrymen regardless of which side those countrymen supported. As correspondent Stephen Bonsal reported from Mexico City after the major Maderista victory at Ciudad Juárez, "While it seems to me that the people are overwhelmingly sympathetic to the revolution, all Mexicans here are united in a feeling of national pride over the gallant resistance the Federal troops made at Juarez against the overwhelming numbers of insurgents."[23]

After the hard-fought victory at Ciudad Juárez, Francisco Madero paroled General Navarro and his twenty-seven officers, invited them to dinner, and allowed them to sleep at night in their own headquarters. Outbursts of "Viva Madero," hats thrown in the air, and a wave of federal soldiers joining his force met Madero when he told captured Díaz soldiers that they could choose parole or join his army of liberation and that in the meantime they would be treated "as brothers, not as foes."[24] Madero set a precedent later followed by other groups willing to welcome deserters from the opposition as brothers in a national struggle. With Huerta gone, Villa and Zapata reduced in power, and Carranza predominant in 1917, a continued sense of camaraderie officially reigned. As the Carrancista press emphasized, the elections that named

23. *The New York Times*, May 11, 1911, p. 2:3.
24. *Ibid.*, May 11, 1911, p. 2:1.

Carranza president of Mexico in March, 1917, evoked considerable enthusiasm even among many of the Mexicans who had not voted directly.[25] These reiterated calls to patriotism and the prevalent sense of national camaraderie suggest that one impulse of revolutionary participants was the pursuit of a wider national identification.[26]

The nationalistic euphoria of the Revolution, however, should not be overemphasized. John Lind was probably correct when he observed that "if love of country is meant by patriotism, I believe that it may truthfully be said that no people on earth feels a more intense love for its native land than the Mexican people."[27] But no hard data from research surveys corroborate Lind's observation for the 1910 to 1917 period, and the persistence of sentimentally isolated groups many years after the Revolution belies its generalization in quantitative terms. The understanding of revolutionary principles among the common soldiers should also not be exaggerated, for many soldiers lacked detailed knowledge of proposals and dedication to what their commanders and propagandists were calling "the sacred principles for which they are offering their lives."[28] The personalistic loyalty of troops to their own *jefes* outweighed any sense of loyalty to a broad national community, even though later invocations of the *jefes* as national heroes induced more national identification. Without overemphasizing the extent of a wider sense of nationalism, one can still note its force in the Revolution and, what is more, its effects.

25. "El pueblo, poseído de patriótico entusiasmo, acudió ayer en masa a las urnas electorales," *El Demócrata*, March 12, 1917, pp. 1:1-4, 7:6.
26. Contemporary statements that the Revolution was fought in part as a search for national identification include Gustavo Dresel, *A un pueblo errado, un nuevo sermón de la montaña* (México: Eusebio Gómez de la Puente, 1913), pp. 10, 95; and Miguel Galindo, *A través de la sierra (diario de un soldado)* (n.p.: Imprenta de "El Dragón," 1924), p. 127.
27. Lind, *La gente de México*, p. 25.
28. V. Blasco Ibáñez, *Mexico in Revolution*, Arthur Livingston and José Padin, trans. (New York: E. P. Dutton & Company, 1920), p. 184.

INDIANISM

A prime effect of revolutionary nationalism was a shift in attitude toward the Indians. Contending factions needed Indians as fighters, and as fighters the Indians helped to determine the outcome of internecine warfare. As leaders promised reforms to aid them, they came to feel that they had a stake in the governmental structure and resorted to violence when reforms were not immediately forthcoming. From the promises made to Indian groups during the Revolution there arose a lasting commitment to "Indianism," a concept of Indian glorification that has since attempted to bring isolated Indian groups into the economic and social life of the national community. As part of this program, Indianist leaders have emphasized the need to imbue Indians with a sense of nationalism, to make them "know that they are Mexicans." By linking nationalist values to a positive appreciation of the Indian heritage of the national community, leaders have erased the conceptual barriers to Indian assimilation and have both changed the nature and enlarged the internal appeal of Mexican nationalism. Although barriers of economic isolation and Indian localism have proved much more resistant to change than the intellectual concepts of the Mexican elite, progress has been made toward the goal of economic and social assimilation. The continued adherence to Indianist goals by national leaders suggests that economic and cultural assimilation will continue.

The need for Indian support after 1910 reversed the prevailing *cientifico* view that effectively excluded most Indians from membership in the national community. Although supporters of the Porfirian regime on occasion made nationalistic statements that appeared to include the Indians, the expropriation of Indian lands indicated lack of true concern for them. The conceptual exclusion of Indians from the national community by Mexican leaders is reflected in a story told by the mother of Félix Díaz. Young Félix, at the age of six, was asked whether certain dead men that President Díaz had shown him were Mexicans, and he answered that two were Mexicans but "the others were Indians."[29] The participation of Indian fighters in the Revolution altered this viewpoint. At the battle of Santa María in which the Yaqui completely defeated and disarmed a large federal force,[30] for example, Mexican Indians gained prestige from their part in the revolutionary struggle. Pascual Orozco tried to win Indian support away from Madero, and Indians formed the core of Zapata's forces. The 1910 Revolution incorporated the Indian groups that had remained isolated in the struggles of the nineteenth century, as the vortex of the contest drew in Indian communities that for centuries had had only fleeting contacts with the Spanish and mestizo nucleus of the national population.[31]

While many Indians took part directly as fighters, others suffered invasions by contending forces and the privations of the years of violence. The Revolution increased contacts between Indians and other Mexicans, as Indians left their own communities to fight and as mestizos came into the Indian areas. As Indians mixed more freely with other Mexicans in a situation that underscored their inherent importance in the national framework, revolutionary leaders promised them land, opportunity, and national recognition.[32] These promises created a feeling that something

29. *The New York Times*, February 16, 1913, Part 5, p. 1:7.
30. Roberto Guzmán Esparza, ed., *Memorias de don Adolfo de la Huerta, según su propio dictado* (México: Ediciones "Guzmán," 1957), pp. 43-44.
31. Alfonso Caso and others, *Métodos y resultados de la política indigenista en México* (México: Ediciones del Instituto Nacional Indigenista, 1954), p. 260.
32. Madero's Plan of San Luis Potosí, Zapata's Plan of Ayala, Carranza's Veracruz decrees, and Article 27 of the 1917 Constitution formalized promises of the return of Indian lands. For a documentary summary of Indianist legislation with introductory comments, see Francisco González de Cossío and others, eds., *Legislación indigenista de México*, Instituto Indigenista Interamericano, Ediciones Especiales Núm. 38 (México: Unión Gráfica, S.A., 1958), pp. 79-110.

was coming to them, a sense that they should partake of the promised benefits of the state. After Madero's victory over Porfirio Díaz, American Consul Samuel E. Magill at Guadalajara reported Indian bands to be arming throughout his district in order to dispossess landholders. These bands did begin to take lands that once belonged to their ancestors, protesting that "Madero promised we should have them."[33]

The failure of promises to materialize immediately led Indians to renewed revolutionary activity and to an ultimate realization that they could participate, were in fact participating, in a broad national struggle beyond their isolated communities. The renewal of violence by the Yaqui Indians after Madero's triumph is a case in point. For several months after the Madero victory, the state government of Sonora fed the Yaqui, and their greatest mischief was stealing horses and cattle. Because they had aided Madero and his party, they were "promised everything" they asked. One promise that the Yaqui regarded as made was the restoration of all the lands they claimed on the Yaqui and Mayo rivers. Since much of this land belonged to innocent purchasers, including a number of American citizens, the promise was unfulfilled, and the Yaqui once again resorted to violence.[34] This action began with the wanton killing of two Mexicans in December, 1911, and continued with the deliberate burning of a railroad car with men, women, and children inside. In the case of the Yaqui, Orozquista rebels carefully cultivated the "non-fulfillment-of-promises sentiment," even though those in charge of this anti-Madero propaganda neither wanted nor expected the promises to be fulfilled.[35] In turn, the continuance of Indian agitation, participation, and destruction evoked renewed promises and new protestations of the Indians' importance to the national community. Initially

33. Samuel E. Magill to Knox, August 5, 1911, /2282.
34. Louis Hostetter to Knox, December 14, 1911, /2661.
35. Letcher to Knox, March 20, 1912, /3424.

arising to make the Indians fight for particular factions, these protestations now endeavored to channel the demands for land and opportunity into peaceful resolution.

While precedents arose in nineteenth-century Mexico for the *indigenismo* that flowered after the Revolution,[36] the equalitarian thrust of the Revolution itself precipitated the immediate and continuing ideological commitment to incorporation of the Indians in the Mexican national community. In 1913 Pedro Lamicq's *Piedad para el indio!* strongly pleaded for the material and moral uplifting of Mexico's Indian population and for their public acceptance as an integral part of the Mexican national community. Lamicq claimed that Indian toil produced the substance on which other Mexicans lived, argued cogently for full acceptance of the Indian as a "Mexican," and refuted depictions of the Indian as an outsider by sympathetically interpreting the common charges of Indian laziness and drunkenness.[37] Mexican anthropologists pointed out Indian achievements and capabilities, and reasoned polemics such as Manuel Gamio's *Forjando patria* showed the need for social and economic change while effectively pleading the cause of Indian assimilation. Mexicans found ample reason for nationalist resentment toward foreigners like Professor Albert Bushnell Hart at Harvard University who claimed, ethnocentrically and inaccurately, that "the fundamental trouble in all Latin-American countries, and particularly in Mexico, seems to be that the population is substantially of native American origin" and that the 14 million Mexicans not "of unmixed European race" have "not acquired the coolness and political reasonableness which are the basis of modern civilized governments."[38]

36. See Martin S. Stabb, "Indigenism and Racism in Mexican Thought: 1857-1911," *Journal of Inter-American Studies*, Vol. 1, No. 4 (October, 1959), especially 422-23.

37. Crater [Pedro Lamicq], *Piedad para el indio!* (México: n.p., 1913).

38. Albert Bushnell Hart, "The Postulates of the Mexican Situation," *The Annals of the American Academy of Political and Social Science*, Vol. 54 (July, 1914), 137.

Programs and attitudes in Mexico became frankly Indianist. After 1917 the Revolution gave rise to systematic and scientifically planned programs of Indian acculturation, programs specifically designed to incorporate the Indian groups into the national life of Mexico.[39] After purposefully detailing various contributions to Mexican society, Pastor Rouaix in 1929 candidly indicated the purpose and unifying significance of much Indianist literature by concluding that "as Mexicans we must strive so that in our Motherland differences disappear in order to unite us all. . . . We work, therefore, in this book of union and of love between the members of the great Mexican family, so that the eighty per cent of our fellow citizens, working class Indians and mestizos, may unite themselves and identify themselves with us."[40] Literature here reflected a shift in attitude and a new sense of self-discovery among Mexican leaders and intellectuals; the Indian rose to full citizenship in his country as far as the attitudes of the great majority of his fellow citizens were concerned. As Frank Tannenbaum noted, one purpose of the Indianism that followed the Revolution was Indian incorporation into the national community "as a means toward nationalism."[41]

Mexicans began to look back with great pride on the Indian heritage. Saying that "we Mexicans must know what are the true origins of our nationality," Francisco G. Cosmes had typically linked Mexican nationality to the Spanish inheritance and proudly proclaimed Hernando

39. For a retrospective statement of the programs' purpose by a leading Indianist, see Miguel León-Portilla, "La emancipación de la población indígena," in Norman Thomas and others, *Homenaje a la Revolución Mexicana, Combate,* edición especial, Vol. 2, Núm. 13 (noviembre, 1960), 43. For analysis of the changing attitudes that underlay the program, see Luis Villoro, *Los grandes momentos del indigenismo en México* (México: El Colegio de México, 1950).

40. Pastor Rouaix, *La influencia azteca en la República Mexicana* (Tacubaya, D.F.: Talleres Gráficos de la Secretaría de Agricultura y Fomento, 1929), p. 15.

41. Frank Tannenbaum, "Agrarismo, Indianismo, y Nacionalismo," *Hispanic American Historical Review,* Vol. 23, No. 3 (August, 1943), 420.

Cortés as "the first father of our nationality."[42] With the rise of *indigenismo* in the Revolution, however, Mexicans enfranchised the Indian element of the population by symbolically replacing Cortés with the Indian figure of Cuauhtémoc. For many years students of Indianism have emphasized that Mexico abounds with statues of Cuauhtémoc while statues of Cortés can not be found. Cuauhtémoc has become a truly national hero, and Mexican school texts, pictures, pamphlets, and histories recite Cuauhtémoc's bravery in defending the Aztec capital against Cortés and in withstanding the torture of the Spaniards who tried to make him reveal the hiding place of Aztec treasure. "Cuauhtémoc" has become a favorite first name in revolutionary Mexico.

In embracing the Indian heritage, Indianism also exalted the virtues, dances, songs, dress, and art of the Indians. While Mexicans showed new concern for the artistic and musical forms of the Indians themselves, Mexican artists depicted the previous exploitation of the Indian in a manner that demanded his present incorporation. Although a strain of "forthright criollismo" that José Vasconcelos came to represent rebutted Indianism,[43] many Mexicans with equally strong attachment to the church and to xenophobic nationalism came to look back with approval on the Catholic missionaries of the conquest as the first Indianists in Mexico.

While the predominance of Indianist material in Mexican art has fallen away, Indianism continues today to form an important part of the commitment of Mexican political leaders. President Gustavo Díaz Ordaz, in his successful 1964 campaign as candidate of the dominant Partido Revolucionario Institucional, emphasized Indianist themes in campaign speeches in the states of Oaxaca,

42. Francisco G. Cosmes, *La dominación española y la patria mexicana* (México: Imprenta de "El Partido Liberal," 1896), pp. 5-8, 80.

43. See Robert A. Potash, "Historiography of Mexico Since 1821," *Hispanic American Historical Review*, Vol. 40, No. 3 (August, 1960), 401.

Chiapas, Yucatán, Veracruz, Hidalgo, and Chihuahua. Finding 10.5 per cent of the Mexican population to be still separated as Indians by ethnic and linguistic characteristics from "the mestizo remainder of the population," Díaz Ordaz defined the Indian problem as cultural and economic rather than racial. He praised the ancient Indian civilizations, lauded Juárez and Altamirano as Indians, and affirmed José Martí's statement that "Mexico will be saved by her Indians." Decrying the fact that some Mexicans who happened to be Indians did not know that they were Mexicans, he committed his party to provide full national resources for combating poverty in Indian areas and assimilating isolated Indian groups into the nationalist framework.[44] This continuing political commitment to Indianism maintains an important impetus to assimilation, even though the size of the task that remains to be done underscores the difficulties of past efforts at assimilation.

While the significance of the national commitment to Indian assimilation should not be underestimated, neither should the practical difficulties of effecting assimilation. In 1922 the monumental field study of *La población del valle de Teotihuacán* directed by Manuel Gamio specifically addressed the question of the extent to which Indian groups had acquired a sense of Mexican nationalism. The study concluded that the Indians in rural areas surrounding Mexico City were "incapable of understanding the idea of the Motherland" and that, through ignorance, they had neither love for Mexico nor a desire to defend her national autonomy. The Indians were ignorant not only of the names of elected officials but of the political divisions the officials represented, and they frequently asked Gamio's investigators questions that showed a complete lack of contact with national events, such as whether Yankees still held the Veracruz coast. Elucidating the intense rivalry between

44. *Partido Revolucionario Institucional: Ideario de su candidato, Gustavo Díaz Ordaz* (3 vols.; México: n.p., 1964), Vol. 1, pp. 143-52, Vol. 2, pp. 141-46, Vol. 3, pp. 109-19.

individual Indian communities which spurred parochial allegiances, Gamio notes that the only manifestation of solidarity among the rural Indian groups was their local loyalty, "the absolute and almost irrational love which they feel for their town."[45]

Assimilation progressed only gradually after Gamio's survey. In the 1930's when Mexican educators went to Indian communities to study their incorporation into Mexican national life, as did Moisés Sáenz in the remote town of Carapan, Michoacán, they frequently encountered unexpectedly strong and persistent resistance to change and to national incorporation among the Indians.[46] After spending some months a decade later with the predominantly Indian population of the Chiapas interior, Dr. Sol Tax, an anthropologist from the University of Chicago, reported that "Mexico to almost all of them is a far away country as vague as Tibet is to us."[47] Recent Mexican studies of community development show Indian groups remaining isolated from the national community in the 1960's and maintaining their traditional forms of social organization and cohesion.[48] Accepting Díaz Ordaz' estimate of the Indian proportion of the national population at just over 10 per cent, between 3 and 4 million Mexicans still remain economically and culturally isolated in this group.

Although heavy financial commitment by the national government to economic development and education are the main prongs in its attack on Indian isolation, other programs also support the Indianist design. Mexican books and museums are providing a strong sense of national pride

45. Manuel Gamio, *La población del valle de Teotihuacán* (3 vols.; México: Dirección de Talleres Gráficos, Dependiente de la Secretaría de Educación Pública, 1922), Tomo 2, pp. 263-69.

46. Moisés Sáenz, *Carapan: Bosquejo de una experiencia* (Lima, Perú: Librería y Imprenta Gil, S.A., 1936), pp. vii, 48-56.

47. Sol Tax, "The Problem of Democracy in Middle America," *American Sociological Review*, Vol. 10, No. 2 (April, 1945), 195.

48. Ricardo Pozas Arciniega, *El desarrollo de la comunidad* (2d ed.; México: Universidad Nacional Autónoma de México, 1964), pp. 44-45.

in the pre-Columbian past. Such books as the colorful and provocative *Esplendor del México antiguo*[49] receive prominent display in Mexican libraries. While the Indian displays of local and regional museums have for some time given Mexicans a greater sense of connection with the Indian past, contemporary museums, such as the arresting new Museum of Anthropology that President López Mateos opened in 1964, consciously and effectively give Mexicans a sense of national pride in their Indian heritage.

The difficulties of implementing Indianist policies within Mexico is matched by resistance outside Mexico to accepting the Mexican ideal of racial harmony. France and Brazil stand out in their similar racial tolerance, but old resentments still thrive in areas like South Africa and parts of the United States. Communist China threatens the world with a racism in reverse which denigrates all whites. In contrast to Mexico, the incorporation of Indian elements in other Latin American countries with large Indian populations is either unconsidered, as in Ecuador, or only recently enunciated as a national problem and a national goal, as in Peru. The concept of racial equality has now won more general acceptance, however, than it had in the recent days of Kipling's white man's burden and of Nazi racial persecutions. Difficulties of implementation notwithstanding, the early and continuing Mexican acceptance of the ideal of Indian incorporation has resembled the advanced social doctrines of the 1917 Constitution in bringing Mexico racial and social attitudes that later in the twentieth century have gained salience in other parts of the world.

Mexico's prominence as an exemplar of the ideal of national integration is significant in the study of comparative politics regarding the question of why Indianism increased. The fact that before the second half of the twentieth century other Latin American countries with large Indian populations enjoyed no Indianist movements despite

49. Carmen Cook de Leonard and others, *Esplendor del México antiguo* (2 vols.; México: Centro de Investigaciones Antropológicas de México, 1959).

increasing miscegenation suggests that Mexican Indianism
did not advance simply because the mestizo and Indian elements gradually won overwhelming numerical dominance
over *criollos*. The increase in the size of the combined
Indian and mestizo group and their growing power in commercial and industrial enterprises were important, but they
do not fully account for the Indianist phenomenon. The
fact that successive Mexican governments imbued with
Indianist values have actively *fostered* economic growth
for the Indians suggests that Indianism has been more
than a societal response to twentieth-century requirements
for a type of co-ordinated industrial and agricultural society in which the activity of national populations works
for the common benefit. The elements of numerical dominance and developmental requirements have significance,
but the immediate impetus to Mexican Indianism came from
the activist spirit of Indian participation and equalitarianism of the 1910 to 1917 Revolution. Here, as in other areas,
Mexican pride in the social thrust of the Revolution is
indeed justified.

WORKERS

The participation of workers and trade unionists in the
military struggle after 1910 resembled that of Mexican
Indians in both nature and effect. Workers, who under
Porfirio Díaz had tried unsuccessfully to establish strong
organization and the right to strike, gained new organizational strength under Madero's permissiveness. Their importance as supporters and fighters provoked appeals to
them which promised rights and benefits in exchange for
adherence. Besides acknowledging labor's right to bargain
and to strike, appeals tried to win the backing of Mexican
workers by infusing a sense of "national purpose" into
their movement. The resulting military support of specific union detachments for the Carrancista victors in the

revolutionary contests provided, in addition to the formalization of labor demands in the 1917 Constitution, for the evolution of labor as one pillar of support for subsequent regimes and ultimately for the official Revolutionary party. The binding of the Mexican labor movement within the nationalist framework, which began through labor participation in the Revolution, has in the long run made it resistant to the foreign call of communism and has encouraged it to work through effective channels for the benefit of its members and of other Mexicans.

The Maderista victory over Porfirio Díaz in 1911 opened the door to new possibilities for organization and political activity by Mexican labor. Díaz had never allowed strikes to interfere with continuing business operations, and, by curtailing labor's bargaining power through this withholding of the right to strike, he had also prevented effective labor organization. Francisco Madero, basically in sympathy with the grievances of the workingman, allowed both strikes and union organization. The Casa del Obrero Mundial arose to spread anarchist I. W. W. propaganda similar to that of Flores Magón's followers. As the Casa built up its membership through the new freedom to proselytize, it gained in political power. Laborers and labor leaders awakened to the realization of their new privileges and began to look upon those privileges as rights. As they did so, strikes erupted throughout the republic which seriously added to the problems of instability facing the Madero government.[50] The early Maderista phase of the Revolution thus created an atmosphere of permissiveness in which a labor movement, which was to take an increasing part in the Revolution, grew in strength and self-confidence.

With approval of new powers for labor came appeals for labor support from the revolutionary factions. Madero's electoral program of August, 1911, Carranza's Veracruz decrees of December, 1914, and even the platform of

50. "Labor Unrest in Mexico," *The New York Times,* January 13, 1913, p. 10.

Félix Díaz' Reconstruction party promised major benefits to labor.[51] These appeals for support through concessions to labor demonstrated the political effect of labor's growing organizational strength and the possibility that labor might tip the military balance between competing groups.

Support from organized labor actually did help Álvaro Obregón win the decisive series of engagements with Pancho Villa. Illustrating the need for factions to grant recognition of rights in return for individual and group support, six ''Red Battalions'' of workers from the formerly syndicalist Casa del Obrero Mundial joined Carranza and Obregón against Villa in return for political recognition.[52] Even at their first engagement, the Red Battalions made a substantial military contribution through efficient handling of their rifles and impeccable discipline.[53] Through this military service, the Casa del Obrero Mundial won the right to organize labor behind the advancing Carrancista lines and influenced Obregón to back favorable labor legislation at the upcoming Constitutional Convention. The 1910 Revolution here differed from the major Mexican conflicts of the nineteenth century in that industrial workers and labor union members participated in the struggle as workers and unionists. Union members here used their military capability to win political leverage and national recognition.

Acceptance of workers and workers' organizations within the emerging nationalist framework resulted only partly from their participation in the revolutionary struggle. The simple fact that workers and peasants made up the armies

51. On August 31, 1911, *The Mexican Herald* published a copy of the Madero platform which is enclosed in Fred Morris Dearing to Knox, September 1, 1911, /2334. A copy of the Félix Díaz platform is enclosed in John H. Stephens to Bryan, September 12, 1913, /8837.

52. For a copy of the pact between Carranza and the Casa del Obrero Mundial, see Rosendo Salazar, *La Casa del Obrero Mundial* (México: Costa-Amic, Editor, 1962), pp. 129-31.

53. Antonio Rivera de la Torre, *El Ébano: Los 72 días de su heroica defensa* . . . (México: Imprenta del Departamento de Estado Mayor de la Secretaría de Guerra y Marina, 1915), p. 26.

of the 1910 Revolution did not, in itself, create commitment among Mexican leaders to the interpretation that the Revolution had been fought in their interests. Workers and peasants had formed the basis for all Mexican armies.[54] But by 1910 incipient industrialization was beginning to create an urban proletariat, and the direct participation of labor union troops in the later contests of the Revolution differentiated their role sharply from that of the artisans who fought in nineteenth-century armies. Champions of workers' rights, including delegates at the Constitutional Convention of 1916 and 1917, were able to argue that workers' wishes must be satisfied because workers had formed contingents in the revolutionary armies. The participation of workers in the armed conflict came consistently to serve as a handy justification for introducing social legislation and maintaining government policies in the interests of this group. Once Article 123 of the 1917 Constitution had enunciated its extensive goals and guarantees for Mexican labor, these goals could gradually be implemented as increasing Mexican prosperity made it possible. Reiterations of labor's dedication to national goals would inspire concern for raising productivity as well as wages and so would advance reinvestment and economic growth by not demanding that wage increases exceed increases in productivity. Acceptance of workers within the national framework continued, therefore, not simply because they had participated in the Revolution but also because their continued acceptance was in the long-term interests of labor, of the political leaders, and of the Mexican people.

Labor legislation and pro-labor government statements and policies fitted the needs of Mexican society by diverting the early radicalism of Mexican trade unionism into manageable collaboration. As the size of the industrial labor force increased later in the twentieth century, the new cadres of Mexican workers came into a system already

54. Víctor Alba, *Las ideas sociales contemporáneas en México* (México: Fondo de Cultura Económica, 1960), pp. 414-15.

officially dedicated to workers' welfare. The labor Congress of Tampico in October, 1917, and the formation of the Confederación Regional Obrera Mexicana (CROM) in May, 1918, marked the end of strong anarchosyndicalist influence within the Mexican labor movement. Under Lázaro Cárdenas, Vicente Lombardo Toledano organized the Confederación de Trabajadores de México (CTM) to swing labor support to the national leadership. Although Lombardo Toledano left the CTM and the Revolutionary party and has long worked in opposition to them, the CTM has continued to be the dominant voice of Mexican labor and today operates effectively within the structure of the Partido Revolucionario Institucional. As CTM leader Fidel Velázquez emphasizes, the CTM sees itself as a genuine product of the Mexican Revolution and, by eschewing foreign influences, works for the benefit of Mexican workers and the Mexican people.[55] This nationalist orientation has made labor a central element in the revolutionary power structure and counteracted the persistent efforts of Mexican Communists to subvert the Mexican labor movement into subservience to the international interests of the Soviet Union. Here, as in the earlier rejection of anarchosyndicalism, a nationalist orientation has won benefits for Mexican labor by making its power work with, rather than against, the power of other elements of Mexican society.

WOMEN

The Revolution of 1910 gave women new roles in Mexican society. Military technology allowed them to bear arms easily, and lady soldiers or *soldaderas* came to fight alongside men in the revolutionary armies. Advances in technology associated with the Industrial Revolution provided a host of new jobs for women to fill behind the lines, and in many tasks, women proved as capable as men. As the

55. Víctor Alba, *Historia del movimiento obrero en América Latina* (México: Libreros Mexicanos Unidos, 1964), pp. 443, 450-51.

Mexican soldiers' only commissariat, large numbers of women traveled with the troops to forage for food and to provide encouragement and companionship. Other women worked as clerks and secretaries, scouted for military intelligence, and smuggled in ammunition. A movement for feminine equality gained strength as revolutionary leaders recognized women's contributions and made nationalistic appeals to them. Like the technological advances that facilitated women's contributions, the organizing and demonstrating of suffragettes in western countries such as Britain and the United States in the years after 1910 had repercussions in Mexico. In addition to the influences of foreign feminism and of technological change, the situation of civil war molded the extent and nature of the Mexican movement for feminine equality.

The participation of women in the Revolution led, both during the period of violence and afterwards, to an ideological shift toward feminine emancipation. Although some special functions of the *soldaderas* terminated with the gradual return of domestic tranquility after 1917, women continued to fill many of the posts they had acquired during the Revolution as industrialization increased the demand for their services. A new spirit that stressed feminine participation in the Revolution and sought the inclusion of Mexican women in the national community continued unabated. Heroines, not only of the Revolution, but of the nineteenth century as well, gained new status in the national hagiology. As they did so, Mexican women as a group gained new status and national recognition that in turn affected their attitudes toward the national community.

Participation in the Revolution altered the pattern of familial loyalties, feminine subjugation, and isolation from national affairs that had long prevented Mexican women from acquiring a sense of membership in the national community. Before 1910, Mexican women lacked the contacts that would have given them a strong sense of nationalism. Their isolation significantly limited the rise of Mexican nationalism because, although discussions of nationalism usually fail to differentiate between masculine and feminine attitudes, the attitudes of women are important, not only in themselves, but also as they reappear in the attitudes that children derive at an impressionable age from their mothers and other female members of the household. The distinction between masculine and feminine attitudes had particular relevance in the nineteenth century when tradition gave women a pattern of life far different from that of men. During the colonial period and throughout the nineteenth century the ideal and primary role for *criollo* and mestizo women was the nurturing of children, and their daily routine was one of household and family affairs. The fact that only 8.82 per cent of Mexican women were economically active in 1910 evidences the widespread seclusion of women up to the time of the Revolution.[56] When their lives were primarily taken up in home and family affairs, it was only natural that women's primary loyalty should be to the family.

With scant educational opportunities to supplement their familial orientations, Mexican women manifested pronounced religious loyalties. Few Mexican women received any formal education. Rather than study subjects such as geography and national history, which might have given them some sense of a national community, the aristocratic ladies who received "an education" in the nineteenth century took up foreign languages and the fine arts. The nineteenth-century feminist movement in Europe and the United States influenced Mexico only slightly, and Mexico produced no pre-1910 counterparts of Susan B. Anthony and Mrs. Henry Fawcett. The few representations to the government made in the name of Mexican women during the nineteenth century exemplified their dedication to the

56. Daniel Moreno, *Los factores demográficos en la planeación económica* (México: Ediciones de la Cámara Nacional de la Industria de la Transformación, 1958), p. 240.

Catholic church, as did the plea for more church power which was sent to the framers of the 1857 Constitution with the names and apparent endorsements of nearly five hundred Mexican ladies.[57] Mexican women notoriously felt greater loyalty to the church than did the men. Carmen Díaz, the wife of don Porfirio, embodied the sentiments of many Indian and mestizo as well as *criollo* women when she promoted the interests of an ecclesiastical authority as it competed for loyalty with the nation and attempted to recover some of the power over national affairs that it had lost under Juárez. The fact that the church generally exercised much more influence over Mexican women than over Mexican men and opposed radical social and political reforms adds increased significance to the new role of women in the Mexican Revolution.

The travel and new occupations of Mexican women in the Revolution disrupted the pattern of isolation and exclusively familial and ecclesiastical loyalties. With the exception of Yaqui Indian troops, the Mexican soldiers in both federal and revolutionary ranks took their women along with them in the railway cars that carried belligerents from one part of Mexico to another. The *soldaderas* or *galletas* ("cookies," as they were sometimes called) provided a commissariat for Mexican troops, and both federal and revolutionary chieftains regularly provided for their transportation along with the troops in the major campaigns. The numbers of women who traveled with revolutionary armies was probably somewhat less than the number of men, but a great number of women from diverse parts of the republic participated in migrations of varying lengths during the long years of violence. Forced migrations also affected Mexican women. Victoriano Huerta's press gangs regularly conscripted women to cook and to

57. *Representación que las señoras de Guadalajara dirigen al soberano congreso constituyente sobre que en la carta fundamental que se discute, no quede consignada la tolerancia de cultos en la República* (Guadalajara, Jal.: Tipografía de Rodríguez, 1856).

work in the powder mills. In a tragic instance of forced migration, the Huerta government took three hundred Morelos peasant women from their families and sent them to Quintana Roo in hopes of forming a colony with the men who had been deported to that territory. Such a violent scramble for the women occurred when they reached Quintana Roo that officials shipped the women back to Veracruz and dumped them on the beach. There, separated from their families by hundreds of miles and completely lacking in food, clothing, and guidance, almost every woman bore a child.[58]

The *soldaderas* were exposed to various geographical regions and social groups from which they had previously been isolated, thus acquiring a deeper personal appreciation of the diversity that comprises the Mexican nation. In addition to new encounters, their travel removed them from regular family relationships. Huerta's conscription forceably removed women from family groups, and other women became separated when their husbands, fathers, and brothers left to fight and failed to return. Although *soldaderas* regularly attached themselves to individual soldiers and remained true to them, the women shifted to new protectors when their soldiers were killed or cast them off. This provided *soldaderas* with no regular family life, and it created a similarly unstable family pattern for the children by various fathers whom they carried with them.

Soldaderas came to play an unexpectedly significant role in the Revolution. Describing in detail the participation and leadership of numerous Mexican women, a 1911 article in *The New York Times* commented with surprise that "women have taken a spectacular part in the revolution."[59] Foreign journalists such as Tito L. Foppa, whom the Argentine review *Fray Mocho* sent to Mexico after the Madero assassination, marveled at the hardships the *sol-*

58. Edith O'Shaughnessy, *A Diplomat's Wife in Mexico* (New York: Harper & Brothers, 1916), pp. 58, 67, 124-25.
59. *The New York Times*, May 10, 1911, p. 2:5.

daderas underwent and praised them as martyrs of the Revolution.[60] Improvements in military technology made it feasible for women to participate militarily; guns were not only far more plentiful but also lighter and easier to carry than they had been in nineteenth-century Mexican engagements. With the shift from machetes and the cumbersome rifles of earlier revolts to improved weapons, many *soldaderas* took part in the actual fighting of the Revolution. Commonplace in collections of revolutionary photographs are pictures of these determined women with full skirts, cartridge belts over their shoulders, and six-shooters strapped at their waists. Some *soldaderas* showed such military proficiency that they were promoted to the rank of sergeant or lieutenant, and such women as Margarita Neri assumed command of large groups of followers. Besides fighting and supplying food, *soldaderas* fulfilled the less heroic but equally necessary tasks of providing fuel, clothing, and companionship for Mexican soldiers of all factions. They foraged for their men, nursed them, and buried them. With a degree of self-abnegation that surprised contemporary observers, they provided companionship that kept up morale and labor that provided the amenities on which the revolutionary armies subsisted.

The revolutionary situation itself propelled women into a wide range of new occupations. They were especially suited to the task of smuggling arms across the United States border, and during certain periods, women were caught nearly every day.[61] American soldiers searched all men on the streetcars running from El Paso into Ciudad Juárez, but women in only selected cars were forced to get off and be searched by an inspectress. Women came up to the front lines carrying medicines, ammunition, clothes, food, mail, military equipment, and information on the enemy. Behind the lines, women worked as dispatchers of

60. Tito L. Foppa, *La tragedia mexicana* (Barcelona: Buigas Pons y Ca., n.d.), p. 110.
61. George W. Wickersham to Knox, July 9, 1912, /4397.

trains, telegraphers, nurses, druggists, office employees, reporters, newspaper editors, businesswomen, and teachers.[62] As in belligerent countries during World Wars I and II, women assumed new occupations when men were needed elsewhere. Once women assumed the new jobs, they remained in them, as it became clear that technology permitted and encouraged their participation.

During the 1910 Revolution, Mexican men thus became united in new relationships to Mexican women. For the first time in Mexican history, women developed their potentialities on a large scale beside the men and won recognition as companions, mates, and partners.[63] Feminists publicized the new relationship, and Hermila Galindo proudly held Mexico up to other women of Latin America as a country where women worked profitably and fought valiantly side by side with men.[64] Both the participation and the publicity supported an enduring movement for female emancipation that championed wider activity for Mexican women within the national community.

Female participation in the revolutionary struggle reinforced the movement for emancipation, as leaders appealed to Mexican women with promises of greater equality of rights and privileges. Revolutionaries enacted legislation designed to aid women, and they upbraided practices such as prostitution that cut women off from national loyalties. Appeals and legislation added momentum to the civic participation of women's groups and the movement for women's suffrage that formed between 1910 and 1917. As the nascent movement for female emancipation gained force and acceptance, it established a basis of public sym-

62. Laura Palavicini, ''La mujer en la historia de México,'' in Thomas and others, *Homenaje a la Revolución Mexicana*, p. 51. See also [María de los] Angeles Mendieta Alatorre, *La mujer en la Revolución Mexicana* (México: Biblioteca del Instituto Nacional de Estudios Históricos de la Revolución Mexicana, 1961).

63. Santiago Ramírez, *El mexicano: Psicología de sus motivaciones* (3d ed.; México: Editorial Pax-México, 1961), p. 127.

64. Hermila Galindo, *La doctrina Carranza y el acercamiento indolatino* (México: n.p., 1919), p. 188.

pathy and support on which its objectives won implementation after 1917.

The revolutionaries appealed to women as Mexicans to support their causes and become participants in the Revolution. In the short manifesto against Pancho Villa published on November 17, 1914, Obregón exclaimed on behalf of the Constitutionalists, "Mothers, wives and daughters!: kneel before the Altar of the Motherland and bring to the ear of your sons, husbands and fathers the sacred call of Duty, and cursed be those who, forgetting every principle of honor, place themselves in the hands of treason to stab the Motherland."[65] General Salvador Alvarado stated an ideological basis of such appeals by declaring, "UNLESS WE ELEVATE WOMAN, IT WILL BE IMPOSSIBLE FOR US TO CONSTRUCT A MOTHERLAND."[66] As part of his program for the economic reconstruction and social regeneration of Yucatán between 1915 and 1918, General Alvarado consciously tried to implement promises made to Mexican women. A leading revolutionary, he worked to raise and dignify their status through a program of educating women in the rights of citizenship, through the convocation of feminist congresses, and through propaganda designed to make all citizens of Yucatán respect the rights of women.

As a result of the appeals of revolutionary leaders and attempts at implementation, persistent calls developed for the incorporation of Mexican women into the national community. Most literary recreations and tributes to the Revolution contain sections on the role of Mexican women and often use such praise of female participation to underscore pleas for acknowledgment of the full membership of Mexican women in the Mexican nation.

Legislation also tried to substantiate the appeals made to Mexican women. Carranza's family legislation, which made it possible for women to obtain divorces on a variety

65. Obregón, *Ocho mil kilómetros en campaña*, p. 227.
66. Salvador Alvarado, *Mi actuación revolucionaria en Yucatán* (México: Librería de la Vda. de Ch. Bouret, 1918), p. 45. The capitalization is Alvarado's.

of grounds including prolonged absence of the husband, was formulated with the express purpose of giving women legal equality and preventing male domination.[67] Article 123 of the 1917 Constitution provided working women with childbirth benefits and with protection against night work and certain types of heavy and dangerous labor. By emphasizing the rights given to natural sons and "blotting out" the stigma of illegitimacy,[68] revolutionaries tried to aid the mothers of illegitimate children as well as the children themselves.

The campaign for women's welfare included efforts to alleviate the condition of prostitutes, whose numbers were inordinately great before the Revolution and swelled alarmingly during the revolutionary upheaval. In 1905 Luis Lara y Pardo found that Mexico City alone had 11,554 registered prostitutes in a total population of 368,000 and that the concentration of prostitutes between 15 and 30 years of age meant that, for this age group, 120 women per thousand were registered prostitutes in the Inspection of Health. This did not include the number of unregistered prostitutes, of whom 4,371 were apprehended in 1905.[69] As in the French Revolution,[70] the number of prostitutes in Mexico increased sharply after 1910. Hunger, the specter that stalked all Mexican cities and especially Mexico City, forced women into prostitution. Girls who had just reached puberty practiced prostitution to acquire the bean and bran bread that was substituted for corn tortillas.[71] Foreign

67. *Ley sobre relaciones familiares expedida por el C. Venustiano Carranza, primer jefe del ejército constitucionalista, encargado del poder ejecutivo de la nación* (México: Imprenta del Gobierno, 1917), pp. 7, 27.

68. Luis Cabrera, *El balance de la Revolución* (México: n.p., 1931), p. 30.

69. Luis Lara y Pardo, *La prostitución en México* (México: Librería de la Vda. de Ch. Bouret, 1908), pp. 19-20, 27.

70. For comparative statistics, see Pitirim A. Sorokin, *The Sociology of Revolution* (Philadelphia, Pa.: J. B. Lippincott Company, 1925), p. 94.

71. Manuel González Ramírez, ed., *La caricatura política* (Vol. 2, "Fuentes para la Historia de la Revolución Mexicana"; México: Fondo de Cultura Económica, 1955), p. 77. See also U.S., Congress, Senate, Committee on Foreign Relations, *Investigation of Mexican Affairs*, 66th Cong., 2d sess., Sen. Doc. 285 (2 vols.; Washington, 1920), Vol. 1, p. 1434.

prostitutes were known to inhabit certain areas. Charles Jenkinson observed that of the several hundred prostitutes who established themselves in Veracruz immediately after the American occupation about one-half were Mexican while the others were French, Spanish, Cuban, and North American.[72] Although some prostitutes in the republic were foreign, most of the girls whom hunger and revolutionary disorder forced into prostitution were Mexican.

Nationalism had little chance to spread among the prostitutes who were of Mexican nationality. Their profession did not automatically prevent these women from holding nationalistic values, but it did tend to produce a group lacking fixed allegiances, to the nation as well as to the family and to individuals. Painters like José Clemente Orozco uncompromisingly condemned prostitution in paintings such as the "House of Tears" series done as early as 1912 and 1913 and the later works "Loca," "La Victoria," and the "Catharsis" fresco in the Palace of Fine Arts.[73] The high incidence of prostitution during the Revolution stimulated new concern for Mexican women and for bettering their condition.

Another reason for concern with women's welfare was the organized strength they demonstrated in the Revolution. *Ad hoc* and enduring women's groups, which sprang up in various parts of Mexico, gave women practice in organizing and pointed up women's political significance. With other groups, the feminist club Hijas de Cuauhtémoc marched in protest against the Porfirio Díaz regime in Mexico City on September 11, 1910.[74] More than a thousand Mexican women signed a petition asking for Díaz' resignation, which finally caused his wife to advise his with-

72. Charles Jenkinson, ''Vera Cruz, What American Occupation Has Meant to a Mexican Community,'' *Survey*, Vol. 33, No. 6 (November 7, 1914), 137.

73. James B. Lynch, ''Orozco's *House of Tears*,'' *Journal of Inter-American Studies*, Vol. 3, No. 3 (July, 1961), 376-77.

74. Blas Urrea [Luis Cabrera], *Obras políticas del lic. Blas Urrea . . .* (México: Imprenta Nacional, S.A., 1921), p. 327.

drawal.[75] When Félix Díaz capitulated after his eight-day occupation of Veracruz in October, 1912, a group of ladies visited President Madero to plead for Díaz' life. Although they withdrew indignant and angry when Madero promised only impartiality,[76] Madero soon commuted the court-martial sentence on Díaz from death to life imprisonment. As these and other female groups made active political demands, national leaders began to take them into account even though the women lacked the right to vote. In addition to the groups that made demands on behalf of particular candidates and factions, other women's groups formed to promote special projects. The ladies of Puerto Mexico joined together in February, 1913, to form a city betterment committee; elected a president, secretary, and treasurer; and planned public celebrations with the purpose of raising money to reconstruct the public park.[77]

Female groups working for factional interests and public projects complemented those groups working directly for women's rights. Suffragist sentiment solidified early in the Revolution, and in May, 1911, several hundred women signed a letter to interim President de la Barra which requested votes for women and pointed out that the 1857 Constitution did not bar them from voting since it made no mention of the sex of voters.[78] Declaring it to be time that Mexican women recognized that their "rights and obligations go much farther than just the home," a manifesto of the Cuauhtémoc feminist league called for political enfranchisement and the full emancipation of Mexican women in their "economic, physical, intellectual and moral struggles."[79] Violence sometimes attended the early suf-

75. *The New York Times*, May 8, 1911, p. 2:2.
76. Stanley R. Ross, *Francisco I. Madero: Apostle of Mexican Democracy* (New York: Columbia University Press, 1955), pp. 273-74.
77. *El Imparcial*, February 22, 1913, p. 4:6-7.
78. *The New York Times*, June 1, 1911, p. 2:2.
79. A translation of the manifesto appears in C. J. Velarde, *Under the Mexican Flag: The Mexican Struggle Outlined* (Los Angeles, Calif.: Southland Publishing House, Inc., 1926), pp. 307-8.

frage movement in Mexico. At one suffrage demonstration, nine persons were reported killed and many wounded when *rurales* tried to preserve order in a crowd that began to parade with Mexican women in Santa Julia, one of the poorest districts of Mexico City, on June 5, 1911.[80]

The concern of Mexican women for suffrage came partly from events abroad. The literate women of leisure discovered, during the Revolution, a series of feminist articles and reports in Mexican periodicals such as the *Revista de Revistas*. In 1913 and 1914 alone, for instance, the *Revista de Revistas* carried fourteen articles on female equality in England, Europe, the United States, and Japan, extensive illustrated descriptions of suffragette activities, and moving statements of women's intellectual equality and their need for legal equality. It printed articles by Mrs. Carrie Chapman Catt and Lady Lillian Glenworth; descriptions of women entering new fields such as law, police work, and the armed services; and references and quotations from such feminist literature as Olive Schreiner's *Women and Labor* and Cicely Hamilton's *Marriage As a Trade*.[81] With its basis of demands made during the 1910 Revolution, political enfranchisement became a formalized goal of Mex-

80. *The New York Times,* June 6, 1911, p. 1:1.
81. While Mexican newspapers gave extensive coverage to the suffrage movement along with their major coverage of the Revolution, local events, and World War I, the *Revista de Revistas* contained far more suffragette information than did other periodicals such as the humor magazines. In lieu of voluminous content analysis of the coverage of the suffrage movement by a wide range of periodicals for the 1910 to 1917 period, a comprehensive view of the kinds of information and ideas imparted to Mexican women may be found in the 1913 and 1914 issues of the *Revista de Revistas.* See ''El porvenir de la mujer,'' *Revista de Revistas,* Año 4, Núm. 155 (26 enero 1913), 16; Jean Finot, ''La mujer del porvenir,'' *ibid.,* Núm. 168, p. 14; Francois de Tessan, ''La odisea de una sufragista,'' *ibid.,* Núm. 169, p. 20; 'Las mujeres-gendarmes,'' *ibid.,* Núm. 170, p. 21; ''Lo que piden las mujeres,'' *ibid.,* Núm. 174, p. 23; ''Intelectualidad feminina,'' *ibid.,* Núm. 176, p. 22; ''Mi feminismo,'' *ibid.,* Núm. 189, p. 16; Francois de Tessan, ''Las nuevas mujeres del Japón,'' *ibid.,* Núm. 200, p. 20; ''La sufragista de las rosas,'' *ibid.,* Año 5, Núm. 207, p. 6; ''Impresiones de una sufragista,'' *ibid.,* Núm. 216, p. 7; ''El celibato contra las sufragistas,'' *ibid.,* Núm. Extra (17 mayo 1914), 7; ''Los triunfos del feminismo,'' *ibid.,* Núm. 218, pp. 5-7; Lillian Glenworth, ''Por que soy sufragista,'' *ibid.,* Núm. 223, p. 7; and ''Literatura sufragista,'' *ibid.,* Núm. 236, p. 13.

ican women in a long series of conferences in the 1920's and 1930's.

Feminist pressure gradually won enfranchisement. On May 14, 1925, Chiapas became the first state to grant women complete equality to vote and to serve as candidates in state and municipal elections. Throughout the republic, women gained the right to vote and to be elected in municipal elections in 1947. When women won full suffrage in national elections in 1953, the victory represented not only the culmination of a successful campaign but also acquiescence to a demand initiated during the violence of the Revolution.

National heroines received greatly increased recognition with the coming of the Revolution. Praise abounded for both revolutionary heroines and a host of pre-1910 heroines whom feminists resuscitated and glorified as champions of Mexico. The creation of national heroines, like the revolutionary participation of Mexican women and the movement for female emancipation, showed the 1910 Revolution to be a turning point in the commitment of Mexican women to participation in national affairs.

The women in President Francisco Madero's family displayed a quiet dedication and heroism that makes them well remembered as revolutionary heroines. Sara Pérez de Madero, the president's wife who was described as ''a dark type of New England woman'' who ''gives an impression of valiance without any hint of worldliness,''[82] followed her husband constantly throughout his long political campaigns, revolutionary battles, and uneasy presidential term. Maderista troops and chroniclers took pride in the fact that she shared the ideals and hardships of her husband. One of many descriptions of her popularity was reported by *The New York Times* after the triumph over Porfirio Díaz:

A few moments later down the main thoroughfare was heard the galloping of horses, and soon the insurrecto standard, the

82. Edith O'Shaughnessy, *Diplomatic Days* (New York: Harper & Brothers, 1917), p. 75.

Mexican national colors, flashed in the sunlight. Behind it rode Mrs. Francisco I. Madero, Jr., and an escort of cavalry. Her face was beaming with joy, her black dress covered with dust. She spurred her horse to her husband's side. The shouting increased as the two embraced and entered the municipal building. . . .[83]

During the military engagements, she devoted her time to caring for the wounded and improving sanitary conditions, and she personally toured battle areas to see that proper burial was given to the dead.[84] Later she supported numerous altruistic projects, including an attempt to ameliorate the lot of Mexican women by organizing a lace and embroidery industry.[85]

The other women of the Madero househould—Francisco's mother Mercedes González de Madero, his sisters Mercedes and Angela, and the wives of Alfonso and Gustavo Madero—aided the Revolution by encouraging the insurgents, by embroidering a flag, and even during Madero's plotting in the United States, by singing around the piano to allay the suspicions of the North American police.[86] The Madero women all made heavy financial sacrifices to support the Revolution, and young Angela even gave up such inexpensive pleasures as going to the movies to buy cartridges for the fighting in Chihuahua.[87]

The Revolution produced a host of other heroines who won recognition from Mexican citizens. By exhorting Madero's cause, the women in the family of Aguiles Serdán came to share his famous martyrdom, and they fought to the death in his scheduled but premature uprising against the Díaz regime. Each faction had its heroines, from Delfina Morales, another early martyr of the Maderistas, to Elisa Acuña y Rossetti, who worked for Flores Magón's Liberals in Mexico City and signed the manifesto of February 27,

83. *The New York Times,* May 11, 1911, p. 2:1.
84. *Ibid.,* May 12, 1911, p. 2:5.
85. O'Shaughnessy, *Diplomatic Days,* p. 335.
86. Federico González Garza, *La Revolución Mexicana: Mi contribución político-literaria* (México: A. del Bosque, 1936), p. 255.
87. Roque Estrada, *La Revolución y Francisco I. Madero: Primera, segunda y tercera etapas* (Guadalajara, Jal.: Imprenta Americana, 1912), p. 442.

1903. The latter went into exile with other Liberals and returned to Mexico with the Revolution to fight for Emiliano Zapata until his death. Women also demonstrated ability to command troops; Margarita Neri kept seven hundred Indian troops in reserve and sent three hundred Indians into a battle in which, under the command of an eighteen-year-old girl who was wounded fighting in the front rank, they finally defeated the opposing federals.[88]

Such heroism quite naturally received sympathetic interpretation from Mexican artists. Depicting *soldaderas* in individual portraits, battle scenes, and on the covers of widely distributed popular ballad sheets, José Guadalupe Posada uniformly portrayed them as beautiful, well-groomed, and determined young ladies.[89] Today even the comic books that are so popular in Mexico paint a romanticized but flattering picture of the lady revolutionaries. In "La coronela," in the *Leyendas de Pancho Villa* series, for instance, a poor peasant girl from the mountains becomes the respected leader of a revolutionary band that steals from the rich to give to the poor. She finally engages a teacher to instruct her men in reading after she sees that they lack education.[90]

Secretaries and suffragettes also became heroines. Soledad González, noted for her patriotism and revolutionary dedication, successively served as private secretary for Francisco Madero, Álvaro Obregón, and Plutarco Elías Calles. When, in an interview with a newspaperman, Señorita González was asked how and why she had become imbued with the ideals of the revolutionary cause, she candidly explained that her contact as a youth with Francisco Madero had given her the civic fervor that Madero

88. *Washington Herald*, August 18, 1911, in U.S., Library of Congress MSS collection, *Newspaper Clippings pertaining to Mexico, 1911-1913*, 3 vols.; III-48-C,1, Ac. 6194, Vol. 2.

89. Jaled Muyaes, ed., *La Revolución Mexicana vista por José Guadalupe Posada* (México: Talleres "Policromía," 1960), pp. 38, 44, 48.

90. Roberto Durón, adaptor, "La coronela," *Leyendas de Pancho Villa*, Año 1, Núm. 38 (10 junio 1964).

later instilled in other Mexicans.[91] One who later became a heroine of the women's suffrage movement, Señora Hermila Galindo de Topete, also worked before her marriage as a private secretary for Venustiano Carranza, and it is possible that she influenced his liberalization of divorce legislation in the Decree of December 29, 1914, and the amendment of the Civil Code of the Federal District and Territories in January, 1915. Carranza allowed her to spread feminist literature in the states of Veracruz, Tabasco, Campeche, Yucatán, San Luis Potosí, Coahuila, and Nuevo León. In September, 1915, with Artemisa Sáenz Royo and others, she founded the feminist magazine *Mujer Moderna,* which continued publication until 1919. It was she who persuaded General Salvador Alvarado to hold the first feminist congress in Yucatán, and she sent the Constitutional Convention at Querétaro a strong plea to grant women the franchise.[92]

In addition to creating contemporary heroines, the revolutionary impetus to feminism and nationalism revived heroines of the past. Mexican periodicals took new interest in the heroines of the Mexican independence movement a hundred years earlier. The *Revista de Revistas* celebrated Josefa Ortiz de Domínguez, whose indispensable warning to Miguel Hidalgo has given her a well-recognized place in Mexico's pantheon, and also the lesser known heroines Leona Vicario, Gertrudis Bocanegra de Lazo de la Vega, Mariana Rodríguez de Lazarín, Manuela Medina, Rita Pérez, and Luisa Martínez, whose credentials range from serving as captain among the insurgents to suffering long prison terms for financing and planning the independence movement.[93] As the feminist movement gained strength

91. Clodoveo Valenzuela and Amado Chaverri Matamoros, *Sonora y Carranza* . . . (México: Casa Editorial ''Renacimiento'' de G. Sisniega y Hno., 1921), p. 515.

92. Ward M. Morton, *Woman Suffrage in Mexico* (Gainesville, Fla.: University of Florida Press, 1962), pp. 2-6.

93. Noé Aguilar, ''Heroinas de la independencia,'' *Revista de Revistas,* Año 4, Núm. 185 (14 septiembre 1913), 16-17.

during the Revolution, articles appeared alleging that famous Mexicans of the past, among them novelist José Joaquín Fernández de Lizardi, had in fact favored feminine emancipation.[94] Writing in 1917, Jesús Romero Flores dedicated a full chapter in his *Labor de raza* to the "glory and honor" of the "forgotten" heroines of the independence.[95] In popular fiction, as well as histories since 1917, the lionization of national heroines from all periods of Mexican history has not only continued but increased substantially.

Women of all social classes in Mexico today look back on the Revolution of 1910 as the significant initiator of their political rights and their social emancipation. Feminists allegorically describe the effect of the Maderista and Constitutionalist revolutions on female national participation as eyes opening for the first time, a door opening upon sunlight, or a bird finding its wings. Without exception, in interviews and discussions with Mexican women, one is struck by the unanimity with which they ascribe the initiating role of the Revolution and the sharp break in the year 1910 to their participation in national affairs. Linking the change in attitude to national awareness, feminists emphasize that by the end of the period of revolutionary violence the feelings of "the Mexican woman" had changed totally and she had come to feel that she "must be prepared to aid in the development of her motherland and her people."[96] Although studies of the psychology of Mexican women stress their passivity, subordination, and familial loyalty, their daring and energy as evidenced in the Revolution are also depicted; Adelita and Valentina, heroines of the Revolution, are found to be the essence of

94. José de J. Núñez y Domínguez, " 'El Pensador Mexicano,' feminista," *Revista de Revistas,* Año 5, Núm. 242 and subsequent numbers.

95. Jesús Romero Flores, *Labor de raza* (Morelia, Mich.: n.p., 1917), pp. 35-41.

96. Ana María Flores, "La mujer en la sociedad," in *La vida social* (Vol. 2, *México, cincuenta años de Revolución;* 4 vols.; México: Fondo de Cultura Económica, 1960-62), p. 333.

Mexican femininity; and it is suggested that Mexican women of the Revolution followed as partners the same path as Mexican men because they shared the same ideal.[97]

Amid a welter of women's organizations and substantial female participation in high professional posts, women's activities in Mexican national life today receive official endorsement and encouragement that reflect the praise of Mexican women of the past. Official encouragement reflects the fact that, with a keen sense of national dedication and public service, numerous Mexican women have assumed prominent positions in the fields of higher education, library directorship, medicine, journalism, government service, music, and literature.[98] Mexican women now belong to many interest and professional organizations such as the Ateneo de Mujeres, the Alianza de Mujeres de México, the Club Internacional de Mujeres, and the Asociación de Escritoras y Periodistas de México. Their political influence is crystallized in the Sociedad de Técnicas y Profesionales and the Mujeres Revolucionarias in the Popular sector of the dominant Partido Revolucionario Institucional.

Retrospective views of the Revolution are not, however, all positive. The abuse and sexual license that occurred during those years alienated certain individuals, particularly women, from revolutionary "heroes" and revolutionary goals. The negative view is typified in Gabriel Almond and Sidney Verba's illustrative case history of Señora S., who has no pride in her country and says that the Mexican Revolution meant "nothing more than going around stealing and violating girls."[99] Furthermore, cultural attitudes still retard full national participation among

97. M. Loreto H., *Personalidad (?) de la mujer mexicana* (México: Impresora Galve, S.A., 1961), pp. 153-54.

98. See the biographies and representative statements in Rosalía d' Chumacero, *Perfil y pensamiento de la mujer mexicana* (México: Edición de la Autora, 1961), published by the Asociación de Escritoras y Periodistas de México.

99. Gabriel A. Almond and Sidney Verba, *The Civic Culture: Political Attitudes and Democracy in Five Nations* (Princeton, N.J.: Princeton University Press, 1963), p. 428.

Mexican women; for the most part they remain subservient within the Mexican family structure and do not utilize advanced divorce legislation for fear of social ostracism.[100] As in other countries, cultural attitudes inherited from the past retard the national participation that can only gain impetus from the need to raise living standards for all citizens by utilizing the brainpower potential of Mexican women. In Mexico the cultural lag is not so great as in other developing countries, however, specifically because of the movement for feminine incorporation initiated in the Revolution. Here, as in the cases of Indians and organized labor, participation in the Revolution led to a pattern of increased participation in national affairs.

100. Nathan L. Whetten, *Rural Mexico* (Chicago: University of Chicago Press, 1948), p. 396.

VI
Xenophobia and the Revolution

Between 1910 and 1917, repeated outbursts of xenophobia helped to solidify and extend the self-consciousness of the Mexican national community. Motivated by economic jealousy and personal antagonism, by patriotic fear and by factional advantage, xenophobia became manifest in intense and demonstrable forms throughout the republic. As Frederick Palmer predicted after visiting Mexico to write a series of articles for *The New York Times,* the direct result of xenophobia was that citizens in all parts of Mexico, "both the men of the plateau and the men of the lowlands," came gradually to ascertain that they were "all Mexicans."[1]

North American actions stimulated xenophobia by stirring Mexican fears. The mistreatment of individual Mexicans, the diplomatic intrigues of Henry Lane Wilson, and such official acts as successive army mobilizations, the occupation of Veracruz, and Pershing's expedition aroused Mexican resentment and increased fears of more widespread American intervention. Reinforcing Mexicans' mistrust of the United States was their characteristic sensitivity, their inherent tendency to mistrust all men and ideas, and their inclination to perceive casual gestures and

1. *The New York Times,* November 20, 1910, Part 5, p. 9:7.

words as a personal affront.[2] Protestations of patriotism in both the North American and the Mexican press only inflamed antagonisms already kindled by the rivalry with foreign soldiers in the revolutionary armies, by the rousing of Mexican youth against the United States, and by the antagonizing of specific revolutionary factions through the failure to recognize Huerta and the subsequent alienation of Villa. Fears of actually precipitating United States intervention limited the extent of xenophobia, however, as did individual attitudes caused by isolation, economic interests, or personal friendships. Despite such limitations, the outbreaks of antiforeignism that initially stimulated Mexican nationalism between 1910 and 1917 have since that period come to serve as a principal focus for the continuing growth and development of nationalism in Mexico.

THE INTENSITY OF XENOPHOBIA AND ITS MANIFESTATIONS

Some of the most violent manifestations of xenophobia during the Revolution were those directed against Chinese immigrants. Far from being aggressive troublemakers, these immigrants seemed inoffensively industrious, but anti-Chinese sentiment erupted dramatically in the Torreón massacre of 1911. In a vicious battle that ran from May 13 to May 15, Maderista troops, with slight apparent provocation,[3] massacred Chinese in and around the city of Tor-

2. For an extended and generally accepted discussion of the implications of Mexican national sensitivity, see Samuel Ramos, *El perfil del hombre y la cultura en México* (3d ed.; Buenos Aires: Espasa-Calpe Argentina, S.A., 1952), pp. 58-60.

3. One cause of the Torreón massacre reported in *The New York Times* was several bottles of poisoned cognac that the Maderistas looted from a courthouse storeroom where the cognac had been placed after a court investigation of a wholesale poisoning attempt several years before. The looting Maderistas allegedly took the cognac to a Chinese restaurant, where they drank it with breakfast, and assumed incorrectly that the Chinese were responsible for the resultant poisoning which killed several of the breakfasters and made the rest ill. See *The New York Times*, June 11, 1911, p. 4:3. Even if this report is accurate, it provides only the initial impetus to the massacre. The grotesque proportions that the massacre assumed and the

reón. Dr. J. W. Lim, one of the wealthiest Chinese in northern Mexico and head of a Chinese banking institution, "was dragged, at the end of a rope which had been tied around his neck, around the plaza until his body was badly crushed" and then was shot.[4] On May 15, the final day of the massacre, rioters indiscriminately shot down or stabbed the Orientals, killing a reported 206 Chinese.[5] A number of Chinese bodies remained for some time in the wells into which they were thrown and were still there in June when Wu Lan-pee, an official of the Chinese Legation who investigated the massacre, announced that over 300 Chinese had been killed.[6]

Outbreaks of anti-Chinese mob violence in Sonora, Sinaloa, Chihuahua, Durango, and Nuevo León followed the Torreón massacre. American consuls reported that scores of Chinese were robbed and cruelly mistreated. Chinese stores were raided and their owners beaten, and stripping Chinese naked in the streets became a common type of persecution.

No single explanation fully accounts for the Chinese persecutions and the underlying xenophobia they reveal. China was too weak to protest effectively, so in one sense, the Chinese became victims of a general xenophobia that might have been demonstrated toward Americans or Europeans had their governments not been capable of making reprisals. Furthermore, the Chinese were easily distinguished by physical characteristics and their poor ability to speak Spanish; they were more "visible" objects of hatred than other groups, like the Spaniards, who could not be so readily identified among the Mexican population. More basic reasons for the violence, however, were economic competition and the general belief among Mexicans that the Chinese had become a wealthy and privileged

---

later Chinese persecutions still amply demonstrate the depth of anti-Chinese feelings.

4. *The New York Times*, May 22, 1911, p. 3:3.
5. *Ibid.*, May 23, 1911, p. 2:3.
6. *Ibid.*, June 9, 1911, p. 22:1.

group.[7] Continuing antagonism and the competition for feminine companionship—Chinese colonists were overwhelmingly composed of male workers and shopkeepers—resulted not only in revolutionary violence but also in the 1923 and 1930 Sonoran laws that forbid both marriage and concubinage between Mexicans and Chinese. The violence and frustration of battle encouraged revolutionaries to give vent to these underlying antagonisms, especially when the Chinese shopkeepers refused to sell their goods at the prices demanded. The persecutions of Chinese are significant, therefore, in that they demonstrate an intensity of xenophobia not leveled at better protected and less "visible" groups and also reveal underlying feelings of jealousy and competition.

Manifestations of hostility toward Spaniards also became particularly strong during the Revolution. When over forty Spaniards had been killed by April, 1911, Spanish subjects in Mexico sent a petition with 20,000 signatures to King Alfonso XIII informing him of the "deplorable situation."[8] Throughout his career, Pancho Villa felt a deep personal repugnance for Spaniards, and Villistas became known for their lack of leniency with Spanish prisoners. One of Villa's first acts after taking Chihuahua in December, 1913, was to decree the explusion of all Spanish subjects from the state, allowing them under penalty of death only ten days to depart.[9] While many Americans went unharmed through Zapata's territory in and around the state of Morelos, Zapatistas showed no similar leniency toward Spanish subjects.

The cause for anti-Spanish sentiment was based on the same competitive antagonism made evident in the Chinese persecutions. Memories of Mexico's long struggle with Spain between 1810 and 1824 made it easy to stir popular

7. Charles C. Cumberland, "The Sonora Chinese and the Mexican Revolution," *Hispanic American Historical Review*, Vol. 40, No. 2 (May, 1960), 206, 210-11.

8. *The New York Times*, April 29, 1911, p. 2:2.

9. Marion Letcher to William Jennings Bryan, December 11, 1913, /10167.

resentment against individual Spaniards. The antipathy
toward Spain evidenced by Mexicans after 1810 and 1910
has remained active in an interesting form today. Despite
their enthusiastic hospitality to defeated Spanish Republicans and Republican organizations after the Spanish
Civil War of 1937 to 1939, Mexicans have remained adamantly hostile to General Franco's Spain. There remain
staunch and conservative Hispanophiles in Mexico today,
as there have been at each stage of Mexico's history, but
as a whole, the Mexican national community has continued
uniquely united in its warm support for the exiled Republican cause and its firm opposition to the ideological tenets
of the Franco regime. In 1910, however, rather than representing an admired intelligentsia who helped to staff Mexican universities and periodicals as did the Republican
émigrés, Spaniards still owned many of the small commercial establishments. The fact that Spaniards controlled
the grocery and liquor traffic and usually owned the general
stores in small towns made them particularly liable to loss
of property and the resentment that caused xenophobic
attacks. With Spaniards predominant as overseers on
haciendas and as principal owners of pawnshops, the every-
day duties of many Spaniards further aroused Mexican
anger.[10]

The resentment against Spaniards as managers and
property holders raises the more general question of economic motivation for Mexican xenophobia. Competition
for jobs, for property, and for economic status apparently
did make many Mexicans dislike individual foreigners and
by extension dislike "foreigners" as a whole. The often
repeated phrase that under the Díaz administration Mexico had become "the mother of foreigners and the step-
mother of Mexicans" emphasizes the connection most Mexicans saw between the preferential treatment given to

10. Edith O'Shaughnessy, *A Diplomat's Wife in Mexico* (New York:
Harper & Brothers, 1916), p. 94.

foreigners and their own exclusion from the *científico* conception of the national community.

Taking advantage of the absence of restraining central authority between 1910 and 1917, Mexicans manifested their pent-up feelings concerning foreign predominance and changed the governmental regulations that formed the ground rules for competition with foreigners. The Madero administration dropped all American employees from the Mexican railroad system and replaced them with Mexican nationals. By the summer of 1911, reports came from various Mexican cities that Mexicans were replacing Americans not only in the railroad positions but also in many other "places of trust" that had formerly been the province of foreigners.[11] Although some foreigners stayed in Mexico throughout the Revolution and some of those whom revolutionary violence drove away later returned, the exodus of foreigners and the revolutionary sentiment in favor of Mexican nationals permitted Mexicans to acquire a great number of positions once held by foreigners. Meanwhile, state authorities were gradually circumscribing the foreigners' ability to compete with Mexicans. On August 14, 1913, Governor José María Maytorena published decrees prohibiting foreigners from acquiring property in the state of Sonora.[12] In February, 1916, the government of Yucatán prohibited foreigners from acquiring land in the state, as the depreciation of paper Mexican currency and the consequent premium on American dollars was allegedly allowing Americans to buy valuable properties for "fictitious" prices.[13]

In declaring void the concessions of the Díaz period, in guaranteeing the subsoil rights belonging exclusively to the Mexican "nation," and in curtailing the outright foreign ownership of property, the Querétaro Constitution

11. Luther T. Ellsworth to Philander C. Knox, June 30, 1911, /2196.

12. Frederick Simpich to Bryan, September 9, 1913, /8886.

13. U.S., National Archives, Department of State, Record Group 84, post records of the American Consulate at Progreso, Yucatán, 1916, Vol. 2, 852.

of 1917 established the ultimate legal foundation for subsequent restrictions upon foreigners. The constitution
provided that, with increasing technical competence, Mexicans could take over the staffing of their own enterprises,
with the idea that the enterprises would then make increased contributions to Mexican public welfare. In so
doing, the constitution removed the real sting of foreign
competition, forced foreigners to work not merely for themselves but also for the integral benefit of the Mexican national community, and thus made acceptance of the benefits
of foreign technology, personnel, and capital compatible
with the short-run interests as well as the long-run advantage of the Mexican people.

Although Mexican xenophobia became manifest with
varying intensity in respect to other foreign nationals between 1910 and 1917, the most prolonged and the most
widespread xenophobia directed itself against North Americans. Reminders of the territory lost in the War of 1847
and the constant antagonism of conservative and clerical
factions had maintained a strong element of anti-Yankeeism
throughout the nineteenth century, and one reason for the
failure of Confederate colonization attempts in Mexico
after the American Civil War had been the deep hostility
that Mexicans continued to feel.[14] Differences in attitudes
and cultural values continued to separate Mexicans and
North Americans, for, as Samuel Guy Inman observed, the
Americans worshipped "truth and action" while the Mexicans revered "politeness and form."[15] With these inherited
antagonisms and cultural differences added to the revolutionary breakdown of authority and fears of fresh United
States intervention, anti-Americanism pervaded the period
of Mexican revolutionary struggle. While consular and
diplomatic reports, newspaper articles, and memoires in-

14. George D. Harmon, "Confederate Migration to Mexico," *Hispanic
American Historical Review*, Vol. 17, No. 4 (November, 1937), 482, 487.

15. Samuel Guy Inman, *Intervention in Mexico* (New York: George H.
Doran Company, 1919), p. 142.

dicate a marked lack of anti-Americanism among certain groups at particular times, the manifestations of anti-Americanism demonstrated strongly increased Mexican awareness of the need for a unifying national mystique.

In response to a State Department request for information on anti-Americanism during March, 1911, American consuls in many parts of Mexico reported it to be deep and widespread. Consul Samuel E. Magill at Guadalajara reported to Secretary of State Knox that "the anti-American sentiment is almost universal among rich and poor alike," adding that at the national celebration commemorating Hidalgo's Grito de Dolores on September 15 Mexican mobs paraded through the streets crying "Death to the Americans."[16] Linking anti-Americanism with general xenophobia and hostility to the Díaz regime, Consul Clarence A. Miller reported considerable anti-American, anti-foreign, and anti-government feeling throughout the state of Veracruz.[17] While Lewis W. Haskell at Salina Cruz was reporting the state of Oaxaca to be decidedly anti-American,[18] Consul Charles M. Freeman at Durango wrote that "this district is 95% anti-American, and that is a most conservative estimate for I have yet to meet a Mexican who has any love for the people of the United States as a whole. There are cases where individual Mexicans have a real affection for individual Americans, but even such cases are not common."[19]

Antipathy to Americans appeared even in the most isolated regions of Mexico, and American representatives throughout Mexico reported deep dislike at various times during the Revolution. One of the most isolated peasants whom John Reed met while he was traveling in Mexico told

16. Samuel E. Magill to Knox, March 20, 1911, /1126. For detailed discussion of Mexican-American diplomacy at this time, see Berta Ulloa, "Las relaciones mexicano-norteamericanas, 1910-1911," *Historia Mexicana*, Vol. 25, Núm. 1 (julio-septiembre, 1965).

17. Clarence A. Miller to Knox, March 18, 1911, /1106.
18. Lewis W. Haskell to Knox, March 20, 1911, /1135.
19. Charles M. Freeman to Knox, March 19, 1911, /1105.

Reed that the United States coveted his country and that gringo soldiers would come in the end to take away his goats.[20] In Yucatán, where strong separatist sentiment during the nineteenth century had shown a decided lack of Mexican nationalism, Mexicans hissed films showing the American flag and threatened maltreatment of Americans in the event of intervention.[21] Anti-Americanism pervaded even the southern section of Baja California, a region then remote from national life, which even today remains a territory and is only being gradually incorporated through transportation improvements such as the extension of roads and the new ferry service from Mazatlán to La Paz. In January, 1913, when the American consul at La Paz reported a complete absence of political or revolutionary disturbance in his district during the last two years of the Madero revolution, he also reported a strong undercurrent of anti-American feeling which, fanned by the "little paper printed in La Paz," had increased sharply throughout his district and seemed especially strong in the interior.[22] As the revolutionary struggle continued and fears of American intervention mounted, reports of deep hostility toward Americans came from Acapulco, Veracruz, Aguascalientes, and what is now Piedras Negras.[23]

Although some demonstrations of xenophobia only frightened or goaded Americans, its over-all effect was to prompt Americans to leave Mexico while exclaiming about the ferocity of Mexican patriotism. One victim of the day-by-day expression of xenophobia was Mrs. Anna Sherwood, the American proprietress of a hotel in Manzanillo on the Pacific coast. She reported to the American consul in April,

20. John Reed, *Insurgent Mexico* (New York: D. Appleton and Company, 1914), p. 170.

21. Wilbur T. Gracey to Bryan, September 3, 1913, /8730.

22. U.S., National Archives, Department of State, Record Group 84, post records of the American Consulate at La Paz, Baja California, Lucien N. Sullivan to Knox, January 4, 1913, 800.

23. Ellsworth to Knox, September 27, 1911, /2392; William W. Canada to Knox, March 12, 1912, /3314; Clement S. Edwards to Knox, February 12, 1913, /6110; and Gaston Schmutz to Bryan, January 29, 1914, /10897.

1912, that the Mexican railroad employees who boarded with her were constantly intimidating her and "speaking ill" of Americans. She had become particularly nervous when the Mexicans had threatened to shoot her, at the first sign of United States intervention, and to seize the American consul, tie weights to his feet, and throw him off the wharf.[24] Another incident revealing anti-Americanism occurred in Zacatecas; Judge Marentes, believed to be "notoriously anti-foreign," sentenced an American mechanic, J. A. Farrell, to ten years in prison for lending a pistol that later became a murder weapon. Farrell's lawyer and the Secretary of the American Embassy declared that there was "not sufficient evidence against Farrell to justify his being detained for one hour," and the American residents of Zacatecas sent out an appeal for aid on the basis of judicial prejudice.[25]

As a result of such incidents as the threats to Mrs. Sherwood, the questionable trial of Farrell, and the general atmosphere of incipient violence, Americans like the wealthier Mexicans frequently decided to leave the country. The American population in various areas declined sharply; for example, the number of American residents in the consular district around San Luis Potosí fell between 1910 and 1912 from 1,500 to fewer than 600.[26] What is interesting from the standpoint of Mexican nationalism is that the returning Americans reported an intensification of nationalism and its xenophobic overtones as prime reasons for their exodus. M. S. Largey, a banking and mining operator from Butte, Montana, explained after his return that "the great masses of the population hate Americans with an intensity that is awful to contemplate."[27] North Americans who were born and reared in Mexico came to

24. Milton B. Kirk to Henry Lane Wilson, May 1, 1912, /3823.
25. *The New York Times*, March 2, 1911, p. 1:4.
26. Wilbert L. Bonney to Knox, April 30, 1912, /3814.
27. "Took Hint and Left Mexico Just in Time," *The New York Times*, February 17, 1913, p. 2.

the United States pointing out that Mexicans were becoming "an intensely patriotic people."[28]

Anti-Americanism, no matter how harmless some of its manifestations may have been, also resulted in the murder and molestation of a large number of American citizens. While it is difficult to judge accurately the number of Americans attacked and murdered during the Mexican Revolution, the documented estimates by groups pressing for United States intervention show the number to be large. On December 29, 1919, Edward R. Sartwell, a publicity agent employed by the National Association for the Protection of American Rights in Mexico, furnished a subcommittee of the Senate Foreign Relations Committee with a "Murder Map of Mexico," showing the locations of the killings of 550 Americans in Mexico and along the border between November 20, 1910, and October, 1919. Compiled from lists by Senator Albert B. Fall, Thomas E. Gibbon, and the State Department, the map was purported to be authentic and included Americans murdered by troops, by bandits, and by their own Mexican servants.[29] A second list prepared from testimony before the Senate subcommittee shows 785 American civilians and soldiers killed, wounded, or outraged in Mexico and in American territory along the border from 1910 to May 20, 1920.[30] While the particular incidents on which these statistics are based resulted from a variety of causes—and while the statistics lose some of their shock value when compared with statistics indicating the number of Americans lynched within the United States during the same period—they nevertheless indicate a high level of hostility toward Americans.

Factional wrangling heightened the level of anti-Amer-

28. U.S., Congress, Senate, Committee on Foreign Relations, *Investigation of Mexican Affairs*, 66th Cong., 2d sess., Sen. Doc. 285 (2 vols.; Washington, 1920), Vol. 1, p. 1278.

29. For a copy of the map with a detailed explanation, see *ibid.*, Vol. 1, pp. 845-66.

30. *Ibid.*, Vol. 2, p. 3382.

ican sentiment, and in one sense anti-Americanism also grew by feeding upon itself. Revolutionary groups described rival factions as being led by Americans, trying in this way to gain support for themselves by making their opposition appear non-national. A Porfirista circular attacking the American press in Mexico found the Monterrey *News* to "smell of Maderoism" and declared that it was Americans who gave the Madero mutiny the character of a revolution.[31] The United States served as the scapegoat in a variety of later factional disputes. Querido Moheno, leader of the government faction in the Chamber of Deputies after Huerta's take-over, announced that the secessionist movement defying Huerta in the state of Sonora was in fact a preliminary step in a plan by former President Roosevelt and "Yankee bankers" to partition Mexico into several small republics that would be at the mercy of the United States.[32] As was the case with partisan assertions that the United States was siding with the opposition, the xenophobic actions and statements of Mexican leaders frequently generated further xenophobia. The long-standing sentiment in Mexico against foreign ownership of Mexican resources such as oil or mining properties prompted restrictive "anti-American" actions in Carranza's oil decrees and Article 27 of the 1917 Constitution. When these decrees in turn aroused severe protest and proposals for intervention from the United States, these North American statements further heightened Mexican fear and animosity. In this manner the original Mexican xenophobia and nationalism initiated a progression of events that ultimately strengthened and fortified its own tenets.

The extent of anti-Americanism should not be overemphasized, of course. In March, 1911, while other American diplomats were reporting underlying antagonism toward Americans, the consuls in Monterrey, Hermosillo,

31. Ellsworth to Knox, April 26, 1911, /1555.
32. *The New York Times,* March 12, 1913, p. 2:4.

Mazatlán, Acapulco, and Tapachula were reporting hostility only in specific personal incidents.[33] Throughout the remainder of the revolutionary conflict, particular areas reported at various times either a lack of anti-Americanism or the effective stemming of such sentiment by government officials.[34] The relief felt by Mexicans when full-scale American intervention failed to materialize in the Revolution caused some amelioration of antagonism. Before the revelation of Ambassador Wilson's part in Madero's overthrow, for example, Consul General Hanna was prompted to write in February, 1913, that "today the Mexican people, regardless of political faction, hold the United States in higher esteem than at any time during the last two years."[35] During periods of both greater and lesser fear of American intervention, robbery rather than antipathy was the reason for many of the attacks on Americans. Since troops were stationed only in the larger towns and brigands were difficult to distinguish from revolutionaries, bandits such as Luis Mora in Durango attacked the property holders who were often American.

The United States did on occasion gain outspoken praise rather than invective from Mexican leaders. Francisco Madero, now one of Mexico's most widely respected national heroes despite his attitude toward Americans, stands out for the consistency of his attempts to maintain American friendship. In an interview printed in *The New York Times* in February, 1911, Madero said that the "great and honest sympathy of the American people for the revolutionists of Mexico is a beautiful thing. About 95 per cent. of the Mexicans appreciate it, and return their sym-

33. William E. Alger to Knox, March 19, 1911, /1113; Harry K. Pangburn to Knox, March 19, 1911, /1136; Albert W. Brickwood to Knox, March 19, 1911, /1412; Philip C. Hanna to Knox, March 20, 1911, /1111; and Louis Hostetter to Knox, March 25, 1911, /1134.

34. For reports indicating limitations on anti-Americanism and effective government action, see Magill to Knox, September 13, 1912, /5035; and Hostetter to Knox, November 9, 1912, /5549.

35. Hanna to Knox, February 22, 1913, /6484.

pathy to Americans. Honestly; we like Americans, I do, anyway."[36]

An atmosphere of cordiality apparently marked the "magnificent" banquet at the American Club on November 25, 1911, where, against a background of intertwined Mexican and American flags, the American colony of Mexico City entertained Madero and his ministers. Responding to continued criticism of the United States, Madero observed that other Latin American states had not come to Mexico's aid in 1828, 1838, 1847, or 1862 and declared simply, "Mexico's peace and prosperity depend upon a continuance of friendly relations with the United States."[37]

Mexican leaders after Madero attempted to maintain as much American support as possible without alienating Mexican nationalists. Huerta persistently sought American recognition, and Villa's violence against Americans erupted only after the rival Carrancistas received American backing. When seeking support in the United States for the Constitutionalists, Roberto Pesqueira declared that Americans were generally held in higher esteem than any other group of foreigners and that Mexican laborers sought out American employers not simply for higher wages but because of the Americans' reputations for fair treatment.[38] José Vasconcelos notes in his memoires and, in passing, denounces the lack of strong anti-Americanism and national loyalty in Pesqueira and other northern leaders.[39] Finally, looking back upon the events of the 1910 period, such Mexican statesmen as Isidro Fabela can now express their conviction that imperialists formed only a fraction of the population and that the North American people as

36. *The New York Times*, February 20, 1911, p. 3:4.
37. *The Daily Mexican*, February 1, 1912, clipping enclosed in Henry Lane Wilson to Knox, February 2, 1912, /2757.
38. Roberto V. Pesqueira, "The Constitutionalist Party in Mexico: What It Is Fighting For," *The Annals of the American Academy of Political and Social Science*, Vol. 54 (July, 1914), 172.
39. José Vasconcelos, *La tormenta, segunda parte de ulises criollo* (7th ed.; México: Ediciones Botas, 1948), p. 96.

a whole were pacific, fair, and respectful of foreign rights.[40] Despite such protestations of friendship, however, the manifestations of anti-Americanism in the 1910 period itself have stimulated and through reiteration continue to stimulate the Mexican sentiment of nationality and national separation.

NORTH AMERICAN PROVOCATIONS

On the eve of the Revolution, a brutal instance of injustice turned Mexican sentiment sharply against the United States. Mexicans reacted violently when a mob lynched twenty-year-old Antonio Rodríguez from Las Vacas, Mexico, by burning him at the stake in Rock Springs, Texas, on November 4, 1910. Rodríguez had asked Mrs. Lem Henderson, a rancher's wife, for food while neighboring ranchers were away on a roundup, and when Mrs. Henderson "talked mean" to him, he had shot and killed her. After Rodríguez confessed to the crime and entered the Rock Springs jail, ranchers battered down the jail doors. The mob outside had a fire waiting for him, watched while he burned, and dispersed when he was dead. The coroner's jury reported only that "an unknown Mexican met death at the hands of an unknown mob."[41]

When news of the Rodríguez burning spread through Mexico, it rekindled resentment, and violence erupted in Mexico City and Guadalajara. Mexican newspapers published severe attacks on Americans; *El Diario del Hogar,* in typical fashion, called the people of the United States "giants of the dollar, pigmies of culture, and barbarous whites of the North." On the night of November 8, after a number of inflammatory speeches and the passage of resolutions, a crowd of a thousand marched on the Mexico

40. Isidro Fabela, *Historia diplomática de la Revolución Mexicana (1912-1917)* (2 vols.; México: Fondo de Cultura Económica, 1958-59), Vol. 1, p. 369.

41. *The New York Times,* November 11, 1910, p. 2:5.

City offices of *The Mexican Herald,* an American-owned daily newspaper printed in English for the American colony. The crowd attacked the *Herald* building with stones, broke a number of windows, and pelted the managing editor with mud and rocks when he tried to speak from the balcony. On the morning of November 9, Mexicans attacked American houses, hotels, and such establishments as Sanborn's drugstore and the American Club. Seeing an American flag flying in front of the Imperial Restaurant, members of the mob pulled the emblem down, tore it apart, trampled and spat upon it while ten Mexican policemen stood by. Police finally curbed the rioting on the night of November 9 when a large, belligerent mob committed further vandalism, including the demolition of the pro-American government newspaper *El Imparcial.* The police made many arrests, and one Mexican was run through when police charged the crowd with drawn swords.[42]

In Guadalajara, Mexican students, like the several hundred university and medical students who participated in the Mexico City riots, organized a demonstration in which hundreds of Mexicans shouted, "Mueran los gringos." Rioters burned an American flag, beat and kicked American railroad employees, and caused an estimated damage of between $5,000 and $10,000 to American property. The musicians of Guadalajara even signed an agreement not to play American music.

In commenting on the basic Mexican hostility toward the United States, the American vice-consul in Mexico City stated that the anti-American rioting was not so much a protest against the Rodríguez burning as it was a sign of "jealousy of American success" and the fact that Americans had come to control some of Mexico's most productive industries and lands.[43] Confirming this viewpoint, Amer-

42. Extensive descriptions of the reaction in Mexico City to the Rodríguez burning appear in Henry Lane Wilson to Knox, November 9, 1910, /357; Henry Lane Wilson to Knox, November 10, 1910, /385; and *The New York Times,* November 10, 1910, p. 1:3.

43. *The New York Times,* November 12, 1910, p. 5:2-3.

ican Consul Samuel E. Magill reported that the riots resulted primarily from "a deep seated jealousy or hatred of all things and persons American." He felt that "the lynching of an alleged Mexican was only incidental, and a large proportion of the populace engaged in the riots knew little and cared less about it."[44] By bringing this underlying Mexican jealousy and antagonism toward Americans to the surface, the Rodríguez burning prompted Mexicans to perceive the later events between 1910 and 1917 in an anti-American and nationalistic manner.

As the Madero revolt gained momentum along the northern tier of Mexican states, mobilizations of American troops along the border stirred widespread fears of American military intervention and so sustained the intense sentiment of anti-Americanism roused by the Rodríguez burning. Although the main purpose of the successive American mobilizations was to limit filibustering and to protect American citizens, Mexicans consistently interpreted these movements as signs of American intervention, impending invasion, and territorial expansion.

President Taft inaugurated a program of naval surveillance and substantially increased deployment of American troops along the border which the Woodrow Wilson administration later maintained. The deployment began with the mobilization of twenty thousand American troops and two naval divisions near the Mexican border in March, 1911. Throughout the Revolution, incidents occurred along the border which aroused animosity. Four Mexican soldiers were killed when two troops of the Ninth United States Cavalry came to the assistance of American soldiers who had been fired upon while patrolling the border near Douglas, Arizona.[45] American, British, German, and even Cuban warships patrolled Mexico's extensive Atlantic and Pacific coasts after 1910 and frequently evacuated foreign refugees threatened by revolutionary violence.

44. Magill to Knox, January 11, 1911, /615.
45. *The New York Times*, March 4, 1913, p. 10:2.

This continuing naval encirclement and the maintenance of a large American army along the border increased Mexican fears of American motives. The general Mexican opinion, coinciding with that frequently expressed in Europe, was that these mobilizations ultimately presaged a large-scale invasion with the objective of safeguarding business interests and acquiring territory. To Mexicans like Gonzalo Rivero, the troop movements ordered by President Taft appeared to be mobilization for war rather than simple frontier vigilance.[46] As the extensive American military and naval vigilance continued, Consul Alphonse J. Lespinasse in the coastal city of Frontera reported that all classes shared the idea that American intervention was inevitable and might be expected at any moment.[47] Mexican reviews of Mexican-American relations, like that of Gonzalo Travesí, published before the Veracruz occupation and Pershing expedition stated that Wall Street control of the American government was forcing President Wilson to armed intervention in Mexico.[48]

Foreign opinion also saw American mobilization as a prelude to invasion. The Tsarist press, for example, basing its view of international affairs upon an appreciation of national interests which the succeeding Soviet regime was increasingly to adopt, found the incorporation of Mexico into the United States to be inevitable because it was "necessitated by the vital national interests of the United States." With Mexicans as well as foreigners believing that the "imperial interests" of the United States indicated a need to capitalize on internal disorder to acquire further Mexican territory, many Mexicans wondered when Americans would give up what the Russians called their "su-

46. Gonzalo G. Rivero, *Hacia la verdad: Episodios de la Revolución* (México: Compañía Editora Nacional, S.A., 1911), p. 62.

47. For a definitive statement of the Mexican belief in intervention with the added implication that Mexicans should openly defy the United States since intervention was inevitable, see Alphonse J. Lespinasse to Knox, March 9, 1912, /2981; and Lespinasse to Knox, April 8, 1912, /3649.

48. Gonzalo G. Travesí, *La Revolución de México y el imperialismo yanqui* (Barcelona: Casa Editorial Maucci, 1914), pp. 219-20.

perfluous hypocrisy.''[49] When armed intervention came, therefore, it appeared to those who had predicted it as a confirmation of their fears.

The implication of United States Ambassador Henry Lane Wilson in the overthrow and death of President Francisco Madero produced a wave of anti-Americanism that has reverberated ever since. During the period of severe fighting for control of Mexico City between Madero's government forces and the insurgents of Félix Díaz, which began on February 9, 1913, the American ambassador put considerable pressure on Madero to resign. It was in meetings at the American Embassy on February 16 and 17, ostensibly held to discuss a truce for evacuating foreigners from the danger zone and for clearing the streets of debris and dead bodies, that representatives of Díaz and Huerta arranged for Madero's ouster. Wilson overtly encouraged Huerta's *coup d'état* by informing the general's representatives that he would recognize any regime that was able to restore order in the city.[50] His telegram to Secretary Knox of 4 P.M. on February 17, the day before the coup, indicates that Huerta sent a final messenger to assure Wilson of the upcoming ouster and that, instead of remaining neutral or warning the government to which he was accredited, Wilson acquiesced to the plan with the single reservation that "no lives be taken except by due process of law."[51]

No evidence links Wilson directly with Madero's murder, although he continued to support Huerta as staunchly after the murder as before. Wilson bears responsibility in

49. Translation of an April 18, 1911, editorial in *Novoe Vremia*, the chief Saint Petersburg newspaper, enclosed in William W. Rockhill to Knox, April 19, 1911, /1634.

50. Lowell L. Blaisdell, ''Henry Lane Wilson and the Overthrow of Madero,'' *Southwestern Social Science Quarterly*, Vol. 43, No. 2 (September, 1962), 131-32. See also Isidro Fabela, ''La actitud del embajador Wilson durante la 'decena trágica,' '' *Ciencias Políticas y Sociales*, Año 2, Núms. 5, 6 (julio-diciembre, 1956); and John P. Harrison, ''Henry Lane Wilson, el trágico de la decena,'' *Historia Mexicana*, Vol. 6, Núm. 3 (enero-marzo, 1957).

51. Henry Lane Wilson to Knox, February 17, 1913, /6225.

that the coup he encouraged permitted the murder, and he failed to use his influence to prevent the murder, but it is difficult to prove that he actually expected Madero and Pino Suárez to be assassinated or that he consciously abetted the assassination through inactivity. Despite personal dislike of Madero, Wilson did not wish his death, as Wilson did not share Huerta's desire to permanently eliminate a rival whom he had betrayed. What is comparatively clear is that the ambassador based his policy recommendations, and perhaps his perception of events as well, upon an overriding desire to achieve peace, to provide safety for American residents of Mexico, and so ultimately to allow American business interests to flourish as they had under Porfirio Díaz. Wilson's desire for peace and his partial indifference to the methods of its achievement clarify his support of Huerta's coup and the persistence of his pleading after Madero's murder that Huerta be granted full recognition.[52]

No matter what degree of reprehensibility foreigners may ascribe to Ambassador Wilson, the Mexican studies that have shaped Mexican opinion on the subject unanimously and often violently condemn him. In helping to end the carnage in Mexico City, Wilson's actions did bring a sense of immediate relief to many Mexicans, and his complicity certainly pleased the followers of Huerta who clustered around the presidential palace. Wilson's ephemeral popularity is described in a newspaper report that, after Harry Berlinger carried Ambassador Wilson's message of peace to the arsenal of Félix Díaz and the palace of Huerta, the crowd outside the palace learned of his mission and produced "an outburst of applause rarely heard for an American in Mexico. Crowds filled the Zocalo and San

52. In his dispatch of February 24, only two days after the murder, Wilson was already asking the State Department to inform the American public "of the friendly disposition of this Government towards the United States" and declaring his own disposition to consider the murder "a closed incident." For expression of Wilson's strongly pro-Huerta and anti-Madero sentiments shortly after the assassination, see Wilson to Knox, February 24, 1913, /6353; and Wilson to Knox, February 26, 1913, /6394.

Francisco Street, along which the automobile picked its way, and from man to man the shout 'Viva Los Americanos' swept along, keeping pace with the progress of the automobile.''[53] Huerta's supporters formed only part of the polity, however, and with Madero's martyrdom, opinion in Mexico turned decisively against Henry Wilson.

A number of contemporary books typified in Pedro Lamicq's *La parra, la perra y la porra*[54] bitterly condemned the ambassador. Even comparatively unemotional historical accounts published during the Revolution such as Ramón Prida's *¡De la dictadura a la anarquía!* found Wilson's actions to be rationally inexplicable and his complicity in Madero's overthrow "truly odious."[55] The American ambassador's role seemed especially reprehensible when compared with that of Cuban Minister Manuel Márquez Sterling. By remaining with former President Madero during part of his confinement and later writing a book that champions the martyred president, Márquez Sterling gained unanimous admiration from Mexican writers and students. One of the streets running off the Ciudadela has been named in his honor.

Recent Mexican studies continue the attack on Wilson, frequently linking it with attacks on the United States. Popular histories depict the ambassador as "a classic representative of yankee imperialist policy" whose attitude was perpetually against Madero, the Revolution, and the interests of the Mexican people.[56] Widely read books by Jesús Silva Herzog and Isidro Fabela similarly assert that Wilson's actions were an affront to all Mexican people and reprint anti-Wilson selections. Luis Manuel Rojas' caustic *Yo acuso al embajador de los Estados Unidos* and

53. *The New York Times*, February 20, 1913, p. 2:5.
54. Pirra-Purra [Pedro Lamicq], *La parra, la perra y la porra* (México: Oficina Editorial Azteca, n.d.), pp. 168, 181.
55. Ramón Prida, *¡De la dictadura a la anarquía!* . . . (El Paso, Texas: Imprenta de ''El Paso del Norte,'' 1914), p. 678.
56. José Mancisidor, *Historia de la Revolución Mexicana* (México: Ediciones el Gusano de Luz, 1958), pp. 164-65.

the condemnation of Wilson by Sara Pérez de Madero in her 1916 interview with Robert Hammond Murray are frequently quoted.[57] Younger Mexicans who never knew the ambassador have developed hostility toward him as the result of the republication of the classic indictments, such as that of Ramón Prida which contains appendices of more recent studies that underscore Wilson's guilt.[58] These reiterated attacks against Henry Lane Wilson as an individual and as a representative of the United States are significant in the nation-building process because they provide a continuing focus for antipathy and anti-Americanism for all Mexican citizens.

The capture and subsequent occupation of Veracruz between April and November, 1914, generated deeper xenophobia in Mexico than any other single occurrence during the Revolution. This potentially explosive confrontation between the patriotic intransigence of Mexico and the United States developed after Mexicans had arrested eight uniformed American seamen from a Navy whaleboat plainly flying the American flag and marched them through the streets of Tampico on April 9, 1914. Huerta's soldiers removed two of the bluejackets from the whaleboat itself, which was technically equivalent to United States territory. The American sailors were set free within an hour and a half, and General Ignacio Morelos Zaragoza immediately provided a written apology for the affront, but the Mexican general refused to fire the twenty-one gun salute demanded by Rear Admiral Henry T. Mayo, commander of the Fifth Division of the United States Atlantic Fleet at Tampico.[59]

57. Jesús Silva Herzog, *Breve historia de la Revolución Mexicana* (2 vols.; México: Fondo de Cultura Económica, 1964), Vol. 1, pp. 302-13; and Fabela, *Historia diplomática de la Revolución Mexicana (1912-1917)*, Vol. 1, pp. 37-191.

58. See Ramón Prida, *La culpa de Lane Wilson, embajador de los E. U. A., en la tragedia mexicana de 1913* (México: Ediciones Botas, 1962).

59. One of the most accurate contemporary accounts of the details of the Tampico incident appears in the *San Francisco Chronicle*, April 16, 1914, p. 3:2. Less detailed corroboration may be found in the April 20, 1914, speech of President Wilson to both Houses of Congress in U.S., *Congressional Record*, 63d Cong., 2d sess., Vol. 51, pt. 7 (April 20, 1914), pp. 6908-9.

When Huerta also refused to jeopardize Mexico's "national dignity" by acceding to American demands for the salute, Woodrow Wilson, with delayed congressional approval, ordered naval forces to capture the key port of Veracruz and so cut off the revenues and arms shipments that Huerta received through it. As the German steamship *Ypiranga* was about to deliver 10,000 rifles, 15,000,000 rounds of ammunition, and 200 rapid-fire machine guns[60] to Huerta on the morning of April 21, President Wilson ordered the seizure of Veracruz to block these arms which, with the crisis created by the Tampico incident, might soon have been used against American troops. In addition to demonstrating Wilson's desire to stop the arms shipment and to remove Huerta from office, the Veracruz occupation exemplifies the manner in which nationalism may work in opposition to national interest. Mexican nationalism and Huerta's position as a national leader precluded making the salute and so threatened Mexico with the specter of American invasion. Similarly, such American jingoes as Senator Chilton of West Virginia invoked the spirit of American nationalism to demand aggressive action, even though this was squarely opposed to the American national interest of maintaining peace with Mexico as World War I approached.

The capture of Veracruz caused the death of many Mexicans who are now remembered as national heroes. After American sailors and Marines had landed on April 21, the citizens of the port led by two hundred cadets from the Naval Academy opened fire and forced Admiral Mayo to withdraw the landing party. On the following day, bombardment from the American cruisers *Chester, San Francisco,* and *Prairie* pounded the Mexican defenders into submission, tearing gaping holes in the stone walls of the Naval Academy and silencing the rifle fire inside. In the seizure of Veracruz, American fire killed at least two

60. *Boston Evening Transcript*, April 21, 1914, p. 1:7.

hundred and wounded another three hundred Mexicans, many of them civilian noncombatants. The American forces counted only nineteen dead and seventy-one wounded. After capturing the port, in order to combat scavengers and the rapid putrefaction caused by the tropical humidity of Veracruz, the American forces resorted to the expedient of piling the Mexican corpses together, covering them with crude petroleum, and setting them on fire rather than providing individual burial.[61]

The American occupation and the deaths it caused further inflamed Mexican nationalism and produced violent denunciations of the United States. Huerta tried to promote his own popularity by evoking national loyalty; *El Imparcial,* the government newspaper, proclaimed the pride of Huerta and the Mexican people in the Veracruz defense and announced rewards for the cadets involved.[62] Fear and mistrust grew when Mexican newspapers proclaimed that this had been the spearhead of an American occupation of the rest of Mexico.[63] Even the *Revista de Revistas,* a notably unemotional weekly review that ordinarily abstained from political discussion, declared that the inhabitants of Mexico must now become "Mexicans before everything else," and the review subsequently carried highly nationalistic articles on the American invasion, extensive discussions of the War of 1847, and pictorial presentations of the Veracruz occupation with numerous photographs of the

61. For a detailed survey of the Veracruz occupation, see Robert E. Quirk, *An Affair of Honor: Woodrow Wilson and the Occupation of Veracruz* (Lexington, Ky.: University of Kentucky Press, 1962). For an interpretation of the literature on the occupation, see Ronald G. Woodbury, "Wilson y la intervención de Veracruz: Análisis historiográfico," *Historia Mexicana,* Vol. 17, Núm. 2 (octubre-diciembre, 1967).

62. "La patria premiara el heroísmo de los defensores de Veracruz," *El Imparcial,* May 4, 1914, pp. 1:3-6, 5:3-6. For discussion of the depth of resentment against the occupation among Carrancistas, which made Carranza fear that he might need to declare war against the United States in order to prevent some of his men from going over to Huerta's side to fight the Yankees, see Charles C. Cumberland, "Huerta y Carranza ante la ocupación de Veracruz," *Historia Mexicana,* Vol. 6, Núm. 4 (abril-junio, 1957).

63. See "Cuarenta mil Americanos ocupan Veracruz y se preparan a invadir el interior de la República," *El País,* May 6, 1914, pp. 1:3-7, 6:4-6.

Mexican dead.[64] Mexican attacks became less violent after the May 18 peace talks with the mediation of Argentina, Brazil, and Chile lessened fears of a republic-wide American conquest, but active hostility to the American invaders was manifested until their departure in November.

The coalescing sense of Mexican nationalism evident in this unwavering hostility to the occupation can be attributed to the fact that, although many American diplomats and private citizens protested the occupation, the American public statements that were most apparent to the Mexicans supported Wilson's intervention. Private citizens, socialists, YMCA secretaries, missionaries, and most of the diplomats involved did oppose intervention.[65] Unfortunately,

64. "Frente al enemigo," *Revista de Revistas*, Núm. Extra (26 abril 1914), 1. Later, uncharacteristically emotional invocations of nationalism in response to the Veracruz occupation appeared in the *Revista de Revistas*: "La invasión norteamericana en 1847," (3 mayo 1914), pp. 8-10; "El conflicto con los Estados Unidos," (10 mayo 1914), pp. 1-3; "La invasión norteamericana en 1847," (17 mayo 1914), pp. 9, 10; and "El ejército norteamericana y la cuestión de México," (24 mayo 1914), p. 5.

65. For strong statements of the position of American socialists which denounce the intervention allegedly advocated by big business and assert that the American working class should not allow Wilsonian invocations of American "national honor" to force it into war against the Mexican people, see "The Honor of the Nation," *The New York Call*, April 16, 1914, p. 6:1-2; and "Helping the Jingo Exploiters Will Further Enslave American Workers," *The New York Call*, April 22, 1914, p. 1:2-4. A telegram from Edward L. Doheny to President Taft on behalf of American petroleum, gas, and construction companies in Mexico indicates that the American business interests decried by the socialists had also opposed intervention, since the "only gainers thereby would be British and other foreign interests." Doheny and others to Taft, May 5, 1911, /1666. Letters from the secretary of the American Board of Commissioners for Foreign Missions and the secretary of the Presbyterian Board of Foreign Missions contain detailed reports from American missionaries in Mexico opposing intervention on the grounds that it would occasion the death and suffering of the Americans already in Mexico. James L. Barton to Knox, February 24, 1912, /2896; and A. W. Halsey to Knox, October 10, 1912, /5218. For anti-intervention appeals to the American government from secretaries of the Young Men's Christian Association in Mexico and the American Peace Society, see G. I. Babcock and A. E. Turner to William Knowles Cooper, May 5 and May 10, 1911, /1872; and Benjamin F. Trueblood to Knox, April 23, 1912, /3698. Supporting nonintervention pleas, such as those of Arthur Thompson in *The Conspiracy against Mexico* (Oakland, Calif.: n.p., n.d.), Americans like Austen G. Fox opposed military intervention on the realistic grounds that it would not bring self-government to the Mexicans and that it would "be easy enough for us to go in, but it may, at least, be impossible to get out, except accompanied by the confession

however, the opposing letters and diplomatic dispatches did
not reach the Mexican people as readily as did the clamors
for general intervention from American jingoes, the Republican opposition, and certain business interests. Congressional speeches and newspaper editorials indicate that,
while many Americans strongly opposed the war with
Mexico, extended American conquest and occupation would
have been supported. Representative Mann, the Republican
minority leader in the House who himself opposed war,
summed up the basis of many Mexican fears when he observed: "I do not believe it is possible for us to have war
with Mexico and ever leave Mexico. I think that when our
troops land in Mexico City when the war is over we will
own Mexico. . . . I know that when the time comes I will
join with a majority in this House who will say the flag
must never come down; that our boys planted it there."[66]

Even if Arthur Link is correct in his controversial view
that Wilson's policy of intervention lacked popular American support,[67] Mexicans quite naturally assumed that most
Americans backed belligerent action because the official
position of the American government and the reiterations of
the American press—the main evidence on which Mexicans
had to go—showed increasing endorsement of armed occupation.

Since 1914, the Veracruz intervention has given Mexicans a rallying point and provided international opponents
of the United States with an emotionally charged weapon

that the so-called Mexican problem remains unchanged." Austen G. Fox,
"Mexico," *The Annals of the American Academy of Political and Social
Science*, Vol. 54 (July, 1914), 184. Other Americans such as Leslie C. Wells
criticized intervention on the grounds that domestic problems of social wel-
fare could keep us fully occupied, that foreign dependencies would invite
great corruption in our public service, and that we should avoid unnecessary
entanglement in the church-state controversy inherent in the revival of the
Mexican clerical party. Leslie C. Wells, "The Remedy for Mexico," *The
Annals of the American Academy of Political and Social Science*, Vol. 54
(July, 1914), 216-17.

66. *San Francisco Chronicle*, April 21, 1914, p. 5:3.

67. Arthur S. Link, *Woodrow Wilson and the Progressive Era, 1910-1917*
(New York: Harper & Brothers, 1954), p. 125.

of propaganda. José Mancisidor, one of Mexico's most anti-American novelists, was born in Veracruz in 1895 and personally took part in the resistance to the United States invasion in 1914. *Frontera junto al mar* (1953), his sixth, penultimate, and most widely read novel, shows the Veracruz invasion as a heroic resistance of the Mexican people. In Mexican literature generally, the intervention ranks with, if not ahead of, the War of 1847 as the instance most frequently and forcefully invoked to demonstrate the importance of Mexican unity and national strength in the face of potential foreign domination.

Besides creating a central focus for Mexican nationalism, the intervention has laid the United States open to effective criticism from a series of opponents, from Germany in the years of William II to Soviet Russia and Communist China today. Soviet writers, for example, in propagandistically detailing the machinations of United States "imperialism" during the "recent" 1910-1917 period, try consciously to promote antagonism between Mexico and the United States by picturing the Veracruz occupation as a carefully planned invasion by the North American "bourgeoisie." They emphasize the destruction caused by North American troops and judiciously select quotes from participants and reputable sources to depict the North Americans as inherently anti-Mexican "imperialists." Although most Mexicans would reject the Soviet portrayal of Carranza as the leader of Mexico's own "national bourgeoisie" who opposed American intervention only because he feared losing the support of the Mexican "masses" if he failed to oppose the Americans,[68] the Veracruz occupation has, nevertheless, given Soviet historiography a series of events

68. See M. S. Alperóvich and B. T. Rudenko, *La Revolución Mexicana de 1910-1917 y la política de los Estados Unidos,* Makedonio Garza and others, trans. (México: Fondo de Cultura Popular, S. de R. L., 1960), pp. 194-211. On pp. 326-28 Alperóvich and Rudenko provide a handy checklist of other Soviet publications that have tried to use Mexican nationalism to stir up friction between Mexico and the United States.

that may easily be manipulated to stimulate Mexican nationalism in an anti-American direction.

Although the expeditionary force sent into Mexico under General John J. Pershing excited less anti-Americanism than did the occupation of Veracruz, it played a significant part in arousing Mexican apprehension and national pride. Pancho Villa occasioned the intervention when, by reproaching increased American support for Carranza and by attempting to provoke a general American invasion by which he might win leadership from Carranza, he massacred seventeen Americans in Santa Ysabel on January 10, 1916, and killed nineteen American citizens in a daring night raid on Columbus, New Mexico, on March 9, 1916.[69] In retaliation, President Wilson ultimately mobilized 150,000 militia along the southern frontier and sent 12,000 men under General Pershing to pursue Villa through the large Mexican state of Chihuahua.

Although Pershing's troops never captured Villa and had entered Mexico with Carranza's grudging consent, they encountered mounting Mexican hostility and resistance before returning to the United States in February, 1917, after an exhaustive, ten-and-a-half-month penetration. Tension grew during the months the expedition remained in Mexico. After two American soldiers and forty Mexicans

69. On Villa's anti-Americanism, see Clarence C. Clendenen, *The United States and Pancho Villa: A Study in Unconventional Diplomacy* (Ithaca, N.Y.: Cornell University Press, 1961). Considerable disagreement occurs between primary sources and American and Mexican secondary sources on the numbers killed at Columbus, as it does for the number killed at Santa Ysabel, Carrizal, the Veracruz seizure, and other Mexican-American conflicts. The varying estimates of secondary sources generally develop from discrepancies in dispatches and newspaper reports and from the fact that men initially reported as wounded later died of the wounds received. As in the underestimated preliminary and official reports of the Mexican casualties in the Veracruz invasion, variations in estimates also resulted from the fact that no accurate count was ever made and from the tendency for Mexicans to remove dead or wounded friends from the scene of battle before any count was taken. Mexican estimates are the most useful for the study of Mexican nationalism, because they indicate the bases of judgment and exhortation by the spokesmen of the Mexican national community. The present study uses Mexican estimates, therefore, where they are consistent with primary sources and with the best American estimates.

died in a battle at Parral some 340 miles south of the American border on April 12, 1916, Villista raids on Glen Springs and Ygnacio, Texas, on May 5 and June 15 killed eight Americans.[70] Mexicans arrested American naval officers and fired on a boat crew at Mazatlán on June 19, and two days later Carrancistas killed twelve American soldiers and captured twenty-three others in a battle near Carrizal.

Pershing's troopers kindled resentment and national pride in both the Mexicans whom they encountered and the Mexicans who wrote or read about them. Cries for American conquest again arose in the United States as American soldiers fought and died in Mexico, and again such outcries stirred national fear and resentment among the Mexicans. As Pershing's columns proceeded into Villista territory, through the very towns in which Villa had recruited many of his men for the Columbus raid, the hostility and lack of co-operation they encountered along the route reflected the personal as well as the national antagonism that the Mexicans felt for the Yankee soldiers who sought their friends and relatives.[71] Mexicans took and continue to take considerable national pride in the rout of American forces in the major encounter at Carrizal, where a column under Captain Charles J. Boyd met ignominious defeat because of Boyd's overconfidence and tactical errors.

The Pershing expedition stimulated nationalistic condemnation of Woodrow Wilson as typified by Carlos Pereyra, a former Mexican professor of sociology at the University of Mexico who became a member of the Hague Court. Pereyra remarked bitterly that Americans would learn that "the *greaser* bandits will defend their Motherland." He ridiculed President Wilson for sending the Pershing expedition after his earlier friendship for Villa,

70. H. A. Toulmin, *With Pershing in Mexico* (Harrisburg, Pa.: The Military Service Publishing Co., 1935), pp. 11-12.

71. For a firsthand statement of the attitudes and nonco-operation of the Mexicans encountered, see Frank Tompkins, *Chasing Villa: The Story Behind the Story of Pershing's Expedition into Mexico* (Harrisburg, Pa.: The Military Service Publishing Company, 1934), p. 100.

belittled Wilson's bellicosity toward Mexico while he displayed timidity in entering World War I, and proudly announced that Wilson lapsed into an attitude of cordiality to Mexico only after seeing his North American troops routed at the battle of Carrizal.[72] Actually the increasing sentiment of national unity during the period of Carranza's leadership was favored by Wilson's ultimate restraint. Despite his interventions, Wilson basically sympathized with Mexico's social and democratic aspirations, and upon the advent of World War I, the attention and energies of the United States and the powerful European states were diverted from Mexico's civil war.[73] Denunciations of President Wilson and of the Pershing expedition similar to those of Pereyra, however, have pervaded subsequent Mexican historiography. As was the case with the Rodríguez burning, President Taft's preparations for intervention, Ambassador Wilson's machinations, and the Veracruz occupation, the Pershing expedition has shaped the Mexican sense of national community through its immediate impact and through subsequent invocations of it as a lasting part of the Mexican national mystique.

A MULTIPLICITY OF ELEMENTS

In addition to the reactions to North American provocations, a multiplicity of other causal strands are woven into the pattern of anti-Americanism and xenophobia in relation to the Mexican Revolution. The foreign participants who came from many parts of the world to join the revolutionary cause aroused a surprising degree of jealous rivalry and xenophobia among their Mexican peers. Agitators consciously instilled Mexican youth with anti-American sentiments as a means of winning them over to participation in

72. Carlos Pereyra, *El crimen de Woodrow Wilson* . . . (Madrid: Imprenta de Juan Pueyo, 1917), pp. 112-41.

73. Floyd Ford Ewing, ''Carranza's Foreign Relations: An Experiment in Nationalism'' (unpublished Ph.D. dissertation, University of Texas, 1952), pp. 368-69.

Mexico's internal conflict, and the 1910 schism in Mexican Freemasonry produced a division of Masons in Mexico along lines of nationality which has persisted ever since. Furthermore, Woodrow Wilson's inveterate opposition to Huerta and his alienation of Pancho Villa estranged the United States from two revolutionary factions while creating no redeeming cordiality from the rival Carrancistas. For a variety of subjective reasons, in addition to the more objective resentment of direct United States intervention, therefore, Mexicans gained an increasingly personal awareness of their nationalism and national distinctiveness.

A large and militarily significant contingent of foreign volunteers originally formed a portion of Francisco Madero's revolutionary army. Well-intentioned fighters from many foreign countries came to participate in what seemed to be a struggle for democracy against dictatorship, and a particularly large group of North Americans responded to advertisements in United States newspapers that regularly solicited the services of young Americans. American volunteers became so numerous, in fact, that all foreign participants came to be spoken of as Americans.[74] The military experience or mechanical know-how of the foreigners often raised them to positions of leadership and prestige in the early years of the Revolution, and foreigners in the Maderista ranks came to manage the more complex duties such as handling the machine guns.

Exemplary expatriates who were outstanding for their participation ranged from W. H. McKenzie, a Canadian who led the famous Maderista attack on Ciudad Juárez on May 8, 1911, to Giuseppi Garibaldi, grandson of the Italian liberator, and General Ben Viljoen, the Boer War veteran. A foreign contingent of former soldiers from America, Canada, and Europe, led by Garibaldi and variously called the "American Legion" and the "Foreign Legion," stood out in the heavy fighting for Ciudad Juárez which brought

74. Canada to Bryan, December 5, 1913, /10067.

Madero victory and toppled the Díaz regime. It was Garibaldi who received General Juan J. Navarro's sword at the surrender of the city. Garibaldi and Viljoen became two of the four brigadier generals in Madero's army of five thousand. As Minister of Finance José Yves Limantour lamented from his parlor at the Plaza Hotel in New York after returning from a year in France negotiating Mexican bonds, "If it had not been for American filibusters and adventurers the revolt in Mexico would have been put down in two weeks."[75]

Jealousy and the fact of foreignness underlay the hostility that many Mexicans developed toward the exogenous revolutionaries. Mexican subordinates became suspicious of the high rank and accolades awarded to the foreigners in the struggle for Mexican liberation, while it became apparent even to Mexican foot soldiers that these outsiders usually got the more important and more prestigious jobs. The national ethnocentrisms of both the Mexicans and the foreigners also set them apart. Such foreign volunteers as General Viljoen often spoke no Spanish or spoke it only with considerable difficulty. The spirit of adventure and a manifestly Anglo-Saxon enjoyment of robust activity among some volunteers estranged them from the more dedicated Mexican revolutionaries, while other volunteers maintained the attitude that they had come to bring Mexicans a brand of "liberty" and political democracy not shared by the Mexicans or only dimly understood. Further resentment toward Americans serving with the revolutionists sprang up in such individual cases of reprehensibility as that of the disgruntled American volunteer who set fire to a Mexican flag and then swam across the Rio Grande to an American cavalry patrol that prevented his punishment.[76]

The increasing jealousy the Mexican Maderistas felt for

75. *The New York Times*, March 12, 1911, Part 5, p. 14:1; May 9, 1911, p. 2:1; May 10, 1911, p. 2:1; May 14, 1911, p. 2:1; and June 1, 1911, p. 2:2.
76. *Ibid.*, May 7, 1911, p. 2:1.

the Foreign Legion under Garibaldi coincided with a personal animosity that Francisco Villa felt for Garibaldi himself. Three days before the battle of Juárez, Villa disarmed Garibaldi and a group of Americans under his command at gun point only to have Madero release them. After the battle, Villa and two companions crossed over into El Paso hunting for Garibaldi but were disarmed and sent back to Juárez by Mayor Kelly and members of the United States Secret Service. Mexican Maderistas derided the significance the American press placed on Garibaldi's troops in the battle of Juárez. When Villa by chance met Roque González Garza, at that time a major designated as historian of the battle of Juárez, Villa made it plain that he rather than Garibaldi should receive proper credit in the battle reports. When Villa and Pascual Orozco threatened Madero for his alleged slighting of their interests after the Juárez victory, General Viljoen and other members of the Foreign Legion protected Madero. Tempers flared when Americans who had served under Madero attempted to recross the Rio Grande into Juárez after a one-day visit in El Paso for which they had obtained permission, and the Mexicans refused to admit them, saying that the Americans' services were no longer required and that they could not re-enter Mexico for the duration of hostilities.[77]

For this variety of reasons, Mexicans came to resent the foreigners. After the victory at Ciudad Juárez, the foreign volunteers recognized that they were not a welcome part of the Mexican success and that Madero would be prudent to rid himself of them, so the officers of the Foreign Legion —Garibaldi, Viljoen, Captain Lewis, and Captain Malan —sent their resignations to Madero. Chronicling the military campaign against Díaz, Maderista writers reject charges that Madero was "soft" on foreigners, and they defend his revolution as being eminently Mexican. Pedro Lamicq, for example, stoutly defends Madero's patriotism

77. *Ibid.*, May 14, 1911, p. 2:1; May 18, 1911, p. 2:2; and May 21, 1911, p. 2:1.

by noting that Garibaldi and Viljoen were subordinate to their Mexican chiefs and pointing out that other foreigners —Lafayette in America, Byron in Greece, and Cochrane in Chile—had participated in national revolutions.[78] Antagonism to the foreigners spread, however, despite such advocacy, prompted in part by a segment of the Yankee press that denounced the expatriates as common criminals.[79]

Besides the animosity that the foreign volunteers aroused in the Mexican Maderistas with whom they served, an additional antagonism developed in the revolutionary factions against the foreigners serving with the opposition. Díaz supporters, many of them clerically-oriented conservatives who had traditionally flayed the detestable United States, hated to see foreigners join in Madero's revolt. They overemphasized the foreigners' influence in their own minds and also in the public statements by which they tried to discredit Madero. Only a small number of Mexicans followed Ricardo Flores Magón in his support of Stanley Williams, Simon Berthold, and their crew of largely English and American socialist adventurers who tried through insurrection to establish a separate socialist republic in Lower California.[80] Zapatistas looked warily not only upon all foreigners but even upon Mexicans from outside their *patria chica* of Morelos.

As the Revolution progressed, the resentment and xenophobia that built up against foreigners in each faction tended to curtail the outsiders' participation. Governor Carranza refused to let any "foreigners" serve in the Constitutionalist ranks and forced the Japanese and other foreigners serving under him to become Mexican citizens.[81]

78. Crater [Pedro Lamicq], *Madero por uno de sus íntimos* (México: Oficina Editorial Azteca, n.d.), pp. 116-17.

79. *New York Tribune*, March 15, 1911, in U.S., Library of Congress MSS collection, *Newspaper Clippings pertaining to Mexico, 1911-1913*, 3 vols.; III-48-C,1, Ac. 6194, Vol. 1.

80. On the socialist campaign, see Lowell L. Blaisdell, *The Desert Revolution: Baja California, 1911* (Madison, Wis.: University of Wisconsin Press, 1962).

81. Ellsworth to Bryan, July 9, 1913, /8046.

The new ferocity of Mexican nationalism prevented the reconstitution of fighting units such as Garibaldi's Foreign Legion. This Mexican hostility toward foreign participation developed, of course, not only as the foreign participants themselves stimulated xenophobia but also as the foreigners became objects of the wider Mexican nationalism and xenophobia that forces beyond the control of the expatriates were producing.

Mexican youth during the Revolution, like the youth of Mexico and other Latin American countries during later periods of the twentieth century, proved to be outspoken nationalists and particularly fierce opponents of North American encroachments. Yankee provocations produced especially determined resistance in Mexican students, that educated segment of Mexican youth who had already developed an allegiance to the national community. In early 1911, Consul General Shanklin stressed to Secretary Knox that students, like the lower and middle classes in Mexico City, combined strong anti-Americanism with their resolute support for the Madero revolution.[82] During the anti-American campaign in Huerta's newspapers in July, 1913, a poster signed by student representatives appeared in all of the public schools of Mexico City asking students to carry Japanese flags to the railway station to greet the new Japanese minister. Demonstrating a clear sense of participation in the national community by the student activists, the poster asked fellow Mexican students to show support for Japan, the United States rival, "now that our nationality is put to the test by the imperialistic ambition of strong peoples."[83]

The threat of military invasion by the United States occasioned widespread voluntary participation by Mexican youth in the preparations for Mexican-American conflict. In May, 1911, correspondent Stephen Bonsal reported that

82. Arnold Shanklin to Knox, March 21, 1911, /1104.
83. *The Mexican Herald*, July 12, 1913, clipping enclosed in Nelson O'Shaughnessy to Bryan, August 6, 1913, /8412.

patriotic societies had formed all over Mexico which stimulated "excitement among the younger generation" to resist United States invasion. In societies with such names as Friends of the Country, Lives of the Country, and the Society for National Integrity, Bonsal "conservatively" estimated that between twenty thousand and twenty-five thousand men were drilling half an hour every day.[84] In Tampico, an estimated two thousand Mexicans signed a paper circulated by a committee of young nationalists with the sanction of the miltary commander which called for volunteers to meet daily at the barracks for military drill and instruction to prepare for the defense of the city.[85] On the morning after the circular was issued, about fifty enthusiastic young men reported for drill.[86]

Student activity remained strong throughout the republic as a result of successive rumors of Yankee invasion. In Durango, during May, 1912, when the populace generally believed American intervention to be inevitable, students drilled actively and showed considerable enthusiasm for the prospective encounter.[87] After a night rally in August, 1913, in which 3,000 residents of Nuevo Laredo heard Huerta agitators proclaim that a war with the United States was imminent, since "the noble and illustrious Huerta would brook no insult or humiliation from the Yankees," about eighty persons underwent an initial training course given by an army officer appointed by General Joaquín Téllez to instruct citizens desiring military training.[88] With the same prevailing impression that war was inevitable, about one hundred "young men of the better class" drilled with Mexican Army troops in Acapulco during September, 1913, after volunteering for anti-invasion service.[89]

84. *The New York Times*, May 13, 1911, p. 3:2.
85. Miller to Knox, May 10, 1911, /1716.
86. Miller to Knox, May 11, 1911, /1728.
87. Theodore C. Hamm to Knox, June 1, 1912, /4240.
88. Alonzo B. Garrett to Bryan, August 31, 1913, /8641.
89. Edwards to Bryan, September 19, 1913, /8926.

An underlying reason for the arousing of Mexican youth was, as Vice-Consul Richard M. Stadden explained in an interesting dispatch to Secretary Bryan, that the volunteer forces drilled allegedly for local use in the event of American invasion were actually raised as a means to get men into the regular army. As Stadden observed, Mexican federal, state, and local authorities throughout the republic were appealing to an expression of patriotism which made clerks and laborers march through the streets and drill in the use of arms in preparation for a Yankee invasion. The three hundred volunteers who gathered at Colima in the summer of 1913, for example, had been led to believe that they would be used for the defense of Colima alone. Gradually these men were issued arms and uniforms, and in September, they became part of the federal troops and were listed as the irregular infantry of the 13th Regiment. Although these volunteers, like other Huerta conscripts, resented being sent away from their *patria chica*,[90] they gained an increased sense of Mexican nationalism from their travel and their active participation in the anti-gringo cause. Like the student demonstrators who fiercely built up their own sense of nationalism, the youth in whom agitators stimulated anti-Americanism developed a sense of their nationality through fear of another nation.

Resentment among liberal Mexican Freemasons arose in 1910 when American, British, and Canadian Freemasons supporting the Díaz regime for reasons of business interests took over the Valley of Mexico Grand Lodge to the exclusion of Mexican Masons. Resident English-speaking foreigners in independent Masonic lodges openly challenged the pro-Madero Mexican lodges, accusing Mexican Masons of "never really understanding Freemasonry" and of "possessing Latin minds incapable of grasping Freemasonry." As this split contravened Masonry's unifying principles, it emphasized the potential divisiveness of nationalism and economic self-interest.

90. Richard M. Stadden to Bryan, September 25, 1913, /9212.

The 1910 break between Mexican and English-speaking Freemasons led to a continuing schism with the founding of the York Grand Lodge of Mexico by the foreigners. Today the York Grand Lodge still conducts its rituals in English, competes for exclusive jurisdiction with the far larger Mexican lodges, and has gained recognition from more grand lodges in the United States than the giant, Mexican-oriented, and Mexican-staffed Valley of Mexico Grand Lodge. Although a lack of unity exists among Mexican Masonic organizations such as the Confederation of Regular Grand Lodges, the old Rito Nacional Mexicano, and the blue lodges of the "Cárdenas Rite," the major conflict among Masons in Mexico has been the foreign-national antagonism between the Mexican lodges and the York Grand Lodge of the Anglo-Saxons.[91]

Woodrow Wilson's refusal to recognize Victoriano Huerta's regime alienated the Mexican faction that, despite Villa's apparent friendship, was the most ready to cooperate with the United States. Huerta courted American support from the time negotiations for Madero's overthrow were made at the American Embassy, and it was only later, with Wilson's nonrecognition and the occupation of Veracruz, that he attempted to rally Mexicans behind him against the United States. President Wilson, who took office just ten days after the assassination of Madero, could have maintained Huerta's support by following the lead of England, Germany, France, and Japan in quick recognition of the new regime. *The New York Times* had commented before the assassination that recognition was a "formality" that "probably will fall to the Administration of President-elect Wilson."[92] Wilson had ample precedent for recognition and could have found numerous vocal backers in both Mexico and the United States for his support

91. For a terse and sympathetic account of Mexican Freemasonry since the Díaz era, based on sources that are generally unavailable in the United States, see Frank Brandenburg, *The Making of Modern Mexico* (Englewood Cliffs, N.J.: Prentice-Hall, Inc., 1964), pp. 195-204.
92. *The New York Times*, February 19, 1913, p. 1:3.

of Huerta. Furthermore, Wilson knew that his negation of Huerta could not in itself create political democracy or teach Mexicans to elect "good men." He himself had written many years before, "Self-government is not a thing that can be 'given' to any people, because it is a form of character and not a form of constitution."[93]

Despite such reasons for recognition, President Wilson elected a policy that probably contributed more than that of any other single individual to Huerta's overthrow. As supporters of Huerta commented, without American recognition, Huerta more closely resembled the president in an operetta than a veritable chief of state.[94] Huertistas and Mexicans desiring an end to civil war expressed increasing hostility toward Americans at the initiation and maintenance of the nonrecognition policy.[95] The policy cut the United States off from those Mexicans who, in the manner of Porfirio Díaz, were still willing to exchange Mexican encouragement of American business interests for cordial American friendship. Although Huerta's defeat within Mexico reduced evidences of the support that he once had, one should not underestimate the size or the power of the faction that the United States antagonized by its opposition to him.

Like the followers of Huerta, Villistas later became estranged from both Woodrow Wilson and the United States. In the summer of 1914, Wilson looked to Pancho Villa as the new leader of Mexico. Wilson appreciated Villa's coming to his defense during the Veracruz crisis and noted Villa's apparent willingness to accept United States guidance in the reconstruction of Mexico. Villa

93. Quoted in L. S. Rowe, "The Scope and Limits of Our Obligations Toward Mexico," *The Annals of the American Academy of Political and Social Science*, Vol. 54 (July, 1914), 225.

94. León Cárdenas Martínez, ed., *Memorias ineditas escritas por Victoriano Huerta en la prisión de Fort Bllis* [sic.] *Tex., E. U. A.* (Durango, Dgo.: Redacción de "El Azote," 1917), p. 36.

95. See Henry Lane Wilson to Bryan, April 25, 1913, /7273; Letcher to Bryan, May 3, 1913, /7427; Lespinasse to Bryan, May 18, 1913, /7732; and Canada to Bryan, May 31, 1913, /7662.

appeared to be the most likely instrument of agrarian and social reform, and favorable press reports on Villa in the United States created support for him in a large segment of American opinion.[96] No evidence indicates that the Wilson administration seriously considered recognizing Villa. The Villista faction became incensed, however, when, as the tide of battle turned against Villa within Mexico, the United States deprived him of what had been tacit support. The United States needed to stabilize Mexican-American relations so that it could turn to considerations of the European war. The shift of support to Carranza and the final recognition of his regime, which resulted largely from Robert Lansing's personal influence,[97] thoroughly alienated the Villistas and occasioned the attacks that created further Mexican-American antagonism.

The shift of Wilson's support which alienated Villa caused no warm friendship for the United States among Carrancistas. An outspoken nationalist whose opposition to the Veracruz occupation had originally made Wilson look more favorably on the deceptively amiable Villistas, Carranza consistently rested his claim to leadership on his protection of the Mexican "nation" from foreign domination, just as Huerta and Villa had done. With the Pershing expedition deployed on Mexican soil and military encounters creating a real possibility of a second Mexican-American war, the xenophobia of Carranza's followers further prevented his close co-operation with the United States. Carrancistas resented the fact that they had once been counted out by the American administration, while many of them execrated the vested foreign interests that appeared to oppose social reforms.

The withdrawal of Pershing's troops in February, 1917, and *de jure* American recognition of Carranza on March 13

96. Arthur S. Link, *Wilson: The Struggle for Neutrality, 1914-1915* (Princeton, N.J.: Princeton University Press, 1960), pp. 239-41.

97. Louis G. Kahle, "Robert Lansing and the Recognition of Venustiano Carranza," *Hispanic American Historical Review*, Vol. 38, No. 3 (August, 1958), 367.

prevented military co-operation between Carranza and the Central Powers. Henry P. Fletcher, the new American ambassador, nevertheless found resentment seething against the United States in the Mexican populace and the new Carrancista Congress. Mexico remained a haven for German agents, and the German request for Mexican assistance in return for the restoration of Mexico's "lost territory" in Texas and California contained in the Zimmermann note appealed strongly to the coalescing sense of Mexican nationalism. The Constitutionalist leaders of what was to become the institutionalized Revolution in Mexico had, therefore, like the Mexican soldiers antagonized by foreign participants, the youth goaded to anti-Americanism, the estranged Mexican Freemasons, and the defeated followers of Huerta and Villa, developed a personal antipathy and a profound sense of separation from foreigners residing both inside and outside the Mexican Republic.

VERBAL ATTACKS

Incendiary publications on both sides of the border dramatized the conflicts of interest between Mexico and the United States during the years of revolutionary violence. Books, articles, plays, and even the reporting of events mirrored the hostility to the United States which increasingly set Mexicans apart in the realization of their own nationality.

Looking back on the coverage of the 1910 Revolution in the foreign press, Mexicans still denounce it as a defense of Saxon imperialism and are convinced that newspaper space was sold to Mexican reactionaries.[98] Mexicans leveled particularly fierce criticism against the newspaper chain of William Randolph Hearst, a spokesman for North American interventionists who had himself inherited a ranch in northern Mexico larger than the state of Rhode Island.

98. María del Carmen Ruiz Castañeda, ''El periodismo y la Revolución Mexicana,'' *Ciencias Políticas y Sociales,* Año 4, Núm. 14 (octubre-diciembre, 1958), 449.

Juan T. Burns, a onetime Mexican consul general in New York who violently attacked American trusts and American capitalism, spoke out strongly against the interventionism of the Hearst editorials. Burns characterized Hearst as "the fiercest enemy of Mexico" and "a veritable boss of public opinion in the United States."[99] Informing Hearst of "the wave of hatred which your conduct has roused in us against the whole American people," another Mexican in an open letter to the publisher claimed—with more enthusiasm than accuracy—that "even the most isolated Indian of our country is aware of the existence of a Mr. Hearst who owns many newspapers; knows that he is constantly maligned by that gentleman; and that the major part of that person's statements is false."[100]

Yankee books and articles also rasped on Mexican sensitivities. Mexicans took umbrage at repeated North American presumptions of racial superiority that, like those of Henry Morris, pictured Mexicans as members of an inferior race that would be effortlessly defeated and then "saved" in the manner of the Philippines and Puerto Rico by a forthcoming Yankee invasion.[101] Particularly insulting was the flood of superficial sensationalistic accounts of the Mexican people which interest in the Revolution stimulated in the United States and other foreign countries. Offensive accounts such as Henry Neil's *Exciting Experiences in Our War with Mexico* provoked Mexican anger by describing "the average Mexican" as savage, bloodthirsty, and indolent; by declaring that Mexican Indians still practiced the "hideous" sacrificial rites of the Aztecs; and by self-righteously claiming that the present troubles in Mexican-American relations resulted from the "purity of motive," the "unselfishness," and the "fine ideals" of Americans

99. Juan T. Burns, *El pulpo* (Madrid: Editorial Reus, S.A., 1921), p. 349.

100. "Open Letter of Mr. M. C. Rolland to Mr. W. R. Hearst," included as the second part of a pamphlet entitled "Intervene in Mexico, Not to Make But to End War, Urges Mr. Hearst" (New York, 1916).

101. Henry Morris, *Our Mexican Muddle* (Chicago: Laird & Lee, 1916), especially Chs. 2, 11.

in the face of Mexican "brigandage."[102] Furthermore, Mexican Constitutionalists keenly resented the unbridled attacks against them by the Roman Catholic clergy of the United States. In the widely circulated pamphlet entitled "The Religious Question in Mexico," Luis Cabrera summed up Constitutionalist resentment in a definitive reply to the barbed and biased North American indictments of restrictions on the Mexican church such as those of Francis Clement Kelley.[103]

Partly in response to such North American pressure, local newspapers throughout Mexico kept up constant denunciations of the United States between 1910 and 1917. The reports of American diplomatic representatives and a content analysis of particular Mexican newspapers show one of the most constant prods toward anti-Americanism to have been the Mexican press. The Mexican press also projected an ideal of national unity before a large segment of the Mexican people during a period when the successive contests of civil war delayed actual unity. As Tampico's *El Insurgente* proclaimed two days after the issue of a xenophobic and unifying circular, consciousness of the Yankee menace seemed to be "the only thing which can raise us to harmony, the only thing which will permit these Mexicans to exhibit their capacities to sacrifice everything and to see yesterday's enemy as an ally and a brother when trying to defend the honor and integrity of the nation."[104]

Posters displayed on walls and billboards throughout

102. Marshall Everett [Henry Neil], *Exciting Experiences in Our War with Mexico* . . . (Chicago: The Bible House, 1914), pp. 22, 238, 296-300.

103. Cabrera's study was published at Veracruz, in *Forum* magazine, in pamphlet form by the Carrancista junta in New York, and in several Mexican newspapers in the United States. For a bitter and righteously indignant indictment of the Mexican revolutionaries by North American Catholics, which includes many "eyewitness" accounts of atrocities and persecutions of the Catholic clergy in Mexico, see Francis Clement Kelley, *The Book of Red and Yellow: Being a Story of Blood and a Yellow Streak* (Chicago: The Catholic Church Extension Society of the United States of America, 1916), pp. 8-15, 39-43, 79, 147.

104. *El Insurgente*, March 16, 1912, clipping enclosed in Miller to Knox, March 17, 1912, /3350.

the republic at the various periods during the Revolution both frightened North Americans and incited Mexicans against them. Americans began to leave Mexico when, at the beginning of Madero's revolt, they began to see posters such as those covering Pachuca which read "Death to the Yankees!" "Down with Gringos!" and "Kill Díaz and his Yankee friends." An editorial published in *El Tiempo* on April 28, 1912, was reproduced and widely distributed in Mexico City as a twelve-by-sixteen-inch poster. It denounced the supposed Anglo-American invasion and called for the Mexican people to rise up, repel the invaders, and make sure that "each bullet fired goes to strike the heart or the forehead of the profaner of our soil."[105]

Recruiting handbills and fliers appealed to illiterates through such devices as pictures of President Wilson and the American eagle and shield. As part of Huerta's anti-American recruiting campaign, a handbill urged men to volunteer for informal military training, asked them to defend the "immaculate national colors," and suggested that those from all occupations and social groups, "being Mexicans," should apply at once.[106] On February 9, 1914, a bitter but not atypical flier was sold on the streets of Saltillo at 10 cents per copy. In violently anti-American language, it attacked historical and contemporary American invasions of Latin America and suggested nine means of repelling American attack, including the extermination of all American residents in Mexico, the counterinvasion of American territory, and the propagation of smallpox, yellow fever, and other diseases along Mexico's frontiers and coasts.[107]

Mexican cartoons lampooned the United States in a lighter vein. A three-column, front-page cartoon in the

105. A copy of the poster is enclosed in Henry Lane Wilson to Knox, May 6, 1912, /3875.

106. Enclosures in William B. Davis to Bryan, July 18, 1913, /8210.

107. John R. Silliman to Bryan, February 11, 1914, /10928, and enclosures.

daily newspaper *Redención* on August 9, 1917, showed a beautiful, nude, and languishing woman in a liberty cap being burned at the stake. Around the burning woman, who was labeled the Mexican Revolution, lay fresh logs marked "U.S.A.," "Yankees," and "Yankee-lovers."[108] Woodrow Wilson in one revolutionary cartoon leers lecherously at the feminine form of Baja California; in another, Wilson is Goliath, carrying a silver dollar shield and the blood-dripping sword of "ambition," standing by David, a small Mexican boy with the simple inscription "pueblo," who twirls the sling of "justice."[109] These cartoons and the others like them that filled the Mexican press during the Revolution could communicate even with the illiterate soldiers and peasants into whose hands they occasionally fell.

The books and plays produced during the Revolution also portray the United States as a predator intent on destroying Mexico's national independence. Books published in the first years of the Revolution, even before the interventions of Ambassador Wilson and Veracruz, berate the United States determination to hold Mexicans strictly responsible for loss of American lives and property and depict Uncle Sam as a gleeful observer of Mexican destruction.[110] Contemporary accounts of the Revolution describe the United States as being in league with betrayers of the Mexican Motherland in a plot to divide the states of Mexico one from another.[111] A number of plays and short stories such as *Tenorio-Sam* and Filiberto C. González' *Proyectos de un yankee,* produced in the atmosphere of revolutionary xenophobia, show Uncle Sam bested by a Mexican Indian girl and picture despicable Americans who speak very

108. Carl W. Ackerman, *Mexico's Dilemma* (New York: George H. Doran Company, 1918), pp. 57, 284.

109. Manuel González Ramírez, ed., *La caricatura política* (Vol. 2, "Fuentes para la Historia de la Revolución Mexicana"; México: Fondo de Cultura Económica, 1955), Figs. 378-418, especially Figs. 378, 381, 396, 400-1, 409, 412.

110. Héctor Ribot, *Las últimas revoluciones* . . . (México: Imprenta la. de Humbodlt [sic.] Número 5, 1910-11), pp. 258-59.

111. G. Núñez de Prado, *Revolución de México: La decena trágica* (Barcelona: F. Granada y Comp., 1913), pp. 298-99.

bad Spanish and grasp at Mexican territory.[112] Intellectual and racial antagonisms recur through the references of revolutionary writers and commentators to the *angloamericanos*, the *yanquis, norteamericanos*, and *estadounidenses*. Such books as *El porvenir de México y sus relaciones con Estados Unidos* by Enrique E. Schulz outspokenly plead for greater Mexican nationalism and national unification. Since history, geography, and race have made the United States and Mexico unalterable enemies, Schulz and other nationalists argue, Mexicans must group together in resistance by means of military preparations and an educational system that would make all Mexican citizens unwaveringly loyal to the Motherland.[113]

Rómulo Velasco Ceballos and Querido Moheno made especially convincing indictments of American policy and American society. As a prelude to his study of the invasion of Baja California by North American filibusters in 1911, Velasco Ceballos traced the history of United States interventions in Mexico from the plots against New Spain by Aaron Burr, "the founder of United States imperialism." Velasco Ceballos discourses at length on the differences between "us" Mexicans and "those" Yankees.[114] In what professes to be a series of letters written in 1915 from the United States to an aunt in Mexico, Querido Moheno, with bitter irony and understatement, attacks the entire fabric of North American society. Using frequent comparisons that show in what ways Mexico surpasses the United States and numerous quotations that show how barbarous other foreigners find the United States to be, Moheno belittles

112. *Tenorio-Sam. Humorada satírica de autores mexicanos, escrita en un acto dividido en tres cuadros, sobre el drama de Zorrilla y contra la tragicomedia yankee. Estrenada en el Teatro Principal de México, con éxito extraordinario, la noche del 28 de febrero de 1914* (México: Imprenta de "Novedades," 1914); and Filiberto C. González, *Proyectos de un yankee* (México: Tip. 1a de Humboldt No 5, 1914).

113. Enrique E. Schulz, *El porvenir de México y sus relaciones con Estados Unidos* (México: Tipografía Económica, 1914), pp. 1, 32-35, 49.

114. R. Velasco Ceballos, *¿Se apoderará Estados Unidos de América de Baja California? (La invasión filibustera de 1911)* (México: Imprenta Nacional, S.A., 1920), pp. 1-30.

such customs as the North American use of leisure time in which the women play cards at their club while the men stay at home to cut the grass. He quotes a spokesman for the Women's Christian Temperance Union on the shocking number of prostitutes and clandestinely immoral women in the United States and describes how Negroes are relegated to separate waiting rooms and separate churches in *"such a Christian, such a free and such an equalitarian"* society. In the promotion of nationalism, like other forms of verbal conflict between Mexico and the United States, Moheno's indictment effectively executed his stated purpose of making Mexicans as a group feel "somewhat higher" by showing the low life of their North American neighbors.[115]

THE LIMITATIONS ON XENOPHOBIA AND ITS OVER-ALL EFFECT

The objective situation and subjective attitudes of the leaders, participants, and isolated populace of the Mexican Revolution imposed limitations on their acquisition of xenophobic attitudes. Because of the United States military superiority and power to support rival factions by nonbelligerent means, the verbal and military provocations of Mexican leaders did not exceed certain limits. For many of the participants and onlookers who by means of the Revolution became engaged in national activities outside the scope of familial and *patria chica* relationships, friendships for individual foreigners reduced the depth and temporal extent of xenophobia. For individuals still isolated by barriers of geography, illiteracy, and language, this isolation prevented xenophobia from altering their modes of perception. Despite these very real limitations during the 1910 to 1917 period, however, an extension of xenophobia has since that time become an important ingredient of Mexican nationalism.

115. Querido Moheno, *Cosas del Tío Sam* (México: Talleres Tipográficos de "Revista Mexicana," 1916), pp. 2, 12, 65, 75, 102-3. The italics are Moheno's.

In the case of each factional leader, the practical danger of provoking foreign pressure and so jeopardizing the achievement of particular political objectives circumscribed his use of nationalistic xenophobia as a rallying device. Porfirio Díaz endeavored to prevent manifestations of xenophobia from undermining the cordial relationships his regime had established with foreigners, while Francisco Madero, more than any other revolutionary leader, recognized the importance of friendly relations with foreigners. Carranza held anti-Americanism within bounds when the offer of a German alliance encouraged its fermentation, and knowledge of American military strength prevented even Pancho Villa from launching more than sporadic military raids in United States territory. Zapata's dream of indigenous agrarian reform excluded foreign *hacendados,* but it did not presuppose continuing opposition to foreigners as long as they left Zapatistas alone. Even without direct Pershing-style military actions in support of one faction, the United States could exercise considerable leverage by embargoing arms shipments and recognizing a group's belligerent status. Even though American blockade proved ineffective, as in the case of the Veracruz occupation when the *Ypiranga* simply sailed south and unloaded its cache of arms for Huerta at the secondary port of Puerto Mexico, still American policy could substantially affect the flow of arms. It had done so after American *de facto* recognition of Carranza and the embargo on arms shipments to all other Mexican groups in October, 1915. A primary limitation on xenophobia as a rallying point, therefore, was its limited feasibility.

Secondly, the existing isolation of Mexican groups and the limited nature of American intervention imposed restrictions on the pervasiveness of the resulting anti-Americanism. The Veracruz invasion and Pershing expedition did stimulate Mexican resistance and nationalism, but the lack of a full-scale American invasion and occupation con-

fined the tide of xenophobia. Only a small proportion of
the Mexican population personally confronted Pershing's
troopers and the Americans who occupied Veracruz. All
citizens could listen to the anti-foreign harangues and discussions, but illiteracy prevented many from sharing directly in the journalistic attacks on Americans. A sense of
the immediacy of the Yankee danger was diffused only with
great difficulty in linguistically isolated Indian groups and
in areas other than those in which North American power
was most readily apparent. Furthermore, acquiring the
daily necessities of food and shelter and maintaining interpersonal relationships prevented xenophobia from preoc-
cupying many Mexicans. As Oscar Lewis' documented
re-creation of revolutionaries' attitudes indicates, a search
for justice or vengeance and the fulfillment of personal
drives motivated their actions far more often than did vague
fears of foreign oppression.[116]

The personal friendship or economic interdependence
of individual Mexicans and foreigners further lessened the
intensity of xenophobia. In actual interpersonal relationships, the stereotyped Mexican image of Americans as
covetous and presumptuous was no more generally true than
was the American stereotype of the indolent Mexican. Like
other foreign residents, a large number of the 50,000 to
75,000 North Americans who had become residents of Mexico before 1910 had established genuine bonds of friendship
with individual Mexican citizens. Some foreigners performed admirably during the Revolution, as did John Hayes
Hammond, a wealthy American mining engineer owning
660,000 acres in Mexico, who offered to conciliate the Yaqui
Indians by giving them a large portion of his land for farming and tried to persuade the Mexican government to give
them land as well.[117] Xenophobia is reduced even when
individual Mexicans find a foreigner to be *simpático*, and

116. Oscar Lewis, *Pedro Martínez: A Mexican Peasant and His Family*
(New York: Random House, 1964), pp. 73-110.
117. *The New York Times*, January 12, 1913, p. 18.

they describe him as uniquely unrepresentative of the foreign group.

Before, during, and after the Revolution, many Mexicans enjoyed economic benefit from their contacts with foreigners. Rivalry with some animosity has persisted, but foreign financing and technology have employed and given managerial responsibility to many Mexicans who know that cordial relations with foreigners and foreign states further their own interests. Economic self-interest, as well as personal friendship, has contributed to counteracting anti-foreign attitudes.

Xenophobia as a passion that forcefully shapes thought and action is a phenomenon of comparatively short duration without repeated provocation. A North American traveling in Mexico today as a tourist, student, or businessman may—depending more upon his own character than upon his national origin—find in the friendliness of Mexicans of all social classes little to remind him of the anti-Americanism of 1910 to 1917. When individual Mexicans express resentment of United States influence, it tends to focus on such phenomena as Madison Avenue advertising or unpleasant experiences with individual North Americans rather than on the United States itself. Since the Good Neighbor policy of Franklin Roosevelt and the revered presidency of John Kennedy, Mexicans have little reason to fear American policy.

Xenophobia became intermittently weaker after 1917. Despite the genuine affection that Mexicans came to feel for Ambassador Dwight Morrow, an underlying antagonism shaped largely by the earlier American interventions labeled even this outstanding representative of the new American policy of active co-operation as a *yanqui* responsible for halting the social progress of the Mexican Revolution.[118] Lázaro Cárdenas' nationalizations of foreign oil properties

118. See Stanley Robert Ross, ''Dwight Morrow and the Mexican Revolution,'' *Hispanic American Historical Review*, Vol. 38, No. 4 (November, 1958), 506-7.

in 1938 rejuvenated xenophobic attitudes, which became dormant again during the Mexican-American co-operation programs of the 1940's.

A strong undercurrent of anti-Yankee feeling pervades Mexico today. Mexicans who experienced the xenophobia of the revolutionary years are being replaced by younger generations. Many of the most violently anti-American tracts of the 1910 to 1917 period received only limited printings and today gather dust on library shelves, read by scholars but largely ignored by the general Mexican public. Revolutionary participants have conveyed attitudes to their children and grandchildren, however, and the ideas of the early anti-American books still appear in a variety of popular genres. Mexicans still resent examples of North American "presumptuousness," the smug boasting and display of material wealth, the tourist's insistence on speaking English in Mexico without even an attempt to learn Spanish, and the distasteful attitudes of racial or religious superiority found in some Americans. Heightened by leftist propaganda that depicts the "economic imperialism" of Yankee capitalism, anti-gringo sentiment finds support in the American invasions and xenophobia of the past. Mexicans who remember the North American invasions of their country hold out against breaking relations with Fidel Castro's Cuba even under concerted pressure from the Organization of American States. Although anti-American rantings in such magazines as the Communist organ *Politica* represent only a small fraction of the Mexican people, the equally consistent and more clever anti-Yankeeism of *Siempre!* accurately reflects the sentiments of a large part of the Mexican national community.

Anti-Yankeeism has also shaped the spirit of "Latin Americanism," which theoretically competes with Mexican nationalism. Providing an excellent focus for xenophobia, the United States has encouraged Latin American states to maintain a feeling of comradeship toward each other. Common fear of the United States has, in fact, been one of the principal causes for the degree of Latin American solidarity and camaraderie that now exists—more important perhaps than the dubious, if often reiterated, ties of common language, geography, and history. Latin Americans continue to face what appears to be economic and cultural, if no longer political, danger from the northern colossus, and discord within the area would seriously fragment its influence on United States policies. The spirit of Latin Americanism has, however, in no sense seriously challenged nationalism for the effective loyalty of the Mexican people. Xenophobia, in conjunction with the social bases of Mexican nationalism, has made nationalism a far more potent and pervasive force.

VII
Literature, the Arts, and Nationalism

Literature both registers growing awareness of nationalism among the inhabitants of a given territory and cumulatively increases that awareness as successive generations develop common attitudes from "their own" literature. Mexican literature, in its various genres, is a primary source by which we may measure the extent and nature of nationalism in consecutive periods of Mexican history, considering the extent to which the cumulative growth of nationalistic expression has in turn stimulated national consciousness both during and after the period of composition. The interrelationship of literature and nationalism encompasses what literature fails to say as well as what it says, so that the lack of emphasis upon indigenous art forms and the extent of extra-Mexican thematic and stylistic material created during the nineteenth century evidences an absence of full cultural autonomy in Mexico before 1910. Mexican literature, music, and art in both the nineteenth and twentieth centuries have contained an abundance of introspective and romantic material that bears virtually no relevance to nationalism. The beginning of conscious formulation of a national literature coincided in the nineteenth century, however, with literary works that either directly or indirectly furthered the individual attitudes made possible by an enlarged national community. During and since the events of 1910 to 1917, in novels, histories, plays, poetry, films, murals, and popular ballads, Mexicans have both memorialized the events and pleaded the cause of national solidarity and social justice for which they have made the events stand.

The importance of literature in the process of nation-forming gives particular relevance to the kinds of functions the literature is performing as Mexicans see it. In developing nations, such as the newly created states in Asia and Africa, the benefits that nation-states derive from ideological unity encourages a degree of "cultural management," a shaping of culture into national molds that achieve unity of purpose and a measure of consensus among the diverse peoples inhabiting the national territory.[1] Just as the manipulation of nationalist symbols is one of the most appropriate and significant functions of political leaders in developing nations, so the effective although frequently less conscious, manipulation of literature by national writers and artists may influence the goals, aspirations, and forms of competition within a national polity. By stressing cohesive nationalism and social equality, literature can shape the way in which a national populace and its leaders perceive their own relation to the goals and problems of inter-group competition within the national community. The cultural impact of literature gives social significance to the fact that Mexicans see the 1910 Revolution as creating a "new sensibility" among Mexican artists and writers,[2] establishing the "Mexicanization of the national culture,"[3] and bringing Mexico *"a truly social conscience"* and the desire for *"a homogeneous national life."*[4]

1. Lloyd A. Fallers, "Ideology and Culture in Uganda Nationalism," *American Anthropologist*, Vol. 63, No. 4 (August, 1961), 677-78.

2. José Mancisidor, *Historia de la Revolución Mexicana* (México: Ediciones el Gusano de Luz, 1958), p. 272.

3. Julia García, "Factores sociales de la cultura mexicana," *Ciencias Políticas y Sociales*, Año 2, Núms. 5, 6 (julio-diciembre, 1956), 57.

4. J. M. Puig Casauranc, *La aspiración suprema de la Revolución Mexicana*

Analyses of the social relevance of literature must avoid the twin problems of overestimating literary permeability and overgeneralizing the literature chosen for analysis. Illiteracy and cultural isolation, which variously affect the different media of artistic expression, have greatly restricted the permeability of Mexican literature among the Mexican people. A large body of Mexican literature patently espouses cohesive nationalism and castigates foreigners, racial and geographical divisiveness, and economic and social inequalities, but exclusive consideration of this body of literature creates the danger that the discussion of literary nationalism may turn into an extended bibliographical essay that focuses on selected literary themes. For most passages and viewpoints cited to illustrate the modes of nationalist expression, similar or opposing sentiments could be culled from other literary works. Furthermore, although the aggregate audience for Mexican literature is large and growing larger, the number of Mexicans studying any single piece of art or literature is comparatively small. While most Mexicans with whom one talks readily agree that the Revolution had a great nationalistic impact, they frequently show little familiarity with nationalist literature and seem satisfied with knowing the Revolution's effects rather than studying its historical details. The basic fact that Mexican literature has had a decided and increasing significance in manifesting and shaping patterns of national loyalty necessitates exploration of the mainstreams and some of the rivulets of various Mexican genres in order to see how they have affected the growth of nationalism.

ANTECEDENTS AND THE MEXICAN NOVEL

Although the rise of literary nationalism may be most clearly traced in the gradual development of the Mexican

(México: Imprenta de la Secretaría de Relaciones Exteriores, 1933), pp. 11, 19. The italics are Puig Casauranc's.

novel after 1810, Mexicans find the roots of their national literature to lie in the pre-Columbian, colonial, and independence periods. While destruction of the early Indian texts has created a paucity of materials from which to work, Mexican scholars proudly reproduce what remains and regard the great Maya and Náhuatl literatures as part of their own inheritance.[5] Extrapolating *indigenismo* into the past, critics conclude that Mexicans have "an older and more profound tradition of national consciousness" than do the Argentineans or Chileans because of "the importance of our cultural Indian past and the solidarity which the Mexican feels for that past."[6]

In colonial literature, such figures as Sor Juana Inés de la Cruz, Bernardo de Balbuena, and Francisco Javier Clavijero add the hallmark of antiquity to Mexican literature, just as Puritan writers like Cotton Mather and Anne Bradstreet do in the United States. Mexicans trace the intellectual foundations of Mexican nationalism to a series of colonial writers.[7] The acceptance of colonial writing as part of the Mexican tradition reflects in the fact that nearly half of Carlos González Peña's standard *Historia de la literatura mexicana* deals with the period before Mexico became an independent state.

Before considering the rise of nationalistic tendencies in the nineteenth-century Mexican novel, it is well to remember that many novels of the period reflected foreign influences or embodied a romanticism and sentimentality that had nothing to do with nationalism. French and Spanish writers, and particularly Walter Scott whose work was widely read in Mexico, strongly influenced Mexican novelists. Zola's influence, for instance, is evident in the natural-

5. For a concise statement of present attitudes with descriptions and reproductions of the Indian literature, see Miguel León-Portilla, *Las literaturas precolombinas de México* (México: Editorial Pormaca, 1964).

6. José Luis Martínez, *La emancipación literaria de México* (México: Antigua Librería Robredo, 1955), p. 57.

7. See Rafael Moreno, "Creación de la nacionalidad mexicana," *Historia Mexicana*, Vol. 12, Núm. 4 (abril-junio, 1963).

istic novels such as Martínez de Castro's *Eva,* in which Eva's attitude changes from one of idealism to predatory malevolence after her rape by a group of soldiers. Many writers followed Scott in the idealization of characters, particularly women, and sentimentality predominates in the works of the lesser novelists, Fernando Orozco y Berra, Juan Díaz Covarrubias, and Florencio M. del Castillo.[8] Religious themes of José Francisco Sotomayor and others only diverted attention from nationalism.

Despite foreign influences and extranational concerns, a revealing and influential national consciousness initially evident in the work of Fernández de Lizardi came to full maturity in the novels and doctrine of Ignacio M. Altamirano. Novels came to contain the best expression of nationalism that Mexican literature manifested, and no other genre was so widely read by the general public. It is indicative of later trends that Fernández de Lizardi's *El Periquillo Sarniento,* an essentially picaresque work generally conceded to be Mexico's first novel, contained enough nationalism to cause its suppression after the publication of the eleventh chapter in 1816. Lizardi is appreciated as a nationalist as well as the nation's first novelist, and the lasting influence of *El Periquillo Sarniento* is evident in the fact that over 100 million copies have reputedly been sold.

National consciousness developed during the Reforma period, and the French intervention came to have a direct influence on Mexican literature through the work of Altamirano, just as that literature may in turn have effected the later rise of nationalism. Victory over the French and Maximilian gave a nationalistic impetus and fervor to

8. José Luis Martínez, ''Las letras patrias,'' in Jaime Torres Bodet and others, *México y la cultura* (México: Secretaría de Educación Pública, 1946), p. 402. For a comparative study of Mexican novels, see John S. Brushwood, *Mexico in Its Novel: A Nation's Search for Identity* (Austin, Texas: University of Texas Press, 1966).

Mexican novels which the Revolution of 1910 revived and continued.[9] Altamirano, who became the champion of national literature, took part in the revolt of Ayutla, the War of the Reform, and the French intervention. A full-blooded Indian of humble birth whose contemporary portrait shows a look of fierce determination, Altamirano kept his work free from xenophobia but consciously developed national sentiment in the Mexican scenes that he chose to depict. Altamirano indicated both the superior utility of the novel as a vehicle for nationalism and its use in facilitating social integration when he wrote that "the novel is the book of the masses. . . . Perhaps the novel is called to open the way to the poorer classes so that they may arrive at the height of this privileged circle and be blended with it."[10]

Altamirano's hope that the Mexican novel could promote nationalism in the sense of both patriotism and social integration was partially realized even before the appearance of the revolutionary novel after 1910. The crystallization of nationalism appeared in such novels as Juan A. Mateos' *El cerro de las campanas,* a patriotic interpretation of the French intervention which paints the clergy as traitors to Mexico and ridicules *afrancesados* in the persons of Mr. and Mrs. Fajardo who ludicrously wear wigs and try to marry their daughter to the first French soldier who proposes.[11] Social themes predominate in realistic novels like Arcadio Zentella Priego's *Perico* (1885), which was somewhat similar to *Uncle Tom's Cabin* in that it stimulated ideas of social justice. Perico, a peon and in effect a slave, kills his tyrannical master who is about to molest Perico's sweetheart, only to find that the representatives of the law

9. Doris King Arojona and Carlos Vázquez Arojona, "Apuntes sobre los origenes del nacionalismo en la novela mexicana," *Revue Hispanique,* Vol. 81, 2d part (1933), 440-41.

10. Quoted in Irma Wilson, *Mexico: A Century of Educational Thought* (New York: Hispanic Institute in the United States, 1941), p. 268.

11. J. Lloyd Read, *The Mexican Historical Novel, 1826-1910* (New York: Instituto de las Españas en los Estados Unidos, 1939), pp. 215-17.

serve the rich rather than justice.[12] By portraying the destruction of an Indian group, Heriberto Frías in *Tomóchic* (1894) attacked the Díaz regime in revolutionary terms. Mexican authors and critics laud *Tomóchic* for the nationalism of its form and content, and Mariano Azuela writes that the novel "reproduces authentically national events and evidences Mexicanness in each of its figures, with their appearances, expressions and manners which are exclusively ours."[13]

In order not to place too much emphasis on the influence of novels as an initiator of national values or even of the Revolution itself, we must remember the limitations of both the novelists' social criticism and the permeability of their ideas in Mexican society. It is difficult to find Mexican literature in the Díaz period to be a direct cause of the Revolution because, instead of favoring revolution, the novelists who criticized social conditions in Mexico saw revolution as an obstacle to progress. Mariano Azuela's *Los fracasados* and *Mala yerba* received very little attention when they were published in 1908 and 1909, and their revolutionary content was scarcely noticed until the revival of interest in Azuela's early work long after the publication of *Los de abajo*. Furthermore, even the novelist's advocacy of limited means to effect social change could not reach the masses in a society where the official rate of illiteracy was 85.3 per cent in 1895 and 78.4 per cent in 1910. This illiteracy greatly restricted the immediate impact of nationalistic literature despite the fact that the literate segment of the Mexican population had disproportionate political and economic influence. In the novel, as in other forms of literature, it is important to remember the sharp distinction between the culture of the elite and the culture of the people.[14]

12. Ralph E. Warner, *Historia de la novela mexicana en el siglo XIX* (México: Antigua Librería Robredo, 1953), p. 92.

13. Mariano Azuela, *Cien años de novela mexicana* (México: Ediciones Botas, 1947), p. 217.

14. Bernardo Canal Feijóo, *Confines de occidente: Notas para una sociología de la cultura americana* (Buenos Aires: Editorial Raigal, 1954), p. 108.

The Revolution of 1910 introduced subject matter and attitudes of reform and social solidarity that have characterized many of the most important Mexican novels of the twentieth century. Mariano Azuela's *Los de abajo* became the most influential of a long series of revolutionary novels. Azuela's pre-revolutionary novels, which strongly indict the inequalities of Mexican society, demonstrate the social conscience that prompted Azuela to participate in the Revolution. *Los fracasados,* written in 1906 and published in 1908, illustrates the corruption of a small town during the Díaz epoch, while *Mala yerba* (1909) unsentimentally depicts a family of Spanish immigrants who exploit and outrage the Mexican peasants around them. *Sin amor,* published in 1912, criticizes the Mexican elite in the story of a middle-class girl who sacrifices her dignity to marry a rich *hacendado* in what becomes an unhappy and loveless union. *Andrés Pérez, maderista* (1911), with a passing description of the Serdán martyrdom, compares the idealism and opportunism of the Revolution in the figures of Toño Reyes and Andrés Pérez. *Los caciques,* written in 1914 and published in 1917, exposes the local bosses, the robber barons who prey upon the inhabitants of small-town Mexico, and upholds the power and honesty of the Revolution in the murdered figure of Rodríguez.[15]

Mariano Azuela, a trained medical doctor, had first become affiliated with the Maderistas. He became a local *jefe político* under Madero's administration and a fugitive from the Huertistas after Madero's assassination. After traveling extensively with a Villista chieftain while serving in his capacity as a doctor, a disillusioned Azuela emigrated to the United States. Disenchanted when he found that what he called "the spirit of love and sacrifice"[16] of the early Maderista revolutionaries had disappeared, Azuela

15. The best study on Azuela, with an excellent bibliography, is Luis Leal, *Mariano Azuela, vida y obra* (México: Ediciones de Andrea, 1961).

16. Quoted in Antonio Magaña Esquivel, *La novela de la Revolución* (México: Biblioteca del Instituto Nacional de Estudios Históricos de la Revolución Mexicana, 1964), Vol. 1, p. 99.

published *Los de abajo* in an El Paso, Texas, newspaper in the last months of 1915.

Los de abajo presents the need for love of country by portraying men without patriotism and the need for human and national goals by showing the brutality of a situation determined by circumstance and private concern. Demetrio Macías, who leads his men through many encounters only to watch them die in the end, lacks national consciousness. The blond Margarito embodies a ferocity that became commonplace with revolutionary violence, while the opportunist intellectual, Luis Cervantes, has no dedication to the principles upon which the Revolution is presumably being fought. Irony and an embittered optimism deny the suggestion that with these revolutionaries "our motherland will be filled with glory."[17] Clarifying Azuela's evocation of the apparent pointlessness of the Revolution is Alberto Solís, a dedicated revolutionary who is disillusioned with the Revolution's failure to implement its goals. Through Solís and the presentation of the immediate irrelevance of pre-1916 violence, Azuela suggests the national cohesion and the altruism needed in the subsequent constructive phase of the Revolution. It is precisely by showing the lack of unifying ideals that Azuela emphasizes the need for them.

Although isolated novels approached revolutionary themes in the aftermath of the struggle itself, it was not until after literary controversy called wide attention to *Los de abajo* in 1924 that other novelists began to grapple with Azuela's theme and their own interpretations of the Revolution. Two of the most successful, whose message parallels that of Azuela, are Nellie Campobello and José Rubén Romero.

In *Cartucho* (1931) Nellie Campobello presents the

17. Mariano Azuela, *Los de abajo* (México: Fondo de Cultura Económica, 1964), p. 61. On the general relevance of this theme in Latin America, see Seymour Menton, "In Search of a Nation: The Twentieth-Century Spanish American Novel," *Hispania*, Vol. 38, No. 4 (December, 1955).

brutality of the Revolution as described by a little girl. Although some figures appear valiant—as Pancho Villa actually did to the authoress, who grew up in Durango during the revolutionary years of Villa's fighting there— the brutality and bloodiness of the Revolution rather than lionization of its heroes characterizes the novel. With an apparent indifference and objectivity of description that emphasizes the horror of the events described, *Cartucho* effectively condemns the hatred between brothers which makes killing seem justified. Nellie Campobello's appeal for a greater sense of brotherhood among Mexicans becomes clear when she describes the enemies that the revolutionaries are preparing to fight as their own "cousins, brothers and friends." One character in the book declares that "the war between ourselves is what makes me sad."[18]

José Rubén Romero joined Madero's revolt, worked at various jobs during the Revolution, including that of secretary to two governors of Michoacán, joined the Ministry of Foreign Relations in 1920, and rose to become Mexican ambassador to Brazil and Cuba between 1937 and 1945. His novels on the Revolution, which trace in part his own actions through the revolutionary years, include *Apuntes de un lugareño* (1932), *Desbandada* (1934), *El pueblo inocente* (1934), *Mi caballo, mi perro y mi rifle* (1936), and *La vida inútil de Pito Pérez* (1938). Like Azuela, Romero suggests that the violence of the Revolution must be vindicated by the implementation of revolutionary ideals. At the conclusion of *Desbandada,* after graphically portraying the hardship and injustice of revolutionary violence, Romero sums up the major burden of his narratives by stating that "pillage and sacking are not Revolution. Revolution is a noble ardor for uplifting, and I will uplift; it is the hope for a life with more justice, and I cling to it."[19]

18. Edna Coll, *Injerto de temas en las novelistas mexicanas contemporáneas* (San Juan, Puerto Rico: Ediciones Juan Ponce de León, 1964), pp. 117-21.

19. José Rubén Romero, *Obras completas* (México: Ediciones Oasis, S.A., 1957), p. 195.

Mexican participants have also inspired a spirit of Mexican nationalism by creating realistic descriptions of the scenes and heroes of the Revolution. Francisco L. Urquizo, one of the most dedicated Carrancistas, successively served in Francisco Madero's Presidential Guards, became Carranza's aide after Madero's assassination, rose to brigadier general and chief of operations at Veracruz, and loyally followed Carranza on the final flight from Mexico City to the peasant hut at Tlaxcalantongo where he died. After years of exile in Europe, Urquizo returned to Mexico in 1930 and became an outstanding figure in the Mexican Army after resuming his position as brigadier general in 1934. In addition to a radio drama and numerous stories written between 1933 and 1953, General Urquizo produced popular biographies of Carranza and Morelos, *Venustiano Carranza, el hombre, el político, el caudillo* (1935) and *Morelos, genio militar de la independencia* (1945). General Urquizo also wrote novelistic re-creations of Mexican revolutionary history. *México-Tlaxcalantongo, mayo de 1920* (1932) sympathetically re-creates the flight from Mexico and murder of Carranza, while *¡Viva Madero!* (1954) depicts the life of Francisco Madero from the time of his return from foreign travels to his death following the *decena trágica*.

Urquizo's best known novel, *Tropa vieja,* elicits nationalistic responses in a more indirect manner. A peon-soldier, Espiridión Sifuentes, here relates the story of his conscription into the army under Porfirio Díaz, his conversion to Madero's side after the Ciudad Juárez victory, and his loss of an arm in fighting for Madero in the *decena trágica*. By picturing the hardship and injustice of Espiridión's early life on the hacienda of a *gachupín* landholder, Urquizo delineates the causes of the Revolution of 1910. Although Espiridión comes to represent the conscripted federal soldier who fought indiscriminately for those in power, he has both a strong sense of Mexican nationalism and an appreciation of revolutionary heroes and events.

A sense of nationalism is clearly demonstrated in the scene in which Espiridión and other conscripts swear allegiance to the Mexican flag. His battalion shouts affirmation when the colonel asks, "Soldiers, do you swear constantly and faithfully to follow this flag, symbol of our Motherland, toward which every Mexican has duties and obligations to fulfill?" Espiridión forgets all of his suffering as the flag passes, and he comments, "With what willingness would I have shouted a *Viva México!* with all my heart!, with what rage would I have fought against an invader." Urquizo evokes an appealing sense of the nationalistic sentiments of federal troops in Espiridión's description of "all the guys in uniform, brothers in suffering and hunger; orphans abandoned by all, with only one mother, with only one sheltering tricolor flag. . . ."[20] As the flag scene demonstrates the conscripts' sense of patriotism, the conclusion of *Tropa vieja,* a frequently quoted section of the novel, shows their appreciation of the revolutionary movement. Declaring that those who are free will fight on, Espiridión refuses to accept the pessimism of those who say that the army has all gone over to Victoriano Huerta and prophesies that a new Madero will arise.[21] Here, as elsewhere in the novel, which has been reprinted in inexpensive editions and anthologies and is widely read as one of the best revolutionary novels, readers gain a heightened sense of patriotism and sympathy for the Revolution by sharing the conscript's viewpoint.

The Indianist novels written after the Revolution portray Indians not simply as individuals with curious customs or as "noble savages" degraded by civilization but as Mexicans beset by social problems in contemporary Mexico. *El indio* (1935), like the other Indianist novels of Gregorio López y Fuentes, illustrates and reprehends the barriers that exist between the Indian groups and other Mexican

20. Francisco L. Urquizo, *Tropa vieja* (México: Talleres Gráficos del Departamento de Publicidad y Propaganda de la Secretaría de Educación Pública, 1943), pp. 80-81.
21. *Ibid.,* p. 349.

citizens. Widely read in Mexico, *El indio* gained immediate
popularity and won Mexico's National Prize for Literature
in 1936. Similarly championing social improvement for the
Indians in *Tierra* and *Huasteca,* López y Fuentes again
shows the Indians without the roads and schools promised
to them, still exploited after the Revolution.[22] These novels
of social reform, like the earlier revolutionary novels, match
with their outspoken nationalism much of the historical and
pedagogical writing done since the Revolution.

HISTORIES AND SCHOOL TEXTBOOKS

The approach to nationalism that citizens derive from the
study of national history depends largely on the content and
slant of the histories and the informal milieu with which
they are surrounded. Mexican formal histories, school
textbooks, and extracurricular sources of information present Mexican history and the Revolution with patriotic
intonations that arouse loyalty in the national community.
To bear primary relevance to the ongoing process of nation-
forming, however, national history must invade the consciousness of the great majority of citizens rather than
serve as a plaything of historians that reaches only a thin
literate stratum of society. The interpretations that Mexican historians and anthropologists put upon the past is
important, but even more important in quantitative terms
is the fact that increasing literacy permits a growing
number of the Mexican people to derive a sense of personal
involvement with the national past. Although illiteracy and
lack of school attendance still limit opportunities for basic
historical study in Mexico as in other developing nations,
Mexico's expanded school budgets and the present reduction of illiteracy to about 23 per cent have opened a sig-

22. Hubert E. Mate, ''Social Aspects of the Novels by López y Fuentes
and Ciro Alegría,'' *Hispania,* Vol. 39, No. 3 (September, 1956), 287, 289.
For a comparison of the Indianist attitudes of Mexican novels, see Aída
Cometta Manzoni, *El indio en la novela de América* (Buenos Aires: Editorial Futuro, 1960), pp. 65-77.

nificantly expanding market for texts dealing with the past and present.

Mexican historians have long provided the literate segment of the Mexican people with a wealth of material that creates loyalty to the national community. Rather than chronicling facts or interpreting events in the providential manner of clerical writers, Mexican historians in the nineteenth century viewed events in terms of their social and national significance. Differences between such nineteenth-century histories as those of the respected conservative Lucas Alamán and the radical Lorenzo de Zavala reflect the opposing views of their period, while at the end of the century the contrast between the criticism of Francisco Bulnes and the scholarly patriotism of Justo Sierra provided Mexicans with both a challenge to their sense of nationalism and an optimistic faith in its eventual triumph. Manuel Orozco y Berra directed the monumental *Diccionario de historia y geografía* that honored Mexican culture, and his *Geografía de las lenguas indígenas* and *Historia antigua de México* increased awareness of Mexico's unique heritage. In 1862 Pérez Hernández dedicated his *Estadística de la República Mejicana* to the "Mexican nation," evidencing a national pride that he may have imparted to others in his chronicle of Mexico's highest mountains, her volcanoes and gorges, her flora, and national monuments. Finally, a series of highly patriotic, popularized histories also appeared in the last half of the nineteenth century: Enrique de Olavarría y Ferrari's *Episodios nacionales;* Ireneo Paz's hero studies on *Hidalgo, Morelos,* and *Guerrero;* and José Severino de la Sota's piece, *El Grito de Dolores.* While, as Ralph E. Warner suggests, these works contain more "patriotism than inspiration,"[23] they did foster the common national pride on which a sense of community could be based.

The Revolution of 1910 has intensified the nationalistic tone of most Mexican historical writing. Typical of a long

23. Warner, *Historia de la novela mexicana en el siglo XIX*, p. 76.

series of state and campaign histories that appeared during and after the Revolution is T. F. Serrano's early *Episodios de la Revolución en México* (*Estado de Chihuahua*). With biographies of revolutionary leaders and detailed accounts of battles and campaigns, these histories re-create, memorialize, and glorify the events of the Revolution. Post-revolutionary Mexican philosophers now engage extensively in defining the meaning of "Mexicanness," pointing out connections between "Mexicanness" and other aspects of life in the long *México y lo mexicano* series.[24] Like the philosophers, writers of general and specialized histories frequently tie their interpretations of events to Mexico's struggle for unity. Partisan writing on the Revolution has so long been common that impartial students of revolutionary history must identify sources as being Maderista, Zapatista, Carrancista, Villista, or Obregonista. Despite the partisanship of individual factions, however, all factions esteem "the Revolution." Members of the inclusive revolutionary "family" join together to laud Madero's revolt, deride Huerta's coup, and praise the struggle for social reforms embodied in the 1917 Constitution.

Although objectivity has increased substantially in the writing of Mexican history since the early 1950's, most histories still bear a strongly nationalistic imprint and frequently overemphasize revolutionary achievements in what Howard F. Cline calls a "modified Chamber of Commerce tone."[25] While appearing somewhat ephemeral to the professional historian, even the most flagrantly nationalistic writings promote the growth of nationalism. They record the predilections of their writers and indicate what is thought saleable to a national audience. In turn they mold the thinking of their audience, depending on the

24. For outside criticism of this preoccupation with "Mexicanness," see John Leddy Phelan, "Mexico y lo mexicano," *Hispanic American Historical Review*, Vol. 36, No. 3 (August, 1956).

25. Howard F. Cline, review of *México, cincuenta años de Revolución*, Vol. 2, *La vida social*, by Julio Durán Ochoa and others, *Hispanic American Historical Review*, Vol. 43, No. 2 (May, 1963), 291.

degree of sophistication of the audience as well as on its size.

School textbooks are the introduction to national history for a majority of young Mexican citizens today. The growth of nationalism in Mexico as elsewhere has increased the importance of scholars and teachers. They no longer simply seek knowledge or instruct youth but also, in their writing and teaching, give the national community the propagandistic justification that facilitates communication and social interaction within it.[26] Mexicans get their first detailed impressions of civics and history from textbooks and many students lack the opportunity to pursue studies beyond this level. Poverty and the pressures of a rapidly expanding population oblige many children to drop out of school before reaching the sixth grade, and with the increasing technological complexity of Mexico's emerging society, most of the students who go on to study medicine, agriculture, science, or literature have little time to pursue historical studies beyond the level of a *secundaria* text.

On the covers of many of the government textbooks, which are distributed free to children in primary school, appears the figure of a beautiful woman with flowing black hair and somewhat Indian features who carries an unfurled Mexican flag. An insert on the title page of each book explains that the woman ''represents the Mexican nation advancing with the impetus of her history with the triple impulse—cultural, agricultural, industrial—which the people give her.'' *Primaria* textbooks and workbooks amplify this idea of the Mexican nation. The geography texts, for example, give schoolchildren an excellent idea of the physical proportions of the Motherland and stress the geography of Mexico as a whole rather than pointing up differences among the states. Typically, the fourth-grade geography book contains fifty-nine colored pictures that show the physical characteristics of Mexico, and only two of them

26. Elie Kedourie, *Nationalism* (London: Hutchinson of London, 1960), p. 49.

indicate state divisions.[27] Supplementing the geography texts, the third-year workbook contains eight pictures of Mexico which the children can color, and the fourth-year workbook contains thirty-one.[28]

Primary-school texts are specially designed to give students a sense of cohesive nationalism. A reading book for second-grade students, for example, focuses on Mexican racial unity. With pictures of red, brown, and white hands joined together and of five boys of distinctly varying racial characteristics with their arms around each other, a section entitled "Comrades" states that "all the boys who are part of the second year group are friends and play together at recess."[29] The third-year course continues the nationalist indoctrination at a slightly more advanced level. The third-grade reader presents a colored picture of the fluttering Mexican flag saying "young Mexicans, look well at my three colors: green, white and red. . . . I represent the Motherland, this Mexican land in which you saw light for the first time." Emphasizing the patriotic heroism of Mexican youth, the reader contains the story of Narciso Mendoza, the twelve-year-old boy who in February, 1812, on his own initiative, fired a cannon at the Spanish to aid José María Morelos in the siege of Cuautla.[30]

Secondary-school textbooks, like the textbooks of the *porfiriato,* introduce a strong note of xenophobia to evo-

27. Rita López de Llergo, *Mi libro de cuatro año: Geografía* (México: Comisión Nacional de los Libros de Texto Gratuitos, Dependiente de la Secretaría de Educación Pública, 1960), pp. 41-123.

28. Carmen Domínguez Aguirre and Enriqueta León González, *Mi cuaderno de trabajo de tercer año: Geografía* (México: Comisión Nacional de los Libros de Texto Gratuitos, Dependiente de la Secretaría de Educación Pública, 1961), pp. 28-34, 41; and Rita López de Llergo, *Mi cuaderno de trabajo de cuatro año: Geografía* (México: Comisión Nacional de los Libros de Texto Gratuitos, Dependiente de la Secretaría de Educación Pública, 1960), pp. 18-19, 32-33, 38-52.

29. Paula Galicia Ciprés, *Mi libro de segundo año* (México: Comisión Nacional de los Libros de Texto Gratuitos, Dependiente de la Secretaría de Educación Pública, 1960), pp. 164-81.

30. Carmen Domínguez Aguirre and Enriqueta León González, *Mi libro de tercer año: Lengua nacional* (México: Comisión Nacional de los Libros de Texto Gratuitos, Dependiente de la Secretaría de Educación Pública, 1960), pp. 27-117.

cations of nationalism. José R. del Castillo's *Curso elemental de historia patria,* a government-endorsed textbook issued after the Díaz government had already opened Mexico to foreign investment, arouses nationalism by repeated praise for the Mexicans' "extraordinary valor" and "heroic opposition" against the advancing armies of Taylor and Scott in 1846.[31] Ángel Miranda Basurto's long-standard textbook states that President Polk ordered General Taylor to allow the Mexicans to attack first only to give the false impression that Mexico was the aggressor in the war. Providing a large map demonstrating the extensiveness of the huge provinces that the United States took from Mexico, it describes many alleged abuses of North American soldiers and their looting of the churches after taking Mexico City. The textbook also stirs resentment against later intervention. Proudly noting that Maximilian cost France "900 million francs and the lives of 65,000 imperialists," Miranda Basurto reminds his young Mexican readers that the French intervention was important for Mexico "because during the development of the struggle the people were becoming unified and awakening their *national consciousness.*"[32] Textbook history written from this national standpoint—in whatever country it may be found—quite naturally gives secondary students a sense of pride in their national community.

Popular literature reinforces the attitudes expressed in the school texts. *La bandera de México,* a children's book with a cover picturing a forward-rushing Mexican flag that overspreads both Mexicans brandishing rifles and a serene view of Mount Popocatepetl, traces the history and significance of the national flag.[33] Special coloring books il-

31. José R. del Castillo, *Curso elemental de historia patria* (México: Imprenta, Litografía y Encuadernación de Ireneo Paz, 1898), pp. 174-83, 259.
32. See Ángel Miranda Basurto, *La evolución de México (de la independencia a nuestros días): Segundo curso de historia de México para las escuelas de segunda enseñanza* (9th ed.; México: Editorial Herrero, S.A., 1960), pp. 162, 181, 183, 191, 194, 260, 344, 357, 370-72. The italics are Miranda Basurto's.
33. *La bandera de México* (México: Fernández Editores, S.A., 1961).

lustrate the physical and human geography of the diverse Mexican regions so that the Mexican child may acquire a comprehensive idea of his nation.[34] Supplementing revolutionary comic books like the *Leyendas de Pancho Villa,* the *Biografías Selectas* comic books glorify the whole gallery of national heroes from Guadalupe Victoria to Venustiano Carranza.[35]

One of the most interesting media through which Mexicans acquire pride in their common history is a series of colorful foldout pamphlets that cover such subjects as the winning of national independence, the War of 1847, the national anthem, and the careers of national heroes. With eight or more pictures in brilliant colors on a long sheet and lengthy descriptions of each picture on the reverse side, small pocket-size pamphlets sketch historical events in a highly nationalistic manner. One pamphlet describes the events of the Maderista revolution, showing Madero with his wife formally accepting the presidency from León de la Barra, discussing conditions in Morelos with Zapata, under arrest by Huerta, and riding above the masses against the background of the Mexican flag. Juárez appears as a boyhood shepherd in Oaxaca, as a student, and as a triumphant national leader in the war against the French. In one of the most violent picture pamphlets, fierce Mexican soldiers are shown slashing, strangling, and shooting North American soldiers in the War of 1847. Supplementing the small

34. *Conoce a tu patria*, Serie 250, Núms. 1-4 (México: n.p., n.d.).

35. See "El Pípila," Año 2, Núm. 34 (junio, 1959); "El niño artillero," Año 2, Núm. 41 (agosto, 1959); "Los Niños Héroes," Año 3, Núm. 156 (octubre, 1961); "¡1862! Batalla de 5 de mayo," Año 3, Núm. 184 (mayo, 1962); "Moctezuma Ilhuicamina," Año 3, Núm. 115 (enero, 1961); "La Malinche," Año 2, Núm. 103 (octubre, 1960); "La Corregidora," Año 2, Núm. 94 (agosto, 1960); "Leona Vicario de Quintana Roo," Año 2, Núm. 100 (septiembre, 1960); "Vicente Guerrero," Año 2, Núm. 99 (septiembre, 1960); "Morelos," Año 2, Núm. 36 (julio, 1959); "Guadalupe Victoria," Año 3, Núm. 164 (enero, 1962); "Hidalgo, el padre de la patria," Año 2, Núm. 46 (septiembre, 1959); "El grito de independencia y sus héroes," Año 2, Núm. 98 (septiembre, 1960); "Benito Juárez, el indio heroico," Año 2, Núm. 102 (octubre, 1960); and "Venustiano Carranza," Año 2, Núm. 79 (abril, 1960).

pamphlets are large, full-color pictures of national heroes with accounts of their exploits printed on the reverse. Sold in Mexico the year around, these pamphlets and pictures are particularly popular on national holidays such as September 16.

Nationalist handbooks and advertising campaigns add to the national content of the Mexican milieu. An effective inculcator of nationalism, which has sold over 130,000 copies in its three editions and is now officially approved for use in schools by the Mexican Ministry of Education, is the nationalist's handbook, *Yo soy mexicano: Lo que todo ciudadano debe saber,* by Francisco Vargas Ruiz. In addition to an up-to-date copy of the Mexican Constitution and the various "plans" of revolutionary leaders, the book contains biographies of twenty-one national heroes and describes the lives of the heroes buried in the Rotonda de los Hombres Ilustres. Sold inexpensively and at reduced bulk rates, it also provides Mexicans with numerous national statistics, a copy of the national anthem, and a long calendar of important events in Mexican history.[36]

Even the advertising techniques of modern sales campaigns promote Mexican nationalism. As a promotional device to stimulate sales, a leading Mexican bank recently issued a scrapbook in which depositors might paste brightly colored stamps that picture Mexican troops in action, the architectural and industrial achievements of modern Mexico, and Mexico's heroes, monuments, and murals. Stamps are issued with each deposit, and upon filling the book the depositor receives a 256-page history, *La nación mexicana.*[37] In this type of sales campaign, the devices designed to promote sales have the same effect as the patriotic histories, textbooks, and popular paraphernalia that also stir Mexican nationalism.

36. Francisco Vargas Ruiz, *Yo soy mexicano: Lo que todo ciudadano debe saber* (3d ed.; México: Enrique Sáinz Editores, S.A., 1964).

37. See *Historia del himno nacional* (México: Sistema Bancos de Comercio, 1964).

Poetry, plays, and oratory all serve as means of nationalist expression in Mexico even though their impact is not as great as their content might indicate. Poetry affects the dissemination of some nationalist attitudes, but it is not as clear a mirror for the advancement of nationalism as the Mexican novel, the histories, and the school textbooks. Although sometimes adding artistic intensity, poetic form makes its expression of nationalism more esoteric than the direct approach of novels and histories. Stage plays have some influence as a medium for the inculcation of nationalism, but they have become less significant in post-revolutionary Mexico than the cinema, which reaches a far wider audience in remote areas of the republic. Mexican oratory since the nineteenth century has expressed nationalist sentiments with varying levels of fervor and sincerity.

Although one may point to numerous patriotic Mexican poems, the most widely respected Mexican poetry has not been nationalistic. During the nineteenth century, patriotism became manifest in a number of Francisco Ortega's poems and even in such religious poetry as Manuel Carpio's ode to the Virgin of Guadalupe. Patriotic poems like Quintana Roo's ode to September 16 replaced the dearth of civic poetry during the colonial period, and Guillermo Prieto's epic of independence, *El romancero nacional,* is often compared with the work of Fernández de Lizardi. The appearance of the "modernist" school and the publication of the *Revista Azul* in 1894, however, marked an advance in aesthetic expression and encouraged poets to write for a small group of readers rather than for the masses. Many Mexican poems regained a nationalistic tone during the Revolution of 1910. Themes of revolutionary novels reappeared in poetry, as the Revolution stimulated Ramón López Velarde's intimate expression of sadness at revolutionary destruction.[38] Poetry also asked Mexicans to unite behind opposing factions in defense of their Motherland.[39] Under the revolutionary impulse, patriotic verse appeared in various volumes as well as national reviews.[40]

Many of the best and most widely known Mexican poets of the twentieth century, such as Jaime Torres Bodet and José Gorostiza, have rejected nationalist themes. Patriotism and national solidarity, nevertheless, receive frequent, if often superficial, poetic treatment. Anthologies and special editions of nationalistic poetry keep its message in circulation.[41] Children's editions of patriotic poetry feature the importance of national holidays, the Niños Héroes and other heroes, the national flag, and the Revolution.[42] The social effect of these poetic themes has grown and may continue to grow, as education gradually increases the number of Mexicans writing as well as reading and listening to poetry.

Drama did not add greatly to the consolidation of the Mexican national community during the nineteenth century. The Mexican theater had failed to convey patriotic ideals at the time of independence, and it continued to lack the patriotic characteristics of other genres once independence was achieved. The fact that, despite the extreme factionalism within Mexican society, theatrical productions flourished during the first half of the nineteenth century under

38. José Luis Martínez, ''La literatura mexicana y la Revolución,'' in Norman Thomas and others, *Homenaje a la Revolución Mexicana, Combate,* edición especial, Vol. 2, Núm. 13 (noviembre, 1960), 90.

39. See the Carrancista poem ''Canto a la Revolución,'' in Marcelino Dávalos, *Iras de bronce* (n.p.: Publicada bajo los auspicios de la Revolución de 1913, 1915), pp. 109-11.

40. For strikingly nationalistic examples of revolutionary poetry, see Antonio Guzmán Aguilera, *Los motivos del águila: Cantos a la raza y a los héroes* (México: Departamento Editorial de la Dirección General de Educación Pública, 1917), pp. 37-38, 53-54, 63, 67-76, 95-104, 115-20, 131-33; and Emilio Fernández, *Revolución 1910 a 1916* (n.p.: Editorial Hispano-Mexicana, n.d.).

41. Manuel Puig Vitria, ed., *Poesías patrióticas mexicanas* (México: Editorial Divulgación, 1957).

42. *Poesías y discursos patrióticos* (México: Fernández Editores, S.A., 1964).

such men as Manuel Eduardo de Gorostiza, Fernando Calderón, and Ignacio Rodríguez Galván indicates that drama may be an inferior vehicle of nationalism. Plays can certainly embody political themes, and drama may prove emotionally moving to a small audience, but as a medium for nationalism, the theater encounters the serious problems of high admission fees, confined seating capacity, and limitations of stage setting, all of which set it off from a medium like the cinema. Furthermore, the wealth of classical plays performed in Mexico lacks national subjectivity and spoofs narrow national allegiance. That drama, like orchestral music, better presents universalistic than nationalistic conceptions reflects in the fact that critics seldom consider *Henry V* to be one of Shakespeare's better plays.

When the Mexican theater turned to more nationalistic themes in the second half of the nineteenth century, it lost much of its earlier brilliance. Some material, in addition to promoting patriotism in a superficial sense, did support nationalism as a cohesive social force or stated the case for social reforms basic to the rise of nationalism. Alberto G. Bianchi's *Patriotismo y deber* (1877) illustrates the unpatriotic futility of civil strife by presenting the conflict of two brothers who die fighting as enemies in opposing political parties. Federico Gamboa's *La venganza de la gleba* (1904) presents a theme of social criticism in the situation of Damián, a peon and illegitimate son of a hacienda owner who falls in love with Blanca, the owner's legitimate daughter, without knowing that she is his sister.[43] The majority of the "nationalistic" plays appearing before 1910 treat only the trappings of nationalism, however. José Peón y Contreras, a major figure in the late nineteenth century, thus took up the nationalist doctrine of Altamirano merely by setting the scenes of his works in Mexican places.

The 1910 Revolution initiated a spate of nationalism in

43. Antonio Magaña Esquivel and Ruth S. Lamb, *Breve historia del teatro mexicano* (México: Ediciones de Andrea, 1958), pp. 91, 102.

Mexican plays.[44] The heroic peasant, revolutionary soldier, wicked landowner, and corrupt politician developed into theatrical stereotypes. The brand of Spanish spoken on stage became that which was actually spoken in Mexico. Dramas incorporated the revolutionary impetus to social transformation with frequent references to patriotism and the Mexican Motherland.[45] Antonio Mediz Bolio, a Maderista exiled by the Huerta regime, exemplifies Indian heroism and Spanish cruelty during the conquest in *La flecha del sol* (1918). The same Indianist spirit pervades his famous presentation of Maya courage in *La tierra del faisán y del venado.* In Mediz Bolio's *La ola* (1917), Jaime, an illegitimate son, gives workers in his family's factory the higher wages and improved working conditions that they are shown to deserve.

Many revolutionary plays evidence strong xenophobia. When John Lind first arrived in Mexico as President Wilson's envoy, Leopoldo Naranjo produced an anti-American satire on the local stage in Saltillo which a North American consular representative described as "most scurrilous."[46] Not only locally produced dramas but also plays with a national audience castigated North American involvement in Mexican affairs. Francisco Monterde's *Oro negro* (1927) is typical in its attack on foreign exploitation of Mexican oil. Epitomizing the anti-Americanism of revolutionary drama is *Tío Sam y la patria,* a short play in verse published in 1919. In this encounter between Uncle Sam and the Mexican Motherland, the Motherland soliloquizes on North American treachery and calls Uncle Sam an imbecile, a thief, and a serpent. Uncle Sam extols the power of his

44. See Armando de María y Campos, *El teatro de género dramático en la Revolución Mexicana* (México: Biblioteca del Instituto Nacional de Estudios Históricos de la Revolución Mexicana, 1957); and Frank Dauster, "The Contemporary Mexican Theater," *Hispania,* Vol. 38, No. 1 (March, 1955).

45. For a selection of these references used in different contexts in twentieth-century Mexican plays, see Chris N. Nacci, *Concepción del mundo en el teatro mexicano del siglo veinte* . . . (México: Impresora Económica, 1951), pp. 55-57.

46. John R. Silliman to William Jennings Bryan, February 11, 1914, /10928.

armies while the Motherland, represented as a beautiful girl of about sixteen years who repulses Uncle Sam's licentious advances, is confident that she has noble and valiant sons to defend her. Finally, when Uncle Sam draws two pistols and shoots at the resisting Motherland, she runs him through with a dagger while holding the Mexican flag. Uncle Sam falls dead, after sputtering a few dying words in very bad Spanish to the effect that his cannons and airplanes have done him no good, and the Motherland marches off with her flag at the head of the Mexican public. To the sound of trumpets she proclaims, "This, Mexicans, this is the way the Yankee is beaten."[47]

Mexican revolutionary ideals have also gained dramatic expression in somewhat subtler forms. Rodolfo Usigli's *Corona de sombra* presents a widely read, sympathetic, and sensitively nationalistic interpretation of Maximilian as a Mexican national hero. In the prologue, Usigli aptly comments that "a nation and a national conscience are things which are slowly formed, and for me the conscience and the truth of a nation reside in its theatre."[48] In Usigli's *El gesticulador* (1937), a history professor named César Rubio impersonates a murdered Mexican revolutionary general who bore the same name. Although initially impersonating the general only as a trick for personal profit, Professor Rubio finally develops a deep and patriotic appreciation of revolutionary goals. These dramas are more restrained than the earlier plays such as *Tío Sam y la patria*, but they still present the elements of Mexican nationalism in a direct manner which is impossible to miss.

Mexico enjoys a long tradition of patriotic oratory. Conservative as well as Liberal combatants in the first fifty years of Mexican independence often couched their appeals in terms of patriotism, and the Díaz regime could claim fine orators like Justo Sierra to praise civic virtue. Ora-

47. Miguel C. Gutiérrez, *Tío Sam y la patria* (México: Librería de la Vda. de Ch. Bouret, 1919), pp. 5-24.

48. Rodolfo Usigli, *Crown of Shadows*, William F. Stirling, trans. (London: Allan Wingate, 1946), p. 100.

torical calls for national unity mark the beginning of independent life in Mexico, and men like Francisco Zarco, Ponciano Ariaga, Ignacio L. Vallarta and Vicente Riva Palacio expressed nationalistic sentiments later in the nineteenth century. Among audiences that heard Francisco Madero's oratory with its interchange of promises and *vivas* from the crowds, there arose an immediate sense of participation and hopes for future fulfillment of the promises.[49] Orators denounced the United States from the beginning of the 1910 Revolution, as even in 1911 they received the most enthusiastic responses from their audiences in attacking, not Díaz or the Terrazas family fortune, but gringo economic domination.[50]

Oratory, no matter how inspiring or persuasive it may be, rarely in itself wins listeners over to attitudes of self-sacrificing nationalism. Oratorical exclamations in Mexico have been important, however, in that they have reached the illiterate audience that is closed off from nationalist literature. As in the long series of speeches throughout Mexico which have become part of Mexican presidential campaigns, orators and politicians observe needs and make promises to diverse groups with invocations of national unity. Crowds are moved and a rudimentary conception of nationalism is gained even when the oratory stresses pat phrases and glosses over basic problems of conflicting interests within Mexican society. The sheer repetition of emotional phrases arouses nationalistic responses, however superficial they may be.

MUSIC

Music can also impart a sense of nationalism to the wide audience that illiteracy cuts off from the written forms of

49. Edith O'Shaughnessy, *Intimate Pages of Mexican History* (New York: George H. Doran Company, 1920), pp. 160-61.

50. *New York Herald*, March 7, 1911, in U.S., Library of Congress MSS collection, *Newspaper Clippings pertaining to Mexico, 1911-1913*, 3 vols.; III-48-C,1, Ac. 6194, Vol. 1.

national literature. Although, even with radio and free public concerts, only a limited segment of the population has ready access to the national themes in the orchestral compositions of Carlos Chávez and Silvestre Revueltas, virtually everyone is exposed to Mexican folk music. Played on streetcorners and in homes, cantinas, and even buses, folk music pervades contemporary Mexico. The themes of folk music have social relevance in Mexico as elsewhere, as folk songs provide a means of social commentary in the common emotional experience that unites performers and listeners. After spending twenty-five years in research and study of folk music, Alan Lomax concludes that it performs the important social function of giving the listener a feeling of security, of symbolizing the place where he was born, his childhood satisfactions, community relationships, courtship, and work.[51] Granting this assumption, it is most important from the standpoint of nationalism to include the national community in this sense of security. The increasing use of nationalistic musical themes then augments the loyalty of a people to the nation, reshaping their values to include a sense of security within the national community.

Nationalism has gradually developed in Mexican orchestral music and popular songs since the beginning of the nineteenth century. The nationalistic music of nineteenth-century Mexico, with its highly restricted audience, largely copied the nationalistic expressions of such European composers as Chopin and Liszt. While suggesting that orchestral music is more a universalistic than a nationalistic means of communication, Carlos Chávez observes that "musical nationalism" does not improve the work of a composer who lacks talent and that the "Mexican 'musical nationalism' of the nineteenth century did not produce great works because there were no great composers."[52]

51. Alan Lomax, "Folk Song Style," *American Anthropologist*, Vol. 61, No. 6 (December, 1959), vii, 929.
52. Carlos Chávez, "La música," in Jaime Torres Bodet and others, *México y la cultura* (México: Secretaría de Educación Pública, 1946), pp. 520, 527, 535.

Like Mexican novels, orchestral compositions reached a peak of nationalist expression in the 1930's with the work of Chávez and Silvestre Revueltas. While some sincere exponents of nationalism have followed the nationalist styles of the 1930's, many Mexican composers today follow the contemporary European trends from neoclassicism to the twelve-tone system. Even the best nationalist composition still appeals only to a sharply limited audience.

The introduction of the Mexican national anthem in 1854 provided the Mexican people with an effective means of promoting their sense of national community. Individual citizens could now not only take an increasing pride in hearing it sung and played but also gain a sense of active participation by singing it themselves. The national anthem, with its music that stirs emotional responses and its words that praise national unity, is an excellent propagator of nationalism. Mexicans do not play their national anthem at soccer, football, or baseball games as is done in the United States, but reserve the playing of it for national holidays. Reinforcing the view that the national anthem is not something to be played casually, the anthem becomes more moving because of being reserved for intrinsically emotional occasions. Extramusical attempts to create pride in the anthem range from long journalistic descriptions of its history and significance to booklets that come complete with illustrations, story, and a 45 RPM recording.[53] Agustín Cue Cánovas, in his recent *Historia mexicana,* devotes an entire chapter to the development of the national anthem. For him, as for the other members of the national community, it is an "immortal song," a "song of the people," and a "precise definition and a creative aspiration of motherland and nationality" which invites "the union of all Mexicans."[54]

53. "El himno nacional," *Revista de Revistas,* Año 5, Núm. 231 (13 septiembre 1914), 10; and *Mexicanos al grito de guerra . . .* (México: Fernández Editores, S.A., 1964).

54. Agustín Cue Cánovas, *Historia mexicana* (México: Editorial F. Trillas, S.A., 1959), pp. 177-84.

Other musical reactions to the foreign wars that stimulated the militant stanzas of the Mexican national anthem were evident in Mexican popular music during the second half of the nineteenth century. "La pasadita," a song originating in the War of 1847, ridicules the Mexican women who consorted with the Yankee soldiers. The nationalistic tone of other popular music appears in the sharply satirical composition "Adiós, mamá Carlota," a song about Maximilian's childless wife. Another ballad on the French intervention shows Mexican mothers sending their sons off to war and troops refusing to sell out the Motherland despite their poverty. Here a Mexican fighter tells his companions, "If my luck is to die in the campaign / defending my motherland and my honor, / Mexicans, adorn my tomb / with the colors of my flag."[55]

During the campaigns of the 1910 Revolution, a series of old and new songs gained a popularity that they still manifest today. During the factional conflict, songs such as "La Adelita," "La Valentina," "El pato," and "La cucaracha" became a part of the revolutionary emotion.[56] Songs of love and impending death, sung of such beautiful women as Adelita and Valentina, today re-create a nostalgic mood of the Revolution in Mexico, where boys still whistle and sing them. "La cucaracha," one version appearing in an 1818 work by José Joaquín Fernández de Lizardi and another denouncing the French intervention of the 1860's with praise for the "valiant don Porfirio," became a favorite of revolutionary soldiers. While popular with Villistas and Carrancistas in the north, "La cucaracha" appeared also in a southern Zapatista version that belittled Carranza by ridiculing his glasses and beard. The refrain of the ballad, telling of a cockroach who can travel no further for need of marihuana, had particular appeal for the soldiers

55. Vicente T. Mendoza, *La canción mexicana: Ensayo de clasificación y antología* (México: Universidad Nacional Autónoma de México, 1961), pp. 311-14.

56. Dr. Atl [Gerardo Murillo], *Las artes populares de México* (2 vols.; México: Librería México "Cvltvra," 1921), Vol. 1, p. 122.

for whom travel and fighting had become a way of life. These widely-known songs of the Revolution, far from having lost their prestige, have become more popular with the passage of time. They are part of the shared emotion of the Mexican people.

Some of the clearest and most popular musical expressions of Mexican nationalism are found in the *corrido,* a narrative ballad in the Spanish style whose origins Mexicans trace in part to Mexican Indian music. *Corridos,* rather than creating fiction, retell historical events with great feeling. They may embellish a story and frequently recount folkloric interpretations of events, but their strong factual basis provides a sense of historical relevance and authenticity that often develops into nationalistic invocations.

Arising as a distinctive form in the late nineteenth century, the *corrido* reached its apogee between 1900 and 1930. Although many marching songs were current during the Mexican independence movement, no *corridos* were produced at that time. The *corridos* that celebrate independence heroes today were composed long after the events they relate. *Corridos* poked fun at the Yankee invasion in 1847, and during the struggle against the French intervention, they described beautiful girls showering flowers upon Juárez' warriors. During the *porfiriato,* Mexican *corridos,* in a spirit of quiet revolt reminiscent of Negro spirituals in the United States, reproved the bondage of Mexicans impressed into the army, imprisoned in San Juan de Ulúa, and enslaved in the Valle Nacional. The *corrido* reached major proportions during and after the Revolution, and after 1930 it declined as a form of popular art. Since 1930, although it has been artificially revived to celebrate subjects such as national and municipal political candidates, it no longer exists as an authentic popular genre. Some *corridos* commemorate Mexican bandits and bullfighters, cities and airplane disasters, and even, on occasion, such foreign events as the Japanese attack on Pearl Harbor in 1941. A major impetus to Mexican nationalism comes, however, from the mass of other *corridos* that honor the epic themes of revolutionary history, heroism, and social change.[57]

The *corridos* of the Revolution emphasize patriotism and the significance of Mexican nationality. La Patria, the Motherland, reappears over and over again in the ballads, watching over her sons, granting laurels to the brave, and calling Mexicans to their duty. *Corridos* memorialize the exploits of revolutionary heroes and portray the entire sweep of the Revolution; the *soldaderas,* the dynamite bombings, the heroes, all are there. Often narrated in the first person singular by a fictional revolutionary participant, the ballads gain an added sense of intimacy by addressing famous personages in the familiar second person.

The *corridos* exude romantic nationalism. After Halley's comet shone with extraordinary size and brilliance over Mexico in early 1910, balladeers employed the old technique of hero-creation in composing a *corrido* that interpreted this omen to announce the benefits Francisco Madero would bring to Mexico. In the folk tradition of Robin Hood, another *corrido* describes how Madero "saw the Motherland subdued / in blackest and most cruel slavery," how he escaped from the San Luis Potosí jail, and how "at his call / came those of the North and those of the South." Illustrating female participation in the Revolu-

57. For an excellent selection of the different types of *corridos,* with an anthology that includes music as well as lyrics, see Vicente T. Mendoza, *Lírica narrativa de México: El corrido* (México: Universidad Nacional Autónoma de México, 1964). The following discussion of nationalistic *corridos* is based on analysis of the *corridos* collected in the Mendoza volume; in Armando de María y Campos, *La Revolución Mexicana a través de los corridos populares* (2 vols.; México: Biblioteca del Instituto Nacional de Estudios Históricos de la Revolución Mexicana, 1962); in Vicente T. Mendoza, *El corrido de la Revolución Mexicana* (México: Biblioteca del Instituto Nacional de Estudios Históricos de la Revolución Mexicana, 1956); and in John Reed, *Insurgent Mexico* (New York: D. Appleton and Company, 1914). For a more extensive discussion of personalities, events, and historical movements as reflected in Mexican *corridos,* see Merle E. Simmons, *The Mexican Corrido as a Source for Interpretive Study of Modern Mexico (1870-1950)* (Bloomington, Ind.: Indiana University Press, 1957).

tion, "La chinita maderista" appealingly plays upon the
rhyme of "cuánto te quiero! . . . ¡Que viva Madero!" and
concludes, "If you love me as I love you, let us both go to
fight for Madero." A ballad on Pancho Villa's assassination typically makes him the man of trust by Madero's side
and a patriot killed by political traitors who feared "his
great heart." Here Villa's dying words are: "I truly
wanted to do great things for my motherland."

Corridos bizarrely associate the constructive programs
resulting from the Revolution with outbursts of revolutionary nationalism. Agrarianism is tied to fierce patriotism and
xenophobia, as an agrarian *corrido* proclaims:

> We sing a *corrido,*
> labor companions,
> for all the united
> patriots and agrarians.
>
> . . . .
>
> To defend our soil
> and our beloved Banner,
> with courage we will fight
> against the Foreign Nation.
>
> . . . .
>
> We will yoke our oxen
> and join the reaping line,
> all the partisans united
> in the fight and the work.
>
> With Agrarianism among all
> we will make the country great,
> until it appears enriched
> with corn and wheat.
>
> Yes, although life it costs!
> all united we will die
> for our beloved motherland.
>
> . . . .

Here in balladry, as in economic fact, the agrarian movement in Mexico works significantly to increase productivity
as well as rural welfare through appeals to cohesive nationalism.

The unifying role of xenophobia implicit in the agrarian
corrido appears more dramatically in a series of frankly
xenophobic ballads. Among the many nationalistic and
anti-gringo songs recorded by John Reed on a trip to Mexico in 1913, a typical song chides, ''The Gringos are all
fools, / They've never been in Sonora, / And when they
want to say: 'Diez Reales,' / They call it 'Dollar an' a
quarta' . . . .'' Another *corrido* begs the benediction of the
Virgin of Guadalupe for a soldier who goes to defend Mexico against the Yankees, telling the Virgin that her soldier
will gladly give his blood to keep ''another nation'' from
trampling the flag and that internal conflict must cease
because of the gringo menace. It concedes North American
power with the warning that ''the rich also die.'' A similar
corrido to the heroes killed in the 1914 capture of Veracruz
shows gringos furiously attacking the young naval cadets
and the boys fighting on for eight hours without ceding a
foot of Mexican territory. It claims that cowardice and
lack of confidence prompted the Yankee withdrawal for the
long naval bombardment. Here, in a re-created defense of
Veracruz, Mexican soldiers, shoemakers, women, and cap-
italists again join together to fight the invader.

The vaunted unity of the Mexican people against foreign invaders gives over in other ballads to appeals for
unity and equality within the Mexican populace itself. One
ballad cries, ''What disgrace for us, / those who are Mexicans! / we kill each other / as if we were strangers.'' The
theme of equality provides a theoretical basis for appeals
for unity. Although rough and without conceptual com-
plexities, the ideal of equality before the law comes out
strongly in Mexican folk music. Trusting in the social
change of the Revolution, a ballad states that ''the naked,
the underdogs, / now have bread for all; / equality, justice,

work / have changed customs and ways.'' With wry indication of the equality of all Mexicans in the face of death during the Revolution, a *corrido* comments, ''Friend, don't distinguish yourself / by riches or stature; / for we are all equal: / matter for the grave.'' This theme of unity and equality propounded by the *corridos* reappears graphically in the huge murals of Mexican revolutionary art.

ART

Mexican art shifted strongly to propagandistic aims and nationalistic content in the period roughly coincident with the Revolution. During the nineteenth century, the commissioned art of Mexico chiefly manifested extra-national preoccupations. With the 1910 Revolution, however, a strong urge to nationalism, partially anticipated in political cartoons, appeared in the work of José Guadalupe Posada. The nationalist impetus reached a culmination during the constructive phase of the Revolution in the work of the Mexican muralists, especially that of Diego Rivera and José Clemente Orozco. While even the most famous pieces of twentieth-century Mexican art are probably not as influential in shaping social values as their creators had hoped, the inclination of Mexican art and particularly the impact of the Revolution upon art still help to diffuse the same nationalistic values evident in other forms of Mexican expression.

Mexican painting in the nineteenth century lacked both the thematic and the stylistic material that would have furthered nationalism. The subjects of Mexican painters were varied but not nationalistic; portraits, religious themes, urban and country scenes, and still lifes of fruit and flowers predominated.[58] Individual portraits of gen-

---

58. María Ester Ciancas, ''La pintura mexicana de siglo XIX'' (unpublished Master's thesis, Facultad de Filosofía y Letras, Universidad Nacional Autónoma de México, 1959), pp. 10, 24. See also Jorge Alberto Manrique, ''Arte, modernidad y nacionalismo (1867-1876),'' *Historia Mexicana*, Vol. 17, Núm. 2 (octubre-diciembre, 1967).

erals, wives, and children show that Mexican paintings were designed to please the small group that could commission them, and the subjects chosen for commissions again indicate the aristocracy's close family loyalties rather than any loyalty to the wider national group. The continuance of particularistic loyalties in the twentieth century reflects in Diego Rivera's 1923 complaint to Bertram Wolfe that "the middle class has no taste, least of all the Mexican middle class. All any of them wanted was his portrait, or that of his wife or his mistress."[59] Family portraits inspire as little national loyalty as the multitude of banquet and supper-table scenes of nineteenth-century Mexican art that appeal in subject matter only to the gourmet. In pre-1910 Mexican painting, even a potentially nationalistic subject like the "Execution of Maximilian"[60] appears with its far-off, inanimate, miniature figures only as the record of a formal event, completely lacking the magnetism of Rivera's and Orozco's murals that were to inspire Mexicans with a national consciousness.

Much of the art to which nineteenth-century Mexicans were regularly exposed was the ornate painting, sculpture, and architecture of Mexican churches. It inspires religious awe to the exclusion of national loyalty, with the exception of the shrines to the Virgin of Guadalupe. Although Chapultepec Castle or the Zocalo government headquarters might inspire some sense of national pride, the high colonial and nineteenth-century proportion of churches, such as those that still line the route from Mexico City to Puebla, indicate that the imposing structures seen by Mexicans were more often religious than secular. Today, while many Mexican churches still provide a sense of traditional reverence, the twentieth-century flourishing of secular Mexican

59. Quoted in Bertram D. Wolfe, *The Fabulous Life of Diego Rivera* (New York: Stein and Day, 1963), p. 144.

60. Roberto Montenegro, *Mexican Painting, 1800-1860* (New York: D. Appleton-Century Company, 1933), painting No. LIV.

architecture has caught Mexicans up in appreciation of their distinctively national structures. From the early heavy and imposing schools built soon after the Revolution to the remarkable Museum of Anthropology, the housing projects and the Latin American tower in Mexico City, the handsome auditoriums and office buildings built in Yucatán, and the project to rejuvenate the northern border area, Mexicans are now surrounded by artistically impressive examples of change. Thus the sustained economic advance following the 1910 Revolution has, by helping to finance and to stimulate imposing new national forms of art and architecture, reinforced the very tendencies toward nationalistic social cohesion that are themselves an element in sustained economic growth.

Before and during the Revolution, cartoons aroused interest and reaction by representing the Motherland and commenting from various viewpoints on the relationships of opposing groups within the Mexican polity. The caricatures that appeared in revolutionary periodicals implanted slogans and ideas with graphic emphasis and humor, even though their impact on the Mexican people was greatly reduced by their limited circulation and the fact that interpretation of the cartoons often required a literate audience.

In the decade before 1910, cartoons mocked the Díaz dictatorship, repeatedly stirred political awareness, and advocated wider participation of the Mexican people in political and economic affairs. A 1901 anticlerical cartoon shows the 1857 Constitution run through with a spear marked "conciliation," a weeping Miss Liberty, and a demented monk laughing gleefully. Ridiculing the false *científico* nationalism that did not see all Mexicans as part of the national community, a 1900 cartoon pictures Bernardo Reyes as a high priest at an altar on which Yaqui Indians lie sacrificed. Reyes lifts toward a graven image of Porfirio Díaz a container of incense from which emerges the smoke of "patriotism."[61]

In the decade after 1910, many cartoonists lacked the previous fervor for reform and placed themselves at the service of reactionary groups. Cartoons of all periods are partially the tools of political factions, and it is not surprising that after 1910, with Madero's freedom of the press and Huerta's coercion, cartoons opposed the very Maderista and Constitutionalist forces that are looked back upon with pride today. Particularly interesting from the standpoint of nationalism is the fact that the reactionary cartoons also used national welfare and national loyalty as the touchstones of their messages. In contrast with the cartoons of the Díaz era which jest lewdly at the idea of a Motherland,[62] are the conservative pictures of the same Patria drawn in such a way as to discredit revolutionary reformers. A 1912 edition of *Ojo Parado* displays the Mexican nation as a beautiful supine woman lying under a huge stone marked "Suspension of Guarantees," while the tiny figure of Francisco Madero perches on top of the slab, telling the nation that he does not know when the suspension of guarantees will be removed.[63]

The revolutionary paintings by Mexican artists resemble the cartoons in their presentation of nationalist themes. Artists painted with social purpose, sometimes with the hope of influencing political decision-makers to attack the problems of poverty and inequality. As Francisco Goitia commented on one painting, "I like it that a half nude skinny child should hang in the office of a Subsecretary, as if saying 'Look, don't get up too high, here

61. For some of the best examples of these themes in pre-1910 cartoons, see Manuel González Ramírez, ed., *La caricatura política* (Vol. 2, "Fuentes para la Historia de la Revolución Mexicana"; México: Fondo de Cultura Económica, 1955), Figs. 7, 11, 16, 42, 70, 128, 151, 159, 180-96. On the evolution of Mexican cartoons before, during, and after the 1910 Revolution, see also Victor Alba, "The Mexican Revolution and the Cartoon," *Comparative Studies in Society and History*, Vol. 9, No. 2 (January, 1967).

62. See *Frivolidades*, Año 1, Núm. 36 (4 septiembre 1910), 16.

63. *Ojo Parado*, Año 1, Núm. 3 (18 enero 1912), 16.

I am.' ''[64] Goitia traveled as a recording secretary with
Villista forces under Felipe Ángeles from 1912 to 1917.
His early paintings, "Dance of the Revolution" and "The
Old Man of the Dump Heap" done in 1916, underscore the
initial social consciousness of Mexican revolutionary art.
The drawings that José Clemente Orozco made for the
Carrancista propaganda paper *La Vanguardia* in 1915
attack Huerta and caricature both clerics and conservative
ladies. Illustrating the role of women in the Revolution,
the Orozco drawings attempt to raise morale by showing
brave and attractive women helping their men or waiting
for them to return.

Although largely devoid of xenophobic content, the
sketches and illustrations made by José Guadalupe Posada
before his death in 1913 provide the most influential artistic
advocacy of nationalist values before the revolutionary
murals. Posada's prints gained an extensive audience
among the illiterate as well as the artistically inclined during the Revolution as they were illustrations for the widely
distributed ballad sheets. These prints stimulated concern
among the emerging generation of Mexican artists with
Mexican themes and the Revolution, and today the prints
are still widely circulated throughout Mexico in books and
magazines. Posada speaks out strongly for greater social
equality, as he depicts *hacendados* whipping peons tied to
trees, peons being deported to the Valle Nacional and working at hard labor there, and conscripts for the army being
dragged away from their protesting women. Showing Zapatista attacks, the loading of troop trains, machine gunners
in action, and portraits of Zapata, Genovevo de la O,
Huerta, and others, Posada compiled a complete record of
the Maderista movement in his popular sketches.[65]

Manuel González Ramírez suggests that the death theme

64. Quoted in Anita Brenner, *Idols Behind Altars* (New York: Payson
& Clarke, Ltd., 1929), p. 296.
65. Jaled Muyaes, ed., *La Revolución Mexicana vista por José Guadalupe
Posada* (México: Talleres "Policromía," 1960), Figs. 1, 27-29, 35, 37, 39,
40, 42-43, 47, 51, 53-56, 58.

pervading Posada's art represents the idea of equality. This theme is particularly apparent in Posada's stylized skeletons—the skeleton in female attire who swings a lasso while riding over skeleton children, the mustachioed Madero skeleton with bottle in hand, the skeleton with rifle and sombrero who brandishes the Jolly Roger while riding over skulls, and the death's-head spider whose many legs reach out for skulls and bones. Death is ever present in the graphic but less abstract sketches of the firing squad in action, the revolutionary who has been hanged, the machine gunners, and the ferocity of Zapata's attack. After viewing the awesome leveling of such revolutionary scenes, one readily agrees with González Ramírez that "the symbol of death, in different ways, represents the idea of equality: in the face of death all values, all differences, all protestations lose the deceit that social conventions lend to them."[66] Certainly if other Mexicans consciously or unconsciously agree with González Ramírez in finding the predominance of the death motif in early revolutionary art to be symbolic of their increasing equality, this motif and the art itself significantly propagate one of the concepts required for an enlarged national community.

Mexican murals embody what Lucio Mendieta y Núñez analyzes as the "nationalist exaltation" that both arose from and in turn influenced Mexico's social revolution.[67] Although a more conservative trend in Mexican art has become accentuated since 1940,[68] revolutionary murals remain as mute pleas throughout Mexico for an all-inclusive national community. Murals are the best artistic example of the nationalist movement, since the artists consciously used this medium to influence social values. It is true that, to be wholly understood in their political and social context, many revolutionary murals require a famil-

66. González Ramírez, ed., *La caricatura política*, p. xl.

67. Lucio Mendieta y Núñez, "Sociología del arte," *Revista Mexicana de Sociología*, Año 11, Vol. 11, Núm. 3 (septiembre-diciembre, 1949), 415.

68. See Virginia B. Derr, "The Rise of a Middle-Class Tradition in Mexican Art," *Journal of Inter-American Studies*, Vol. 3, No. 3 (July, 1961).

iarity with Mexican and world history not usually possessed by the peasants and workers to whom the murals are dedicated. Many Mexicans in isolated districts remain ignorant of the existence of these nationalistic paintings; however the majority of the people has been significantly and increasingly influenced by them.

One of the most striking evocations of Mexican nationalism is the "Allegory of Mexico," a mural done by José Clemente Orozco in the Gabino Ortiz Library in Jiquilpan, Michoacán, in 1940. The mural shows a handsome Indian woman, standard symbol of the Mexican Patria, riding a jaguar through a field of cactus. A large eagle and a serpent, the Mexican national emblem, rise behind the woman and protect her from a second jaguar that represents foreign imperialism. Three women with crowns and rifles stand guard enfolded in one of the eagle's wings, while with the other wing the eagle pushes back the attacking jaguar. Behind the scene spreads the red, white, and green of the tricolor Mexican flag. The mural has a strong over-all effect. The observer wants to stand with the powerful eagle and snake in protection of the Patria and warn the Motherland of the bared fangs of the domestic jaguar on which she is riding.[69]

Murals also impart nationalist interpretations of Mexican history. Diego Rivera's famous murals in the National Palace celebrate Mexican events with elaborate sections on the legend of Quetzalcoatl, the Mexican wars for independence, the American intervention in 1847, the Constitution of 1857, the execution of Maximilian, and the Revolution of 1910. In murals done at the Guadalajara Government Palace in 1937, José Clemente Orozco presents the figure of Hidalgo with a flaming torch in hand exhorting the Mexican people to revolt and seek independence. The censure of church privilege and militarism evident in the Guadalajara murals reappears in Orozco's 1948 fresco of

69. Bernard S. Myers, *Mexican Painting in Our Time* (New York: Oxford University Press, 1956), pp. 164-66. For a different perspective on the mural, compare Luis Cardoza y Aragón, *Pintura mexicana contemporánea* (México: Imprenta Universitaria, 1953), Fig. 9 in the series of Orozco reproductions.

"Juárez and the Reform" in the National Historical Museum at Chapultepec Castle which shows Juárez and his soldiers triumphant over grotesque forms of the high clergy, the military, and the mummified body of Maximilian. Upholding nationalistic actions after the Revolution, Orozco's 1941 "National Riches" mural, in which a jaguar wrapped in the Mexican flag leaps protectively over symbols of oil, gold, silver, iron, and copper, lauds President Lázaro Cárdenas' nationalization of the oil industry and its confirmation by the Mexican Supreme Court.

The revolutionary murals evince strong Indianist attitudes. Rivera's murals in Cuernavaca commissioned by American Ambassador Dwight Morrow in 1929 evoke pride in the Indian past and urge Indian incorporation into Mexican society by portraying the Spanish conquest, the degradation and oppression of the Indians, and finally Zapata's struggle to assure Indian rights. Rivera's murals in the National Palace, illustrating the Aztec capital and the Tarascan, Zapotec, and Totonac civilizations, vividly depict the grandeur of Mexico's Indian inheritance. Like the Cuernavaca murals, those in the National Palace also show the Spanish invasion and enslavement of the Indians as well as the later invasions of France and the United States. Orozco and David Alfaro Siqueiros also incorporate Indianist values in their murals. Orozco's striking "Cortés and Malinche" over the staircase of the national Preparatoria represents the union of Spanish and Indian elements in their Mexican synthesis, while "The Conqueror-Builder and the Indian Worker" suggests, through the quiet strength of the Indian figure, the fashioning of modern Mexico with Indian labor. A Siqueiros mural in the National Institute of Fine Arts effectively shows Cuauhtémoc withstanding torture as the Spaniards burn his feet. Siqueiros' "Cuauhtémoc against the Myth" presents the powerful Indian figure, representing the Mexican people's resistance to foreign domination, sending an obsidian-tipped spear against the huge Spanish horseman who is hurling a sharpened cross down upon him.

Murals sum up the social, xenophobic, and even the educational thrusts of Mexico's national history. Orozco's last completed work, located in the half-dome of the Chamber of Deputies in the Guadalajara Government Palace, represents slaves struggling to loose their chains while the compassionate figure of Hidalgo writes a decree abolishing slavery. Below, amid upthrust bayonets and a document marked "Reform," stand the sympathetic figures of Morelos, Juárez, and Carranza. Opposition to the United States as well as to the inequalities of wealth appears in Diego Rivera's "The Night of the Rich," "Bourgeois Reformers," and "The Billionaires" in the 1928 and 1929 murals at the Ministry of Education. Rivera's murals in the Court of Labor criticize social inequalities and laud the ideals of the Mexican Revolution. In "Weighing of the Grain," an arrogant and menacing *hacendado* stands over the bent figures of Mexican peasants, and in "Exit from the Mine" a well-dressed and light-skinned foreman searches the anonymous, dark-skinned miner whose hands are raised in the form of a crucifix. "The New School," a famous and often reproduced mural in which a mounted revolutionary soldier stands guard with rifle in hand while a teacher instructs Mexicans of all ages and men construct a school building, memorializes the revolutionary ideal of education for all Mexicans. The social commentary of these murals matches in its interpretation of the Revolution the images often presented in the Mexican cinema, a medium that grew up at the same time and with many of the same themes as the muralist movement.

FILMS AND THE NEW MEDIA

Mass media afford particularly significant channels of communication in developing countries in which barriers of illiteracy block the dissemination of nationalist literature to a large segment of the population. Part of the Mexican population remains cut off from the mass media just as it is removed from nationalist literature, but the mass media do affect many individuals who pay little attention to literary nationalism in any form.

The cinema took predominance over other spectator entertainment by the mid-1930's, and the legitimate theater had fallen into comparative obscurity by the late 1940's. Of the 52 million seats sold in Mexican cinemas, dramatic theaters, bullfights, cockfights, sports events, and circuses in 1934, 70.1 per cent were in the 282 movie houses then in Mexico and only 22.5 per cent in the 239 dramatic theaters. Of the 115 million seats sold in 1947, 92.4 per cent were in 1,726 cinemas and only 1.7 per cent in the 28 theaters with stage productions.[70] The Mexican government still holds down the price of cinemas, and even in Mexico City admission to elegant new movie houses costs only about three Mexican pesos or twenty-five cents in North American currency. As the size of the audience for Mexican films expands, the films provide a prime medium for the inculcation of nationalistic values.

Through the work of Salvador Toscano Barragán, Mexico possesses a cinematic record of the 1910 Revolution which instills patriotism and pride as it is shown to Mexican audiences today. Toscano Barragán, who imported equipment from Paris to make local newsreels in Mexico in 1900, recognized the significance of the 1910 Revolution and made a film history of it. Shooting his film under fire and frequently escaping across rooftops,[71] Toscano covered battles from Chihuahua to the southern border as well as the American invasion of Veracruz. He recorded the gestures of Madero, Pancho Villa, Zapata, Obregón, and Car-

70. José E. Iturriaga, *La estructura social y cultural de México* (México: Fondo de Cultura Económica, 1951), pp. 206-7.
71. Irene Nicholson, "Mexican Films: Their Past and Their Future," *The Quarterly of Film, Radio and Television*, Vol. 10, No. 3 (Spring, 1956), 248-49.

ranza. When Señora Carmen Toscano de Moreno Sánchez edited her father's film into an hour-and-a-half production entitled *Memorias de un mexicano* after his death in 1947, she added her own commentary. The added sound track increases the film's emotional impact with a background of Mexican music and the interspersion of shouts and crowd noises. First shown and enthusiastically received in Mexico City on August 24, 1950, this photographic record of the Revolution has been widely shown throughout the republic, with the shots of Victoriano Huerta and the American landing at Veracruz eliciting catcalls from Mexican audiences.[72] Mexican schools still use the film to give students a vivid and patriotic impression of revolutionary history.

Although other attempts to create a film record of the Revolution did not materialize, the various films produced conveyed the patriotic sentiments of the time. Pancho Villa was given $25,000 in American currency by the Mutual Film Corporation for the motion-picture rights to his campaigns. Mutual photographers took action shots and staged a shelling scene with a battery of light field guns, but Mexican audiences have never had an opportunity to see these Villista reels.[73] Even if the reels had been made available, they might have had little effect on the conservative and often anti-revolutionary audiences that made up a portion of the Mexican moviegoing public during the Revolution. In a report that Consul General Arnold Shanklin made after attending a "motion picture show" in December, 1912, he indicated the unreceptive attitudes of the small and privileged class of moviegoers. Shanklin described how, when pictures of President Francisco Madero appeared on the screen, hisses from the audience became so loud that the picture was hurriedly discontinued.[74]

72. Irene Nicholson, ''Memoirs of a Mexican,'' *Sight and Sound,* Vol. 23, No. 1 (July-September, 1953), 15.

73. Terry Ramsaye, *A Million and One Nights: A History of the Motion Pictures* (2 vols.; New York: Simon and Schuster, 1926), Vol. 2, pp. 670-73.

74. Arnold Shanklin to Philander C. Knox, December 18, 1912, /5757.

Although contemporary audiences demonstrated what now appear to be unpatriotic attitudes, attempts to play up the patriotism of these audiences had already begun. In 1910, to celebrate the centennial of Mexican independence, Felipe de Jesús Haro produced an eminently patriotic film on Hidalgo's insurrection, *El Grito de Dolores*. Despite rudimentary cinematic techniques, the film created great public excitement. With the triumph of the Revolution, new nationalist subjects appeared. The Indianist influence reflects in the 1918 production of *Cuauhtémoc,* the life of the Aztec warrior based on a piece by Tomás Domínguez Yáñez. *Juan soldado,* a film produced for the Ministry of War in 1919, glorified the exploits of the common soldier and the *soldaderas* of the Revolution. The Ministry of War simultaneously underwrote other nationalistic films such as *El precio de la gloria* and *Honor militar*.[75]

During the Revolution, Mexicans took sharp offense at any motion picture scenes that could be construed as anti-Mexican. When a North American film called *Fighting Through,* shown in Nogales, Arizona, depicted an American soldier forcing a Mexican to salute the American flag, the Mexican vice-consul at Nogales stationed himself as a picket in front of the theater and advised Mexicans not to patronize it, and he later refused to allow the owner and operator of the theater to cross the border into Mexico.[76] Resentment occasioned by anti-Mexican scenes in American films increased as these films began to fill the Mexican market. In 1923 First National Pictures set up its own distributing offices in Mexico, and other North American firms, including Universal, Paramount, and Fox, soon followed. Many of the early American films distributed in Mexico unfortunately portrayed the villain as a Mexican with pistol and knife.

75. Emilio García Riera, *El cine mexicano* (México: Ediciones Era, S.A., 1963), pp. 14-19.

76. U.S., Congress, Senate, Committee on Foreign Relations, *Investigation of Mexican Affairs*, 66th Cong., 2d sess., Sen. Doc. 285 (2 vols.; Washington, 1920), Vol. 2, p. 3480.

The anti-nationalist material contained in many Hollywood films led to strict censorship in the 1930's. Mexicans declared that they would censor any film that might "offend against the ideals held by the majority of the Mexican people" or "offend against Mexican history, Mexican people, Mexican institutions, and representative men of Mexico."[77] In 1938, the year of the oil nationalization, Mexican censors removed reference to the War of 1847 from Paramount's *Wells Fargo,* deleted shots showing Mexicans as bandits in MGM's *The Girl of the Golden West,* and banned Columbia Pictures' *Lawless Rider* because it showed a Mexican being kicked and ridiculed.

Although the Mexican film industry has grown since the 1930's, many of the messages carried to Mexican moviegoers continue to be from Hollywood. In the early 1930's, the Mexican government stimulated national production by placing a stiff tax on the importation of foreign films,[78] and in 1937 the Cárdenas administration removed all taxes from Mexican film production.[79] Such aid increased Mexican production from a few films a year in the early 1930's to over fifty in 1938. With a greater film production than any other Spanish-speaking country, Mexico has been producing, since 1950, an average of one hundred feature-length films per year.

North American predominance has continued even with increased Mexican production. Among films shown in Mexico in 1938, the year of greatest national film production in the 1930's, North American films still heavily outweighed Mexican.[80] Of films shown in 1944, 67.7 per cent were North

77. Quoted in John Eugene Harley, *World-wide Influences of the Cinema: A Study of Official Censorship and the International Cultural Aspects of Motion Pictures* (Cinematography Series Number 2, Los Angeles, Calif.: University of Southern California Press, 1940), p. 163.

78. René Jeanne and Charles Ford, *Histoire encyclopédique du Cinéma* (5 vols.; Paris: R. Laffont, 1947-62), Vol. 4, p. 350.

79. Georges Sadoul, *Le Cinéma pendant la Guerre (1939-1945)* (Vol. 6, *Histoire Générale du Cinéma;* Paris: Ediciones Denoël, 1954), p. 248.

80. Harley, *World-wide Influences of the Cinema,* p. 166. Compare Jeanne and Ford, *Histoire encyclopédique du Cinéma,* Vol. 4, p. 351.

American, and only 27.7 per cent were Mexican, while, by 1947, 54.6 per cent were North American and 29.0 per cent were Mexican.[81] In the 1950's and 1960's, Hollywood productions have continued to be the primary influence upon Mexican viewers, despite active competition from Mexican films, a trickle of European films, and a substantial number of Soviet films shown in recent years. Mexican critics often agree with Agustín Aragón Leiva, a disciple of Sergei Eisenstein, who attacked Hollywood in the 1930's for having created an industry based on sex appeal rather than making the cinema a true vehicle of expression.[82] No matter what the artistic merits of Hollywood cinema, however, Mexicans still pay to see it and are influenced by its creation of a fantasy world in which acquisitive values often prevail. Since self-imposed censorship has purged Hollywood productions of the anti-Mexican content of the old cowboy films,[83] it is now Mexican films which, by design, give the major cinematic stimulus to Mexican nationalism.

Mexico has a long history of commercial films whose primary theme is Mexican patriotism. In 1922 Miguel Contreras Torres began directing and producing successful movies with a markedly patriotic flavor which eulogized Mexican heroes and the critical events of Mexican history.[84] Films of frankly patriotic content in the 1930's included Ezequiel Carrasco's *¡Viva México!* (1934), Guillermo Hernández Gómez' *La Adelita* (1937), and Luis Lezama's *El cementerio de las águilas* (1938). In 1942 and 1943, Contreras Torres made two cinematic biographies of José María Morelos, *El padre Morelos* and its sequel, *El rayo del sur,* in which the hero of Mexican independence appears,

81. Iturriaga, *La estructura social y cultural de México,* pp. 204-5.

82. Agustín Aragón Leiva, ''Hollywood y la cinematografía,'' *Crisol,* Año 6, Tomo 11, Núm. 63 (marzo, 1934), 159, 164.

83. Hortense Powdermaker, *Hollywood, the Dream Factory: An Anthropologist Looks at the Movie-Makers* (Boston: Little, Brown and Company, 1950), p. 64.

84. For detailed information on the content of Mexican films, see Emilio García Riera, ''Medio siglo de cine mexicano,'' *Artes de México,* Vol. 6, Núm. 31 (1960); and García Riera, *El cine mexicano.*

respected and rhetorical, fully conscious of the transcendental nature of his acts. Representative of later patriotic films are Joaquín Pardavé's *Primero soy mexicano* (1950) and Juan Bustillo Oro's *El último mexicano* (1959), one of the most ambitious of the patriotic films, which was panned by Mexican critics. In addition to these films in which patriotism is the major theme, other Mexican films have played up patriotism as one of several themes. Typical of this latter group is *El rebozo de Soledad* (1952), which, in presenting a panorama of Mexican social problems, shows a physician whose patriotism leads him into the countryside to serve the Mexican people.

Other commercial films illustrate periods of Mexican history and point up such problems as Mexican emigration to the United States. Contreras Torres' *Juárez y Maximiliano* (1933) typifies the melodramatic approach to Mexican history. Films on Porfirio Díaz range from Bustillo Oro's *En tiempos de don Porfirio* (1939), a nostalgic comedy of the Porfirian era, to Raphael J. Sevilla's *Porfirio Díaz* (1944), in which Díaz appears as a hero. *México de mis recuerdos* (1964) shows Díaz as a generous and forceful leader, and strong sentiments of nationalism are apparent in the closing scene in which Díaz boards the *Ypiranga* saying, ''Adiós, México querido. Adiós,'' while a respectful crowd strews his path with flowers and waves good-by. In a re-creation of recent Mexican history which resembles the patriotic war movies of other countries, Jaime Salvador's *Escuadrón 201* (1945) depicts the participation of Mexican forces in World War II. The concern of Mexican novels for the problem of *bracero* emigration to the United States reappears in the cinema. In *bracero* films such as Contreras Torres' *Soy mexicano de acá de este lado* (1951) audiences see the problems of Mexicans who have been transplanted to the environment of the Yankees. Gilberto Gazcón's *Los desarraigados* (1958) presents a panoramic view of the lives of Mexicans in the United States, and

Alejandro Galindo's *Espaldas mojadas* (1953) strongly attacks Yankee exploitation of Mexican "wetbacks."

In utilizing the heroes and ideals of the 1910 Revolution, Mexican film-makers stir nationalistic reactions while creating a popular commercial product. The cult of Pancho Villa has continued since his death with a long series of films from *La sombra de Pancho Villa* (1932) to the Villa trilogy that Ismael Rodríguez produced in 1957 and 1958, *Así era Pancho Villa, Pancho Villa y la Valentina,* and *Cuando ¡Viva Villa! es la muerte.* Like other Villa films, *Vámonos con Pancho Villa,* on which the extravagant sum of one million pesos was spent in 1935, unapologetically shows how injustice led to the necessary social revolution. Other films mirror the same popular interpretation of the Revolution. Emilio Fernández, who won an international prize for an early interpretation of the Revolution, worked with nationalistic themes in *Soy puro mexicano* (1942), *Flor silvestre* (1943), and *Las abandonadas* (1944). In 1958 Contreras Torres produced two films, *Pueblo en armas* and *¡Viva la soldadera!,* whose nationalistic presentation of the Revolution matches that of the technicolor epics *La escondida* (1955), *La Cucaracha* (1958), and *Juana Gallo* (1960). Like this re-creation of Mexican history, adaptation of nationalistic novels has also given some spur to nationalism. In addition to a 1934 version of Altamirano's *Clemencia* and a 1955 version of Fernández de Lizardi's *El Periquillo Sarniento,* adaptations of Azuela's *Los de abajo* and Martín Luis Guzmán's *La sombra del Caudillo* appeared in 1939 and 1960.

Representative of the revolutionary cinema now produced in Mexico is *El centauro del norte* (1964), a film that builds the story of Adelita into a moving nationalist documentary. Opening with films actually taken during the 1910 Revolution which show the fighting and brief shots of Madero, Zapata, Carranza, and Obregón, it then shifts into a contemporary color movie depicting revolutionary times. The simple plot tells the story of Adelita's aid to Villa, her capture, and eventual marriage to a handsome federal officer who joins the insurgents after taking her prisoner. Like many Mexican films, *El centauro del norte* is partially romanticized. Hypothetical revolutionaries in brightly colored and impeccably clean shirts sing and play shiny new guitars. The film effectively evokes a sense of Mexican nationalism, however, as Adelita tells her federal captors how Pancho Villa is fighting for the people. Villa, Adelita, the Revolution, and Mexico successively receive *vivas* from Mexican crowds. The sole villain of the film is an evil colonel who, representing the *ancien régime* that must be overcome, attempts to rape Adelita and to abscond with the federal funds only to be caught and humiliated by the triumphant revolutionaries. With the single exception of the anti-heroic colonel, everyone in the film becomes a devoted revolutionary, as the federal troops desert *en masse* to the Villistas.

Nationalistic intent becomes most evident and effective at the conclusion of the film where, in the style of a newsreel, it portrays first the epic of revolutionary fighting and then the accomplishments of Mexico today. The camera sweeps grandly over large battles as a narrator explains the later course of the Revolution. The portrayal of modern Mexico shows steel furnaces blazing, handsome athletes parading, an aerial view of Mexico's new forty-four-story Latin American tower, and companies of soldiers marching in the uniforms of Mexico's past. Adelita and her husband, now a representative of Mexico's modern army, watch with their daughter from a balcony as their son parades by. Now, they repeat, the Revolution has "created a Mexico for all Mexicans."

While many commercial films lack the nationalistic approach of *El centauro del norte,* most of the educational films similarly arouse Mexican nationalism. Mexicans produce a host of comedies, musicals, romances, and adventures that have virtually no effect on the national consciousness. The ranch comedies, innocuous "family" movies, stories of divorce and adolescent problems, appealing primarily to women, and films with pretty girls, appealing primarily to men, seldom touch on nationalism. With its own horror movies such as Rafael Portillo's *La momia azteca contra el robot humano* (1957), Mexico, like the United States, produces many movies designed only for diversion. By contrast, the educational films have attempted to disseminate nationalist values since 1933, when Secretary of Education Narciso Bassols set in motion an extensive plan for films "to show Mexico's *reality* to itself."[85] Documentaries on Mexican murals and similar subjects have heightened national awareness. In supplying diverse audiences with information as well as patriotic appeals, educational films increase identification with the national community by providing kinds of data seldom found in the commercial cinema.

The newer media of photography, radio, and television, which have developed since the early period of Mexican independence, now provide new channels for nationalist propaganda. Photographs have made the distant events of the 1910 Revolution more apparent to the Mexican people than those of earlier revolts. Propaganda photographs abounded from the start of the Revolution; newspapers reported in 1911 that Madero's photograph looked out from every window on San Francisco Avenue,[86] much as the photographs of political candidates do today. A proliferation of picture postcards made during the Revolution exhibited photographs of everything from the formal poses of leaders and cabinets to corpses and battle scenes, giving Mexicans in all parts of the republic a look at the turmoil and the personalities that shaped events many miles away. The quantity and variety of revolutionary postcards preserved in library depositories and private collections is indeed surprising. Depicting such scenes as riflemen and

85. Carlos Chávez, "Mexico," *Films*, Vol. 1, No. 3 (Summer, 1940), 20-21. The italics are Chávez'.

86. *The New York Times*, May 3, 1911, p. 3:4.

machine gunners in action, *soldaderas* fighting and aiding
the wounded, Pancho Villa riding at full gallop, and the
huge crowds in Mexico City welcoming Madero's victory,
the postcards undoubtedly sharpened the appreciation of
the Mexicans through whose hands they passed. Photographs illustrating the multiple programs and accomplishments of post-revolutionary Mexico, like the old snapshots
of the Revolution, continue today to give Mexicans an added
appreciation of the history and objectives of their nation.

The rapid transmission of ideas, stories, and pictures by
means of radio and television helps Mexicans to diffuse
specific ideological concepts of the Revolution and their
national community. Although rural electrification and
rising incomes have steadily increased the number of radio
receivers in use, particularly in the countryside, the possession of a radio is still one of the factors tending to make
the acquisition of nationalistic values easier for the urban
than the rural dwellers. The number of radio receivers in
use in Mexico has risen from 750,000 in 1950 to 2.5 million
in 1955 and more than 6 million in 1964, which indicates
one radio receiver for every six persons.[87] Just as the
traditional practice of reading periodicals to illiterates on
city streets once made the impact of newspapers far greater
than their numerical circulation would indicate, the integrating potential of radio and more recently television is
increased by the common practice of group listening and
viewing. Many Mexicans cluster around one receiver, and
merchants use the media to draw customers to their stands
and stores.[88]

As in the case of Mexican art and literature, the content as well as the permeability of radio and television
determines their effect on nationalism. Popular music now
played on Mexican radio exposes inhabitants of different
regions to the same popular milieu, but in a propagandistic

87. Frank Brandenburg, *The Making of Modern Mexico* (Englewood Cliffs,
N.J.: Prentice-Hall, Inc., 1964), p. 303.
88. Marvin Alisky, ''Mexico's Rural Radio,'' *The Quarterly of Film,
Radio and Television*, Vol. 8, No. 4 (Summer, 1954), 405-6.

sense, radio seldom endeavors to stimulate nationalism. The reruns of North American television shows, now common in Mexico, convey the superficial aspects of Yankee culture without affecting Mexicans' conception of their own national community. With an estimated 15 thousand color sets and 2 million black and white sets in Mexico in 1967, Mexican television viewers gave the highest ratings to domestically produced soap operas and still depended on many United States programs such as "Los Beverly Ricos" and "El Avispón Verde" ("The Green Hornet").[89] The long-run impact of television will depend on the programing that takes place as more television receivers come into use. As the number of television viewers increases along with the number of moviegoers, radio listeners, and literate readers, the new media may be expected to share significantly in shaping the kinds of attitudes toward the national community demanded of future Mexican citizens.

89. See the feature article "TV in Mexico," *The Christian Science Monitor,* July 26, 1967.

VIII
An Overview

Although this study of Mexican nationalism has not tried to quantify hypotheses to be tested in other national contexts, it has raised issues that may elucidate the study of nationalism in other areas. Of primary interest is the fact that Mexican nationalism is distinctive, not only in its strength and social pervasiveness but also in its essential characteristics, in its political and economic results. On a world-wide basis, nationalism is the most potent social force of the present era, but its effects in any particular national environment depend upon the peculiarities of that environment. Conditioning environmental features include demography, racial intermixture, language, communications and transportation, class structure, literature, and the social significance of national heroes. The ends for which the dominant political leadership uses patriotic appeals are another feature distinguishing types of nationalism, as are fears of powerful neighboring states, the effects of political turmoil and revolutionary destruction, and the appeals for support made under particular stages of military technology. These features provide a common frame of reference that may be adapted to analyze different national communities. Changes through time in each of the framework features can be studied and compared in various nations and periods.

When analyzed in terms of these environmental features, nationalism in Mexico is most strategically viewed as an element of social cohesion, as a device through which conflict between groups in Mexican society is reduced. As a distinctively cohesive social force, Mexican nationalism has underlain the political stability and economic development that have distinguished Mexico in its Latin American context since the mid-1930's. Under *científico* leadership in the quarter-century before 1910, appeals to patriotism attempted to justify dictatorial control as well as material progress, but with the Revolution, the type of cohesive nationalism expounded by Manuel Gamio and other revolutionaries hoped to inspire a form of social, economic, and political progress that would incorporate all the inhabitants of Mexico. Since the Revolution, verbal reiterations of egalitarian nationalism have smoothed over actual disparities in economic wealth and advanced economic development by encouraging both political stability and domestic reinvestment under a system of highly skewed income distribution.

The role of xenophobia in shaping Mexican nationalism suggests that a fear and hatred of foreigners, which on the surface seems destructive to the bonds that link men together, may be one of the most potent forces unifying disparate groups within the national population. While xenophobia increases internal social cohesion within a nation-state, it does not necessarily provoke international conflict or prevent mutually profitable forms of foreign investment.

Notwithstanding the rise of fierce xenophobia, the disparate character that a variety of antinationalistic forces gave to Mexican society in 1810 was not overcome in the nineteenth century. Despite the sincere plans for independence and internal reform of Morelos and Juárez, which might have established a viable national community whose various members could communicate freely and work harmoniously together, Mexican society, between 1810 and 1910, encompassed a variety of mutually exclusive groups, each putting forward its own interests in the name of the state. The incessant warfare against foreign influences which marked the years from 1810 to 1876 initially produced only the stability of a dictatorship. Under Díaz, the *científicos* placated such groups as the landowners, the clergy, and the foreigners who helped to keep their respective governments favorably disposed toward Mexico, but the *científicos* completely excluded the large Indian element of the population from a sense of national participation.

Nevertheless, the development of Mexico in the nineteenth century did provide the foundations upon which many Mexicans could build a strong sense of national community after 1910. First, the Mexican state itself was created by separation from Spain in 1821, and the territorial state was shorn by the Texas Revolution and the War of 1847 of those vast territories into which a non-Hispanic population was rapidly pouring. The struggles of Mexican citizens against Spain and France had significance for nation-building by producing a wider sense of community in those who fought against aliens and by creating a group of national heroes whom later generations of Mexicans could look back upon with common pride. The bitter struggle against the secular power of the church established a precedent for later contests with any institution that might claim for itself the primary loyalty of all Mexicans. Wars with North Americans, in Texas in 1836 and again in 1847, demonstrated the acute need for national unity and created a neat historical precedent for the xenophobia that would help unite revolutionary factions after 1917. More immediately, the concessions to foreign firms and individuals under Díaz created a common grievance among the mass of the Mexican population which, once Madero's revolution had unseated the figureheads of the old regime, erupted in a mass movement that took on social goals for the entire Mexican community.

Within Mexico, the sharp increase in population and its shift into formerly isolated areas increased the degree of personal contact that was a prerequisite for effective communication among Mexicans. Even in its initial stages, Mexican nationalism seemed a middle-class phenomenon, embodying the mestizo drive to gain the status that Indians saw as too distant and *criollos* felt that they had already achieved. The effects of miscegenation paralleled those of the industrialization that created new worker and managerial groups, and ultimately the status of women was improved, which advanced identification with the national group. The spread of Spanish and the growth of a Mexican dialect reduced the formidable language barriers that still made communication difficult in 1910, while novels and other literary forms both mirrored and stimulated the growth of national consciousness. Education gave the new nationalistic literature permeability in an increasing and influential segment of the Mexican population, and the rise of education itself, like the new supremacy of lay education and the new awareness of education's unifying function, furthered national consciousness both before and after 1910. Railroads and other innovations in communications similarly reduced geographic barriers throughout the nineteenth century and provided a network of facilities that advanced nationalism particularly after 1910. Although foreign and domestic influences on Mexico in the century after 1810 did not in themselves greatly enlarge the Mexican national community, they did help to form the background for the Revolution and the conscious formulation of Mexican nationalism in the next fifty years.

With the coming of the 1910 Revolution, internal migration increased sharply and the old class structure received serious if temporary jolts. Constitutional prescriptions and revolutionary programs like that in education based the acquisition of status increasingly on achievement rather than ascription. Revolutionary pronouncements of the secular equality of all Mexicans gave the competing groups in agriculture and industry a basis for common attitudes and compromise. The Revolution set in motion the final check on secular aspirations by the Mexican clergy and left the profession of Catholic faith a unifying rather than a disruptive element in Mexican society. The heavy destruction, both in human and material terms, that Mexico suffered during the long years of revolutionary violence produced a strong desire for peace and a framework of common loyalty to the national community in which group conflict could be settled without violence.

As the stage of Mexican military technology in 1910 stressed the importance of large numbers of devoted followers and gave rough military equality to Mexicans of each race and class, revolutionary leaders couched their appeals in terms of inclusive nationalism. Leaders acceded to special group interests in order to win support. Previously disenfranchised labor, agrarian, Indian, and even feminist groups gained recognition of their status and needs within the polity. The leaders who had issued the revolutionary pronouncements and appeals became, after their deaths, a new galaxy of national heroes and were invoked to expand participation in national affairs and programs.

While the Revolution loosed pent-up hostility against foreign groups such as the Spanish and the Chinese, anti-Americanism became the most pervasive and intense xenophobia of the Revolution. Individual incidents and barbed attacks on Mexico by American businessmen and a segment of the American press stirred deep resentment. Army mobilizations and naval encirclement roused Mexican fears of an all-out Yankee invasion; the machinations of Ambassador Henry Lane Wilson made him a villain comparable to Victoriano Huerta who unified Mexicans in common opposition; foreign participants in the Revolution provoked jealousy and antagonism in their Mexican counterparts; and after Madero, revolutionary leaders inflamed anti-gringo sentiment in their own championing of Mexican interests. Other factors contributing to the pervading xenophobia were the Masonic schism, Woodrow Wilson's alienating policies, the Veracruz invasion, and the Pershing expedition. The latter two provoked unanimous denunciations of North American aggression and still provoke strong sentiments of Mexican unity as they are reiterated in Mexican literature, art, and popular music.

Themes of social justice and unity as well as xenophobia have pervaded Mexican literature. The nationalistic attitudes that became apparent in nineteenth-century novels and histories anticipated the flourishing of literary nationalism in all forms of expression following the Revolution. Patriotic textbooks, popular literature, and the revolutionary novels now reach an expanded audience as literacy increases. With a heavy nationalist content, *corridos,* murals, and the cinema reach many of the individuals whom illiteracy still cuts off from the written forms of literature. Radio and television, as their audiences expand, offer further opportunities for the dissemination of nationalist attitudes and loyalty. Many of the most effective evocations of nationalism in these diverse media of expression depend for their inspiration on the 1910 Revolution.

As Giuseppi Garibaldi commented in 1911, the Mexican Revolution itself is merely one more manifestation of the world-wide "movement toward real freedom."[1] The continuing process of violent revolution after 1911 stimulated the breakdown of social, political, and economic barriers separating men, and it fostered the expansion of individual loyalties outside the family and the *patria chica.* In doing so, the Revolution came to represent the drive for equality and the pattern of national loyalty in Mexico which have become hallmarks of the twentieth century. Much of Mexican history can be understood in terms of a trend toward equality. Strengthening of the ideals of equality before the law and equality of opportunity for all citizens has been a major element leading to nationalism.

1. Quoted in Edward Marshall, ''Grandson of the Great Garibaldi Fights in Mexico,'' *The New York Times,* May 28, 1911, Part 5, p. 3:3.

Violent revolution is one form of social change, a rapid, unwieldy form that by its nature destroys more in the short run in terms of life, property, and human happiness than it creates. Although mass revolution seems likely to frustrate the desire of any individual or group to shape the ultimate nature of the social change that it brings, in the case of the Mexican Revolution, destruction and violence aroused a desire for cohesive nationalism and an inclusive national community. World-wide advances in science and technology have certainly spurred Mexico's development, but the Revolution has allowed Mexico to capitalize on these advances through the ideological commitment to social justice which has mobilized the energy of the Mexican people in constructive co-operation.

The United States has played a role in this evolution, which, although far from what the American policy-makers had in mind, has worked for the over-all benefit of the United States. Instead of contributing to the "ruin of the Mexican nation" as Mexican writers repeatedly aver, the military, economic, and cultural pressure of the United States has significantly advanced the formation of the Mexican national community. Since 1810 a pervasive awareness of the United States has been diffused in the Mexican population, making Mexicans conscious of their national distinctiveness. While often admiring and fearing the political stability and material progress of the United States, Mexicans unwaveringly proclaim the superiority of their own cultural values.

The resistant nationalism evident in Carranza's insistence on unconditional American withdrawal in both the Veracruz occupation and the Pershing expedition underlies the respect for territorial integrity and national sovereignty that has remained a cardinal tenet of Mexican foreign policy since that time.[2] Heavy pressure from the

2. For concise statements elucidating the Mexican viewpoint, see Jorge Castañeda, ''Revolution and Foreign Policy: Mexico's Experience,'' *Political Science Quarterly*, Vol. 78, No. 3 (September, 1963); and Manuel González

United States on Mexico in the past largely accounts for Mexico's stout championing of national self-determination. Mexican policies such as the long maintenance of diplomatic relations with Fidel Castro's Cuba and opposition in the Organization of American States to the intervention of the United States in the Dominican Republic crisis of 1965 run counter to what some Washington policy-planners define as the national interest. The internal Mexican nationalism and social cohesion—also traceable in part to past pressure on Mexico—has an opposite effect on North American interests. The pressure has here helped to create the stability and national self-confidence that makes Mexico resistant to the inroads of communism.

Political stability and national self-confidence have by no means solved all Mexican problems. The strong sense of nationalism that has developed in Mexico has not eliminated the bribery and corruption that still grease the workings of the business and governmental apparatus. Mexico continues to face serious problems of insufficient domestic capital formation, featherbedding in the public sector, and failure to incorporate peasant groups into the national economic structure despite nationalistic statements of the need to do so. The rise of a sense of cohesive nationalism is no panacea for problems of economic growth and social change.

The effects of Mexican nationalism differ for various social classes. Mexican laborers and farmers lack the directive sense of nationalism that their leaders possess. Although those who lead and those who follow share a common facility of communication within the national community, their personal appreciation of national progress and their perception of the phenomenon of Mexican nationalism itself vary with their roles and levels of indoctrination in the nationalist folklore. In no class or group does nationalism eradicate the loyalties to family, locality,

Ramírez, ''La política internacional de la Revolución Mexicana,'' *Ciencias Políticas y Sociales*, Año 2, Núm. 3 (enero-marzo, 1956).

and deity nor does it subsume individual drives for sustenance, power, and sex. A quarter of the Mexican people
have not become self-conscious participants in the activities of the national community, even though since 1917
both the absolute number of Mexicans with strong national
loyalty and their proportion relative to the total population
have increased substantially.

A particularly important result of the growth of Mexican nationalism before 1917 was its implantation as a social
value in the elite who thereafter directed Mexican political
development. Nationalism became—at an earlier date than
in the other presently "developing" countries of Asia and
Africa and with an emphasis on social cohesion not yet
equaled in other Latin American states—a prerequisite
for effective participation in the direction of Mexican politics and the regulation of power relationships among competing groups. The common commitment to nationalist
values forms the basis of cohesion for the functional interest groups united under presidential leadership in the
dominant Partido Revolucionario Institucional. For Latin
American politics in general, Robert E. Scott has recently
suggested that the multiplication of interests in Latin
America now means that "the pressing political problem
is not so much to counteract a power elite by encouraging
pluralism but to find ways to unite the many elites and
their followers and to harness their political activities for
constructive national integration."[3] It is in this process of
unity-creation among occupational and interest groups and
between social classes in which the Mexicans have excelled,
and the development of their peculiarly cohesive form of
nationalism rests at the base of their success.

In addition to supplying a useful mechanism for promoting social cohesion and the political influence of the
new urban leadership, nationalism has shaped the attitudes

3. Robert E. Scott, "Political Elites and Political Modernization: The
Crisis of Transition," in Seymour Martin Lipset and Aldo Solari, eds., *Elites
in Latin America* (New York: Oxford University Press, 1967), p. 128.

of the leadership itself. A basic reason for the separation of the elite in developing countries from the mass of citizens in its championing of nationalism is that the elite has already undergone the social conditioning that the masses have yet to undergo. The elite has won an education and achieved literacy, traveled in various parts of the nation, and developed a sense of economic competition with foreign managers and foreign interests. The Mexican elite is not authoritarian and makes no claim for its own omniscience and unlimited discretion.[4] One reason for this lack of an authoritarian self-image is the association that present leaders see between themselves and the revolutionaries who attacked the authoritarian regime of Porfirio Díaz and established the goal of mass participation in national affairs.

Mexicans and particularly Mexican leaders must take care that national pride does not stifle the spirit of criticism that is needed to further continued material progress and its extension throughout Mexican society. Nationalism in Mexico is maturing and can accept a degree of constructive criticism. Mexican intellectuals themselves distinguish between the positive and negative aspects of nationalism, between what Carlos Fuentes describes as the "affirmation of our human and economic direction" and the "negative, neopatriotic, chauvinistic and totally inefficacious" nationalism that denounces all criticism of Mexico.[5] By maintaining emphasis on the positive rather than the negative qualities inherent in it, the force of cohesive nationalism in Mexico can continue to help Mexicans realize the national ideals of their Revolution.

4. L. Vincent Padgett, ''Mexico's One-Party System: A Re-evaluation,'' *American Political Science Review*, Vol. 51, No. 4 (December, 1957), 1005-6. On the effectiveness with which this elite has been able to absorb dissident groups into its own ranks, see Bo Anderson and James D. Cockroft, ''Control and Coöptation in Mexican Politics,'' *International Journal of Comparative Sociology*, Vol. 7, No. 1 (March, 1966).

5. Quoted in ''Mexicans Debate Book on Poverty: 'Children of Sanchez' Stirs Anger of the Nationalists,'' *The New York Times*, February 21, 1965, p. 28:1.

Bibliography

Although massive amounts of printed material pertain to Mexican nationalism, comparatively few studies consider it specifically and in detail. Bibliographical guides provide ample source material on the general literature. On nationalism, two of the best bibliographies are Koppel S. Pinson, *A Bibliographical Introduction to Nationalism* (New York: Columbia University Press, 1935) and Karl W. Deutsch, *An Interdisciplinary Bibliography on Nationalism, 1935-1953* (Cambridge, Mass.: Technology Press of M.I.T., 1956). Especially comprehensive bibliographies on Mexico are Luis González, ed., *Fuentes de la historia contemporánea de México* (3 vols.; México: El Colegio de México, 1961-62) and Stanley R. Ross, ed., *Fuentes de la historia contemporánea de México* (2 vols.; México: El Colegio de México, 1965, 1967). Sources on the 1910 Revolution are well covered in Ignacio B. del Castillo, *Bibliografía de la Revolución Mexicana de 1910-1916* . . . (México: Talleres Gráficos de la Secretaría de Comunicaciones y Obras Públicas, 1918) and Roberto Ramos, *Bibliografía de la Revolución Mexicana* (3 vols.; México: Biblioteca del Instituto Nacional de Estudios Históricos de la Revolución Mexicana, 1959-60).

For those wishing more general information or interpretations of Mexican affairs, several studies stand out. The most incisive single study remains Howard F. Cline, *The United States and Mexico* (2d ed.; New York: Atheneum, 1963). Recent Mexican history is well treated in Frank Brandenburg, *The Making of Modern Mexico* (Englewood Cliffs, N.J.: Prentice-Hall, Inc., 1964)

and Howard F. Cline, *Mexico: Revolution to Evolution, 1940-1960*
(New York: Oxford University Press, 1963). Different approaches
to the functioning of the Mexican government appear in Robert E.
Scott, *Mexican Government in Transition* (2d ed.; Urbana, Ill.:
University of Illinois Press, 1964); William P. Tucker, *The Mexican
Government Today* (Minneapolis, Minn.: University of Minnesota
Press, 1957); L. Vincent Padgett, *The Mexican Political System*
(Boston: Houghton Mifflin Company, 1966); and Pablo González
Casanova, *La democracia en México* (2d ed.; México: Ediciones
Era, S.A., 1967). Frank Tannenbaum's study entitled *Peace by
Revolution: An Interpretation of Mexico* (New York: Columbia
University Press, 1933) remains a classic on the revolutionary
period. From the Mexican standpoint, revolutionary history is
well summarized in Manuel González Ramírez, *La revolución social
de México. I. Las ideas—la violencia* (México: Fondo de Cultura
Económica, 1960) and Jesús Silva Herzog, *Breve historia de la
Revolución Mexicana* (2 vols.; México: Fondo de Cultura Económica, 1964). Major insights into Mexican thought are contained
in Octavio Paz, *The Labyrinth of Solitude: Life and Thought in
Mexico*, Lysander Kemp, trans. (New York: Grove Press, 1961)
and Samuel Ramos, *Profile of Man and Culture in Mexico*, Peter
G. Earle, trans. (Austin, Texas: University of Texas Press, 1962).

Other useful sources of information are interviews and the
archives of the United States Department of State. Structured or
unstructured interviewing in the field may well change a research-
er's conclusions on aspects of nationalism, while direct contact with
the national milieu that he studies provides popular literature and
insights not available to the outsider. Inclusion of Mexico in
Gabriel A. Almond and Sidney Verba's study of *The Civic Culture:
Political Attitudes and Democracy in Five Nations* (Princeton,
N.J.: Princeton University Press, 1963) points up the wealth of
information on nationalist attitudes in Latin America which may
be documented through survey research. United States archives
similarly show the relevance of foreign diplomatic reporting for the
study of nationalism. Containing reports on political affairs in
Mexico by United States diplomats and consuls from all over
Mexico, the 812.00 decimal file of the State Department has been
reproduced on microfilm and now appears in many university
libraries throughout the United States. It should be supplemented
by consulting the consular post records in the National Archives,
which document past attitudes and actions in such remote locations
as Yucatán and Baja California. The reports contain a wealth of
newspaper clippings, posters, and manifestoes, although the best

source of newspaper and periodical literature on Mexico is the Hemeroteca Nacional in Mexico City.

While a considerable amount of work remains to be done on the nature and effects of Mexican nationalism, the following studies show some of the work that has been done so far.

Books and Dissertations

Brushwood, John S. *Mexico in Its Novel: A Nation's Search for Identity.* Austin, Texas: University of Texas Press, 1966.

Cantú Corro, José. *Patria y raza.* México: Escuela Tipográfica Salesiana, 1924.

Carreño, Alberto María. *México y los Estados Unidos de América: Apuntaciones para la historia del acrecentamiento territorial de los Estados Unidos a costa de México desde la época colonial hasta nuestros días.* México: Editorial Jus, S.A., 1962.

Carrillo Flores, Antonio. *El nacionalismo de los países latino-americanos en la postguerra.* México: El Colegio de México, 1945.

Castro, J. Rafael de. *La cuestión mexicana, ó esposición de las causas que hacian indispensables la intervención europea y el restablecimiento de la monarquía en México como unicos medios de salvar la nacionalidad y la independencia del país.* México: Imprenta de J. M. Andrade y F. Escalante, 1864.

Ceniceros, José Ángel. *Educación y mexicanidad.* México: Populibros "La Prensa," División de Editora de Periódicos, S.C.L., 1958.

Cosío Villegas, Daniel. *Extremos de América.* México: Tezontle, 1949.

Cosmes, Francisco G. *La dominación española y la patria mexicana.* México: Imprenta de "El Partido Liberal," 1896.

Crater [Pedro Lamicq]. *Piedad para el indio!* México: n.p., 1913.

Ewing, Floyd Ford. "Carranza's Foreign Relations: An Experiment in Nationalism." Unpublished Ph.D. dissertation, University of Texas, 1952.

Galindo, Miguel. *El mito de la patria: Estudio de psicología histórica aplicado a la República Mexicana.* Colima, Col.: Imprenta del Comercio, 1920.

Gamio, Manuel. *Forjando patria.* México: Editorial Porrúa, S.A., 1960.

———. *Hacia un México nuevo: Problemas sociales.* México: n.p., 1935.

Hajj Miguel Aury, Elizabeth. "La nacionalidad mexicana." Tesis,

Escuela Nacional de Jurisprudencia, Universidad Nacional Autónoma de México, 1951.

Masur, Gerhard. *Nationalism in Latin America.* New York: The Macmillan Company, 1966.

Maza, Francisco de la. *El guadalupanismo mexicano.* México: Porrúa y Obregón, 1953.

Michaels, Albert Louis. "Mexican Politics and Nationalism from Calles to Cárdenas." Unpublished Ph.D. dissertation, University of Pennsylvania, 1966.

Molina Enríquez, Andrés. *Los grandes problemas nacionales.* México: Imprenta de A. Carranza e Hijos, 1909.

Nieto, Rafael. *Más allá de la patria . . . Ensayos económicos y políticos.* México: Andrés Botas e Hijo, 1922.

Palavicini, Félix F. *Pro-patria: Apuntes de sociología mexicana.* México: Tip. "La Ilustración," 1905.

Ramírez, Santiago. *El mexicano: Psicología de sus motivaciones.* 3d ed. México: Editorial Pax-México, 1961.

Rivero y Martínez, José Luis. "La nacionalidad, problema de México." Tesis, Facultad de Derecho y Ciencias Sociales, Universidad Nacional Autónoma de México, 1934.

Sáenz, Moisés. *Las inversiones extranjeras y el nacionalismo mexicano: Conferencia sustentada en la Universidad de Chicago, Ill., E. U. A., el mes de julio de 1926.* México: Talleres Gráficos de la Nación, 1927.

Scott, Robert E. "Mexico: The Established Revolution," in Lucian W. Pye and Sidney Verba, eds., *Political Culture and Political Development.* Princeton, N.J.: Princeton University Press, 1965.

――――. "Nation-Building in Latin America," in Karl W. Deutsch and William J. Foltz, eds., *Nation-Building.* New York: Atherton Press, 1963.

Sierra, Justo. *Obras completas de maestro Justo Sierra.* 14 vols. México: Universidad Nacional Autónoma de México, 1948-50.

Singer, Morris. "Growth, Equality, and Mexico's Experience." Unpublished manuscript, 1966.

Travesí, Gonzalo G. *La Revolución de México y el imperialismo yanqui.* Barcelona: Casa Editorial Maucci, 1914.

Trejo Lerdo de Tejada, C. *La Revolución y el nacionalismo: Todo para todos.* Habana: Maza y Ca., 1916.

Vargas Ruiz, Francisco. *Yo soy mexicano: Lo que todo ciudadano debe saber.* 3d ed. México: Enrique Sáinz Editores, S.A., 1964.

Véjar Vázquez, Octavio. *Hacia una escuela de unidad nacional.* México: Ediciones de la Secretaría de Educación Pública, 1944.

Whetten, Nathan L. *Rural Mexico.* Chicago: University of Chicago Press, 1948.

Whitaker, Arthur P. *Nationalism in Latin America, Past and Present.* Gainesville, Fla.: University of Florida Press, 1962.

————. "Nationalism and Social Change in Latin America," in Joseph Maier and Richard W. Weatherhead, eds., *Politics of Change in Latin America.* New York: Frederick A. Praeger, 1964.

————, and David C. Jordan. *Nationalism in Contemporary Latin America.* New York: The Free Press, 1966.

Wionczek, Miguel S. *El nacionalismo mexicano y la inversión extranjera.* México: Siglo Veintiuno Editores, S.A., 1967.

Worthen, Edward Henry. "The Reconquest of Mexico: A Panoramic View of Mexican Literary Nationalism." Unpublished Ph.D. dissertation, University of Michigan, 1965.

Articles

Alexander, Robert J. "Nationalism, Latin America's Predominant Ideology," *Journal of International Affairs,* Vol. 15, No. 2 (Fall, 1961).

Arojona, Doris King, and Carlos Vázquez Arojona. "Apuntes sobre los origenes del nacionalismo en la novela mexicana," *Revue Hispanique,* Vol. 81, 2d part (1933).

Carrión, Jorge. "Efectos psicológicos de la guerra de 47 en el hombre de México," *Cuadernos Americanos,* Año 7, Vol. 37, Núm. 1 (enero-febrero, 1948).

Cosío Villegas, Daniel. "Nacionalismo y desarrollo," *Foro Internacional,* Vol. 3, Núm. 3 (enero-marzo, 1963).

Griffin, Charles C. "An Essay on Regionalism and Nationalism in Latin American Historiography," *Journal of World History,* Vol. 8, No. 2 (1964).

Hamill, Hugh M., Jr. "The Virgin of Guadalupe and the Origins of Mexican Nationalism." Paper read before the Ohio Academy of History, April, 1961.

Hoselitz, Bert F. "Nationalism, Economic Development, and Democracy," *The Annals of the American Academy of Political and Social Science,* Vol. 305 (May, 1956).

Johnson, John J. "The New Latin American Nationalism," *Yale Review,* Vol. 54, No. 2 (December, 1964).

Maza, Francisco de la. "Los evangelistas de Guadalupe y el nacionalismo mexicano," *Cuadernos Americanos,* Año 8, Vol. 48, Núm. 6 (noviembre-diciembre, 1949).

Michaels, Albert L. "El nacionalismo conservador mexicano desde la Revolución hasta 1940," *Historia Mexicana,* Vol. 26, Núm. 2 (octubre-diciembre, 1966).

Moreno, Rafael. "Creación de la nacionalidad mexicana," *Historia Mexicana,* Vol. 12, Núm. 4 (abril-junio, 1963).

Reid, John T. "An Aspect of Symbolic Nationalism in Spanish America," *Hispania,* Vol. 40, No. 1 (March, 1957).

Roura Parella, Juan. "Formación de la conciencia nacional," *Revista Mexicana de Sociología,* Año 16, Vol. 16, Núm. 1 (enero-abril, 1954).

Ruiz, Ramón Eduardo. "Mexico: The Struggle for a National Language," *Social Research,* Vol. 25, No. 3 (October, 1958).

Séverin, Jacques. "Démocratie mexicaine," *Esprit,* 20ᵉ Année, No. 190 (Mai, 1952).

Silvert, K. H. "Nationalism in Latin America," *The Annals of the American Academy of Political and Social Science,* Vol. 334 (March, 1961).

Tannenbaum, Frank. "Agrarismo, Indianismo, y Nacionalismo," *Hispanic American Historical Review,* Vol. 23, No. 3 (August, 1943).

Turner, Frederick C. "The Implications of Demographic Change for Nationalism and Internationalism," *Journal of Politics,* Vol. 27, No. 1 (February, 1965).

Index

Abandonadas, Las (film), 302
Academia Mexicana de la Lengua, 85
Acapulco, 95, 210, 214, 237
Access, political, in contemporary Mexico, 10-11, 314-15; under Díaz, 56; and 1910 Revolution, 156-57. *See also* Women, Mexican; Workers; Indians, Mexican
Action-orientation, as test of nationalism, 4-6
Acuña y Rossetti, Elisa, 196
Adelita, La (film), 300
"Adelita, La" (song), 282
Adelita (heroine of 1910 Revolution), 199; in songs, 282; in films, 300, 302-3
"Adiós, mamá Carlota" (song), 282
Africa, vii, 28, 66, 315; "cultural management" in, 255
Agrarian reform, 132, 166; and Morelos, 31; and Zapata, 110, 117, 118; and 1917 Constitution, 111, 131; and Cárdenas, 118; and Confederación Nacional de Campesinos, 118; since 1940, 118; and Porfirio Díaz, 165; and Villa, 241
Agriculture, 65, 80, 90, 98, 145, 147, 285, 311; in New Spain, 24; foreign investment in, 55; education in, 118; mechanization of, 118, 151; workers in, 118, 311, 314. *See also* Agrarian reform; Irrigation
Aguascalientes, city, 148, 166, 210
Air warfare in 1910 Revolution, 159. *See also* Military technology
Alamán, Lucas, 30, 75, 76, 267
Alessio Robles, Miguel, 119
Alfaro Siqueiros, David 294
Alfonso XIII, 205
Alhóndiga, 32

Alianza de Mujeres de México, 200
Alienation, political, in contemporary Mexico, 10-11; under Porfirio Díaz, 56, 170-71, 180, 184-85, 309; of women, 184-86; and violence of 1910 Revolution, 200
"Allegory of Mexico" (mural), 293
Allende, Ignacio, 30, 198
Alliance for Progress, 155
Almond, Gabriel, viii, 10, 200
Altamirano, Ignacio Manuel, 77, 129, 176, 258, 259, 276, 302
Alvarado, Salvador, 124; on Catholic church, 137; and regeneration plans, 152; and feminist movement, 190, 198
American Club, 215, 217
American Embassy, in Mexico, 211, 220, 239
"American Legion." *See* "Foreign Legion"
American Magazine (periodical), 58
American Revolution, 35n; effect of on development of Mexican nationalism, 29
Americans in Mexico, 58, 67-68, 70, 87, 172, 192, 221; claims by and against, 43; investments of during *porfiriato*, 53-61 *passim;* appreciation of Mexican nationalism by, 131, 202, 210-12, 237; press of in Mexico, 138, 213; investment in Mexico, 154; during 1910 Revolution, 203, 205, 207, 245, 250, 311; Confederate colonization attempts, 208; decline in numbers of during 1910 Revolution, 210; murder and molestation of, 212, 229; as volunteers in 1910 Revolution, 213, 231, 232-36; ownership of Mexican resources, 213;

in Baja California, 235; and Freemasons, 238-39, 242; in contemporary period, 251
Anáhuac, 31
Anarcho-syndicalism, 180, 183. *See
also* Casa del Obrero Mundial; Industrial Workers of the World
Andrés Pérez, maderista (Azuela),
261
Ángeles, Felipe, 111, 291
Anthony, Susan B., 185
Anti-Americanism, during 1810-1910
period, 35-44; and Americans' investment in Mexico during *porfiriato,* 53-61 *passim;* and nationalism, 57-58, 202-53 *passim,* 309;
generating xenophobia, 57-58; and
American presumptions of racial
superiority, 173, 243, 252; and
actions of Henry Lane Wilson, 202,
220-23, 311; and mistreatment of
Mexicans, 202; and Pershing expedition, 202, 229-31, 312; and
Veracruz occupation, 202, 218, 223-
29, 312; and American volunteers in
1910 Revolution, 203, 213, 231, 232-
36, 311; and Huerta, 203; and
Villa, 203; limiting factors on,
203, 213-15, 248, 249-52; personal
friendships as a barrier to, 203,
209, 248, 250; cultural basis for,
208; historical basis for, 208;
American consular reports on, 209-
11, 213-14, 217-18, 219, 236; as
cause for departure of Americans
from Mexico, 210-12; murder and
molestation of Americans, 212;
and wrangling between Mexican
factions, 212-13; counteracted by
Madero, 214-15, 232-35; and Antonio Rodríguez lynching, 216-18;
North American provocations of,
216-31, 311; motivated by United
States mobilizations during 1910
Revolution, 218-20, 229, 231, 311;
and José Mancisidor, 228; and
youth in 1910 Revolution, 231, 236;
effect of schism in Freemasonry on,
232, 312; in posters and handbills,
236, 244-45; in press, 236, 244,
245-46; in books, 246-47, 312; in
plays, 246-47, 277-78; expressed
through pejorative Spanish equiv-

alents for ''Americans,'' 247; isolation as a barrier to, 248-49;
dangers of for revolutionary factions, 249; decline of since 1917,
251, 252; in oratory, 279; in songs,
281, 282, 286; and American films,
298-300; in Mexican films, 301-2;
during 1910 Revolution, 311; in
art, 312. *See also* Latin Americanism; Pershing expedition; Veracruz, causes of United States occupation of; War of 1846-1848;
Xenophobia, Mexican
Anticlericalism, 31, 44-48, 136-44
passim. See also Church-state relations; Catholic church; Constitutionalists
Anticolonialism, 28; as an influence
on nationalism, 28; in Mexico, 28-
35. *See also* Xenophobia
Anti-heroes, 112, 113, 114, 115, 303.
See also Huerta, Victoriano; Santa
Anna, Antonio López de; Wilson,
Henry Lane; Wilson, Woodrow
Anti-Hispanicism, 28-35 *passim,* 205-
6, 311. *See also* Anticolonialism
Apache Indians, 25
Appeals during 1910 Revolution,
stress of on national unity, 163-65;
inclusiveness of, 163-69; invocation
of patriotism in, 164, 166; to
Indians, 171-73; to workers, 179,
180-81, 311; to women, 189-91, 311
Apuntes de un lugareño (Romero),
263
Aragón Leiva, Agustín, 300
Arango, Doroteo. *See* Villa, Fran-
cisco
Architecture, French, 52; Mexican,
288-89; church, 288; as influence
on nationalism, 289
Argentina, 3, 14, 27, 68, 257; population of and Mexican nationalism,
64; and Indians, 69; and Veracruz occupation, peace talks, 226
Ariaga, Ponciano, 279
Aristocracy. *See* Upper class
Arizona, 58, 96
Arms, control of by United States,
249. *See also* Military technology
Army, Mexican, 77, 137, 264; Indians
in, 77; role in Mexican politics,
107; and 1910 Revolution, 122, 168,

171, 197, 237, 238; conscripts in, 122, 123-24, 283, 291; internees in United States, 126-27; and women during 1910 Revolution, 186; in novels, 258, 264-65; in literature, 272; in films, 298, 303. *See also* Military technology
Army, United States, 70, 126, 230, 233, 271, 272; mobilizations of during 1910 Revolution, 218, 229, 231, 312
Art, 287-95; and nationalism, 287; Mexican murals, 287, 292-95; in nineteenth-century Mexico, 287-88; Mexican paintings, 287-88, 290-92; Mexican cartoons, 289-90
Asia, 28, 315; nationalism and xenophobia in, vii, 16; "cultural management" in, 255
"Así era Pancho Villa" (film), 302
Asociación de Escritoras y Periodistas de México, 200
Ateneo de Mujeres, 200
Atl, Dr. (Gerardo Murillo), 137
Atrocities in 1910 Revolution, 149-50. *See also* Violence
"Avispón Verde, El" (television program), 306
Ayutla, 259
Aztecs, 24-25, 85, 243, 294, 298. *See also* Indianism
Azuela, Mariano, 260, 261-62, 263, 302

Baja California, 66, 67, 95, 96, 97, 98, 128, 210, 235, 246, 247
Baja California Norte, 123
Balbuena, Bernardo de, 257
Bandera, Juan, 77
Bandera de México, La (children's book), 271
Bandits, 41, 110, 124, 149, 214, 244, 299
Banking, foreign investment in, 55
Baranda, Joaquín, 92, 93, 94
Barra, Francisco de la, 193, 272
Barradas, Isidro, 33
Barreda, Gabino, 92
Bassols, Narciso, 304
Baudin, Charles, 49
Bell, Wendell, 18
Berlin, 145
Berthold, Simon, 235

Betancourt, Rómulo, 14
Beteta, Ramón, 72-73
"Beverly Ricos, Los" (television program), 306
Bianchi, Alberto G., 276
"Billionaires, The" (mural), 295
Biografías Selectas (comic books), 272
Blanca (character in *La venganza de la gleba*), 276
Blanquet, Aureliano, 167
Boer War, 232
Bolivia, 145
Bolshevik Revolution, 115, 118, 131, 152; and xenophobia, 16-17
Bonney, Wilbert L., 131
Bonsal, Stephen, 168, 236
Bosch García, Carlos, 37-38
"Bourgeois Reformers" (mural), 295
Bourke, John G., 78
Boyd, Charles J., 230
Braceros, 128, 154; in films, 301-2. *See also* Emigrants, Mexican, in United States; Emigration from Mexico
Bradstreet, Anne, 257
Bravo, Nicolás, 32
Brazil, 14, 68, 263; effects of expulsion of Dutch, 16, 17; racial tolerance in, 69, 178; and Veracruz occupation, peace talks, 225
Breve historia de México (Vasconcelos), 37
Bryan, William Jennings, 145, 238
Bulnes, Francisco, 75, 93, 267
Burns, Juan T., 243
Burr, Aaron, 247
Bustillo Oro, Juan, 301
Butler, Anthony, 36-37
Butte, Montana, 211
Byron, Lord, 235

Cabrera, Luis, as hero, 111; observance at death of, 165; reply to American Catholic attacks on Constitutionalists, 244; concept of nationalism, 56
Caciques, power of in Mexico, 39
Caciques, Los (Azuela), 261
Cajeme (Indian leader), 77
Calderón, Esteban B., 58
Calderón, Fernando, 276

California, 23, 37, 38, 39, 40, 41, 43, 242. *See also* Baja California
Callahan, Charles, 43
Calles, Plutarco Elías, 109, 139, 197
Campaigns for presidency in Mexico, 175, 279
Campeche, city, 33, 43
Campeche, state, 123, 198
Campobello, Nellie, 262-63
Canada, 35n, 69, 232, 238
Canadian Bank of Commerce, 54n
Cananea, 57-58
Canning, George, 29
Cantú Corro, José, 143
Carapan, 17
Cárdenas, Lázaro, 153, 183, 251, 294, 299
Cárdenas Rite, 239. *See also* Freemasonry, Mexican
Caribbean, 14, 48
Carillo, Carlos A., 94
Carpio, Manuel, 274
Carrancistas, 85, 164, 168, 179-80, 230, 241, 242, 264, 268, 282, 291. *See also* Constitutionalists
Carranza, Venustiano, 88, 104, 129, 130, 147, 148, 168, 198, 213, 249; and egalitarianism, 108; and Zapatistas, 108, 109-10; as leader of Constitutionalists, 108; early career of, 108; opposition of to United States intervention, 108, 313; political beliefs of, 108; as hero, 108-9, 119; death of, 109, 119, 264; and Querétaro Constitution, 119; and Veracruz decrees, 119; military strategy of, 159; appeals of for support, 163, 180; support of by trade unions, 181; and family legislation, 190, 198; United States recognition of, 215, 229, 241; Soviet view of, 228-29; and Pershing expedition, 229, 231, 313; use by of xenophobia, 235, 241, 249; and Central Powers, 241-42; biography of, 264; in comic books, 272; in songs, 282; in murals, 295; in films, 296-97, 302; and United States occupation of Veracruz, 313
Carrasco, Ezequiel, 300
Carrizal, battle of, 229n, 230, 231
Cartoons, 287, 289; during 1910 Revolution, 245-46, 290; before 1910 Revolution, 289-90
Cartucho (Campobello), 262-63
Casa del Obrero Mundial, 109, 180, 181
Casement, Roger, 17
Castillo, Florencio M. del, 258
Castillo, José R. del, 271
Castro, Fidel, 14, 252, 314
Castro, Rafael de, 42-43
"Catharsis" (mural), 192
Catholic church, 57, 291, 294; in New Spain, 24, 26; influence of, 1810-1910, 44-48; economic position of, 1810-1910, 45; legislation curbing, 45, 47; and 1857 Constitution, 46; and Ley Iglesias, 46; and Ley Juárez, 46; and Ley Lerdo, 46; and Maximilian, 47; during *porfiriato*, 57, 136-37; and the family, 133, 135; and clerical garb, 136, 141; and education, 136, 138, 140; and 1910 Revolution, 136-39, 311; and Catholic party, 137; and men, 137; and women, 137; and Constitutionalists, 137-38; and 1917 Constitution, 138-39; influence of on nationalism, 141-42, 143, 309, 311; Virgin of Guadalupe, 142; and Christian universalism, 143; in contemporary Mexico, 143-44; new compatibility with Mexican nationalism, 143-44; and Indians, 175. *See also* Reforma; Three Years' War
Catt, Carrie Chapman, 194
Caudillos. *See Caciques*
Celaya, 30; battle of, 159
"Cementerio de las águilas, El" (film), 300
"Centauro del norte, El" (film), 302-3
Centennial celebrations of 1910, 102-4
Central America, 14
Central Powers, 242
Cerro de las campanas, El (Mateos), 259
Cervantes, Luis (character in *Los de abajo*), 262
Chamber of Deputies, 213
Chapultepec Castle, 41, 52, 288, 294. *See also* Niños Héroes, Los

Chávez, Carlos, 280, 281; on mestizo music, 74
Chávez, Jorge, 116
Chester, 224
Chiapas, 70, 77, 91, 98, 176, 195
Chihuahua, state, 66, 70, 91, 110, 122, 130, 145, 176, 196, 204, 205, 229, 296
Chihuahua City, 130, 147, 205
Children, 187, 191; in 1910 Revolution, 134-35; school textbooks for, 269-71; books for, 271; coloring books for, 271-72; comic books for, 272; and poetry, 275. *See also* Education, Mexican; Education and nationalism; Students; Youth
Chile, 14, 27, 226, 235, 257
Chilpancingo, 31
Chilton, William Edwin, 224
China, 158, 178, 228
Chincha Islands, 34
Chinese in Mexico, 55, 203; Torreón massacre, 203; Mexican persecution of, 204-5, 311; competition for Mexican women by, 205
"Chinita maderista, La" (*corrido*), 285
Cholula, battle of, 160
Chopin, Frédéric, 280
Church. *See* Catholic church; Church-state relations; Religion and nationalism; Religious loyalty
Church-state relations, 139-41, 143; and 1857 Constitution, 46; and Juárez, 136; during *porfiriato*, 136-37; and 1910 Revolution, 136-39; under Calles, 139; under Cárdenas, 139; reconciliation in, 1930's, 139, 143; in post-Revolutionary period, 139-41. *See also* Catholic church; Religion and nationalism
Cid, El, 143
Científicos, 55-61 *passim*, 82, 92, 170, 207, 308, 309. *See also* Díaz, Porfirio; Nationalism, *científico*
Cinema and nationalism, 295-96. *See also* Films, in Mexico
Citizenship and nationalism, 4-5, 69, 71, 74, 76, 106, 125, 127
Ciudadela, 222
Ciudad Juárez, 71, 96, 168, 188; battle of, 106, 110, 232, 233, 264

Civil Code of the Federal District and Territories, 198
Civil liberties, Mexican, 3
Class structure and nationalism, 89; in Mexico, 55-56, 102, 155; during 1910 Revolution, 131-32, 310; determinants of in Mexico, 132. *See also* Lower class; Middle class; Upper class
Clavijero, Francisco Javier, 257
Clay, Henry, 36
Clayton-Bulwer Treaty, 35n
"Clemencia" (film), 302
Clergy. *See* Catholic church
Cline, Howard F., 268
Club Internacional de Mujeres, 200
Coahuila, 108, 125, 198
Cochrane, Thomas, 235
Colegio Militar, 41. *See also* Chapultepec Castle; Niños Héroes, Los
Colima, city, 238
Colombia, 14
Colonization, 67; enforced, 123, 187
Columbia Pictures Corporation, 299
Columbus, New Mexico, 110, 119, 229
Comanche Indians, 25
Comic books, as nationalist vehicle in Mexico, 197, 272
Commerce, 70, 80, 95, 97, 145-46; foreign investment in, 55
Communications, Mexican, 80, 85; effect of on nationalism, 11-12, 20, 95-100 *passim*, 310; before 1810, 23; changes in, 1810-1910, 95-100 *passim;* telegraph system, 96-97; postal service, 97; telephones, 97
Communism, 154; in China, 118; in Russia, 118; in Mexico, 180, 314
Comte, Auguste, 52
Confederación de Trabajadores de México (CTM), 183
Confederación Nacional de Campesinos (CNC), 118
Confederación Regional Obrera Mexicana (CROM), 183
Confederation of Regular Grand Lodges, 239. *See also* Freemasonry, Mexican
Congress. *See* Mexican Congress; United States Congress
Congress of Tampico, 183

"Conqueror-Builder and the Indian Worker, The" (mural), 294

Conscription, 123, 134, 135, 186-87, 264, 265; under Huerta, 122, 134

Consensus, in Latin American republics, 3, 13-14; and nationalism, 3-21, 255; in Mexico, 3-21 *passim*, 314-16; contrasting levels of, 5. *See also* Social cohesion

Constitutional Convention of 1856-57, 186

Constitutional Convention of 1916-17, 151, 182, 198

Constitutionalists, 87-88, 107-8, 109, 121, 122, 124, 146, 148, 165, 166, 190, 199, 215, 242, 290; Zapatistas as, against Huerta, 109-10; and clergy, 137; and Catholic church, 137-38; rule against foreigners in ranks of, 235; and Catholic church of United States, 244

Constitution of 1857, 46, 48, 53, 136, 186, 193, 289

Constitution of 1917, viii, 109, 119, 151, 181, 182, 268, 273; and agrarian reform, 111, 131, 166; and labor, 119, 131, 166, 180; and education, 131; and illegitimacy, 131, 166; and women, 131, 191; as institutionalization of nationalist promises, 131, 166; provisions of, 131; and Catholic church, 138-39; and economic nationalism, 153; and foreigners, 207-8; and foreign ownership of resources, 213

Contreras Torres, Miguel, 300, 302

Convention of Aguascalientes, 148, 166

Corona de Somba (play), 278

"Coronela, La" (comic book), 197

Corralitos, battle of, 160

Corridos, development of, 283; xenophobia in, 283, 285, 286; revolutionary principles in, 283-87, and romantic nationalism, 284-85

Cortés, Hernando, 24, 48, 174-75

"Cortés and Malinche" (mural), 294

Cosmes, Francisco G., 174

Costa Rica, 14, 27

Court of Labor, 295

Crabbe, Henry A., 43

Creelman, James C., 105n

Criollos, 73, 175, 179, 185, 186, 310; in colonial period, 26-27; and the

rise of nationalism, 72, 78. *See also* Mestizos; Miscegenation and nationalism

Cristeros, 139

Cruz, Juana Inés de la, 24, 257

"Cuando ¡Viva Villa! es la muerte" (film), 302

Cuartelazos, 18-19, 115

Cuauhtémoc, 143; as national hero, 175; in murals, 294; in films, 298

"Cuauhtémoc against the Myth" (mural), 294

"Cuauhtémoc" (film), 298

Cuautla, battle of, 270

Cuba, 34, 36, 118, 145, 218, 222, 263; under Fidel Castro, 14, 252, 314; nationals of in Mexico, 192

"Cucaracha, La" (film), 302

"Cucaracha, La" (song), 282-83

Cue Cánovas, Agustín, 281

Cuernavaca, 294

Cultural patterns and nationalism, 20

Currencies, 148, 207; multiplicity of in 1910 Revolution, 146-47

Curso elemental de historia patria (Castillo), 271

Damián (character in *La venganza de la gleba*), 276

"Dance of the Revolution" (painting), 291

Davis, Thomas, 17

Death, and theme of equality in art of Posada, 291-92

Deaths, in 1910 Revolution, 148-49, 229n; in United States occupation of Veracruz, 224-26

Decision-making and nationalism, 315-16

Deference, 9, 11, 314-15

¡*De la dictadura a la anarquía!* (Prida), 222

Democracy, in contemporary Mexico, 3, 312; Madero's conception of, 104-5; political, 130, 161, 233, 239; economic, 151. *See also* Political culture

Demography and nationalism, 15; in Mexico, 62-81 *passim;* effects of changes in population, 63, 310; national pride in population size, 64; pressure for economic growth, 64-65; rural isolation, 65, 79, 176-77;

geographic isolation, 95, 97, 98. *See also* Emigration from Mexico; Immigration to Mexico; Migration, internal; Miscegenation and nationalism

Denver, 125

Department of Communications and Public Works, 97

Department of State, United States, 209, 212

"Desarraigados, Los" (film), 301

Desbandada (Romero), 263

Destruction, as influence on nationalism, 19, 144-45, 150, 311, 312; in 1910 Revolution, 101. *See also* Violence

Deutsch, Karl W., 11, 13

Diario del Hogar, El (periodical), 216

Díaz, Carmen, 186

Díaz, Félix, 167, 170-71; insurrection of, 107, 148, 193, 220, 221; appeals for support, 163, 164, 181

Díaz, Pascual, 140

Díaz, Porfirio, 26, 84, 94, 97, 121, 123, 129, 130, 138, 162, 165, 186, 195, 196, 213, 235, 245, 271, 278, 282, 316; reaction of to possible United States aggression, 1877, 42, 44; concessions of to foreign investment, 53-61, 221, 240, 309; and increase in xenophobia, 53-61 *passim;* and Indians, 55-61 *passim*, 77, 170-71; and Catholic church, 57, 77, 114, 136-37; and labor, 57-61, 179, 180; and Mormons, 70; and Spanish language, 81, 82; and education, 91, 92; and Madero, 104-6, 168, 172, 233, 234; and Zapatistas, 109; departure of for Europe after overthrow, 113; as hero, 113-15; death of, 114; early career of, 114; in films, 114, 301; in literature, 114, 260, 261, 264; in Spain, 114; political beliefs of, 114; stability of Mexico under, 114; and xenophobia, 114, 206, 209, 249; and France, 137; and workers, 179; and women, 192-93; support of by Freemasons, 238; in cartoons, 289-90

Díaz Covarrubias, Juan, 258

Díaz Ordaz, Gustavo, Indianist themes in presidential campaign of, 175-76

Diccionario de historia y geografía (Orozco y Berra), 267

Diccionario de mejicanismos (Santamaría), 85

Diego, Juan, 142

Diéguez, Manuel M., 58

Divorce, in Mexico, 133, 190-91, 201, 304; in United States, 133

Domínguez, Belisario, 111

Domínguez, Josefa Ortiz de, 198

Domínguez Yáñez, Tomás, 298

Dominican Republic, 34, 314

Dorados, 109, 111

Douglas, Arizona, 218

Duhagon, Adolfo, 126, 127

Dunn, H. H., 119

Durango, city, 145, 209, 237

Durango, state, 161, 204, 214, 263

Eagle Pass, 125

Economic development, in Mexico, viii, 3, 177, 179, 182, 314; and flight capital, 9, 154-55; and nationalism, 9-10, 14, 15, 81, 308; during *porfiriato*, 53-61; effect on of agrarian reform, 118; effect on of violence, 145-46, 150; increases in per capita income, 153-54. *See also* Entrepreneurs, Mexican

Ecuador, 3, 178

Education, Mexican, 120, 132, 266, 275, 295, 297, 304; of Indians, 87, 91, 177; effect on of industrialization, 90; size of school populations, 90, 91, 94; and Catholic church, 90-91; military, 91; during *porfiriato*, 92-94; and Zapata, 118-19; and 1917 Constitution, 131. *See also* Education and nationalism

Education and nationalism, 20, 88-94, 304, 310

Edwards, Thomas D., 71

Egalitarianism, made possible by economic growth, 3, 150-52; and income distribution, 9, 153; and investment, 9, 154; and nationalism, 9-10, 15, 17-19, 110, 151-55, 310, 312; and violent revolution, 18-19, 130; and revolutionary destruction, 50, 152; and women, 64, 183-201 *passim;* and economic equality, 101-2, 150-55, 308; and Madero, 104; and effect on of military technol-

ogy, 160-61; and Indianism, 170-79
passim; in *corridos,* 287; in art,
291-92
Eisenstein, Sergei, 300
Elections to presidency, Mexican, of
Madero, 107; of Calles, 109; of
Obregón, 109; of Carranza, 168-69;
of Díaz Ordaz, 175
Elite. *See* Political elite
El Paso, 127, 188, 234, 262
Embargo, Jefferson's, 35n
Emerson, Rupert, 12
Emigrants, Mexican, in United States,
121, 131, 302; military internees,
124, 126-27; encounters with "alienness," 126, 128; nationalist attitudes of, 127-28; return of to
Mexico, 127-28; effect on of Depression, 127; *braceros,* 128, 154,
301-2. *See also* Demography and
nationalism; Emigration from Mexico
Emigration from Mexico, extent of,
68; to United States, 124-28, 301-2;
causes of, 125, 145; and nationalism, 126. *See also,* Demography
and nationalism; Emigrants, Mexican; Immigration to Mexico; Migration, internal
England. *See* Great Britain
"En tiempos de don Porfirio" (film),
301
Entrepreneurs, Mexican, 9, 132, 153,
154, 155; and foreign investment,
56-57, 154; high rate of investment
by, 154; and political stability, 155;
motivated by cohesive nationalism,
155
*Episodios de la Revolución en México
(Estado de Chihuahua)* (Serrano),
268
Episodios nacionales (Olavarría y
Ferrari), 267
Equalitarianism. *See* Egalitarianism
Equality, 9, 15, 18-19, 20, 290, 292,
310, 312; economic, 9, 57-58, 101-2,
150-55, 256; social, 9, 101-2, 130-
31, 151, 152, 255, 256, 291; myths
of and nationalism, 9-10; racial, 25,
31, 68; legal, 29, 151, 286, 312;
political, 31; of opportunity, 130,
312; military, 160-61, 311; of wom-

en, 184, 194. *See also* Egalitarian-
ism
"Escondida, La" (film), 302
"Escuadrón 201" (film), 301
Escutia, Juan, 41
"Espaldas Mojadas," (film), 302
Esplendor del México antiguo (Cook
de Leonard and others), 178
Esquivel Obregón, Toribio, 60
Estadística de la República Mejicana
(Pérez Hernández), 267
Europe, 113, 116, 131, 157, 164, 185,
194, 219, 231, 232, 300
Eva (character in *Eva*), 258
Eva (Martínez de Castro), 258
*Exciting Experiences in Our War with
Mexico* (Neil), 243
"Execution of Maximilian" (paint-
ing), 288
"Exit from the Mine" (mural), 295
Expropriation, in Mexico, 143, 152-
53; and nationalism, 153. *See also*
Economic development; Interna-
tional trade and nationalism; In-
vestment, foreign, in Mexico

Fabela, Isidro, 108, 122; as hero, 111;
on Americans, 215
Factionalism, 116-17, 163, 164, 165,
168; reduced by nationalistic ethic,
ix, 22; reduced by Partido Revolucionario Institucional, 175, 179-80,
183, 200
Fall, Albert B., 54n, 212
Fall Committee, 54n
Family structure, 166, 201; social
value of, 7, 133; and personal loyalties, 24, 134; among Mexican Indians, 133; changing pattern of in
Mexico, 133; cohesion in, 133; effect on of 1910 Revolution, 133-36;
and extramarital relations, 133-34;
and nationalism, 134; disruptions
in during 1910 Revolution, 135; and
urbanization, 135
Farrell, J. A., 211
Fawcett, Mrs. Henry, 185
Federal District of Mexico, 66, 123
Ferdinand VII, 33, 45, 48
Fernández, Emilio, 302
Fernández de Lizardi, José Joaquín,
199, 258, 274, 282, 302
Fernández Güell, Rogelio, 106-7

"Fighting Through" (film), 298
Filibusters, 43, 128, 218, 233, 247
Films, in Mexico, extent of audience for, 296; documentary of 1910 Revolution, 296-97; content of, 296-304 *passim;* produced during 1910 Revolution, 297; distribution of, 298; produced in United States, 298-300; production of, 299; censorship in, 299-300; foreign-produced, 299-300; commercial, 300; patriotism in, 300-1; educational, 303-4. *See also* Cinema and nationalism
First National Pictures, 298
Flag, Mexican, 41, 53, 215, 233, 245, 278, 282, 286, 293, 294; all factions fight under in 1910 Revolution, 167-68; in novels, 265; in school textbooks, 269, 271; in children's literature, 272, 275
Flecha del sol, La (play), 277
Fletcher, Henry P., 242
Flight capital, 9; and political instability, 155; in Latin America, 155
Flores Magón, Ricardo, 58, 80, 151, 166, 180, 196; and 1905 platform of Liberal party, 111; and *Regeneración,* 111; as hero, 111
Florida, 48
"Flor silvestre" (film), 302
Food production. *See* Agriculture
Foppa, Tito L., 187
"Foreign Legion," support of for Madero, 232-33, 234; Mexican feeling against, 234, 235, 236
Foreign Relations Committee, United States Senate, 54n, 212
Forjando patria (Gamio), 173
Fort Bliss, 112, 126
Fort Rosencrans, 126, 127
Fort Santiago, 113
Fox Film Corporation, 298
Fracasados, Los (Azuela), 260, 261
France, 34, 41, 52, 90, 137, 150, 178, 233, 271, 272, 282, 283, 294; culture of in Mexico, 33, 51-52, 257, 259; and Mexico during colonial period, 48, 258, 259; colonies of in Western Hemisphere, 48; and Mexican nationalism, 1810-1910, 48-53, 309; recognition of Mexican independence, 49; military intervention

of in Mexico, 1862-67, 50, 282; private investment of in Mexico, 55; nationals of in Mexico, 57, 70, 192; recognition of Huerta, 239. *See also* French Revolution; Maximilian; Pastry War
Franco, Francisco, 206
Franco-Mexican War of 1838 and 1839. *See* Pastry War
Fray Mocho (periodical), 187
Freeman, Charles M., 209
Freemasonry, Mexican, 141, 242; and Poinsett, 36; 1910 schism in, 238-39
Frei, Eduardo, 14
French Revolution, 19, 29, 150, 151, 191
Frías, Heriberto, 260
Friends of the Country (patriotic society), 237
Frontera, 97, 219
Frontera junto al mar (Mancisidor), 228
Fuentes, Carlos, 316
Fueros, 55; in colonial period, 26; abolition of proposed by Morelos, 31

Gabino Ortiz Library, 293
Gachupines, 34, 264; in colonial period, 26-27; and Hidalgo revolt, 30. *See also* Spaniards in Mexico
Gadsden Treaty, 41
Galindo, Alejandro, 302
Galletas, 186
Gálvez, José, 116
Gamboa, Federico, 276
Gamio, Manuel, 17-18, 34, 308; as hero, 111; and Indianism, 173; study of Valley of Teotihuacán, 176
Gaona, Antonio, 49
García Cubas, Antonio, 84
García González, Alfonso, 123
Garibaldi, Giuseppi, 233, 234, 235, 236; in battle of Ciudad Juárez, 232; and Villa, 234; on 1910 Revolution as part of a world-wide struggle, 312. *See also* "Foreign Legion"
Garza y Ballesteros, Lázaro de la, 46
Gazcón, Gilberto, 301
Geografía de las lenguas indígenas (Orozco y Berra), 267

Geography and nationalism, 20; in New Spain, 23; in Mexico, 65, 95, 97, 102, 256, 271-72
Germany, 10, 90, 158, 178, 218, 228, 249; nationals of in Mexico, 70, 242; recognition of Huerta, 239; activities of in Mexico during World War I, 242. *See also* Nationalism, German
Gesticulador, El (play), 278
Gibbon, Thomas E., 212
Gill, Mario, 37n
"Girl of the Golden West, The" (film), 299
Glenn, John B., 149
Glen Springs, 230
Glenworth, Lillian, 194
Godines, Blas, 49
Goitia, Francisco, 290-91
Golpes d'estado, 18-19, 115
Gómez Farías, Valentín, 45
González, Abraham, 130
González, Filiberto C., 246
González, Soledad, 197
González Garza, Federico, 55-56
González Garza, Roque, 234
González Peña, Carlos, 257
González Ramírez, Manuel, 291-92
Good Neighbor policy, 251
Gorostiza, José, 275
Gorostiza, Manuel Eduardo de, 276
Gracey, Wilbur T., 134
Graft, 314
Gran Círculo de Obreros Mexicanos, 80
Grandes problemas nacionales, Los (Molina Enríquez), 58
Grant, Ulysses S., 42
Great Britain, 10, 18, 28, 34, 35n, 36, 90, 184, 194, 218, 235; and Pastry War, 49; primary concern of for investments, 49; recognition of Mexican independence, 49; intervention of in Mexico, 1862, 50; private investment of in Mexico, 55; nationals of in Mexico, 70; Freemasons of in Mexico, 238; recognition of Huerta, 239
Greece, 235
Grito de Dolores, 30, 209; in films, 298. *See also* Hidalgo y Costilla, Miguel
"Grito de Dolores, El" (film), 298

Grito de Dolores, El (Sota), 267
Guadalajara, 65, 172, 209, 216, 217
Guadalajara Government Palace, 293, 295
Guadalupe, 96
Guadalupe, Virgin of. *See* Virgin of Guadalupe
Guajardo, Jesús, and assassination of Zapata, 110; as anti-hero, 113
Guanajuato, state, 66, 149
Guatemala, 98; nationals of in Mexico, 70
Guerrero, state, 91
Guerrero, Vicente, 31; biography of, 267
Guerrero (Paz), 267
Gurza, Jaime, 99
Guzmán, Martín Luis, 302

Hacendados, 25, 32, 59, 98, 249, 261, 291, 295
Hague Conference, 1899 declaration of, 158
Hague Court, 230
Halley's comet, 284
Hamilton, Cicely, 194
Hamm, Theodore C., 145
Hammond, John Hayes, 250
Handbills and fliers, 273
Hanna, Philip C., 214
Harlem, New York, 69
Haro, Felipe de Jesús, 298
Hart, Albert Bushnell, 173
Hartford Convention, 35n
Harvard University, 173
Haskell, Lewis W., 209
Havana, 98
Hayes, Rutherford B., 42, 54
Hearst, William R., holdings in Mexico, 242; Mexican attitudes toward newspapers' stand on 1910 Revolution, 242-43
Henderson, Mrs. Lem, 216
Henry, Thomas, 43
Henry V (play), 276
Heraldo Nacional, El (periodical), 125
Hermosillo, 213
Hernández Ignacio, 46, 48
Hernández Gómez, Guillermo, 300
Hero-creation, 16, 267; in Mexico, 34-35, 101, 102-20, 284, 309
Heroes, 104, 105, 200, 273, 311; im-

portance of for nation-building, 19, 309; role of in Mexico, 101, 102-20, 272, 273, 275, 283, 284; availability of in different nations, 116; Mexican invocation of for sanctioning of views, 117, 118, 311; in films, 296-97, 298, 300-1, 302. *See also* Bravo, Nicolás; Carranza, Venustiano; Hero-creation; Heroines; Hidalgo y Costilla, Miguel; Iturbide, Agustín de; Juárez, Benito; Madero, Francisco I., Jr.; Morelos, José María; Niños Héroes, Los; Pípila, El

Heroines, 197, 198; of 1910 Revolution, 282. *See also* Adelita; Hero-creation; Heroes; *Soldaderas;* Valentina

Hidalgo, state, 176

Hidalgo County, Texas, 127

Hidalgo (Paz), 267

Hidalgo y Costilla, Miguel, 45, 100, 106, 138; as leader of 1810 revolt, 30, 142; as hero, 30-31; biography of, 267; in art, 293, 295; in films, 298

Hijas de Cuauhtémoc, 192, 193

Historia antigua de México (Orozco y Berra), 267

Historia de la literatura mexicana (González Peña), 257

Historia de las relaciones entre México y los Estados Unidos, 1819-1848 (Bosch García), 38

Historia de México (Alamán), 30

Historia mexicana (Cue Cánovas), 281

Historia política de la Revolución (Alessio Robles), 119

History and nationalism, reinterpretations of, 16; Bulnes' attitudes toward, 267; Sierra's attitudes toward, 267; in Mexico, 267-69; in Mexican textbooks, 269-71; in popular literature, 271-73. *See also* Hero-creation; Heroes; Literature and nationalism

Hitler, Adolf, 7

Hoffman, Pablo, 145

Hogar Católico, El (periodical), 138

Hollywood, California, 119, 299, 300

Holy Alliance, 29

"Honor militar" (film), 298

Hood, Robin, 284

Hoselitz, Bert F., 9

"House of Tears" (paintings), 192

Houston, 39

Huasteca (López y Fuentes), 266

Huerta, Victoriano, 108, 109, 111, 114, 121, 134, 138, 146, 148, 165, 168, 249, 268, 276, 290, 311; and deaths of Madero and Pino Suárez, 107, 112, 220-21; and Villa, 110; death of, 112; as anti-hero, 112-13; military strategy of, 122, 159, 162; and Catholic church, 137, 138; appeals of for support, 163, 164, 167; and conscription of women, 186-87; and United States, 213, 215; and Henry Lane Wilson, 220-23; and United States occupation of Veracruz, 223-26; and anti-Americanism, 237, 239, 245; and conscription of youth, 238; recognition of regime of, 239; Woodrow Wilson's refusal to grant recognition to, 239; use of xenophobia, 241; in literature, 265, 272; in art, 291; in films, 297

Huertistas, 124, 125, 148, 164, 237, 261

Huicol language, 82

Humboldt, Alexander von, 72-73

Hungary, 162

Ibarra, Carlos M., 98

Illegitimacy, 166; extent of in Mexico, 78; as a measure of nationalism, 79; causes of, 79; effect of on nationalism, 79-80; and 1917 Constitution, 131, 191

Illiteracy. *See* Literacy

Immigrants and nationalism, 20

Immigrants in Mexico, assimilation of, 69; effect of on nationalism, 69, 72, 97. *See also* Americans in Mexico; Chinese in Mexico; Immigration; Spaniards in Mexico

Immigration to Mexico, 57, 68-72; and nationalism, 63, 67-72 *passim;* government policies on, 67-68; and racism, 68. *See also* Demography and nationalism; Emigration from Mexico; Immigrants in Mexico; Migration, internal

Imparcial, El (periodical), 217, 225

Imperial Restaurant, 217

Independence, Mexican, 272, 309; events in Spanish America as factor in, 29; Great Britain's recognition of, 29; Napoleon's conquest of Spain as factor in, 29; Spain's recognition of, 33; in literature, 257. *See also* Hidalgo y Costilla, Miguel; Iturbide, Agustín de; Morelos, José María

India, 83

Indianism, 25, 76, 170-79; after 1910 Revolution, 30, 174-79; reasons for uniqueness of in Mexico, 170; causes for rise of, 173; and culture of past, 175, 257; in art, 175; racial equality of in other countries, 178; in novels, 265-66; in murals, 294-95. *See also* Indians, Mexican

Indians, Mexican, 68, 72-73, 75, 79, 87, 105, 145, 197, 243, 283, 298, 310; in colonial period, 24-25; and Hidalgo revolt, 30; parochial orientation of, 44, 170, 177; in *porfiriato*, 57, 61, 82, 186, 309; numbers of, 1810-1910, 73; barriers to national assimilation of, 1810-1910, 75-78; languages of, 76, 81-84, 99; promises to, 76, 162, 171-73, 311; and Catholic church, 76-77, 141-42; participation of in 1910 Revolution, 77, 157, 170-79; revolts of, 1821-1910, 77-78; attitudes of *científicos* toward, 82, 170-71; and education, 87, 89, 91, 93; barriers to national assimilation of since 1910, 170, 176, 177; as Zapatistas, 171; and Partido Revolucionario Institucional, 175; in pre-Columbia period, 177-78; linguistic isolation of as barrier to anti-Americanism, 250; in literature, 256-57, 260, 265-66; in drama, 277; in murals, 293, 294. *See also* Indianism; Miscegenation and nationalism

Indigenismo. See Indianism

Indio, El (López y Fuentes), 265-66

Industrialization, in Mexico, 67, 80, 310; effects of on nationalism in Mexico, 80-81, 182; effects of on education in Mexico, 90; effects of on women in Mexico, 183-84. *See also* Industrial Revolution

Industrial Revolution, 151, 183. *See also* Industrialization

Industrial Workers of the World, 181

Industry, Mexican, 145, 151, 311

Inflation, 147-48

Inman, Samuel Guy, 208

Input functions, 10-11

Inspection of Health, 191

Insurgente, El (periodical), 244

Integration, political, in Mexico, vii, 121, 156-57. *See also* Nationalism, Mexican

Intellectuals, ix, 132, 174, 206, 316; and 1910 Revolution, 61, 94, 106, 111, 119, 156-57

Interest groups, 309, 315; and Partido Revolucionario Institucional, 3, 180, 183, 200; active participation of in 1910 Revolution, 156-57, 170-201 *passim;* effects on of 1910 Revolution, 156-57, 310-11; cohesion among facilitated by nationalism, 163-201 *passim. See also* Agrarian reform; Catholic church; Labor, Mexican; Trade Unions; Women, Mexican

International trade and nationalism, 15, 60. *See also* Economic development; Expropriation; Investment, foreign, in Mexico

Interviews, as research technique for the study of nationalism, viii-ix, 318

Investment, foreign, 98, 99, 152-53, 251, 271, 309; in Mexico, during *porfiriato*, 53-61 *passim;* American, 54, 55, 58, 219; British, 54n, 55; French, 54n, 55; during 1910 Revolution, 152, 207-8, 241. *See also* Economic development; Expropriation; International trade and nationalism

Ireland, 17

Irrigation, 67, 118, 165

Italy, 10; nationals of in Mexico, 57, 69, 232

Iturbide, Agustín de, 31-32, 36, 56, 76

Ivins, Anthony W., 70

Izabal, Rafael, 58

Jackson, Andrew, 16

Jaime (character in *La ola*), 277

Jalisco, **66**
Jamaica, 18
James, Earle K., 140
Japan, 194; nationals of in Mexico, 235; recognition of Huerta by, 236, 239
Jenkinson, Charles, 192
Jiquilpan, 293
Jockey Club, 130
John Bull, 18n
Johnson, John J., 23
"Juana Gallo" (film), 302
"Juan soldado" (film), 298
Juárez, Benito, 30, 51, 77, 92, 100, 106, 136, 138, 176, 186, 283; relations with United States, 41; as hero, 51, 52-53, 129; early career of, 52; attitude of toward national community, 52-53, 308; in literature, 53, 272; as Indian, 77, 176; in murals, 294, 295
"Juárez and the Reform" (mural), 294
Juárez y la Reforma (Molina Enríquez), 53
"Juárez y Maximiliano" (film), 301
Juchitán, 77

Kekchí language, 82
Kelley, Francis Clement, 244
Kelly, Charles Edgar, 234
Kennedy, John Fitzgerald, 108, 251
Kipling, Rudyard, 178
Kissinger, Henry, 28
Knox, Philander C., 131, 209, 220, 236
Kohn, Hans, 12
Kosterlitzky, Emilio, 127

Labor, Mexican, 105, 166; on railroads, 57, 80, 87, 98-99, 207; strike at Cananea, 57-58; wages, 60-61, 132; 1910 employment statistics, 80; industrial workers, 80-81; and Casa del Obrero Mundial, 109, 180, 191; and Red Battalions, 109, 117; support of for Obregón, 109; and 1917 Constitution, 131; in *porfiriato*, 179; participation in 1910 Revolution, 179-82; and nationalism, 179-83; failure of communism in, 180; appeals to in 1910 Revolution, 180-81, 311; Confederación de Tra-

bajadores de México, 183; Confederación Regional Obrera Mexicana, 183; Congress of Tampico, 183. *See also* Conscription; Trade unions
Labor de raza (Romero Flores), 199
Labor movement. *See* Trade unions
Lafayette, Marquis de, 235
Lally, Frank E., 49
Lamicq, Pedro, on Indians, 173; on Henry Lane Wilson, 222; on "Foreign Legion," 234-35
Language, relationship of to nationalism, 15, 20, 74, 81, 82, 83; diversity of in Mexico, 76, 81-84, 99; Indian languages, 76, 81-84, 99; relationship to Mexican nationalism, 81-88; dialects within countries, 84; and economic transactions, 84; and geographic isolation, 84; differences in patterns among areas, 84-85. *See also* Spanish language
Lansing, Robert, 241
La Paz, 210
Lara y Pardo, Luis, 191
Largey, M. S., 211
Las Vacas, 216
Latifundia, 143
Latin America, 3, 13, 18-19, 29, 59, 84, 115, 116, 189; nationalism in, vii, 14, 15; and flight capital, 155; Indians of, 60, 178; Madero on lack of support from for Mexico in nineteenth century, 215
Latin Americanism, and anti-Americanism, 252-53; cause of, 252-53; weaker than nationalism, 253
Laubscher, Enrique, 92
"Lawless Rider" (film), 299
Lazarín, Mariana Rodríguez de, 198
Lazo de la Vega, Gertrudis Bocanegra de, 198
Leadership, political, 18, uses of nationalism by, 5, 7-8, 11, 255, 308; requirements of in contemporary Mexico, 315-16; self-image of shaped by nationalist mystique, 315-16. *See also* Heroes; Political elite
Lee, Robert E., 51
Lenguas Indígenas de México, Las (Pimentel), 83
Lenin, Vladimir Ilyich, 118
Leo XII, Pope, 45

León, 65
Lespinasse, Alphonse J., 219
Letcher, Marion, 54
Lewis, Capt. (officer in the ''Foreign Legion''), 234
Lewis, Oscar, 133, 250
Leyendas de Pancho Villa (comic books), 197, 272
Ley Iglesias, 46
Ley Juárez, 46
Ley Lerdo, 46
Lezama, Luis, 300
Liberal party of Flores Magón, 88, 91, 111, 151, 166, 196-97
Lim, J. W., 204
Lima, Peru, 116
Limantour, José Yves, 164, 233
Lincoln, Abraham, 108
Lind, John, 123, 165, 169, 277
Link, Arthur S., 227
Liszt, Franz, 280
Literacy, 291, 296; and nationalism, 20, 256, 266, 279, 295-96; and immigrants, 69; statistics on, 91, 260; and Zapata, 118-19; and anti-Americanism, 250. *See also* Education, Mexican
Literature and nationalism, 15, 20; drama, 246-47, 274, 275-78; as measure of nationalism, 254; in nineteenth-century Mexico, 254-55, 257-60, 267, 270-71, 274, 275-76, 278-79; and ''cultural management,'' 255; during and after 1910 Revolution, 255, 261-66, 267-68, 274-75, 276-78, 279; limited effect of because of illiteracy and disinterest, 256, 260; social relevance of literature, 256; in pre-Columbian Mexico, 256-57; in colonial Mexico, 257; novels of the nineteenth century, 257-60, 310; novels of the 1910 Revolution, 261-66; biographies, 264; in contemporary Mexico, 266, 268-73, 275; school textbooks, 266, 269-71; histories, 266-69; popular literature, 271-72; pamphlets, 272; in advertising, 273; oratory, 274, 278-79; poetry, 274-75; music, 279-87; *corridos*, 283-87. *See also* Literacy; Press, Mexican
Lives of the Country (patriotic society), 237

''Loca'' (engraving), 192
Local loyalties, in Mexico, 121, 314; in New Spain, 24; of Indians, 170, 177; of Zapatistas, 235. *See also Patrias chicas;* Regionalism, Mexican
Lomax, Alan, 280
Lombardo Toledano, Vicente, 183
López Mateos, Adolfo, 123, 178
López Velarde, Ramón, 274-75
López y Fuentes, Gregorio, 265-66
Lorencez, Count of, 50
Los Angeles, California, 39, 98
Los de abajo (Azuela), 260, 261-62
''Los de abajo'' (film), 302
Louisiana, 29, 48
Lower California. *See* Baja California
Lower class, 26, 71, 129, 132, 133, 259; left out of *científico* concept of nationalism, 103; acceptance of highly skewed income distribution after 1910 Revolution, 153-54; anti-Americanism of, 236
Loyalties, 6, 63; family, 5, 6, 12, 79, 90, 116, 133, 134, 135, 184, 199, 312, 314; church, 12, 48, 90-91, 116, 136, 139-40, 155; class, 12, 56, 131; group, 89; personalistic, 115-16, 169

Macías, Demetrio (character in *Los de abajo*), 262
Madariaga, Teodoro, 159
Maderistas, 106, 111, 117, 130, 142, 164, 167, 168, 195, 196, 199, 203-4, 232, 233-34, 261, 268, 277, 290, 291
Madero, Alfonso, 196
Madero, Angela, 196
Madero, Francisco I., Jr., 87, 109, 113, 116, 122, 129, 130, 132, 137, 147, 148, 165, 167, 168, 193, 196, 197, 210, 213, 234, 249, 261, 263, 264, 268, 279, 290, 305, 309, 311; early career of, 104; political beliefs of, 104-5, 161; as hero, 104-6, 107-8, 119; and labor, 105; view of the United States, 105, 214-15; campaign against Porfirio Díaz, 105-6, 172, 218; after battle of Ciudad Juárez, 106; assassination of, 107, 119, 187, 239; as president, 107; and Pino Suárez, 107-8; invocation of by Constitutionalists, 107-

8; and Zapatistas, 109; and Villa, 110; activities of women in family of, 136, 195; and Catholic church, 136-37; appeals of for support, 163, 180; and Plan of San Luis Potosí, 166; and Indians, 171; and workers, 179; overthrow of and Henry Lane Wilson, 214, 220-21, 239; and Márquez Sterling, 222; foreign participants in army of, 232-33, 235; and youth, 236; support of by Mexican Freemasons, 238; control of xenophobia, 249; in literature, 264, 265, 272; in music, 284, 285; in cartoons, 290; in films, 296, 297, 302

Madero, Gustavo, 196

Madero, Mercedes González de, 196

Madero, Mercedes (sister of Madero), 196

Madero, Sara Pérez de, 195-96; and Henry Lane Wilson, 223

Madrid, 34

Magill, Samuel E., 172, 209, 218

Malan, Capt. (officer in the ''Foreign Legion''), 234

Mala yerba (Azuela), 260, 261

Mancisidor, José, 228

Mann, James Robert, 227

Manzanillo, 210

Margarito (character in *Los de abajo*), 262

Marines, United States, 224

Márquez Sterling, Manuel, 222

Marriage As a Trade (Hamilton), 194

Martí, José, 176

Martínez, Juan José, 32

Martínez, Luis, 143

Martínez, Luisa, 198

Martínez de Castro, Manuel, 258

Marxists, 154

Mass media and nationalism, 295-96; in Mexico, 296-306; radio and television, 305-6. *See also* Cinema and nationalism; Communications and nationalism; Films, in Mexico; Literature and nationalism; Press, Mexican

Matamoros, 167

Mateos, Juan A., 259

Mather, Cotton, 257

Maximilian, 42, 47, 48, 50, 91, 259, 282; as focus for Mexican nation-

alism, 50-51, 271, 278, 293, 294; in films, 301

Maya, 43, 81, 82, 277; in colonial period, 24-25; literature of, 257. *See also* Indianism

Mayo, Henry T., 223, 224

Mayo River, 172

Maytorena, José María, 207

Mazatlán, 96, 210, 214

McKenzie, W. H., 232

Medina, Manuela, 198

Mediz Bolio, Antonio, 277

Mejía, Tomás, 46, 77

''Memorias de un mexicano'' (film), 297

Mendieta y Núñez, Lucio, on revolution and hero-creation, 115; on Mexican art, 292

Mendoza, Narciso, 270

Menéndez de Avilés, Pedro, 48

Mérida, 146

Mestizos, 72-75, 143, 179, 185, 186, 310; in colonial period, 25; numbers of, 1810-1910, 72-73; influence of on nationalism, 72-76; and education, 89. *See also* Criollos; Indians, Mexican; Miscegenation and nationalism; Race and nationalism

Metro-Goldwyn-Mayer Studios, 299

Mexican Congress, 75, 242

Mexican Herald, The (periodical), 138, 217

Mexican War. *See* War of 1846-48

Mexican Year Book 1909-10, The, 81-82

Mexico, state, 66, 104, 117

Mexico City, 25, 30, 65, 90, 95, 98, 107, 121, 122, 124, 138, 147, 148, 168, 191, 194, 215, 216, 216-17, 217, 220, 227, 236, 245, 271, 288, 297, 305

''México de mis recuerdos'' (film), 301

México-Tlaxcalantongo, mayo de 1920 (Urquizo), 264

México y lo mexicano (series), 268

Mi caballo, mi perro y mi rifle (Romero), 263

Michoacán, 45, 66, 177, 263, 293

Middle class, 94, 131, 132, 133, 260, 261, 288, 310; growth of in Mexico, 60, 131; reasons of for championing nationalism, 60, 132; anti-Americanism of, 236. *See also* Class structure and nationalism

Migrant labor. *See Braceros*

Migration, internal, 67, 72, 95, 101; effect upon of railways, 95; and nationalism, 120-24 *passim*, 310; revolutionary troop movements, 121-23; post-revolutionary rate of, 122-23; enforced colonization, 123. *See also* Demography and nationalism; Emigration from Mexico

Military technology, 148; and alternative patterns of loyalty, 156; and appeals for support, 157-58, 162-63; in medieval Europe, 157-58; in industrialized nation-states, 158; in 1910 Revolution, 158-61; air warfare in 1910 Revolution, 159; and egalitarianism, 160-61, 311; and Mexican women, 161, 183, 188. *See also* Army, Mexican; Navy, Mexican

Miller, Clarence A., 209

Mining industry, 55, 57-58, 80, 145; foreign investment in, 55

Ministry of Education, 273, 295

Ministry of Foreign Relations, 263

Ministry of War, films by, 298

Miranda Basurto, Ángel, 271

Miscegenation and nationalism, 20, 101, 310; in New Spain, 23; in Mexico, 1810-1910, 72-75, 142. *See also* Race and nationalism; Indians, Mexican; *Criollos;* Mestizos

Mixtec language, 82

Moheno, Querido, 213, 247

Molina Enríquez, Andrés, 52-53, 75, 120; as hero, 111, on agrarian reform, 111; on factionalism of Mexican national community, 58; on mestizos, 74

"Momia azteca contra el robot humano, La" (film), 304

Money. *See* Currencies

Monlau, Pedro Felipe, 83

Monroe Doctrine, 29, 42

Monterde, Francisco, 277

Monterrey, 65, 213

Monterrey *News* (periodical), 213

Montezuma, 94

Mora, Luis, 214

Morales, Delfina, 196

Morelos, 104, 109, 117, 118, 187, 205, 235, 272

Morelos, genio militar de la independencia (Urquizo), 264

Morelos, José María, 30, 45, 52, 138, 270, 308; as hero, 31, 117; proposals of at Chilpancingo, 31; biographies of, 264, 267; in murals, 295; in films, 300

Morelos (Paz), 267

Morelos Zaragoza, Ignacio, 223

Moreno, Daniel, 97-98

Moreno Sánchez, Carmen Toscano de, 297

Morgenthau, Hans, 7

Mormon colonies in Mexico, 70-72

Morris, Henry, 243

Morrow, Dwight, 251, 294

Motherland. *See Patria, La*

Motherland (character in *Tío Sam y la patria*), 277-78

Mount Popocatepetl, 271

Mujeres Revolucionarias, 200

Mujer Moderna (periodical), 198

Murals, Mexican, 287, 292-95, 304; and ideals of 1910 Revolution, 292-95 *passim;* and nationalism, 292-95 *passim;* and Indianism, 294-95. *See also* Art

Murillo, Gerardo, 137

Murray, Robert Hammond, 223

Museum of Anthropology, 178, 289

Music, 74, 279-87, 297; Mexican national anthem, 113, 272, 273, 281; social functions of, 279-80; and nationalism, 280; folk, 280; orchestral, 280-81; Mexican popular songs, 282-83, 305; *corridos*, 283-87

Mutual Film Corporation, 297

Myths, national, and economic development, 9-10, 152-55; and national heroes, 16, 309; and nation-building, 16, 309; and the repression of memories, 16, 112-15, 149; in the United States, 16; social functions of, 16; in contemporary Mexico, 309

Nación mexicana, La (distributed by Banco de Comercio), 273

Náhuatl, language, 82, 83; literature, 257

Napoleon I, 29

Napoleon III, 34, 42, 50, 51, 52

Naranjo, Leopoldo, 277

"Nation," as goal in Mexico, 5; contrasted with nation-state, 12; definition of, 12

National anthem, Mexican, 113, 272, 273, 281

National Association for the Protection of American Rights in Mexico, 212

National Autonomous University of Mexico, 93, 119, 230

National character, studies of in Mexico, 8-9, 13, 202-3

National community, definition of, 4; extent of, 4-5, 10-11; increases in size of, 5, 10. *See also* National community, Mexican

National community, Mexican, viii, 38, 206, 275; loyalty to, vii, 12, 106, 116, 266, 267; numbers within, 11, 27, 315; barriers to sense of in colonial period, 23-27; barriers to enlargement of, 27, 103-4, 289, 308-9; and equality as necessary to, 34, 101-2, 110, 292; and anti-heroes, 40; factors favoring, 63-64, 68, 281, 292, 309, 310, 311, 313; and mestizos, 73, 74; and sense of security, 80, 135, 141, 280; and language, 81; and students, 89, 236; and heroes, 116, 117; inclusiveness of, 157, 163, 314; appeals for support of in 1910 Revolution, 163-70 *passim;* and Indians, 170, 173, 174; and women, 184, 185, 189, 190; and United States, 231; relevance to of literature for, 254-56; and histories, 267, 269; and mass media, 305, 306. *See also* National community

National consciousness, 12, 13, 120-21, 258, 262, 310

National Historical Museum, 294

National holidays, 30, 51, 273, 274, 275; and escape from inner solitude, 13

National identity, viii, 12, 115-16, 166, 310; sense of in developing countries, 13-14; and anticolonialism, 28

National Institute of Fine Arts, 294

Nationalism, in Africa, vii, 28, 66, 315; measurements of, viii-ix, 4-5, 7, 10-11, 22, 255; in Peru, 3, 116; defined as social value, 4; definition of, 4, 8; quantitative variations in, 4-5, 63; action-orientation as test of, 4-6; distinguishing features, 4-8; and consensus, 5-6; manipulation of, 5-6, 163-69 *passim;* and resolution of conflict, 5-6; qualitative variations in, 5-6; in Spain, 6; as cover for special interests, 6; and the family, 6-7; as device of social control, 6-7; patriotism as element of, 7; "variants" of, 7; and aggressive foreign policies, 7-8; in Germany, 7, 158, 178; and equality, 9, 74; and social mobility, 9; and economic development, 9-10, 14, 15, 81, 308; in Guatemala, 10; unifying effect of, 10; as cohesive force, 10-14 *passim,* 255; and group loyalties, 12, 59; and individual actions, 12-13; in Brazil, 14; in the Caribbean, 14; in Central America, 14; in Colombia, 14; in Costa Rica, 14; in Cuba, 14; in Uruguay, 14; in Venezuela, 14; in Argentina, 14, 27, 257; in Chile, 14, 257; in Asia, 16, 28, 315; in Russia, 16-17, 131; in Ireland, 17; in the United States, 35, 69, 223-27; in Switzerland, 74, 82; conditioning environmental features of, 15-21, 307; and foreign nations, 20; and immigrants, 20; against national interests, 224; and literature, 254; features of, 307. *See also* Demography and nationalism; Geography and nationalism; Language; Nationalism, Mexican; Race and nationalism; Xenophobia

Nationalism, *científico*, 92, 290; concept of, 55-56; exclusivistic nature of, 82, 103, 170-71, 206-7, 309; and education, 92-94; appeals of to patriotism, 308; alienation under, 309

Nationalism, Mexican, contrasted with nationalism in other Latin American countries, 3, 14, 315; distinctiveness of, 3-4, 14, 307, 308; contrasted with Spanish nationalism, 6; consensus in, 6-7, 8; contrasted with Nazi nationalism, 7; and aggrandizement of Mexico, 8; and egalitarianism, 9-10, 15, 101-2, 150-55, 308, 310, 312; and social cohesion, 11, 13-14, 308, 314; quantitative, 11, 169, 315; paraphernalia of, 13, 102-4; and xenophobia, 15-17, 308, 309, 311-12; resemblance to Irish nationalism, 17; and protonationalist forces, 20-21; limitations of, 1810-1910, 22, 308-9; and anticolonialism, 28-29; foreign influences on formation of, 28-53 *passim;* role of United States in shaping, 35-44, 124-29 *passim*, 202-54 *passim*, 313-14; and Catholic church, 44-48, 136-44, 309, 311; and political elite, 55, 315-16; and *cientifico* concept of nationalism, 55-56, 309; and demography, 62-72 *passim*, 310; and social change, 1810-1910, 62-100; and internal migration, 67, 72, 120-24, 310; and immigration to Mexico, 67-72; and mestizos, 72-75 *passim*, 310; and miscegenation, 72-75 *passim*, 310; and illegitimacy, 78-80; and *criollos*, 78, 310; and industrialization, 80-81, 151-55, 179-83, 310, 313; and language, 81-88 *passim*, 99, 310; and education, 88-94 *passim*, 310; effects on of transportation and communications changes, 1810-1910, 95-100, 310; and social change, 1910-17, 101-55; role of violent revolution in shaping, 101-55 *passim*, 313; and oratory, 102, 278-79; and centennial celebrations of 1910, 102-4; and hero-creation, 102-20 *passim;* and urbanization, 124; and emigration to United States, 124-28; and emigration, 126-28; and class structure, 129-33, 310; and the family, 133-36; and religious homogeneity, 141, 142; and revolutionary destruction, 144-50; and economic equality, 150-55; and social groups, 156-201 *passim*, 310, 314-15; and military technology, 157-63 *passim*, 311; and Indianism, 170-79, 310; and trade unions, 180-83; and Mexican women, 183-201 *passim*, 310; and literature,

246-48, 254-78 *passim*, 310, 312; in advertising, 273; and music, 279-87 *passim;* and art, 287-95 *passim*, 312; and cartoons, 289-90; and murals, 292-95, 312; and films, 295-304 *passim*, 312; and television, 304, 306, 312; and radio, 304-6, 312; as counter to communism, 314; effects of, 314-16; and Mexico's future, 316; studies of, 317-22. *See also* Anti-Americanism; Heroes; Heroines; Xenophobia, Meican

National loyalty, 5, 7, 12, 158, 169; in Mexico, vii, 12, 27, 39, 48, 79, 89, 116, 131, 133, 135-36, 139-40, 157, 159, 189, 225, 266, 267, 311, 312, 314, 315; action-orientation as test of, 12; in China, 158; in Germany, 158; in Russia, 158; in United States, 158

National Palace, 293, 294

National Preparatory School, 92, 294

National pride, 34, 267; and 1910 Revolution, 10; high level of in Mexico, 10. *See also* Heroes; Myths, national

National Prize for Literature, 266

"National Riches" (mural), 294

National unity, 40, 228, 231, 262, 279, 286, 309; invoked during 1910 Revolution, 160, 163-66, 244. *See also* Social cohesion

Naval Academy, Mexican, 224

Navarro, Juan J., 168, 233

Navy, Mexican, 224. *See also* Military technology

Navy, United States, 218-19; 311; at Veracruz, 223-25; at Mazatlán, 230

Nazism, 7, 158, 178

Negroes, 68, 283; in Mexico, 23, 26, 31; alleged revolt in United States, 125; Mexican ridicule for United States attitudes toward, 248

Neil, Henry, 243

Neri, Margarita, 188, 197

New Mexico, 23, 38, 39, 43

New Orleans, 98; battle of, 16

"New School, The" (mural), 295

New Spain, 96; antinationalistic elements in, 23-27; as colony, 24; Indian groups in, 24; economic differences in, 25-26; military groups in, 26; *criollos* and *gachupines* in, 26-27; effect on of Napoleon's conquest of Spain, 29

New York City, 243

New York Herald, 145

New York Times, The, 147, 160, 187, 195, 202, 214, 239

"Night of the Rich" (mural), 295

Niños Héroes, Los, 41, 275

Nogales, Arizona, 298

Normal School for Teachers, 93, 94

Normal School for Women Teachers, 93

Novels, 256-66; as vehicle for nationalism, 254-55; in nineteenth-century Mexico, 257-60; and Indianism, 257, 265-66; on 1910 Revolution, 261-66

Nuevo Laredo, 96, 237

Nuevo León, 198, 204

O, Genovevo de la, 111, 291

Oaxaca, state, 161, 175, 209, 272

Obregón, Álvaro, 67, 104, 116, 122, 129, 148, 197; and constitution of 1917, 109, 119, 181; early career, 109; as hero, 109, 117, 119; as president, 109; death of, 109, 119; military strategy of, 109, 159; opposition to Carranza, 109; political beliefs of, 109; and Zapatistas, 109-10; and Catholic church, 138-42; appeals of for support, 163, 190; support of by trade unions, 181; in films, 296, 302

Obregonistas, 165, 268

Obrero de Tepic, El (periodical), 138

Oil industry, 277, 299; foreign investment in, 55; nationalization of in 1938, 143, 153, 251-52, 294-95

Ojo Parado (periodical), 290

Ola, La (play), 277

Olavarría y Ferrari, Enrique de, 267

"Old Man of the Dump Heap, The" (painting), 291

Oratory and nationalism, in Mexico, 102, 278-79

Ord, Edward O. C., 54

Organization of American States, 252, 314

Organski, A.F.K., 64

Organski, Katherine, 64

Orizaba, 92

Oro negro (play), 277

Orozco, José Clemente, 27, 287, 288, 291, 293, 294, 295

Orozco, Pascual, 160, 167, 171, 234

Orozco y Berra, Fernando, 258

Orozco y Berra, Manuel, 267

Orozquistas, 172

Ortega, Francisco, 274

O'Shaughnessy, Edith, 134, 148

Output functions, 10-11

Pachuca, 245

"Padre Morelos, El" (film), 300

Palavicini, Félix F., 97

Palmer, Frederick, 202

Panama Congress of 1826, 29

"Pancho Villa y la Valentina," (film), 302

Paramount Pictures Corporation, 298, 299

Pardavé, Joaquín, 301

Paredes, Antonio de Jesús, 138

Parnell, Charles Stewart, 17

Parra, la perra y la porra, La (Lamicq), 222

Parra, Porfirio, 93

Parral, 111, 230

Partido Revolucionario Institucional, 3, 175, 180, 183, 200; role of nationalism within, 120, 315. *See also* Interest groups; Leadership, political

"Pasadita, La" (song), 282

Pastry War, 49-50

"Pato, El" (song), 282

Patria, La (Mexican Motherland), 53, 83, 92, 93, 98, 122, 143, 176, 190, 199, 230; symbolized, 18n, 269, 277-78, 284, 293; invoked by competing factions, 163-69; in literature, 246, 264, 275; in art, 277, 293; in music, 281, 282, 285; in cartoons, 290

Patrias chicas, 24, 39, 59, 86, 99, 109, 121, 235, 248, 312. *See also* Local loyalties; Regionalism, Mexican

Patriotism, 5, 56, 210, 212, 264, 266, 267, 275, 276, 277, 278, 284, 288, 300, 304; as element of national-

ism, 7; invoked during 1910 Revolution, 156, 157, 163, 166-68, 203, 238, 308; appeals to by Mexican leaders, 160, 307, 308; revolutionary societies for, 237
Patriotismo y deber (play), 276
Paz, Ireneo, 267
Pearl Harbor, 284
Pearson's Magazine (periodical), 105n
Peasants. *See* Peons
Peons, 31, 60, 61, 80, 98, 110, 114, 118, 121, 123, 130, 132, 134, 146, 147, 152, 153, 159, 160, 181, 182, 197, 259, 261, 264, 276, 277, 291, 295, 314
Peón y Contreras, José, 276
Pereyra, Carlos, 230-31
Pérez, Andrés (Character in *Andrés Pérez, maderista*), 261
Pérez, Rita, 198
Pérez Hernández, José María, 267
Perico (character in *Perico*), 259-60
Perico (Zentella Priego), 259-60
Periquillo Sarniento, El (Fernández de Lizardi), 258, 302
Pershing, John J., 119
Pershing expedition, 108, 119, 219, 241, 249, 250; causes of, 110-11, 229; duration, 229, 241; effects on Mexicans, 229, 230; as stimulant to Mexican nationalism, 230-31
Personalism, and leaders of 1910 Revolution, 52, 115-16, 169, 195-200 *passim*
Peru, 3; difficulties of nation-building in, 116; racial attitudes in, 178
Pesqueira, Roberto, 215
Philippines, 243
Photography and nationalism, 304-5
Piedad para el indio! (Lamicq), 173
Piedras Negras, 96, 125, 210
Pimentel, Francisco, 68, 75, 76, 83
Pino Suárez, José María, 107, 221
Pípila, El, 32
Pius IX, Pope, 46
Plan of Aguascalientes, 166
Plan of Ayala, 166
Plan of Guadalupe, 166
Plan of Iguala, 76
Plan of San Luis Potosí, 166
Plaza Hotel, 233

Población del valle de Teotihuacán, La (Gamio), 176-77
Poetry and nationalism, in Mexico, 274-75
Poinsett, Joel R., 36-37
Política (periodical), 252
Political apathy, 9-11
Political culture, and nationalism, 4-8; characteristics of in Mexico, 8-11, 312, 314-16; and political participation in Mexico, 10-11, 315-16
Political development, and nationalism, 3, 118, 315; and economic development, 9-10, 150-55; effects on of 1910 Revolution, 313-16. *See also* Constitution of 1917; Egalitarianism
Political elite, 82, 92, 103, 170, 207, 308, 309; in contemporary Mexico, 9, 132, 315-16; under Porfirio Díaz, 55-61 *passim*
Political participation, in Mexico, vii, 5, 10-11, 120, 139, 309, 315; encouraged by nationalism, 11, 157, 315, 316; by Mexican Indians, 75, 309
Political recruitment, 11; in 1910 Revolution, 163-69 *passim*; and Partido Revolucionario Institucional, 314-15
Political socialization, 5, 15-21; in Mexico, 88-94, 255, 266-73, 279-80, 296, 305-6, 313-16
Political stability, 3, 68; effects of on 1910 Revolution, 3-4, 144; and economic growth, 51, 153-55; under Porfirio Díaz, 53-61; violence as influence on, 144-50; and nationalism, 308, 314; of United States, 313
Political system, and nationalism, 3, 11; participation in, 10; pride in, 10
Polk, James Knox, 271
Population, Mexican, 269; statistics on, 10, 63-72 *passim*, 91, 124, 148; changes in, 1810-1910, 62-72 *passim*, 310; changes in, 1910-17, 120. *See also* Demography and nationalism
Porfiriato, 53-61, 94, 114, 131, 136, 137, 270, 283. *See also* Díaz, Porfirio; Nationalism, *científico*
"Porfirio Díaz" (film), 301

Portillo, Rafael, 304
Porvenir de México y sus relaciones con Estados Unidos, El (Schulz), 247
Posada, José Guadalupe, 197, 287; nationalistic values in prints of, 291; death themes of and equality, 292
Positivism in Mexico, 55, 92. *See also Científicos*
Postcards, 304
Posters, inciting xenophobia, 244-45
Poverty, 57, 60, 120, 135, 147, 151, 152, 176, 269, 290. *See also* Egalitarianism, Equality
Prairie, 224
"Precio de la gloria, El" (film), 298
Presidential elections. *See* Elections to presidency, Mexico
Presidential Guards, 264
Press, foreign, 113, 219, 242
Press, Mexican, 125, 146, 290, 305; and labor strike at Cananea, 58; and language, 87; and centennial celebrations of 1910, 102; and Madero, 107; denunciations of United States in, 1910-17, 216, 236, 244, 245-46
Press, United States, 38, 232, 262, 311; Mexican attitudes toward, 213; on Veracruz occupation, 227; on battle of Ciudad Juárez, 234; on Americans serving in revolutionary forces, 235; on Villa. *See also* Hearst, William R.
Prida, Ramón, 222, 223
Prieto, Guillermo, 49, 274
Prim, Juan, 34, 35
"Primero soy mexicano" (film), 301
Progreso, 123, 134
Prostitutes, 123, 189; and French Revolution, 191; number of in Mexico before 1910 Revolution, 191; increase in number of during 1910 Revolution, 191; attitudes of toward national community, 192; in paintings of Orozco, 192; nationalities of at Veracruz, 192; in United States, 248. *See also* Women, Mexican
Protestants, 138; in United States, 36; French in Florida, 48

Proyectos de un yankee (González), 246
Public utilities, foreign investment in, 55
Puebla, 65, 288; battle of, 51, 110
"Pueblo en armas" (film), 302
Pueblo inocente, El (Romero), 263
Puerto Mexico, 97, 193, 249
Puerto Rico, 34, 243

Qualitative differences in nationalism, 5, 7-8, 13-14
Quantitative differences in nationalism, 4-5, 27, 315
Querétaro, city, 132
Querétaro Constitution. *See* Constitution of 1917
Quetzalcoatl, 293
Quintana Roo, 96, 123, 187
Quintana Roo, Andrés, 274

Race and nationalism, 15, 20, 269; in Mexico, 3, 31, 68-69, 72-78; in revolt of 1810, 30; in Morelos' proposals, 31; *científico* concept of, 55-56; in Brazil, 178; in France, 178; in Nazi Germany, 178. *See also Criollos;* Indians, Mexican; Mestizos; Miscegenation and nationalism
Radio, Mexican, 305-6. *See also* Mass media and nationalism
Railways, Mexican, 80, 87, 152, 186; foreign investment in, 54, 55, 98; extent of during *porfiriato*, 59; enlargement of, 1810-1910, 95-96; statistics on, 95-96; effect of on nationalism, 95-100 *passim;* nationalization of, 99; and xenophobia, 99, 207; use of during 1910 Revolution, 121-22, 158, 160
Ramírez, Ignacio, 82-83
Ramos, Esteban, 167
Ramos, Manuel, 92
Ramos, Samuel, 121
Ramos i Duarte, Feliz, 86
"Rayo del sur, El" (film), 300
Raza cósmica, La (Vasconcelos), 74
"Rebozo de Soledad, El" (film), 301
Rébsamen, Enrique C., 92-93
Reconstruction party, 181
Red Battalions, 109, 117, 181

Redención de una raza: Estudio sociológico, La (Zayas Enríquez), 76
Redención (periodical), 246
Reed, John, 209-10, 286
Reforma, 46, 53, 136; accommodation to by Catholic church, 136; development of national consciousness during, 258
Regeneración (periodical), 111
Regionalism, Mexican, 23-24, 121; and language differences, 84-87. *See also* Local loyalties; *Patrias chicas*
Religion and nationalism, 142. *See also* Catholic church
Religious loyalty, 12, 48, 90-91, 116, 136, 139-40, 155. *See also* Catholic church
"Religious Question in Mexico, The" (Cabrera), 244
Repression of memories, 16, 112-15, 149. *See also* Myths, national
Republican party, United States, 227
Revista Azul (periodical), 274
Revista de Revistas (periodical), 150, 194, 198, 225
Revolution, different types of and nationalism, 18-19, 115, 313. *See also* American Revolution; French Revolution; Revolution of 1910; Spanish Civil War
Revolution of 1810, 30-31, 32, 45, 142, 293, 298; centennial celebration of, 102-4
Revolution of 1910, as instrument of change, vii; Mexican conception of, 3-4; and cohesive nationalism, 9-21 *passim;* Mexican pride in, 10; effects of compared to other revolutions, 18-19, 115, 150, 191; as catalyst of social change, 101-2, 120-36; national heroes of, 102-20, 195-200; and Catholic church, 136-43; effects of violence and destructiveness in, 144; military technology of, 157-63; leaders' appeals in, 163-69; and emergence of Indianism, 170-73; workers' participation in, 179-82; women's participation in, 183-200; role in of xenophobia, 202-51 *passim;* foreign participants in, 231-36; literature of, 254-56, 261-65, 274-75, 276-78; in histories and textbooks, 266-71; in popular literature, 271-73; in music, 282-87 *passim;* in art, 287, 289, 290-95; in mass media, 296-98, 300-3, 304-5; as part of world-wide movement toward freedom, 312
Revolutionary party. *See* Partido Revolucionario Institucional
Revueltas, Silvestre, 280, 281
Reyes, Bernardo, 107, 113, 164, 289-90
Reyes, Toño (character in *Andrés Pérez, maderista*), 261
Rice, Francis W., 43
Río Bravo. *See* Rio Grande
Rio Grande, 125, 233
Rippy, J. Fred, 37
Rito Nacional Mexicano, 239. *See also* Freemasonry, Mexican
Riva Palacio, Vicente, 279
Rivera, Diego, 27, 287, 288, 293, 294, 295
Rivero, Gonzalo, 219
Robinson, John A., 43
Rock Springs, 87, 217
Rodríguez, Antonio, 87, 216, 231
Rodríguez, Ismael, 302
Rodríguez (character in *Los caciques*), 261
Rodríguez Galván, Ignacio, 276
Rojas, Luis Manuel, 222
Roman Catholic church. *See* Catholic church
Romancero nacional, El (Prieto), 274
Romero, José Rubén, 262-63
Romero Flores, Jesús, 199
Romney, Thomas Cottam, 70-71
Roosevelt, Franklin D., 251
Roosevelt, Theodore, 213
Rotonda de los Hombres Ilustres, 273
Rouaix, Pastor, 174
Rubio, César (character in *El gesticulador*), 278
Rurales, 57, 194
Russia, 131, 158, 300; assumptions on United States imperialism toward Mexico, 219-20, 228-29; consistent views of national interests, 219. *See also* Bolshevik Revolution
Russian Revolution. *See* Bolshevik Revolution
Rynning, Thomas, 58

Sadism, in 1910 Revolution, 149-50
Sáenz, Moisés, 177
Sáenz Royo, Artemisa, 198
Salina Cruz, 97, 209
Salinas, Gustavo, 159
Saltillo, 245, 277
Salvador, Jaime, 301
Sanborn's drugstore, 217
San Diego, California, 126, 128
San Francisco, 224
San Francisco, California, 39, 98
San Jacinto, battle of, 13, 38
San Juan de Ulúa, 33, 35, 49, 283
San Luis Potosí, city, 65, 131, 211, 284
San Luis Potosí, state, 91, 198
Santa Anna, Antonio López de, 13, 33, 38, 39, 40, 45-46, 49, 52, 56, 67, 112, 114
Santa Fe, 95
Santa Julia, 194
Santa María, battle of, 171
Santamaría, Francisco J., 85
Santa Ysabel, 229
Sartwell, Edward R., 212
Schools. *See* Education, Mexican
Schreiner, Olive, 194
Schulz, Enrique E., 247
Scott, Robert E., 10, 315
Scott, Walter, 257-58
Scott, Winfield, 40, 271
Scottish Rite, 36. *See also* Freemasonry, Mexican
Scrip. *See* Currencies
Seamon, William H., 54n
Secret Service, United States, 234
Segura, Andrés, 138
Self-consciousness, national. *See* National consciousness
Self-identification, 20, 314
Serdán, Aquiles, as hero, 111, 261; women in family of, 196
Serrano, T. F., 268
Sevilla, Raphael J., 301
Seward, William H., 41, 42, 43, 51
Sex, 110, 184, 315; as motivation in 1910 Revolution, 149-50, 187; role of in shaping nationalist attitudes, 189, 191-92, 200; in art, 246; in cartoons, 246, 290; in United States, 248; in novels, 258, 259; in plays, 277-78; in *corridos*, 285; in films, 300, 303, 304. *See also* Women, Mexican; *Patria, La;* Prostitutes
Shafer, Boyd C., 7
Shanklin, Arnold, 236, 297
Sherwood, Anna, 210
Siempre! (periodical), 252
Sierra, Justo, 40, 53, 83, 92, 93, 94, 267, 278
Sifuentes, Espiridión (character in *Tropa vieja*), 264-65
Silva Herzog, Jesús, 222
Silvert, K. H., 13, 27
Sinaloa, 204
Sin amor (Azuela), 261
Singer, Morris, 153
Slavery, 31, 59, 294, 295
Smith, Justin H., 36, 37
Social cohesion, and nationalism, vii, 4-15 *passim*, 17, 55, 62, 66, 142, 143, 255, 256, 262, 269, 270, 276, 286, 308, 314, 315, 316; and hero-creation, 115-16, 119
Social communication, 11-12
Social mobility, 130; shift from ascription to achievement, 73-74, 101-2, 129; new patterns in because of revolutionary violence, 129, 132-33; and 1917 Constitution, 130, 131; as element of nationalism, 130-31, 151. *See also* Status, social
Socialist Party of the Southeast, 124
Socialista, El (periodical), 80
Sociedad de Técnicas y Profesionales, 200
Society for National Integrity (patriotic society), 237
Soldaderas, 183, 186, 187, 197, 284, 298, 302, 305. *See also* Heroines; Women, Mexican
Solís, Alberto (character in *Los de abajo*), 262
"Sombra del Caudillo, La" (film), 302
"Sombra de Pancho Villa, La" (film), 301
Somellera, Gabriel, 137
Sonora, 43, 58, 66, 70, 98, 172, 204, 205, 207, 213, 286
Sonora, 159
Sorokin, Pitirim A., 115, 152
Sota, José Severino de la, 267
Sotomayor, José Francisco, 258
South Vietnam, 158

''Soy mexicano de acá de este lado'' (film), 301

''Soy puro mexicano'' (film), 302

Spain, 45, 114, 116, 145, 309; influence of on Mexico during nineteenth century, 23-25, 257; nationals of in Mexico, 26-27, 30, 34, 264; effect of Napoleon's conquest of in Mexico, 29; attempt of at reconquest, 33, 35; recognition of Mexican independence, 33; colonies of in Latin America, 34; intervention in Mexico in 1862, 50. *See also* Nationalism, Spanish; Spaniards in Mexico

Spaniards in Mexico, 57, 70, 73, 75, 192, 261; hostility toward after 1810, 32-33, 34, 35; during *porfiriato*, 55; persecutions of in 1910 Revolution, 205-6, 311; contemporary attitudes toward, 206; Spanish Republicans, 206; in drama, 277. *See also Gachupines;* Spanish Civil War

Spanish-American War, 35n

Spanish Civil War, 19, 162, 206

Spanish language, 76, 93, 128, 233, 252, 276, 278; government efforts to spread after 1910, 27; and immigrants, 69; Mexican variant of as aid to nationalism, 81, 84-86, 99, 310; attitude on in *porfiriato*, 81-82; linguistic assimilation, 81-84, 101; spread of, 81-88 *passim*, 310; differences in between Spanish-speaking countries, 84-86; inclusion of Indian words, 85; Mexican slang, 85; linguistic parochialism, 86, 102; incorporation into of English words, 87; linguistic imperialism, 87-88. *See also* Language

Stadden, Richard M., 238

Starr, Frederick, 73

Status, social, shift from ascription to achievement, 73-74, 101-2, 129, 155, 310; determinants of, 129; in 1910 Revolution, 129, 311. *See also* Social mobility

Strata, social, in Mexico, 131-32; and differing appreciations of nationalism, 314-15. *See also* Class structure and nationalism

Students, demonstrations of, 217; and nationalism, 236; and reports of Yankee invasions, 236-37; anti-Americanism of, 236-37; patriotic societies of, 237. *See also* Education; Youth

Sucesión presidencial en 1910, La (Madero), 105

Suffrage, in Mexico, in *porfiriato*, 56; women's, 184, 193-95, 198

Sufragio Libre, El (periodical), 130

Supreme Court, Mexican, 294

Survey research, and the study of nationalism, vii-x, 165, 169, 176-77, 317

Switzerland, 74, 82

Tabasco, 96, 198

Taft, William Howard, 218, 219, 226n, 231

Tamaulipas, 123, 125

Tampico, 183, 223, 224, 237, 244

Tannenbaum, Frank, 27, 44

Tapachula, 214

Tarahuman language, 82

Tarascan Indians, 294

Tatabiate (Indian leader), 77

Tax, Sol, 177

Taylor, Zachary, 271

Teachers, Mexican, 109, 166; and nationalistic indoctrination, 88, 92-94, 269; and 1910 Revolution, 157. *See also* Education, Mexican; Education and nationalism; Students

Technology, effects of on nationalism, 15, 313. *See also* Industrialization; Industrial Revolution; Military technology

Tehuantepec, Isthmus of, 41

Television, Mexican, 304, 305; as vehicle for nationalism, 306; use of American programs in, 306

Téllez, Joaquín, 237

Tenorio-Sam (play), 246

Tepic, 138

Terrazas, Luis, 279

Texas, 23, 37, 67, 69, 89, 125, 126, 127, 242; annexation of by United States, 37, 41; secession of from Mexico, 37, 40, 43, 309; Republic of, 38; as focus for Mexican xenophobia, 39

Textbooks and nationalism, 255, 266,

269; in Mexico, 256, 269-71. *See also* Education and nationalism
Textile industry, 80
Thatcher, Moses, 70
Third Reich, 7, 158, 178
Three Years' War, 30, 46, 47
Tiempo, El (periodical), 245
Tierra del faisán y del venado, La (play), 277
Tierra (López y Fuentes), 266
Tío Sam y la patria (play), 277, 278
Tlaxcala, state, 67
Tlaxcalantongo, 264
Tobacco industry, 80
Tomóchic (Frías), 260
Tone, Theobald Wolfe, 17
Topete, Hermila Galindo de, 189, 198
Topolobampo, 159
Torreón, 203-4; battle of, 161
Torres Bodet, Jamie, 275
Toscano Barragán, Salvador, 296-97
Totonac Indians, 294
Tourism in Mexico, 124, 154
Trade unions, 132; aid of to Obregón, 109, 117, 181; and 1917 Constitution, 131; appeals to in 1910 Revolution, 162; freedom to organize under Madero, 179, 180; under *porfiriato*, 179, 180; and Carrancistas, 179-80; and failure of communism, 180; participation of in 1910 Revolution. *See also* Casa del Obrero Mundial; Confederación de Trabajadores de México; Confederación Regional Obrera Mexicana; Labor, Mexican; Red Battalions
Transportation, Mexican, 35n, 67, 121, 124, 132, 307; effects of on nationalism, 20, 95-100 *passim*, 310; changes in, 1810-1910, 95-100 *passim;* port facilities, 97; disruption of, 147. *See also* Emigration from Mexico; Geography and nationalism; Migration, internal; Railways, Mexican
Travesí, Gonzalo, 219
Trejo Lerdo de Tejada, C., 130
Treviño, Jerónimo, 42, 44, 54
Trist, Nicholas P., 41
Tropa vieja (Urquizo), 264-65
"Tropical and Sub-Tropical Agriculture" (manuscript), 145
Trujillo, Torcuato, 30

Turner, John Kenneth, 58
Tzotzil language, 82

"Ultimo mexicano, El" (film), 301
Uncle Sam, 18n
Uncle Sam (character in *Tío Sam y la patria*), 277-78
Uncle Tom's Cabin (Stowe), 259
Union of South Africa, 178
Unions. *See* Trade unions
United States, 10, 68, 90, 98, 99, 158, 184, 185, 188, 194, 196, 235, 261, 281, 283, 294, 295, 301, 304; effect of as colonies on development of Mexican nationalism, 28-29; relations with Mexico after independence, 35-44; geographic isolation of, 35n; under Hayes, 42, 54; and filibuster raids, 43, 128, 218, 233, 247; recognition of Mexican independence, 48-49; and Indians, 69; under Woodrow Wilson, 108, 126, 218, 223-32 *passim*, 239-41; racial attitudes in, 178; and Villa, 203, 214, 239-41; and nonrecognition of Huerta, 203, 239; and Madero, 214-15; and Carranza, 215, 241; and Huerta, 215, 220-23; provocations of anti-Americanism, 216-231 *passim;* under Taft, 218, 219, 231; occupation of Veracruz, 223-29; under Franklin Roosevelt, 251; effect of policies of on Mexican nationalism, 313-14. *See also* Americans in Mexico; Anti-Americanism; Investment, foreign, in Mexico; Nationalism, United States; Pershing expedition; Veracruz, causes of United States occupation of
United States Civil War, 19, 42, 162, 208
United States Congress, 227
Universal Pictures Corporation, 298
University of Chicago, 73, 177
University of Mexico. *See* National Autonomous University of Mexico
Upper class, in New Spain, 26; in Mexico, 13, 57, 60, 103, 114, 131, 133, 170, 260, 261, 266, 315-16. *See also* Class structure and nationalism; Nationalism, *científico*
Urbanization, 121; and rural violence, 41; lack of, 1810-1910, 65-66; ef-

fects of on nationalism, 124; temporary, 124; effects of on family structure, 133, 135; beginning of urban proletariat, 182. *See also* Demography and nationalism
Urquizo, Francisco L., 165, 264
Uruguay, 14, 27
Usigli, Rodolfo, 278

"Valentina, La" (song), 282
Valentina (heroine of 1910 Revolution), 199, 282
Valladolid, 30
Vallarta, Ignacio L., 279
Valle Nacional, 283, 291
Valley of Mexico Grand Lodge, 239. *See also* Freemasonry, Mexican
"Vámonos con Pancho Villa" (film), 302
Vanguardia, La (periodical), 291
Vargas Ruiz, Francisco, 273
Vasconcelos, José, and racial attitudes, 25, 74, 175; and anti-Americanism, 37, 39, 42, 215; as hero, 111
Véjar Vázquez, Octavio, 89-90
Velasco Ceballos, Rómulo, 112, 247
Velasco Valdés, Miguel, 85
Velázquez, Fidel, 183
Venezuela, 14
Venganza de la gleba, La (play), 276
Venustiano Carranza, el hombre, el político, el caudillo (Urquizo), 264
Veracruz, city, 95, 96, 97, 108, 109, 113, 114, 119, 127, 148, 164, 187, 193, 210, 219, 228, 229n, 231, 239, 240, 241, 246, 249, 250, 264, 286, 296, 297; Spanish troops in, 34; in Pastry War, 49; Félix Díaz uprising in during 1912, 193; causes of United States occupation of, 223-24; Mexican heroes of, 224-25; Mexican press on, 225-26; peace negotiations, 226; American reactions to, 226-27; as focus for Mexican nationalism, 227-28; as focus for international criticism, 228-29
Veracruz, state, 122-23, 176, 198, 209
Veracruzanos, 86, 87, 113
Verba, Sidney, viii, 10, 200
Verissimo, Erico, 42
Vicario, Leona, 198
Victoria, Guadalupe, 31, 272

"Victoria, La" (painting), 192
Victoria, Rodrigo, 46
Vida inútil de Pito Pérez, La (Romero), 263
Viljoen, Ben, 232, 233, 234
Villa, Francisco, 67, 79, 104, 116, 129, 147, 148, 181, 190, 263, 305; in comic books, 104, 272; in films, 104, 296-97, 302-3; on break with Carranza, 108, 165; military strategy of, 109, 159, 160; and Zapatistas, 109-10; early career, 110; in popular literature, 110; revolutionary activities of, 110, 122, 161, 168; and United States, 110-11, 215, 229-31; as hero, 110-11, 119-20; death of, 111, 119; attitude of toward Spaniards in Mexico, 205; provocation of Pershing expedition, 229; and Garibaldi, 234; and Woodrow Wilson, 239, 240-41; use of xenophobia, 241, 249; in *corridos*, 285
Villistas, 119, 134, 164, 205, 230, 240, 241, 261, 268, 282, 291, 303
Violence, 125, 129; as impetus to nationalism, 101, 124, 144-45, 150, 311, 312; characteristics of in Mexico, 115; effect of on family structure, 133-36; by Cristeros, 139; effect of on economy, 144-55 *passim;* destruction of records, 145; mortality in, 148; atrocities in, 149-50; in novels, 262-63. *See also* Revolution of 1910
Virgen de los Remedios, 142
Virgin of Guadalupe, 96, 141, 167, 274, 286, 288
"¡Viva la soldadera!" (film), 302
¡Viva Madero! (Urquizo), 264
"¡Viva México!" (film), 300
Vocabulario popular mexicano (Velasco Valdéz), 85

Walker, Edmund, 54n
Walker, William, 43
Wall Street, 219
Warner, Ralph E., 267
War of the Reform, 259
War of 1812, 35n
War of 1836, 127, 309
War of 1846-48, 35n, 37, 39, 41, 70, 208, 225, 228, 229n, 241, 271, 272, 282, 283, 293, 299, 309

Wars of Mexican independence, 31, 293

War with Mexico, The (Smith), 37

Washington, George, 31

Webster-Ashburton Treaty, 35n

"Weighing of the Grain" (mural), 295

"Wells Fargo" (film), 299

"Wetbacks." *See* Emigrants, Mexican, in United States

Whetten, Nathan L., 122

Whitaker, Arthur P., 8

Whiteford, Andrew, 132

William II, 228

Williams, Stanley, 235

Wilson, Henry Lane, 134, 311; implication in Madero overthrow, 214, 220-23, 231, 246; and Huerta, 220-23; Mexican studies on, 221, 222-23

Wilson, Woodrow, 125, 126, 165, 218, 245, 277; and Pershing expedition, 108, 219, 229, 230-31; and United States occupation of Veracruz, 224, 226; and Carrancistas, 232, 241; opposition of to Huerta, 232, 239-40; withdrawal of support of Villa, 232; support of Villa, 240; in cartoons, 246

Wolfe, Bertram, 288

Women, Mexican, roles of in 1910 Revolution, 122, 134-35, 157, 161, 183-201 *passim;* enforced migration of, 123, 186-87; and 1917 Constitution, 131; emancipation of, 135, 184, 189-90, 199, 310; and Catholic church, 137, 185-86; alienating influence on of revolutionary sexual license, 149-50, 200; as *soldaderas,* 183, 186, 187-88, 197, 284, 298, 302, 305; and Industrial Revolution, 183-84; and suffrage movement outside Mexico, 184, 194; as heroines, 184, 195-99; loyalties of, 184, 199; attitudes of before 1910, 185; pre-revolutionary education of, 185; appeals to in 1910 Revolution, 189-91, 311; and Salvador Alvarado, 190; in art, 192, 197, 291; organizations of, 192-93, 200; enfranchisement of, 193-95, 198; in comic books, 197; in songs, 197, 282, 284, 285; interpretation

by of 1910 Revolution, 199-200; contemporary professional roles of, 200; political participation of, 200; in art, 291; in films, 300, 302-3. *See also* Family structure; Heroines; Prostitutes

Women and Labor (Schreiner), 194

Women's Christian Temperance Union, 248

Workers, 9, 80-81, 310, 314; and 1910 Revolution, 157, 179-82; appeals to in 1910 Revolution, 179, 180-81, 311; under *porfiriato,* 179. *See also* Trade unions

World War I, 224, 231, 241

World War II, 301

Wu Lan-pee, 204

Xenophobia, as cohesive force, 15; as destructive force, 15; relationship to nationalism, 15, 308; absence of in nineteenth-century United States, 35

Xenophobia, Mexican, and nationalism, 15-17, 202-53 *passim,* 309; compared to Irish xenophobia, 17; during 1810-1910 period, 22-61 *passim;* manifestations of against Spaniards in Mexico, 32-33, 34, 35, 205-6, 311; and railways, 99; and middle class, 132; and religious affiliation, 141, 175; stirred by United States actions, 202, 216-31; and the 1910 Revolution, 202-53 *passim,* 311; manifestations of against Chinese in Mexico, 203-5; use of by leaders, 203-16 *passim,* 235-37, 241, 249; and Díaz regime, 206-7, 213; economic motivation for, 206-8; manifestations of in laws against foreigners' ownership of property and resources, 207, 208, 213; effect on of American press, 213, 216-17, 242-43; role in of Mexican press, 216, 225, 236, 244, 245-46; and students, 217, 242; toward foreign participants in 1910 Revolution, 231-36; effect on of American books and articles, 243; role in of Mexican books and drama, 246-48, 255; limitations upon, 248-52; in textbooks, 271; in plays, 277-78; in songs, 282, 283, 285-86;

stirred by American films, 299. *See also* Americans in Mexico; Anti-Americanism; *Científicos;* France; Investment, foreign, in Mexico; Spain; Spaniards in Mexico; United States

Xochimilco, 148

Yaqui Indians, 104, 250, 289; role of in 1910 Revolution, 171, 186; promises to by Maderistas, 172-73. *See also* Indians, Mexican; Indianism

Yaqui River, 172

Ygnacio, Texas, 230

Yo acuso al embajador de los Estados Unidos (Rojas), 222

York Grand Lodge, 239. *See also* Freemasonry, Mexican

York Rite, 36. *See also* Freemasonry, Mexican

Yorktown, battle of, 29

Yo soy mexicano: Lo que todo ciudadano debe saber (Vargas Ruiz), 273

Youth, and 1910 Revolution, 157, 236-38; attitudes of in contemporary Mexico, 157; and xenophobia, 203, 242; appeals to, 231; effect on of United States mobilizations, 236-37; Huerta's recruitment of, 238; and school textbooks, 269-70. *See also* Education, Mexican; Education and nationalism; Students

Ypiranga, 113, 224, 249, 301

Yucatán, 77, 81, 95, 96, 97, 98, 122, 123, 124, 134, 152, 176, 190, 198, 207, 210, 288; separatism in, 33, 43; during War of 1847, 43

Zacatecas, city, 211

Zapata, Emiliano, 79, 104, 122, 129, 145, 148, 166, 168, 197, 205, 272; as hero, 109-10, 117, 119; and agrarian reform, 110, 118, 161, 249; death of, 110, 113, 117, 119; leftist invocations of, 118; and education, 118-19; and Indians, 171; in art, 291, 292, 294; in films, 296, 302

Zapata County, Texas, 127

Zapatistas, 117, 134, 142, 164, 167-68, 249, 268, 291; Indians among, 57; and agrarian reform, 107, 109; and Carranza, 108; local loyalties of, 109, 235; changing loyalties of, 109-10; victory at Puebla, 110; treatment of Spaniards, 205

Zapotec Indians, 294

Zapotec, language, 82

Zarco, Francisco, 279

Zavala, Lorenzo de, 267

Zayas Enríquez, Rafael de, 76

Zea, Leopoldo, 94

Zentella Priego, Arcadio, 259

Zimmermann note, 242

Zocalo, 30, 221, 288

Zola, Émile, 257-58